The WEEKEND NAVIGATOR

Simple Boat Navigation with GPS and Electronics

Second Edition

Robert J. Sweet

International Marine / McGraw-Hill

Camden, Maine • New York • Chicago • San Francisco • Lisbon • London • Madrid •
Mexico City • Milan • New Delhi • San Juan • Seoul • Singapore • Sydney • Toronto

The McGraw·Hill Companies

Copyright © 2005, 2012 by Robert J. Sweet
All rights reserved. Printed in the United States of America.
Except as permitted under the United States Copyright Act of
1976, no part of this publication may be reproduced or distributed in any form or by any means, or stored in a database or
retrieval system, without the prior written permission of the
publisher.

1 2 3 4 5 6 7 8 9 10 11 12 13 14 15 QDB/QDB 1 9 8 7 6 5 4 3 2 1
ISBN 978-0-07-175996-0
MHID 0-07-175996-4
eBook ISBN 0-07-176041-5

**Library of Congress Cataloging-in-Publication Data is avail-
able from the Library of Congress.**

Photographs and Illustrations by the author unless noted otherwise. Photo on the title page by William Thuss.

McGraw-Hill books are available at special quantity discounts
to use as premiums and sales promotions or for use in training
programs. To contact a representative, please e-mail us at
bulksales@mcgraw-hill.com.
This book is printed on acid-free paper.

Questions regarding the content of this book should be
addressed to
www.internationalmarine.com

Questions regarding the ordering of this book should
be addressed to
The McGraw-Hill Companies
Customer Service Department
P.O. Box 547
Blacklick, OH 43004
Retail customers: 1-800-262-4729
Bookstores: 1-800-722-4726

dedicated to

Harold B. Gores (1909–1993)
Noted educator, adviser to presidents,
my mentor and father-in-law.
He provided inspiration for my business career
and instilled in me the confidence to write.

Contents

Preface and Acknowledgments to the Second Edition

A number of years ago I talked with Jon Eaton and Tris Coburn at International Marine. We discussed the need for an up-to-date, straightforward navigation book for the recreational boater—a book based on using electronics as the primary approach. Most navigation books and courses at that time were based on traditional navigation, and a discussion of electronics was thrown in as an afterthought, at best. Since much of traditional navigation was based on just figuring out where you were, and modern electronics provided location with great precision, we planned the new book to be fundamentally different—learning to navigate could begin from a known location.

Thus, *The Weekend Navigator* was born.

Since publication, a number of organizations have adopted *The Weekend Navigator* as their book to accompany their navigation courses—notably the United States Power Squadrons (USPS) and the United States Coast Guard Auxiliary (USCGA). The principles in the original book are all still vital, and the material remains current and accurate.

So, why write a second edition? The main reason is that electronics are being continually upgraded. The most notable new addition to the marine world is automatic identification system (AIS). A chapter has been added on this new system. The digital world has opened new avenues for performance enhancement, and some of those applied to radar have been added to the radar chapter.

Navigation software has also continued to advance, so Appendix 1, Using Digital Charts, has been updated. This appendix now uses software from Rose Point Navigation, whose assistance is gratefully acknowledged. A free viewer is available and described for the practice exercise.

Electronic navigation has become more and more widespread since the first edition of this book was published. Even those who learned to navigate with paper charts and parallel rules rely more on their chartplotters than on their charts these days. There's a danger, however, in forgetting or never learning the basics of manual navigation. Electronics can and do fail. Batteries die. Lightning can strike. More importantly, the fundamental rule of good navigation is to use every resource available—including your own brain and senses—to keep your boat and crew safe. Included in this edition at the end of Chapter 2 is a section simply called "Oops," outlining some of the pitfalls of relying too much on electronics and not enough on basic skills and common sense.

The other notable change over the past years has been the wide availability of digital charts. In the United States, NOAA offers its entire suite of both raster and vector charts for free download. It is essential that we all use the latest charts for our navigation as many changes are made each year that affect your safety afloat. The Alliance for Safe Navigation has been formed to help make all boaters aware of accurate and up-to-date navigation.

As a result of the ready availability of NOAA charts, producers of chartplotters and cartography have vastly reduced the costs of charts and made updating far easier. Many chartplotters and handheld GPS units come with whole sets of charts pre-installed. Just remember to update them.

Today most navigation equipment is in color (good for charts), and most GPS units—even handhelds—are sold with charting capability. Touch screens are making their way into the mainstream. Bright, waterproof displays are commonplace, and the processors produce faster redraws. Perspective and 3-D views have been added using new high-resolution screens. With all of that, the basic principles remain and are well covered in this book. (For a more thorough resource on GPS, see *GPS for Mariners, Second Edition*.)

Several other books are cited in *The Weekend Navigator, Second Edition*, and should be considered for additional reading. Nigel Calder's *How to Read a Nautical Chart* is an excellent and interesting resource. Charts are essential in navigation, and GPS is useless without them. Some of Nigel's graphics are used in this book. Bill Brogdon's *Boat Navigation for the Rest of Us* is an excellent resource for a practical, commonsense approach to navigation. In my view, Richard Hubbard's *Boater's Bowditch*, which covers a broad range of topics including weather, offshore navigation, and oceanography, in addition to basic piloting, is another valuable reference.

The author would like to acknowledge a number of individuals and companies that have helped make this book and its second edition possible. Prominent among them are Bob David, former National Educational Officer of USPS, and Tony Gibbs, noted author and publisher. A team of folks helped create and review the original concepts in the book, including Frank Lingard, Charlie Perkins, Jerry Daly, Paul Tarr, and Jack Healy, all from USPS. They and others including Dick Kyle, Dick Pfenniger, Ken Griffing, and Bob Potter contributed to integrating this book into the USPS courses. Dick "Doc" Clinchy and Robin Freeman did the same for the Coast Guard Auxiliary. Many more have contributed with input and feedback. One of the most notable was Lance Jensen, past Chief Commander of USPS, who helped us deal with the unusual tides and currents of the Northwest in the simplification of the subject.

Companies including Jeppesen Marine, Raymarine, Standard Horizon, Furuno, Garmin, Weems and Plath, ICOM, OceanGrafix, Danforth, Davis Instruments, Ritchie Navigation, KVH, Vesper Marine, Navico/Lowrance, ACR, Comar, Argonaut, MarinePC, Simrad, L3, Maretron, Airmar, Plastimo, Rose Point Navigation, Nobeltec, NavSim, and Maptech have contributed information and photos used in this book. Government agencies including the Coast Guard, NOAA, and the U.S. Navy have provided photos, charts, and information also used in this book. Many websites have been used in researching material and getting graphics, including those of the companies above. One other that stands out for up-to-date information is www.panbo.com, hosted by Ben Ellison, writer for a number of marine publications.

In addition to reading this book, you can learn a great deal about navigation by attending courses and seminars offered by the U.S. Power Squadrons, Coast Guard Auxiliary, U.S. Sailing, and many other schools. It's all about having an enjoyable time on the water and getting where you want to go safely and comfortably.

Last but not least, I would like to thank Molly Mulhern of International Marine for getting both the first and second editions of the book into your hands.

Good boating,
Bob Sweet
Falmouth, MA

INTRODUCTION

About This Book

In the fog-shrouded past of a generation ago, navigation was still done as it had been for centuries. A navigator would set forth on the wide waters armed with his (or her) charts, dividers, course plotter, compass, eyes, and wits. Along unfamiliar coasts or through bad weather, he "felt" his way from port to port. Any charted navigation buoy or landmark was a valued reference; with bearings and distances from these, he could fix a point on a chart and say with confidence, "I am there!"

But such confidence would be tested if those charted objects ever slipped from view. In darkness or thick fog, the navigator could calculate only his *approximate* position. This calculation, this *dead reckoning,* worked when done well, but it wasn't dead on. Without precise fixes, the navigator could only strain his eyes and ears to hear the reassuring peal of a bell buoy or (heaven forbid) to see the foaming white surge of breakers over lurking rocks in the mist ahead.

But all that has changed.

Just prior to the close of the last millennium, GPS (the Global Positioning System) was born. Within a few years, GPS receivers had become popular and affordable. Nowadays, if you have a hundred bucks and two AA batteries, you can buy a handheld GPS and use it to plot your location anywhere on the Earth's surface. Just one glance at the GPS screen will tell you your precise location, your speed, your heading, and the direction and distance to your next destination. It will even give you the time of day.

GPS has made navigation easy. Within hours you can learn enough to get out on the water. But those AA batteries won't last forever, and neither will your GPS receiver, for that matter. Sure, the quantum leap in technology is impressive, but no one has yet invented electronics that won't eventually break down. Therefore, it's important that you also learn the techniques from a generation past. You should know how to plot courses on a chart with dividers and parallel rules, steer them by compass, fix your position with visual bearings, and dead reckon when no bearings are

possible. In short, you should know how to navigate by your wits.

The Weekend Navigator will teach you how to navigate in the digital age, but it will also teach you the time-honored techniques that never go out of style and never lose their usefulness. You'll learn how to use a GPS receiver as well as a handful of other modern electronic navigation tools, and you'll learn within a context that will strengthen your overall understanding of navigation concepts. Despite all the new technologies, nautical charts remain the single most essential tool of the navigator, and unlocking their language still requires practice. So, it's important that we learn about navigation's past before we can fully understand its future. After all, a straight line may represent the shortest path between two points, but it isn't always the safest.

But here's the good news: with GPS on your side, you can safely do a lot more of your learning *while* you're boating, not before. Round up the recommended navigation tools and spend a weekend with *The Weekend Navigator,* and you'll be ready to start putting your navigation skills into practice. *That's* the GPS revolution.

Navigating This Book

This book can be considered both a "quick start" guide to navigation and a reference guide. The early chapters will quickly get you up to speed and out on the water. The later chapters will provide you with the advanced techniques and tools that only old salts know.

Part I gives you an overview. Using a sample cruise as an example, Chapters 2 and 3 help you see the important differences between traditional piloting and modern-day navigation. You'll learn the key concepts of waypoint navigation, and you'll be introduced to "The Three Steps of Navigation." Chapter 4 introduces the necessary tools, both traditional and digital.

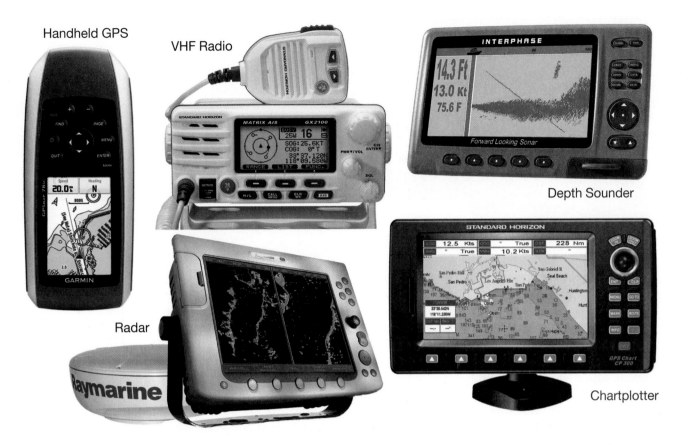

Handheld GPS

VHF Radio

Depth Sounder

Radar

Chartplotter

FIGURE 1-1. *Today's navigation electronics are reliable, easy to use, and quite accurate.*

Part II deals with prevoyage planning—the first of the three steps in navigation. These chapters show you how to plot safe courses on both paper and digital charts and how to enter waypoints into a GPS.

By Part III, we've plotted courses and are ready to follow them across the water. Navigating underway is the second step in navigation, and these chapters teach you how to use a GPS, a computer, and a chartplotter from the helm.

The third and final step in navigation is to confirm your electronics through independent means. Double-checking is the focus of Part IV. These chapters reveal some low-tech tips that will keep you on the right track.

Electronic failures and forces of nature can play havoc with even the most careful navigation. Part V discusses how to prepare for changing conditions.

Part VI is a virtual wish list of high-tech navigation equipment; each chapter demonstrates how to use a particular tool and explains what it does best. Armed with this information, you can decide which tools are right for your boat.

Each of the chapters in Part VII explores an advanced topic in navigation. These tips and techniques are easily referenced and ready to help you develop into a seasoned navigator.

The principles of navigation were established long ago. A GPS receiver fixes your position by crossing circles of equal distance, just as celestial navigators have been doing for centuries and coastal pilots have been doing for millennia. But the electronics revolution is bringing us rapidly evolving tools that allow us to navigate more precisely and with increasing ease and safety. As one example, the downloadable software described in Appendix 1 is updated at least yearly. I invite you to visit www.weekendnavigator.net, where I keep track of updates, tips, and late-breaking information on navigation software and navigation in general.

No other pursuit can set you free the way boating can. The infinite expanse of blue water and sky invites you to leave your everyday stresses behind. Even a short weekend outing on local waters can make you feel as though you're worlds away from home and work. But no matter how far you drift, the skills and techniques you'll learn from *The Weekend Navigator* will ensure that you can always return. (Whenever you're ready, of course.) And regardless of conditions—be it the foggiest day or the darkest night—you will always be able to pull out a chart and confidently state, "I am there!"

What Is Navigation?

Navigating on the water is vastly different from piloting your automobile. In your travels by car, you follow roads. Although it is possible to select the wrong road or route to your destination, you will rarely encounter terrain hazards as long as you stay on the roadway. But there are no roads on the water, and your choices for travel appear virtually limitless. This is at once the great freedom and the challenge of navigating a boat, because unseen hazards may lurk below the surface of what looks like safe water. Consequently, a major part of marine navigation is avoiding hazards while traveling from point A to point B.

In planning for travel on land, you pull out maps and select the appropriate sequence of roads to reach your destination. The roads generally are clearly defined and marked, so they are easily identified while you are underway. Planning for travel on the water is an entirely different matter. You will need to make up your own roads. Once on the water, you may encounter few markings or signs to guide you along your chosen path.

The Three Steps of Navigation

To clarify the process of marine navigation, it is helpful to consider it in three sequential steps, the distinctions among which may blur in practice.

Prevoyage planning—deciding which path to take

Navigating underway—following the selected path

Double-checking—confirming by independent means that you have selected the right preplanned path and are where you think you are

A skilled navigator will not rely only on electronic devices for the latter determination. He will use his ship's compass, his eyes, his charts, and other tools to reassure himself that those marvelous but inscrutable electronic black boxes are still displaying reliable data. But more on this momentarily.

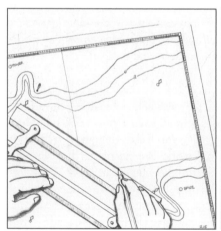  

FIGURE 2-1. *Navigation has three distinct steps. First,* prevoyage planning *identifies safe paths and defines the coordinates for way-points. Second,* navigating underway *involves following those prequalified safe paths. Third,* double-checking *enables the navigator to verify that all is proceeding according to plan.*

FIGURE 2-2. *A bird's-eye view of your harbor suggests that there is open water offering a choice of paths to your destination. (Courtesy: Maptech)*

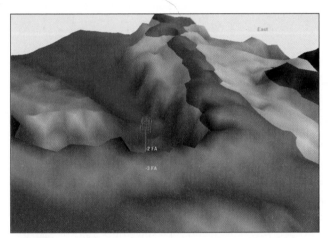

FIGURE 2-3. *If you could see below the surface, you'd discover underwater hills and valleys and any number of potential hazards that preclude safe passage along certain paths. (Courtesy: Maptech)*

Step 1—Prevoyage Planning

Planning before you set out is ideal, but it's a safe bet that you will find yourself planning on the fly as conditions or destinations change. Nonetheless, you need to plan. And to plan, you need charts and the know-how to use them.

How much planning is enough? It depends on the kind of boating you will be doing and the waters and conditions in which you will be doing it. For example, you should consider whether you will be:

- voyaging directly from one location to another
- tacking into the wind or waves
- or meandering freely around a region while fishing or just enjoying your time on the water

How you plan and how you navigate safely are a little different for each.

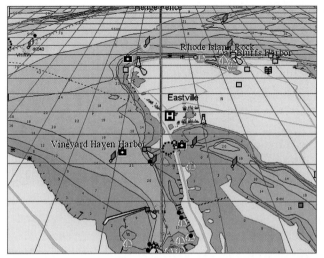

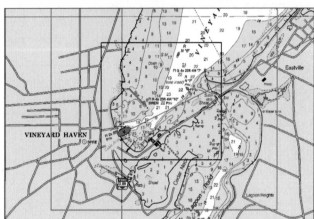

FIGURE 2-4. Top: *This perspective view shows nearby land and underwater features in sharp detail, yet it also provides a general sense of what lies ahead. (Courtesy: Rose Point Navigation)* Above: *The corresponding chart indicates depths and underwater features that are vitally important to the boater.*

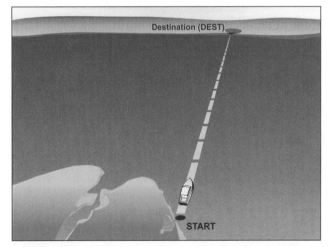

FIGURE 2-5A. *Recreational boaters typically engage in one or more types of boating. Each involves characteristic navigation techniques.* Above: *Point-to-point navigation starts by identifying safe paths from a starting point to a destination.* (illustration continued next page)

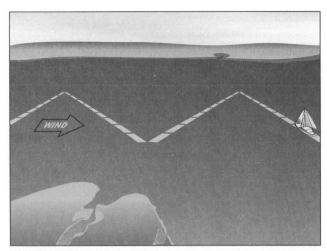

FIGURE 2-5B. Left: *Sailing often involves tacking back and forth across the intended path into the wind to reach your destination. This may require waters on both sides of the intended path to be prequalified. Right: When fishing or cruising around an area, you may have no specific destination in mind. But you still have to avoid obstacles and hazards. In your planning you can plot the hazards so as to more easily avoid them while you're on the water.*

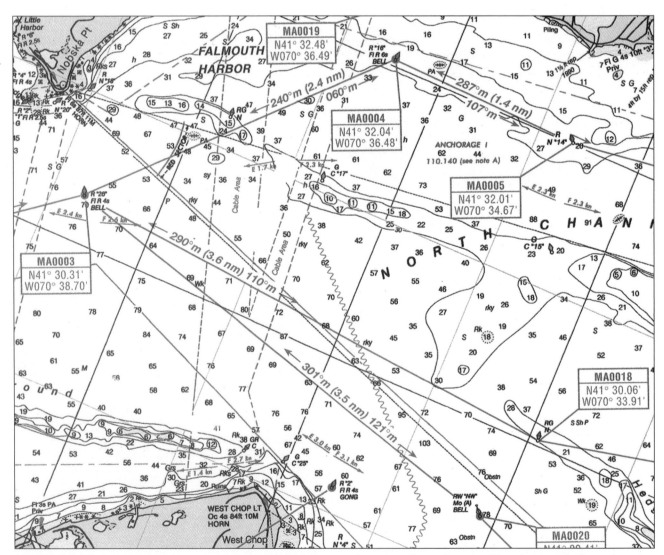

FIGURE 2-6. *The basic approach recommended in this book is to preplan safe paths on the water. To make your plotting tasks easier, commercial chart providers often preplot paths along major channels. These superimposed paths are usually labeled, as here, with courses to steer as well as distances between waypoints.*

PREVOYAGE PLANNING It makes a great deal of sense to preplan for the waters you intend to frequent. You can plan a sequence of point-to-point legs that get you to your destination, or you can isolate areas you want to avoid on a meandering excursion or fishing trip. Then annotate your charts and enter the corresponding information into your electronics. (These are good tasks for evenings or the off-season.) With appropriate preplanning, you will be well prepared for most of the navigating tasks you may face.

You can take a cue from what a number of commercial chart companies provide. For example, Maptech paper chart kits come with course segments preplotted between prominent navigation aids. The distances between these nav aids and the courses to steer from one to the next are already labeled. You can navigate from point to point or buoy to buoy along these segments and be reasonably confident that you will not encounter underwater hazards. The coordinates of the endpoints are often printed on the chart so you can enter them into your GPS, as illustrated in Figure 2-6 and explained in Chapter 5. This is a handy tool.

These preplotted segments don't cover all the paths you may wish to take, however, nor do they extend into harbors or coves you might want to visit along the way. As you venture away from preprinted course lines—or if you're using government charts, which don't include preplotted courses—you will need to plot your own courses. You can customize any paper or electronic chart by preplotting course segments. Then you can measure the coordinates of the plotted waypoints and enter them into your GPS.

On the other hand, while you're fishing or just enjoying a day on the water, you may wish to move around more or less at random rather than follow prescribed paths. In this case, you will be more interested in marking where you do *not* want to go. Navigation then becomes a process of avoiding the hazards you have highlighted on your charts and stored in your electronics.

Preplanning techniques are described in Chapters 5, 6, and 7.

PLANNING ON THE FLY We're all susceptible to impulses, and the impulse to change course is a strong one. But when you do, you must choose a safe path. It's a good idea to keep up-to-date charts near the helm while you're underway. You'll need to plot your present position on the chart and examine your intended path for any potential hazards before you follow a new course. If you use digital charts, you can do the planning in real time on your screen. Planning on the fly is described in more detail in Chapter 13.

Step 2—Navigating Underway

You made your plan; the next step is to follow it. You'll steer clear of any charted obstacles or shallow areas by navigating from waypoint to waypoint along preplotted paths, moni-toring your navigation equipment to make sure you stay on course. Sure, navigation requires attentiveness, but it's far easier than continually trying to figure out where you are and where you are going.

Monitoring your progress along your intended path helps you determine when you're approaching the next waypoint or destination and thus when to execute a turn or look for navigation aids.

On the water, under real-life conditions, it is quite easy to stray from your intended course. How will you know? Your GPS can provide that information (see Chapters 8 and 9). It's also the subject of the third step of navigation—double-checking. If you do get off course, you'll need to regroup and replan. GPS will help get you back on course. Chapters 8 and 9 also describe some relatively simple tips for staying on course in the first place.

Step 3—Double-Checking

GPS and other electronic navigation tools are highly reliable, but they're not foolproof. They can fail or occasionally provide faulty or incomplete information. You might misread your instruments or the chart, or you might enter the wrong waypoint into your GPS receiver. Mistakes happen.

As navigator, one of your chief roles is to confirm that you are where you think you are. Your boat and your crew are counting on it.

There are simple techniques for double-checking your navigation. Most boaters rely on a GPS receiver as their primary position sensor, but experienced navigators confirm their positions using their "seaman's eye." Simply put, you should compare GPS readings against your surroundings—what hikers call groundtruthing. This way you can be sure that your electronics are working and remain aware of any uncharted hazards. You can also use radar or other electronics to check your position independent of GPS. The idea is not to rely solely on any one device. Always cross-check with other sources. Chapters 10 and 11 provide techniques for doing this.

Piloting without Electronics

Traditional piloting is navigation with the aid of landmarks, land features, and charted navigation aids; you use these visual clues to continually update your position while underway. Charted features are also used in the planning process. Whenever possible, your chosen paths will begin and end at navigation aids, so you'll be able to visually verify your navigation. More generally, taking bearings from your boat to any charted objects in your field of view is the time-honored way of figuring out where you are at any given time. This is the foundation of traditional piloting. GPS does exactly the same thing electronically.

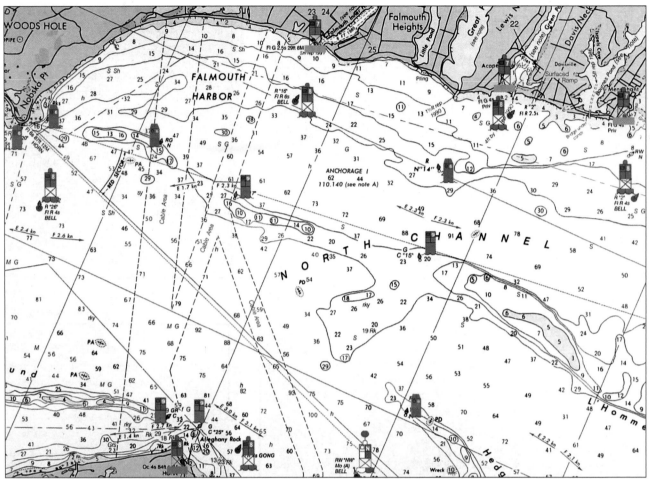

FIGURE 2-7. *Symbols depict a variety of navigation aids. Each aid indicates unique information about what lies below or along your path. In this figure, the symbols have been paired with graphics showing the navigation aids' actual appearance on the water.*

Navigation Aids

As you will learn in Chapter 4, buoys, lights, and other navigation aids mark prominent hazards, channels, and harbors and provide boaters with information of many kinds. Unfortunately, these aids may not be placed in sufficient quantity to mark every hazard or every change of course you might wish to take, particularly in areas away from main channels. Some navigation aids located within harbors are locally managed and may not appear on your charts, or they might even have been moved from their charted locations. Charts showing fine-grained harbor detail are usually prepared only for harbors that receive commercial traffic, so you may need to rely upon the knowledge of local mariners—"local knowledge," it's called—or you may be on your own to mark these locations.

Plotting Courses and Distances

Again, the fundamental task in piloting your boat is to determine and follow safe paths on the water. In traditional navigation, you draw a course line from your starting position on the chart to your intended destination and measure its direc-

tion. This is the course you will steer. You may choose to measure its distance as well, which will also tell you (assuming you can estimate your speed of travel with some degree of accuracy) how long it will take to get there. While you are planning, the course segment is called an *intended course*. When you are underway, your actual course over ground is called a *track* or *line of motion*, which may or may not match your intended course depending upon conditions such as wind, current, or helmsmanship.

To measure the *course direction* on a chart, you will need to use plotting tools as described in Chapter 4. Many plotting tools incorporate a protractor scale for that purpose. To measure distance, you may choose to use a pair of *dividers* (again, see Chapter 4).

Estimating Your Position by Dead Reckoning

GPS tells you where you are at all times while you're underway. Before GPS (and its predecessor electronic navigation devices, loran and SatNav), mariners had to rely on a proce-

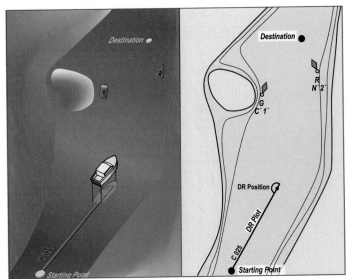

FIGURE 2-8. *There are a number of conventional positioning techniques that enable you to estimate your current location. These methods have been subordinated by GPS but not replaced by it. You still need them to confirm your GPS readings and to keep you going when GPS fails.*

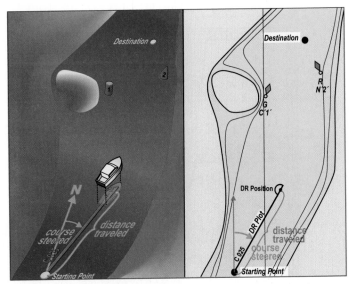

FIGURE 2-9. *The traditional means of tracking your progress is called* dead reckoning. *You plot a line on the chart that reflects your course steered from a known starting point. Your "DR" position (estimated location) is determined by your speed and time of travel but does not account for the effects of wind or current.*

dure called *dead reckoning*—a way to approximate a boat's current position from a known past position and the intervening times, speeds, and directions of travel. Understanding the basic principles of dead reckoning is essential should your electronics fail. It's simple, at least in theory. Let's say, for example, that you begin from a known location and steer a course of 025° for 30 minutes at a speed of 10 knots. You will have traveled a total of ½ hour × 10 nautical miles/hour (knots), which equals a distance of 5 nautical miles. Set a pair of dividers to this distance on the distance scale, then transfer that setting to the plotted course line. The result is called a *DR plot*—or *DR track*. (Dividers are discussed in Chapter 4. More on these techniques appears in Chapter 12.)

A Sample Cruise

Let's look at a practical example of a trip on the water to see how dead reckoning can be used.

You have planned to navigate from just outside Eastham Harbor through Western Channel to a red channel buoy before proceeding out to sea. You'll need to execute a few turns in order to get to the buoy; your chosen path starts diagonally down Oyster Bay and continues from there. The morning weather is clear, so your plan is to monitor your progress using landmarks and thus determine when to turn down channel. Because you'll be steering a compass course, you have plotted a course line and used parallel rules to read the magnetic course direction from the inner scale on the compass rose (more on this in Chapters 4 and 5). The course to steer is 205° magnetic.

With your initial planning complete, you take off at a speed of 10 knots. Unfortunately, the water is still quite

cold, and a gentle, warm, humid breeze causes a dense fog over the water. Suddenly, the fog shrouds the landmarks and shorelines you have planned to use as references. What do you do?

You're steering 205° magnetic as planned, but you need to be concerned about the rocks on the north side of Channel Island. If you go too far, you'll hit them; if you turn to the west too soon, you will encounter the rocks off Dutton Point.

It's time for some dead reckoning. You can determine how far you have traveled along your plotted course line (assuming you have carefully steered that course) using your speed and the known elapsed time. In this example, you departed at 1030 (you did dutifully note the time, didn't you?) and it is now 1106. In 36 minutes at 10 knots, you have traveled 36/60 hour, or 0.6 hour × 10 knots. In other words, you have traveled approximately 6 nautical miles. You can plot this position on your chart as shown in Figure 2-10B. (To get distance, set your dividers on the distance scale and transfer that setting to your course line, with one point of the dividers on your starting point. Alternatively, you can use the latitude scale [vertical scale] for distance, because one minute of latitude is exactly equal to one nautical mile.) After marking 6.0 nautical miles along your course line, you mark the spot, called a DR position, with a half circle and a dot, labeled with the time. Clearly you cannot make your turn yet. You'll need to proceed farther, but for how long?

Using your dividers, you can measure the distance remaining to your turn, which is 1.7 nautical miles. Rearranging the standard speed/time/distance calculation, your remaining time of travel is the remaining distance divided

(continued on page 15)

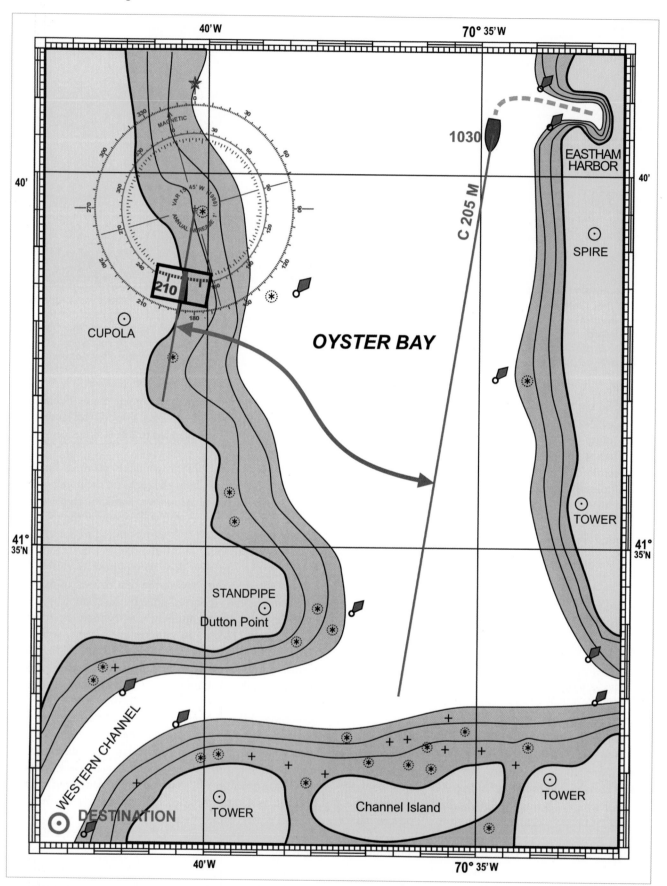

FIGURE 2-10A. *Let's try dead reckoning on Oyster Bay. Your destination is near the mouth of Western Channel on your way out to sea. You can see that you are starting your cruise outside Eastham Harbor at 1030. You have elected a course to steer of 205° magnetic. You could have elected to steer toward the green can buoy off Dutton Point, but a "miss" to starboard would put you among rocks, so you keep to midchannel instead.*

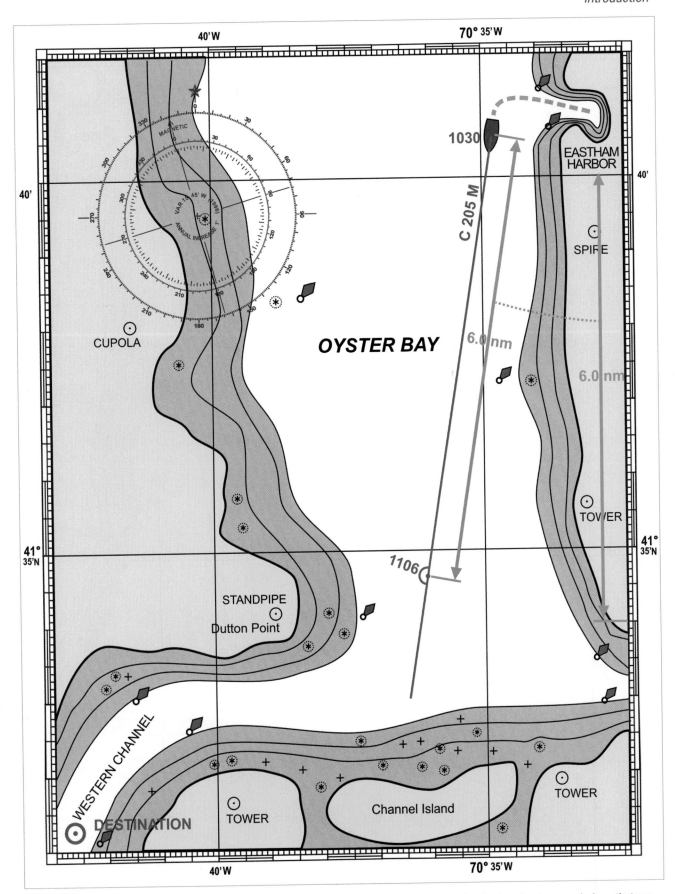

FIGURE 2-10B. *You have encountered fog and need to know where you are at 1106 hours. By dead reckoning you deduce that you have traveled 6.0 nm. You mark your 1106 DR position.*

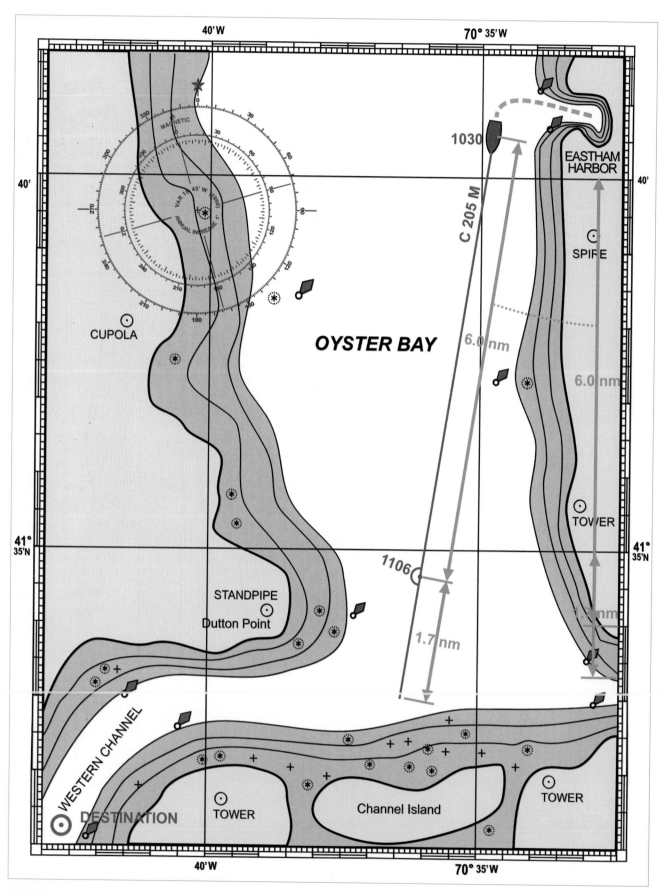

FIGURE 2-10C. *Now you need to know when to make the turn. You will do this with a clock, because you cannot see landmarks. You have determined that you should proceed another 1.7 nm before turning. At your speed, that's another 10 minutes. This is a tricky bit of navigating: if you go too far on your present course, you'll hit the rocks off Channel Island. Not for the first time, you wish there were a midchannel buoy at the head of Western Channel.*

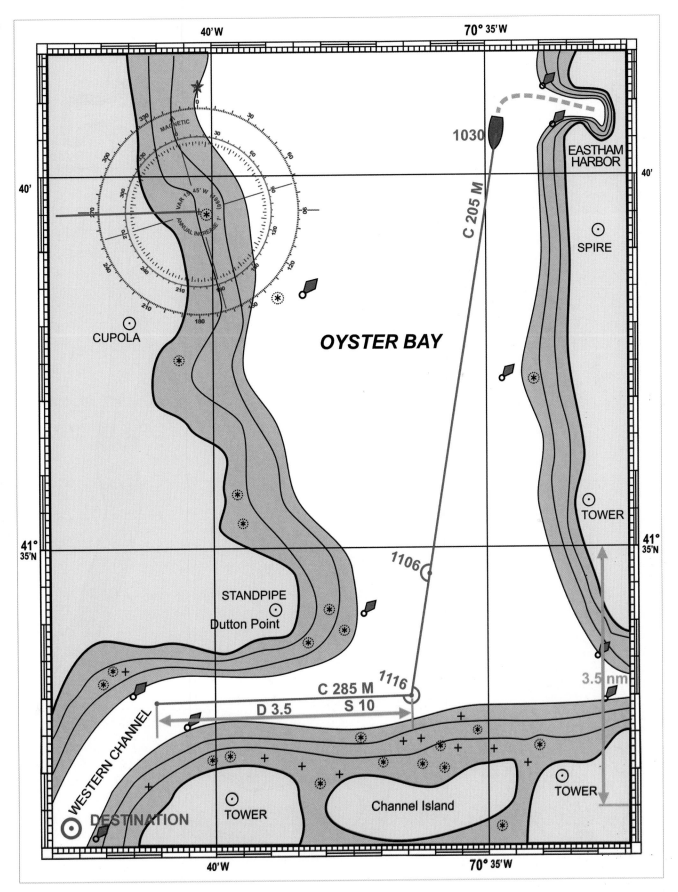

FIGURE 2-10D. *At the appropriate time, you turn toward the green channel buoy in Western Channel. You plot and measure this course to be 285° magnetic. You plan to turn before reaching the buoy for your third and final leg. You measure a distance of 3.5 nm. That will take you 21 minutes at your speed of 10 knots.*

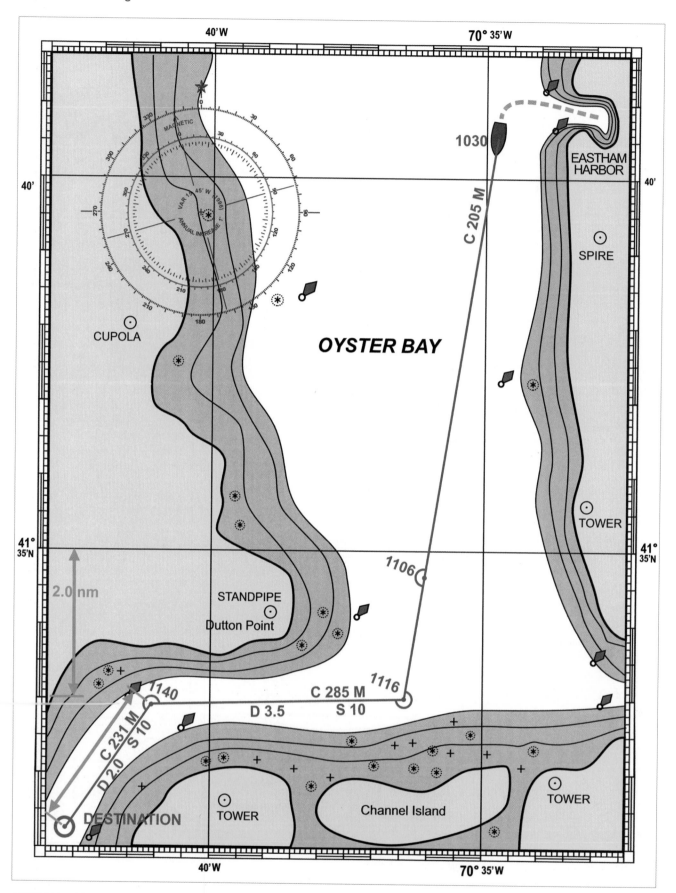

FIGURE 2-10E. *When you reach the spot where you have chosen to turn, you have cleared the fog, so you can see the buoy. Note that this is the first nonfirmation of your position since the fog closed in before 1106. At 1140 you plot the third leg at 231° magnetic and measure the distance to be 2.0 nm. You turn for the final leg and reach your destination at 1152, 12 minutes later.*

(continued from page 9)

by your speed. So 1.7 nautical miles divided by 10 knots will take 0.17 hour, which you multiply by 60 to get approximately 10 minutes. Therefore, you will turn at 1116.

But what course should you steer after that? You need to draw the next course segment and measure its direction using the compass rose or plotting tool. In this case your next course is 285° magnetic, as shown in Figure 2-10D. But, given the uncertain visibility, you also need to know how long you'll be on that course. The distance of that leg is 3.5 nautical miles. You plan to maintain your speed at 10 knots, so the time on that leg will be 21 minutes. Therefore, you will execute your next turn at 1137. Once on this leg, as 1137 approaches, you are able to make out the buoys marking the sides of the channel. This visual confirmation is important, because you were uncomfortable making the final turn in the channel based on dead reckoning alone. Now you have been able to visually check and refine your position. You're running a little late, so you actually make the turn at 1140 based on your visual check.

Finally, you plan the course from your turn to the destination as shown in Figure 2-10E. Using the compass rose or plotter, you determine the course to steer as 231° magnetic. With your dividers, you determine the distance to be 2.0 nautical miles. From that, and assuming you will maintain a speed of 10 knots, you expect to arrive at your destination at 1152.

This sample cruise shows how traditional piloting skills are used to reach a destination. Note that your attention is focused on course direction, speed, and time to estimate your position and when to turn. Obviously, your accuracy is directly tied to your helmsmanship. Less obvious is that your accuracy may also be affected by winds and currents. Although the process is straightforward, it is tedious. Clearly, doing all this plotting and calculating while on the water can lead to mistakes and certainly takes your attention away from the helm. Not only that, you had no way to verify your position until you could see a buoy near the end of the second leg. Navigation by dead reckoning is entirely dependent upon how accurately you can steer your course and how closely you can monitor your speed and time. Even then, external influences such as wind and current may push you from your intended course.

Determining Position by Visual Bearings

Generally you will not be shrouded in fog for extended periods as in the example above. You will be able to check your progress using visual cues on charted objects. The towers, standpipes, buoys, and other objects on the chart samples in Figure 2-10 can be very useful, as you will soon learn. The process of measuring the direction to a charted landmark you can see from your boat is called taking a *bearing*.

Taking bearings is a powerful technique for deter-

mining your position independent of GPS or dead reckoning, or as a quick means of verifying your navigation by other methods. The easiest way to take a bearing is with a *hand bearing compass*, which is simply a magnetic compass designed to be handheld. You align the compass's sight or target line with the sighted object or landmark, and you can read the magnetic direction to that object from the boat.

Assuming the sighted objects or landmarks are marked on the chart, you can plot their bearings on the chart as explained in Chapter 5. Each bearing represents a *line of position*. Because the bearing comes from a direct observation, its reliability is very high. You know that your position lies somewhere along that line—but where? Hopefully, somewhere near where the bearing intersects your course line.

This procedure is reliable unless you have drifted from the intended course line due to winds, currents, waves, inattention, or a malfunctioning compass. This concern can be resolved, however. Given a second bearing line, your position will be at the intersection of the two bearings. This is called a *fix*. Sometimes circumstances may limit how accurately you can read and plot bearings, but clearly a fix is a more precise indication of your true location than an estimate based on dead reckoning alone. By taking a third bearing, you can check the first two. Given the accumulation of small measurement errors in taking and plotting three bearings, you are likely to see that they do not all in-

What Is Navigation?

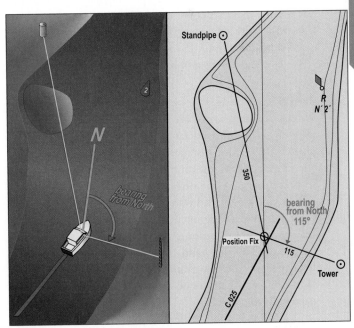

FIGURE 2-11. *You can determine your position on the water by taking visual bearings on charted landmarks. Bearings can be taken using a hand bearing compass. Each bearing represents a line of position, meaning that your position is somewhere along that line. When the bearings are plotted on the chart, their intersection marks your current location, called a fix.*

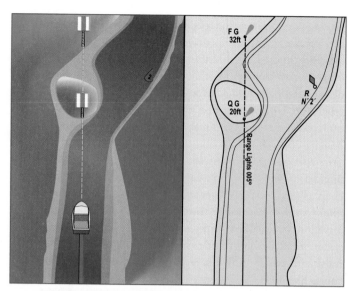

FIGURE 2-12. *A range is a preplotted, convenient way to determine a line of position without instruments. You simply steer your boat to align two visible charted objects. Then you know that your current position is somewhere along the extension of the line between them. Ranges are particularly useful for staying in the center of a channel.*

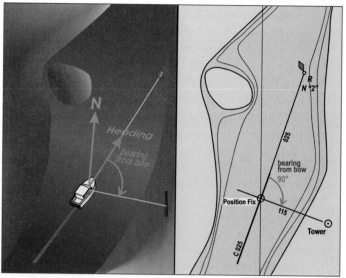

FIGURE 2-13. *On the boat, your frame of reference is the boat itself. Any bearing taken with respect to the bow is called a relative bearing. Often, quick bearings are more conveniently taken relative to the boat itself. In this example, you have pointed the bow at buoy R "2," whose relative bearing is therefore the same as the boat's heading (025°). To your starboard (right) beam you spot a tower. This is a relative bearing of 90°. To plot this bearing you will need to add 90° to the heading of the boat to get the direction of the bearing (115°).*

tersect exactly at a point but form a small triangle. It's usually best to assume that your actual position is in the center of that small triangle. If the triangle is huge, it's time to redo your work.

Taking bearings is essential either to periodically confirm your GPS readings or to refine a position estimate based on dead reckoning. When plotting magnetic bearings on a chart, make sure you use the inner scale on the compass rose, to account for any *magnetic variation*, as described in Chapter 4.

Some special uses of bearings follow.

Ranges

Unlike bearings, *ranges* are often plotted in advance. Any pair of visible charted landmarks—a smokestack and a church steeple, for instance—can constitute a range. You can draw a dashed line on the chart between those two objects and measure the direction of that line on the chart. While you are on the water, when those two landmarks come into perfect alignment from your position, you know that your current location lies somewhere on the plotted range line. This is a handy technique for periodic checks, for staying in a narrow channel, or for locating your harbor. What's more, it requires no compass or measurements. You need only your eyes.

Although any visible pair of landmarks will work, some navigation aids are installed specifically to form a range, and these ranges are printed on charts for your convenience. Range aids are usually installed at the end of a narrow channel. All you need to do to stay within the chan-

nel is make sure that the two range markers stay in alignment as you travel. The nearer mark is lower so as not to obstruct the one behind it.

Relative Bearings

Bearings taken with a hand bearing compass or ship's compass are independent of your boat's heading; that is, they are measured with respect to magnetic north and are the same regardless of what direction your boat happens to be pointing at the time of measurement. Often, however, you will note bearings relative to your boat—say, across your beam or quarter. Any bearing taken with respect to your boat is called a *relative bearing*. These easy references can be valuable but must be converted before you can plot them on a chart. To convert them, you need to consider how many degrees the relative bearing lies clockwise from the heading of your boat, then add that number to your boat's magnetic heading to get the equivalent magnetic bearing. For example, a beam bearing to starboard is a relative bearing of 90°; a beam bearing to port is a relative bearing of 270°. If your boat's magnetic heading is 30°, then a port beam bearing lies at 30° + 270° = 300° magnetic, or 300° M. This bearing can then be plotted on a chart (assuming the object of the bearing is charted).

Relative bearings are described in the "Eye of the Mariner" section in Chapter 11 and also in the section on using radar in Chapter 15.

Oops!

Okay, what can go wrong? After all, you'll eventually find land, right? Well, one of the penalties for faulty navigation is delay in getting there, or more likely arriving at the wrong port. But the one that really hurts is striking something lurking below the surface of the water or masked in fog or darkness. That can downright ruin your day, if not sink your boat.

There is really no reason for this. Navigation is not all that difficult if you develop the skills, and the hydrographic organizations that make charts do a fine job of showing you harbor and water conditions, and in marking navigation hazards on charts.

As pointed out earlier in this chapter, a straight line may be the shortest path, but it may not be the safest. If you set your GPS to guide you to a waypoint without taking time to note with your own eyes that your waypoint is on the other side of a shoal or a jetty, you're obviously setting yourself up for an accident. The more unquestioning confidence you have in your electronics, the faster you may be traveling when you encounter that unpleasant surprise. The point is, the jetty should never be a surprise. Electronic navigation doesn't relieve you of the need to practice the time-honored double-checks that navigators have used to keep their vessels away from danger for many generations. In fact, there's a strong argument that the array of inexpensive, easy-to-use electronic navigation systems available today can lull us into a potentially dangerous complacency. However, there's no need for that to happen. The accuracy and convenience of today's GPS technology and other marine electronics, combined with steady awareness and good habits on the part of the navigator, mean that consistently safe navigation has never been more achievable.

Success in navigation, as in any other pursuit, is difficult to achieve without paying attention. Here are some stories about those who didn't pay enough attention to their navigation. We recognize that after you've finished reading this book, you won't fall prey to these situations, but it's interesting to see how even seemingly experienced mariners can get into trouble.

The Royal Majesty

Let's begin with some professionals. The *Royal Majesty* was a cruise ship that had begun service between Bermuda and Boston in 1995 after serving as a Caribbean cruise ship operating out of Florida since its launch in 1992. What happened is a classic incident that gives us all pause when relying on our navigation equipment.

On the evening of June 10, the ship was returning to Boston with 1,509 passengers onboard. The trained crew had been standing watch and plotting the ship's hourly positions as reported by their GPS. One radar was operating on a six-mile range, and the second was shut down since the weather was clear. The ship also had a Loran-C receiver, and its reported position information had been checked from time to time. Observers believed they had seen a critical buoy on radar near where the sea lanes begin for the approach to Boston. They were confident in their track and position. This was a well-equipped ship with modern electronic navigation equipment.

At about 10:30 p.m., the ship ran aground on Rose and Crown shoal, just east of Nantucket island. It was some 17 miles off course to the west of its presumed track. After unsuccessfully attempting to free the vessel using its engines, the master was contacted by the U.S. Coast Guard, which was responding to a cell phone call from one of the passengers aboard. In the hours following the grounding, an attempt to transfer passengers to ferries was aborted due to growing seas. Ultimately, the ship was refloated and freed by tugs. After a hull inspection showed that the ship was not leaking and was seaworthy, the Coast Guard granted permission for it to complete the remaining six-hour cruise to Boston.

So what happened? A thorough investigation concluded that there was an overreliance on the electronic navigation equipment. Although cross-checks were made, they were not sufficiently verified. The key buoy sighting on radar was not the correct buoy after all. Some telltale warnings went unheeded, such as sighting of red blinking lights off the port side of the ship. It turned out that these were lights on Nantucket that would have been below the visual horizon from ships that were in the proper channel. The

FIGURE 2-14. *Navigation errors are the usual cause of accidents such as the one pictured here. Even professionals have been known to make these errors, resulting in expensive repairs. (U.S. Coast Guard)*

FIGURE 2-15. *This is another example of navigation error resulting in a grounding. Hopefully, this vessel was floated on the next high tide. (U.S. Coast Guard)*

grounding. It cost the owners of the ship about $7 million for repairs and lost revenues, and delayed the return of passengers by quite a few hours—most with a great story to tell.

Some Examples of Recreational Boaters

So, with all of that sophisticated equipment and a seasoned crew, a cruise ship grounded. Obviously, those of us with less equipment and experience can get into trouble as well. But, as with the *Royal Majesty*, it does not need to happen. Here are some typical examples. I am sure that during any boating season you will find similar stories in your local papers. I live on Cape Cod, surrounded by water and boats, so we see our share.

East Dennis, MA. A man was taken to Cape Cod Hospital after his 20-foot Mako boat crashed into a jetty at Sesuit Harbor. It was reported that the boat was returning to the harbor with three persons aboard and apparently missed the entrance to the harbor. It hit and landed on top of the jetty some 100 yards from shore. We can quickly infer that they were not properly navigating.

West Dennis, MA. A man was injured after his boat struck a jetty in Bass River early in the morning. Two men were returning from tuna fishing when the helmsman misjudged their position and ran the 28-foot Grady White sportfishing boat onto the jetty.

Hyannisport, MA. A man was taken to the hospital with facial injuries after his boat rammed into a cluster of rocks at about 9:30 p.m.

These are but a few examples. One might conclude that this is a rock-strewn area, but the south side of Cape Cod is mostly sandy with some rocks. Apparently, these unlucky folks didn't heed safe navigation and became statistics. There are many "soft groundings" that don't make the news or the Coast Guard reports. Lest you think that Cape Cod boaters are unique, let's look at some other examples.

Norfork, AR. Two canoeists were rescued on the White River—located by a helicopter after they failed to return as expected. They had become lost and disoriented.

Wenona, MD. Three people were taken to the hospital after the fishing party ran aground while attempting to leave the harbor around 5 a.m. The boat hit and then landed on top of the jetty.

Westport, MA. One man was rescued from his 40-foot sailboat after he radioed for help. He ran aground hard on a well-marked reef in clear weather.

We could go on. Every year around the country there are hundreds of groundings and collisions with fixed objects resulting in millions of dollars in damages. The vast majority of these accidents are caused by faulty navigation and simple carelessness. You don't need to be in that category, so read on.

crewmembers were so confident in their equipment that these little warnings didn't rise to the level to cause alarm.

It appears that the ship's main GPS navigation system had been operating in its dead reckoning mode for quite some time. In this mode, a navigation system is designed to continue using its last position information if for some reason GPS satellite signals became unavailable. Without an active GPS position, the system assumes that the ship is continuing on the course and at the speed it was just as the signal was lost. It does not take into account helm or throttle changes that take place afterward, or any effects of wind or current. Because there is no electronic verification of position in dead reckoning mode, an alarm and an indication appears on the navigation panel to alert the navigator. Well, in this case there were no alarms.

The investigation concluded that the GPS antenna cable had become separated, resulting in the loss of real-time satellite data and the inability of the navigation system to compute accurate position. The crew thought the GPS was working. Since the system had proven to be very accurate, they appeared to have entirely relied upon it to the point that nothing more than superficial checks had been done. Clearly, those checks were insufficient.

This was not an inexperienced crew. The official report examined a host of major safety concerns. The National Transportation Safety Board determined that the probable cause of the grounding was the watch officers' overreliance on the automated features of the *Royal Majesty*'s modern, integrated bridge system.

Fortunately, there were no injuries resulting from this

Fundamentals of Waypoint Navigation

Waypoint navigation is the process of navigating along a series of straight-line segments, called *legs*. The beginning and endpoints of each segment are defined by their coordinates—commonly their latitude and longitude. These points are called *waypoints*. Because obstacles often lie between your starting point and your ultimate destination, it's usual to have to plot a number of legs for a journey. Often, boaters preplot a matrix of legs between common waypoints in their local waters. By following the appropriate sequence of legs, they can navigate from almost any starting point to any local destination. One of the principal advantages of this approach is that each leg has been prequalified to be free of charted obstacles. By following the legs, you can be reasonably sure that your navigation will be safe. Plotting and measuring waypoints are necessary steps in using GPS to navigate, so a systematic approach to your local waters only makes sense.

Preplotted course segments, especially in open waters, often begin and end at aids to navigation. Each of these locations can be considered a waypoint. Many waypoints you will use have no visible landmarks. For example, the *Titanic*'s track across the North Atlantic on its fateful 1912 maiden voyage followed a great circle route from Fastnet Rock off the tip of Ireland to a waypoint defined by latitude 42° 00' north and 47° 00' west, where most ships of the day en route from England to New York altered course 24° to starboard to follow a rhumb-line course into New York Harbor. Sailors of the day called this waypoint "the Corner." It wasn't marked by a signpost or even a buoy; it was just a featureless spot in a vast, featureless ocean that represented a convenient turning point for mariners intent on avoiding icebergs to the north while traveling no farther than necessary. Unfortunately for the *Titanic*, the strategy didn't work. But that's another story. The point is, if you wanted to go to "the Corner," you could enter its latitude/longitude coordinates into your GPS receiver, and it would tell you how far away the waypoint is and what course to steer to get there. (If you're on the West Coast, it won't tell

you that North America is in the way. That's what charts and navigators are for!)

In waypoint navigation, you sail from waypoint to waypoint along legs or course segments. Any segment that you're currently sailing is known as the *active leg*. A sequence of legs that take you from a starting point to a destination is a *route*. Waypoint navigation is simple and powerful, and it is even simpler and more reassuring when each waypoint is marked by a navigation aid. Waypoint navigation is explained more fully in the next chapter.

To navigate electronically, you need to determine the latitude and longitude coordinates of the endpoints for each leg and enter them as waypoints into your GPS. As you navigate from one waypoint to the next, the GPS computes the *course direction* and *distance* to the waypoint ahead. You

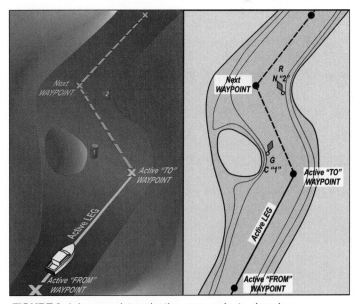

FIGURE 3-1. *In waypoint navigation, you navigate along legs. Each leg is defined by a starting point, or "from" waypoint, and a leg destination, or "to" waypoint. An* active leg *is any leg that you are currently navigating. A leg represents your intended course, which may or may not correspond with your actual path.*

simply follow that course. By contrast, when using traditional piloting techniques, you need to measure course directions and distances on the chart and use that information to steer the boat.

Even though GPS computes courses and distances for you, it's a good idea to measure these the old-fashioned way while you are measuring waypoint coordinates on a chart. Having these labeled on your chart provides you with a convenient means of verifying what the GPS is telling you. In real life, it's not all that uncommon to accidentally select the wrong waypoint name for navigation from the list of waypoints you have stored in your GPS receiver. For example, you might mistakenly select a red nun buoy marked R "2" near Vineyard Haven rather than another R "2" near Woods Hole, depending upon how you named them in your programmed list (a good argument for being as descriptive as possible with these names). Because you must scroll through the stored list to select a waypoint, it is not uncommon to accidentally select the waypoint just above or below the one you intended. On the water, with many distractions, a small keypad, and perhaps with fog or rain on your eyeglasses, it's easy to make mistakes. Should you inadvertently select the wrong waypoint to navigate toward, you could easily put your boat in peril; in any event, you would not reach your intended destination. But if you are also doing your traditional chartwork, you'll know right away when the GPS is directing you somewhere you don't want to go.

Sample Cruise Revisited

Let's revisit our sample cruise from Chapter 2, only this time we'll use waypoint navigation with a GPS. This will illustrate how much easier electronic navigation can be—and the ways in which it differs from traditional navigation.

First, you must do some prevoyage planning. You will need to enter key waypoints in advance before you can use the GPS to navigate to them. Remember, whereas traditional navigation is based on course directions and distances, GPS waypoint navigation is based on navigating from point to point.

This means that you will need to measure the coordinates of the waypoints. Your sample cruise includes a starting point, two turning points, and a destination—four waypoints in all. After you measure the coordinates, you will enter them into the GPS along with a unique name for each, as shown in Figure 3-3.

While locating the waypoints on the chart, you should draw line segments between them, called *legs*, on your chart. Scan along each leg to ensure that the path is clear of charted hazards or shoals.

Now that the waypoints are entered into your GPS, let's repeat the cruise. You will be starting at waypoint

"EH1" outside Eastham Harbor. When you reach that waypoint, you can use the GPS GoTo function to call up your list of stored waypoints on the screen. Select "CITURN," which is the waypoint to the north of Channel Island, and press ENTER. The GPS will compute the course direction (205° M), bearing to the waypoint (also 205° M), and distance to the waypoint (7.7 nm [nautical miles]). The GPS will draw this line on your *Map Screen*. Turn your boat to 205° M, and set your speed. The GPS will display the actual speed and *track* (boat direction) that you are achieving.

As you turn the boat to 205° M, the fog closes in, and you lose sight of the shoreline. Now the advantages of GPS become all the more obvious. Though you are steering 205° M by the compass, your GPS tells you that your track—your boat's actual direction of travel over the bottom—is 215° M. Evidently some factor—most likely a tidal current—is setting you westward of your intended course. The longer this continues, the more the bearing to your next waypoint, CITURN, will differ from the original course line (between EH1 and CITURN). By the time the bearing to CITURN changes from 205° M to, say, 190° M, you will have wandered well west of your intended course, possibly into dangerous waters. To prevent this from happening, steer more to the left until you get back on the course line. Your GPS now tells you that the bearing to CITURN has returned to 205° M and you are back on course. Actually, your compass heading will differ from your track because the boat will be crabbed to counteract the effects that are trying to push you off course. Your compass may now read 195° M, which is your heading "through the water." But because the water itself is moving, your *course over ground* (COG)—that is, your actual track—is 205° M.

Now let's back up a bit and assume for the sake of argument that you've traveled ten to fifteen minutes into this leg steering 205° M by the compass before noticing on the GPS that your actual track is 215° M. The GPS now tells you that the bearing to CITURN is 190° M, and a quick look at the Map Screen shows you to be off course. Should you simply steer left until your track is 190° M? Not without checking the chart, you shouldn't, because you're now navigating in waters that your original course from EH1 to

FIGURE 3-2. Right: *Now, we'll repeat the cruise on Oyster Bay that we did using dead reckoning in Figure 2-10. The same conditions prevail, but this time we'll use GPS and waypoint navigation. In advance of the cruise, you decide on the waypoints, measure their coordinates, and enter them into your GPS. When you begin at EH1, you use GoTo and select CITURN as your first active waypoint. The GPS provides the course to steer (205° magnetic) and the distance (7.7 nm) to the waypoint. You begin your cruise. In addition to fog, this time you are pushed off course to the west. Using the GPS Map Screen you move back to your original course line. You know that you are back on the course line because the bearing to the waypoint and your track (actual direction of travel) both now match your original course of 205° magnetic.*

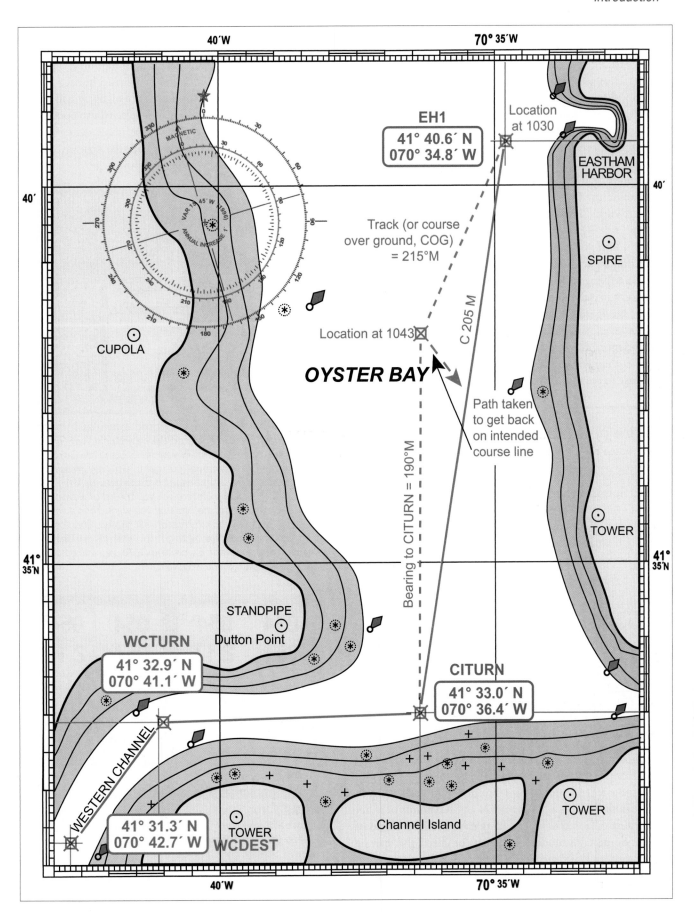

CITURN bypassed. Following a track of 190° M may take you right across a ledge. You won't know until you consult the chart.

Thus, as you progress toward each next waypoint, the GPS will continuously update the bearing and distance to the waypoint. If you choose to display the data field labeled ETA (estimated time of arrival), your GPS will even calculate the expected arrival time based on your current speed. As long as you are on course, the bearing to the waypoint and your boat's track will be the same. As you near your waypoint, the GPS will sound an alarm indicating that you are arriving. This is your cue to get ready to enter the next waypoint.

Once you have arrived at CITURN, use the GoTo function to activate "WCTURN" and repeat the process. Upon arriving at WCTURN, you will activate "WCDEST" and turn in that direction.

Navigation with electronics is unaffected by weather or darkness, so you can proceed to your destination with confidence. In addition, GPS accuracy is significantly greater than you can possibly achieve with dead reckoning. It's easy to see why GPS is so popular.

More on GPS

As part of the planning stage, you'll plot waypoints on your chart, measure their coordinates, then enter and store those waypoints into your GPS, as you did in the sample cruise. Most GPS units offer a GoTo feature. When you're on the water and ready to begin navigating, press GoTo, scroll through your stored waypoints, and activate the waypoint that represents your next destination. The GPS will then draw a line on the Map Screen from your current location directly to the *active waypoint*. It also draws a 3-D highway on the *Highway Screen* corresponding to the same path. The data fields on various screens will display the bearing and distance to that waypoint from your current location, and other information based on which data fields you have chosen to display.

Two of the most popular screens displayed on the GPS are the Map and Highway Screens. The Map Screen presents a two-dimensional plan of the area around your current location. The scale of the map can be adjusted using the zoom feature. On most GPS receivers, you will see a solid arrow representing your current position. The point of the arrow reflects your current direction of motion. You also will see the locations and names of any waypoints or other coordinates stored in your GPS that lie within the field of view. Some GPS models offer maps or charts that can be displayed on this screen (see Chapter 6). When a waypoint is activated, a line is drawn from your current location to that waypoint. That line stays on the screen until another waypoint is activated.

The Highway Screen provides a 3-D view of a virtual highway. Your position is in the foreground at the bottom center of the display. Your direction of motion is indicated in the background at the center of a virtual horizon. When a waypoint is activated, an imaginary highway will appear on the screen extending toward the selected waypoint. Navigating with the Highway Screen is a simple matter of staying on the center of the highway with the highway extending straight ahead toward your waypoint.

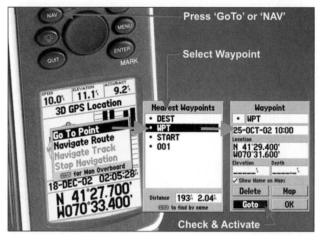

FIGURE 3-3. *Navigating to a waypoint is quite easy. Assuming that you have previously stored the waypoint in your GPS, you can access it from your list of waypoints using the GoTo function or button. In this model, you get to GoTo by pressing a button labeled NAV. That brings up a submenu on which GoTo is an option. Selecting GoTo gives you the list of waypoints from which you select the one that you want. Then a screen with waypoint-specific information will pop up. This screen gives you one more chance to confirm that this is indeed the waypoint that you want. By clicking GoTo, you initiate computation for the path to the waypoint.*

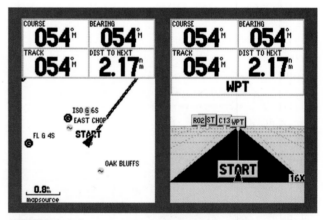

FIGURE 3-4. *As soon as you activate a waypoint in your GPS, it draws a course line from your current position to that waypoint on the Map Screen, and a corresponding highway on the Highway Screen. If you started at one end of an intended leg, this course line and highway represent your active prequalified leg. The course line and highway remain as reference for your intended course while underway. Meanwhile, the GPS will show where you are at all times.*

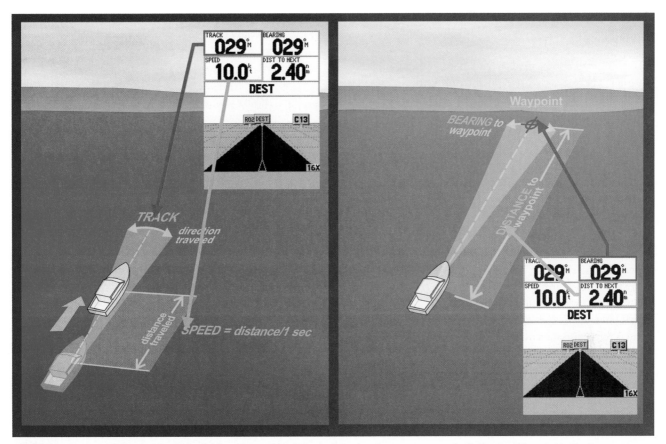

FIGURE 3-5. *Your GPS provides data fields with numeric information about your progress. Left: Track and speed indicate your boat's motion. Track reflects your direction of motion over the ground (on the chart), and speed reflects how fast you are moving in that direction (also over ground). Right: Bearing and distance are computed from your current position to the active waypoint that you have selected. Bearing is the direction to the waypoint. This will differ from your active course line if your actual track (course over ground) has deviated from your intended course. If you are on the original course line or highway (as shown on the Highway Screen) you have prequalified the path; otherwise, you are off course and the direct path to the waypoint could be dangerous.*

Remember, even though you may have preplotted legs and prequalified them on your chart, it's up to you to ensure that you are beginning your navigation from the start of the leg. Please note that the GPS, when activating a waypoint, will plot a course from your current location to the waypoint no matter where you are starting. If you activate the waypoint from another location, it's up to you to qualify the path before proceeding. Although the GPS has just plotted the course, it has no inherent knowledge of what dangers may lurk along that path. This information must come from charts. So before you can proceed safely, you will need to plot your current position on a chart and the path to the active waypoint. Then you need to scan the chart along this path to ensure that it's not rife with obstacles. Only then are you good-to-go.

Now that you're certain your intended course is indeed a safe one, you can steer toward the active waypoint. To help you do this, the GPS displays your actual direction of motion. Again, this is called *track* or *course over ground*

(COG). If this number differs from the original course direction (called *course* data field on some GPS models), you're going off course and you won't hit your target destination. By the same token, if, as you progress toward your objective, the bearing to the destination and your track don't correspond, you are off course. The object is to steer the boat such that the track, bearing, and course numbers match.

Your GPS receiver includes some other handy features as well. For example, it calculates and provides a *speed* display. Plus, as you move, the distance and bearing displays on the GPS will continually update your position relative to the active waypoint. Finally, as you near your waypoint, many GPS units will sound an alarm and display an alert. This is your cue to get ready for your next action, whether docking at your final destination or moving onward to another waypoint.

Believe it or not, you have just mastered the basics of waypoint navigation. We'll discuss the finer points in Chapter 8.

Other Uses for Waypoints

Waypoints can also be used to mark places other than destinations. There are two reasons for doing this. First, if it weren't for obstacles, hazards, and shallow water, you could travel around almost without limits. By using waypoints to mark the places you need to avoid, you can more fully experience the freedom that is promised by an open expanse of water. This is explained more fully in Chapter 7. Second, as explained earlier, an important element of electronic navigation is *double-checking,* or verifying. Often, you will use landmarks and nav aids to visually check your position. If you store landmarks as waypoints in the GPS, you can compare them to your visual sightings.

Navigating to Avoid Hazards

Many GPS models will store a special kind of waypoint called an *avoidance waypoint,* or *proximity waypoint.* These special waypoints are entered through the menu using their latitude and longitude coordinates just as you would any other waypoint. But, unlike other waypoints, you can plot a buffer zone around an avoidance waypoint. This zone is

BASICS OF WAYPOINT NAVIGATION

Select and activate the waypoint.
Use charts to confirm that this is a safe path.
Steer to the bearing indicated on the GPS.
Monitor your progress.
Note when you are approaching your destination.
Select and activate the next waypoint (as appropriate).

called an *avoidance radius.* To plot this buffer, search your chart for a grouping of hazards or any area you should avoid.

More details on this technique are in Chapters 7 and 8.

Using Landmarks

It pays to stay in touch with your surroundings. Despite the ease and reliability of GPS technology, there is still room for human error and electronic malfunction. If you enter navigation aids, buildings, towers, and other visible landmarks into your GPS, you will then see these on the Map Screen as you're boating. If your electronics are in question, you can compare these GPS bearings to landmarks against what you see with your own two eyes.

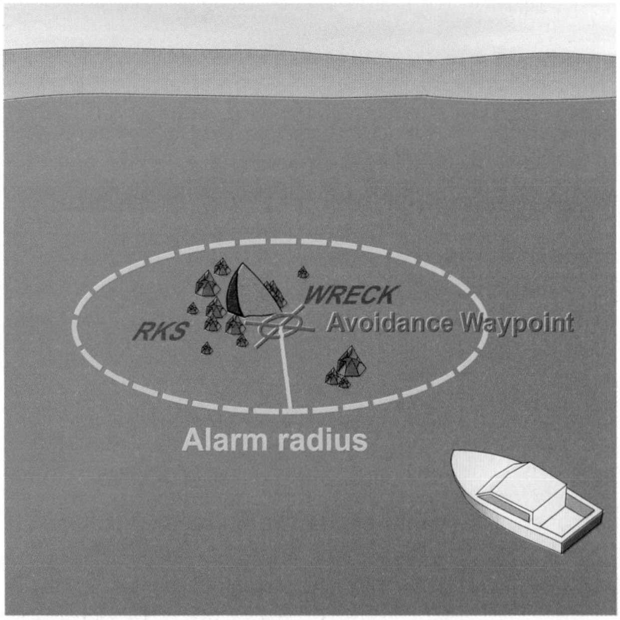

FIGURE 3-6. *Many GPS models allow for a unique type of waypoint. Instead of navigating to this waypoint, you avoid it altogether. You can use these avoidance waypoints to mark hazards and obstacles. Simply program the location of the hazard along with a safe radius around it. Once set, an alarm will sound if you enter that area. This is one of the basic techniques used for sailing or boating about a region.*

FIGURE 3-7. *The GPS is quite reliable but not infallible. Prudent navigators check their position via independent means. One of the best ways to do that is to take a visual bearing on a landmark using a hand bearing compass, then compare that bearing with the GPS reading to that same landmark.*

The Tools of Navigation

It's time to take a look at the "tools of the trade." Knowing how to use navigation tools is essential to your ability to reach your destination safely. While GPS represents a quantum leap in navigation, it alone cannot provide safe navigation. This chapter delves into nautical charts, which store the knowledge of what's where. You will learn what information they provide and how to use them. The means of correlation between charts and GPS is latitude and longitude. You will learn how to measure and plot coordinates. Navigation aids are your signposts on the water and they are marked on your charts. What do they mean? You will learn. Working with charts is aided by the various plotting tools explained here. And last, you'll find an overview of some of the electronic navigation instruments that you'll use on the water. On a clear afternoon in familiar waters, this habitual

piloting will probably take you less time to do than to describe. When you range farther afield or into low visibility, your piloting will need to be more formal and careful. But formal or informal, electronic or traditional, piloting always starts with a nautical chart, and we start our discussion there as well.

Nautical Charts

A chart differs from a map by providing information on and under the water that is useful to the mariner. A chart is a scaled representation of the Earth that accurately portrays shapes, distances, and directions. Unlike highway maps—where roads are already plotted—nautical charts require

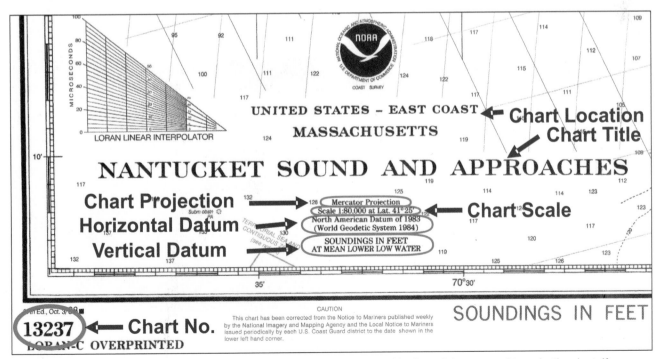

FIGURE 4-1. *The title block provides important information like the vertical and horizontal datums used to make the chart. If your GPS is not set to the same datum, you will not be able to plot your position accurately.*

you to make your own roads. This means you will actually draw on the chart. You will find that charts come in many forms, but their information typically comes from hydrographic organizations within each country of jurisdiction. In the United States, the National Oceanographic and Atmospheric Administration (NOAA) is the source. (Actually, charts are prepared by the National Ocean Service [NOS] which is part of NOAA.) In Canada, the Canadian Hydrographic Service provides charting information. In the United Kingdom, it's the British Admiralty. International standards are developed by the International Hydrographic Organization. Usually, commercial chart companies will scan or copy charting information from these sources and perhaps annotate additional information to them. Updating charts is a constant task. Storms change features, both above and below the water. Navigation aids are moved or replaced, depths change, and so on. The process of updating charts is expensive, so the responsible organizations only do it periodically. It's not uncommon to come across a chart that has not been updated for some time. But, with the advent of satellite imagery and GPS, the entire world of charting has changed. Now, very accurate positional information is available. Today, it's common that your GPS is more accurate than the chart you are using. This poses a dilemma—what to believe? Prudent navigators treat charts as essential, but not absolute. You will learn to use your eyes and observations to refine what they tell you. Nonetheless, they are your primary source of information.

The process of portraying a nearly spherical Earth on a flat chart poses challenges. Over the centuries, cartographers have developed and refined several ways to do that. Today, you will find different projections used for certain applications. For the most part, nautical charts are prepared using one of two projections that will be briefly explained below—*Mercator* and *polyconic*. Mercator maintains directional relationships better over long distances and tends to be the projection of choice for coastal and offshore navigation. The polyconic projection maintains proportions better and tends to be used for inland and lake nautical charts. For many inland areas, there are no charts per se. Here you will need to resort to the use of maps and local knowledge. This book will concentrate on charts, but you can use the techniques on maps as well.

Virtually all coastal and offshore navigation charts are Mercator projections. Imagine a sheet of paper wrapped around a globe to make a cylinder that is in direct contact with the globe only at its equator. Now imagine that globe being lit from within so that its landmasses and other features are projected upon the paper cylinder. The result would be a Mercator chart of the world. In a Mercator projection, all parallels of latitude are horizontal and straight, and all meridians of longitude are vertical and straight. The parallels intersect the meridians at right angles. The result—and this is the great advantage of a Mercator projec-

tion—is that the navigator can measure and plot directions and distances directly on the chart and use them for navigation.

In the real world, of course, meridians aren't parallel. Thus, Mercator projections distort the shapes and relative sizes of landmasses and ocean basins. This distortion becomes exaggerated near the poles. Remember how huge Greenland and northern Canada looked in the Mercator maps in your school textbooks? However, this distortion is so small it's unnoticeable in Mercator charts covering local regions in low and middle latitudes.

Figure 4-3 shows how a Mercator chart is made by projecting the surface of a globe onto a cylinder. Near the equator, the globe and the chart match closely, but the chart stretches as you approach the poles, and landmasses appear larger than they actually are.

The polyconic projection, Figure 4-2, is used for charts of the Great Lakes and some major rivers. An example of this projection can be seen in the paper masters that are wrapped and glued on a sphere to form a globe. When flattened, the result is very complex. Using a polyconic chart to travel over great distances would be difficult. However, charts for local regions are made by peeling the globe so that the center meridian for your region is a straight line. Therefore, if you're traveling locally (especially along the straight centerline of one of the "peels"), the parallels are perpendicular with the meridian, and it's possible to plot a course as you would on a Mercator chart.

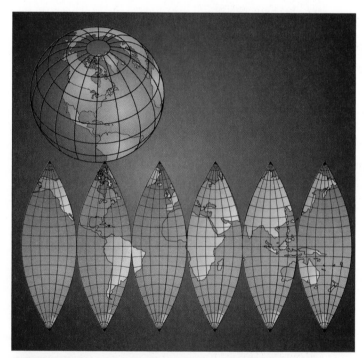

FIGURE 4-2. *Rendering the Earth into a meaningful flat chart is a major challenge. If you simply unfold and flatten the Earth's surface, you will get something like this figure, which is similar to a polyconic projection. Notice that the grid lines are curved. This makes plotting difficult.*

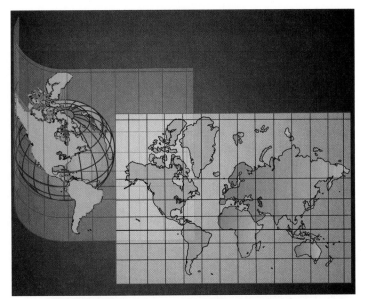

FIGURE 4-3. *Coastal and offshore charts use a Mercator projection. Imagine a light at the center of the Earth projecting the Earth's surface features onto a cylinder that wraps around the equator. The resultant flat projection provides straight and perpendicular grid lines, making plotting easy. Feature shapes and relative positions are accurate, but there is an artificial enlargement of features toward the poles as compared with regions closer to the equator.*

FIGURE 4-5. *When underwater features such as depth contours are added, the map becomes a chart.*

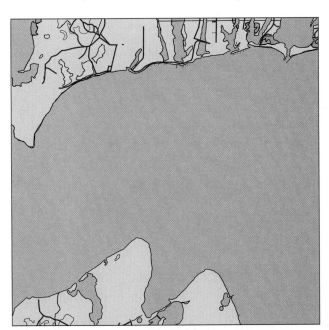

FIGURE 4-4. *A map shows land features but tells little about the water other than the shorelines.*

FIGURE 4-6. *Maps of highways define paths and any marked features along the way. But there are no such features on the water. Therefore, a chart needs to provide a frame of reference. This is indicated by the grid. The grid comprises latitude and longitude lines, and a pair of latitude and longitude coordinates provide your location in numerical form.*

Because charts for many interior rivers and lakes of the United States are scarce, some boaters use U.S. Geological Survey (USGS) topographic maps on these waters. In addition, local maps and guides may be available for popular boating areas. Unfortunately, these charts often do not show underwater features, and you may need to build your own chart using local and personal knowledge.

Nautical charts, unlike topographic and other maps, are rich in details about objects below the surface of the water. This is essential information for the navigator, so you need to understand the symbols the chart uses. Figure 4-4 shows a typical map including a body of water. Obviously, this kind of map wouldn't be of much help to a boater. But the addition of depth contours (similar to the elevation contours you find for land features on a topographic map) gives you some sense of the features under the water's surface, as shown in Figure 4-5.

On a road map, it's easy to see where you are. The map depicts clearly marked roads labeled with street signs. On nautical charts there are no roads. Nautical charts, therefore, need a scale and grid to provide a frame of reference that many maps do not have. Figure 4-6 shows a typical scale and grid, and we'll return to these features shortly.

Depths

Nobody wants to run aground. Fortunately, nautical charts plot depth measurements, known as *soundings*, that help you avoid this unpleasant experience. Figure 4-7 shows how soundings appear on a chart. This might be the single most useful category of information a nautical chart offers.

Because water levels fluctuate, particularly in tidal regions, soundings must be referenced to a vertical *datum*, or standard, that is identified on the chart. Depths on older charts were referenced to *mean low water* (MLW), which is the average local height of all low tides as recorded over a 19-year natural cycle. As a mariner, you could be reasonably sure that the depth you would encounter at a given time and location would be as deep or deeper than its charted sounding. Reasonably sure but not absolutely so. Why? Because in most regions low tides occur twice a day, and one

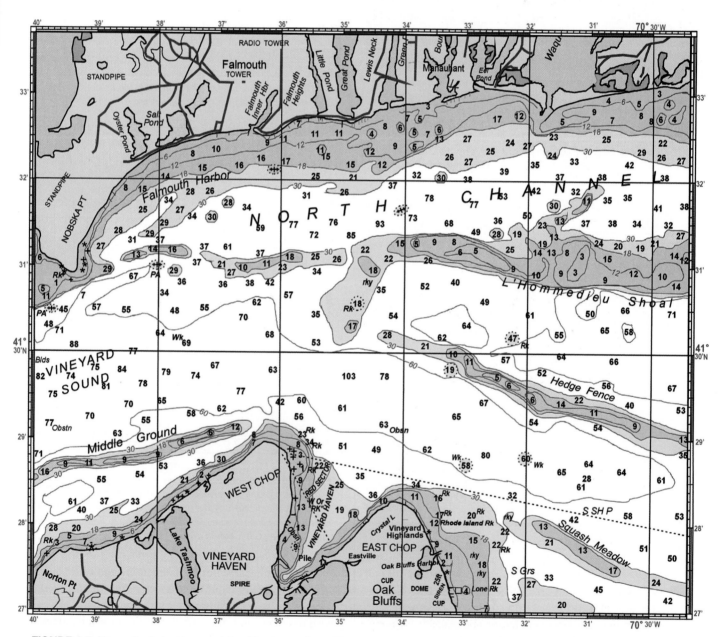

FIGURE 4-7. *No nautical chart is complete without* soundings. *These specific measurements of depth are plotted on the chart to reflect the average least depth at each location. Today, most charts reference these soundings to a tidal datum called* mean lower low water.

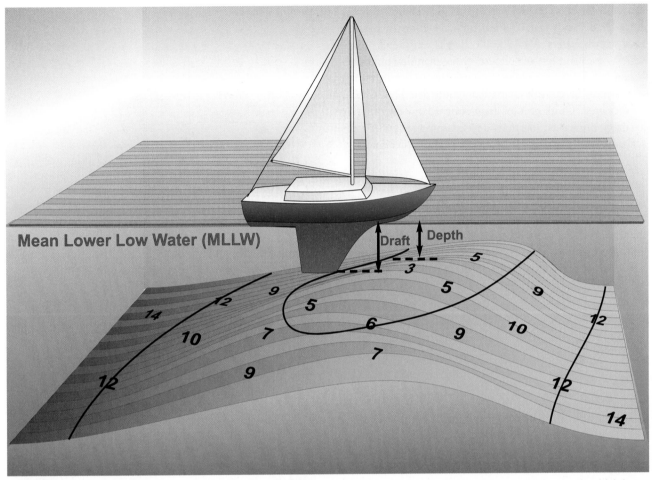

FIGURE 4-8. *Soundings are water depths. You need to consider the draft of your boat to determine your clearance at the tidal datum (which is mean lower low water for these soundings).*

tide is often lower than the other. When boating in such a region, the depths you encounter at the lower of the two daily low tides will be shallower than the average of *all* low tides. To minimize this potential hazard, most new charts use the more conservative vertical datum of *mean lower low water* (MLLW), which is the long-term average of the lower of the two daily low tides. With such a chart, even if you traverse an area at the lower low tide, it's likely that there will be at least as much water under your boat as the chart sounding indicates. (Chapter 14 describes tides and how to predict them.)

On U.S. charts, depths are generally expressed in feet. In Canada and much of the rest of the world, they are expressed in meters. Occasionally, you will see charts in which depths are expressed in *fathoms* (a fathom equals 6 feet). The units for depth are shown on the chart, usually in the title block.

To make charts easier to read, depth contour lines are drawn through points of selected constant depth. For historical reasons, in the United States these contours are generally plotted at some multiple of a fathom (6 feet), so you often see depth contours at 6, 12, 18, 30, and 60 feet. In Canada, the contours are generally plotted in multiples of 6 meters, although other increments may be used. You need to look at the printed depths along the contours. You can tell a contour depth from a sounding because it is oriented with the contour, interrupts the contour line, and is printed in the opposite style of the soundings (italic vs. regular type). Cartographers also use color to help identify information. Shallow water is generally shaded blue; deep water is white. (The definition of what is shallow differs from chart to chart, so take a look at the chart's scale before making any assumptions.) Very shallow water that uncovers at low tide is usually shown in green; land is colored in tan. The type of bottom is often expressed by a combination of abbreviations and symbols, a few of which we'll touch on below.

Scales

Charts come in a variety of scales, with the scale indicated as a ratio. For example, on a 1:40,000-scale chart, 1 inch (or centimeter) on the chart equals 40,000 inches (or centimeters) (approximately half a nautical mile [or 400 meters] in the real world). A 1:20,000 chart is typical for local waters; a 1:10,000 scale may depict a specific harbor; and a 1:80,000 chart depicts a wider boating region. A 1:10,000 chart is considered "large scale"—ideal for navigation in narrow, rock-strewn waters. A 1:120,000 chart is considered "small scale"—excellent for "big picture" cruise planning but insufficiently detailed for picking your way among ledges, buoys, and islands. Large-scale charts show more detail but cover a smaller area. Think of it as "large scale = large detail." The accuracy of charted locations depends on scale. When the scale is larger, charted objects are placed more precisely.

Updates

Although the information on charts is updated regularly, the charts themselves are updated only at intervals. Hydrographic organizations worldwide provide regular updates to charts known as *Notices to Mariners* (NTM). And the U.S. Coast Guard provides updated information in its weekly *Local Notices to Mariners* (LNM), a report that you can access

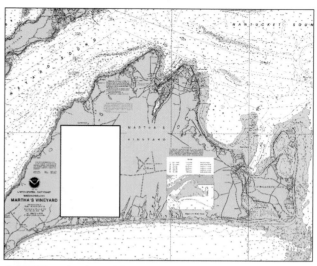

1:40,000 scale chart picks up inshore details you won't find on the 1:80,000 scale chart.

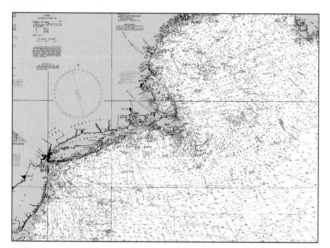

FIGURE 4-9. *A chart's scale is a ratio of the distance between objects on the chart to the distances in the real world. This small-scale chart shows a large area, stretching from the mouth of Delaware Bay to the Gulf of Maine. This is a 1:1,200,000-scale chart; useful for passage planning.*

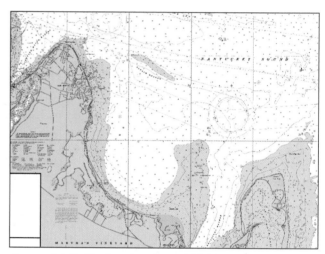

A more detailed harbor chart has a 1:20,000 scale.

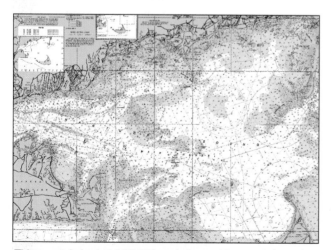

This coastal chart at 1:80,000 scale is good for coastal passages, but you'll need a larger scale to navigate narrow, complicated inshore waters.

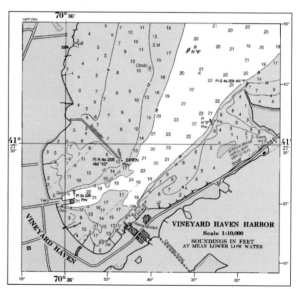

Some popular harbors have very detailed charts of 1:10,000 or even 1:5,000 scale. This is an example of a 1:10,000 chart.

on the Internet. To stay current, review these notices, locate a specific chart by its number (which is printed in the margin of a paper chart or the title block of a paper or digital one), and add the corrections to your copy. Today, commercial services can do this work, and you can purchase copies printed on demand that are updated to the date of printing. Revision dates are listed in the title block of the chart.

Chart Grid and Horizontal Datum

To pinpoint our location on the surface of the Earth, we need a system of coordinates. Most nautical charts use *latitude* and *longitude* for this. Latitude and longitude have already been discussed and are explained further below, but it's important to note that there are other grid systems in use throughout the world. It's imperative that your GPS be set to the same grid system that is employed on your chart.

The Earth's shape is not uniform. Although globes depict a smooth, spherical Earth, our planet is oblong and uneven. Imposing a uniform system of grid lines on the Earth's undulating surface results in inaccuracies. In ancient times, mapmakers would start from a local reference point and build their maps outward by extrapolation. But without a system to account for the Earth's inconsistent shape, as the mapmakers drew farther outward from home, the placement of outlying features became increasingly inaccurate. This became apparent when fellow mapmakers from diverse localities compared their maps. What they needed was a common reference from which they all could build, a framework that took into account the Earth's varying features. This framework is called the *horizontal datum*. Over the centuries—as scientific discoveries and technological advances allowed us to understand more about the Earth's shape—these datums have evolved. Today, most nautical charts reference World Geodetic System 1984 (WGS-84) as the horizontal datum. You need to set your GPS to the datum that was used to create your chart. For example, a few old charts in the United States may not have been updated from the older North American Datum 1927 (NAD-27). If you use the wrong datum in your GPS, you could inadvertently create mismatches of hundreds of yards or more, matches much like those that bedeviled the old cartographers.

Coordinates

An object on a chart can be located using its nautical position address—its latitude and longitude. The chart provides a latitude scale, usually printed in the left and right margins, as shown in Figure 4-7. The longitude scale is usually printed in the top and bottom margins. Looking at Figure 4-10, you will see that latitude is measured from 0° at the equator to 90° N at the North Pole or 90° S at the South Pole. Lines of equal latitude are called *parallels*. Parallels are horizontal slices through the Earth that are parallel to the equator. The parallel lines form the horizontal grid lines on your chart.

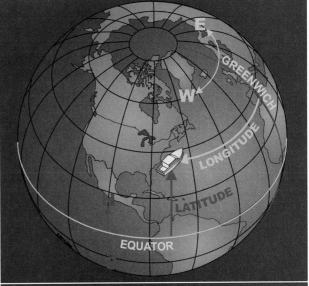

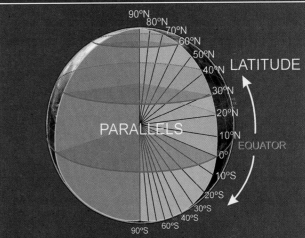

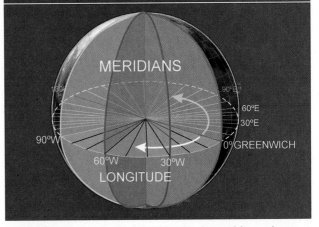

FIGURE 4-10. Top: *Latitude and longitude provide a unique address for every location on the Earth. This grid system is based on a mathematical model for the shape of the Earth. Latitude is measured, either north or south, from 0° at the equator to 90° N or 90° S at the respective poles. Longitude is measured, either west or east, from 0° at the line between the poles that passes through Greenwich, England, to 180° W or 180° E.* Middle: *The horizontal grid lines around the globe, which indicate equal latitudes, form horizontal circular planes that are called* parallels. Bottom: *Lines of equal longitude are vertical planes that intersect an imaginary line through the Earth between the poles, and are called* meridians.

Lines of longitude, or *meridians*, are vertical slices that pass through both poles. Typically, meridian lines are printed at regular intervals on your chart and form the vertical axis of the chart grid. Meridians are numbered from 0° at the prime meridian (which, for historical reasons, passes through Greenwich, England), increasing by degrees both west and east until, on the opposite side of the world, they meet one another again at 180°. All meridians are *great circles*, a great circle being an imaginary line scribed on the Earth's surface by a plane passing through the exact center of the Earth. Except for the equator, however, no line of latitude is a great circle. Any two points on the Earth's surface can be joined by one and only one segment of a great circle, which always defines the shortest distance between those points. But great circles do not make practical courses to follow in coastal navigation, because a great circle course is always curved on a Mercator chart, which would require the helmsman to steer a constantly changing compass course. But no matter. The *rhumb lines*—or courses on a single bearing—we follow in coastal navigation are only slightly longer than their great-circle equivalents. For local navigation, the differences aren't noticeable.

Each spot on the Earth is uniquely identified by its latitude and longitude. Scales on coastal nautical charts are generally divided into *degrees*, *minutes*, and *tenths of minutes* (a minute of angle being ¹⁄₆₀th of a degree). Great Lakes and river nautical charts often have scales divided into degrees, minutes, and *seconds*. (A second of angle is ¹⁄₆₀th of a minute.) One minute of latitude is always exactly equal to one nautical mile. This means that you can use the latitude scale for measuring distance on the chart. A minute of longitude, however, is equal to one nautical mile only at the equator, diminishing to nothing at the poles. Thus, the longitude scale cannot be used to measure distance.

Chart Symbology

Charts use an array of symbols to depict rocks and other obstacles, depending on whether the obstacle is always visible, or is covered only at higher tides, or lies below the surface at all tides. If you run aground on soft bottom, often you need only wait for a higher tide to get off. If you encounter rocks or wrecks, however, you risk damaging your boat and possibly sinking—or at least ruining your afternoon! NOAA charts use a symbol that resembles an asterisk (*) to indicate rocks of unknown heights that are *awash* (breaking the surface at low tide). Underwater rocks often are indicated by a plus sign (+). Broader areas of potential danger are often shaded blue and bounded by a dotted line. For example, rocky regions bounded by a dotted line may be labeled with the term "Rk" or "Rks." Other dangerous zones may be labeled simply "Obstn," for obstruction. A sounding inside the blue area usually indicates the shallowest depth. If no sounding is shown, the depth generally is unknown. Regardless, you should avoid the shaded area altogether.

Wrecks, too, are shown by symbols. If any part of the wreck's superstructure is visible at low tide, it's usually indicated by a profile of a half-sunken boat. If only parts of the boat—such as masts or funnels—are visible, the wreck area is circled by a dotted line, the area within is shaded blue, and a solid line with three intersecting hatch marks is inserted into the middle of it all. (This symbol resembles a three-masted boat, with the long line representing the hull.) Usually, the chart also indicates which part of the wreck is visible at low tide—"Masts," for example. If the wreck is large and well defined, a

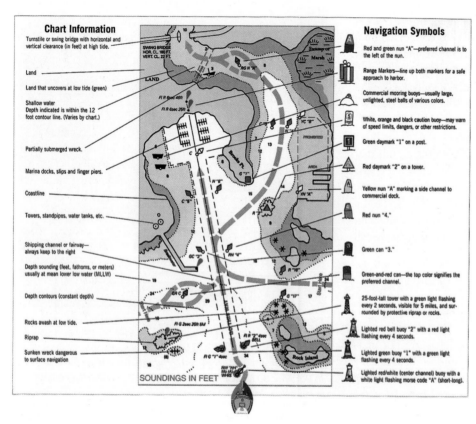

FIGURE 4-11. *Charts use a symbol language to communicate features. Some symbols show visible features and others indicate what you cannot see below the surface—such as rocks. The symbols for navigation aids help you find channels and avoid hazards. (Courtesy: Maptech)*

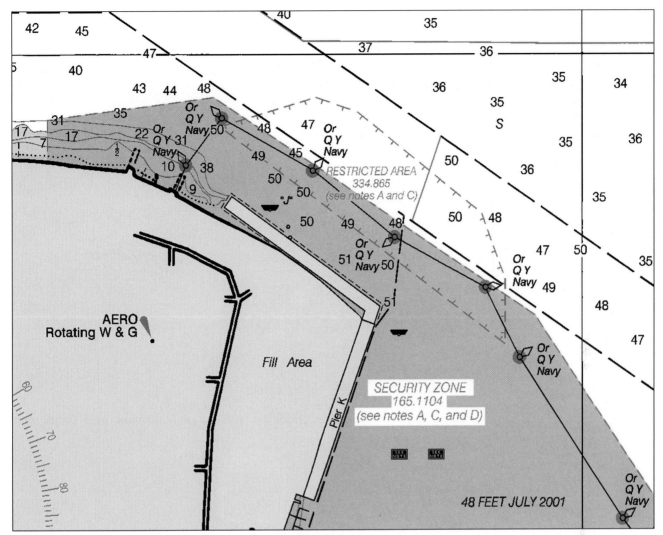

FIGURE 4-12. *Charts also use symbols to define specific areas or restrictions. Recently enacted restrictions provide severe penalties for entering defined zones around military and commercial shipping.*

solid outline indicates a ship above the surface; a dotted outline indicates one below. If the depth is known, it usually is labeled. (See also the discussion in Chapter 5.)

Restricted areas are generally bounded by a dotted line consisting of T-shaped symbols, often in magenta. Alternatively, dashed lines, either in magenta or black, may surround these and other defined areas. Given the heightened security surrounding bridges, naval ships, and other ships and facilities since 2001, you should consult the *Local Notices to Mariners* for updates and append your charts accordingly.

NAVIGATION AIDS Buoys and beacons help define channels as well as mark a variety of underwater conditions or hazards. Navigation aids are either *lateral* or *informational* in North America. (Elsewhere a *cardinal* system for marking isolated offshore dangers is used in addition to the other systems.) Lateral marks indicate the sides and center of a channel. The United States and Canada use the "red-right-returning" rule of lateral marking: keep the red buoys on your right when returning to a harbor, navigating up a river, or traversing the North American coast in a clockwise direction, and keep green buoys to your left. (Elsewhere in the world, the opposite applies.) In serpentine or complex waters, when it isn't absolutely clear which way is toward the nearest harbor or clockwise around the continent, consult your chart. Buoys with red-and-white vertical stripes indicate safe water or a center channel. Informational aids may mark danger or note local rules, such as no-wake zones. Some navigation aids are equipped with lights or audible devices. Charts generally show all significant navigation aids. Though a smaller-scale chart may not show all secondary buoys in inshore waters, it will be apparent from a lack of soundings and other details that larger-scale charts of these waters are needed for safe navigation. However, even a large-scale harbor chart may not show locally maintained, nongovernment navigation aids within a harbor or an approach channel. You'll need local knowledge for these. Gov-

FIGURE 4-13. *The United States uses the "red-right-returning" system. In other words, when you return from the sea, red navigation aids indicate the right-hand side of a navigable waterway; green navigation aids indicate the left side. Navigation aids with vertical red-and-white stripes indicate the center channel and can be passed on either side. Black-and-red aids indicate isolated hazards or danger. If you come to the junction of two channels, the preferred channel is indicated by the top color on a navigation aid. To use the preferred channel, imagine that the junction buoy is the color of the top band. In this figure it is green, indicating that you should keep it to your left. Therefore, the preferred channel is to your right. Buoys are floating navigation aids. Beacons are fixed to the bottom or the shore.*

ernment navigation aids are depicted with abbreviations or symbols that describe their appearance or characteristics. (Please note that charted buoy locations are approximate. Whereas beacons are fixed to the Earth, anchored buoys shift nominally with the tides and can be moved greater distances by powerful storm waves.)

Unlighted fixed nav aids, called *daybeacons*, are usually indicated by a green square or a red triangle. These objects may be on land or in shallow water on poles fixed to the bottom. (Most cartographers further distinguish between fixed and floating nav aids by using italics for the latter.)

Lighted beacons are indicated by symbols that resemble exclamation marks. The solid black dot of the exclamation mark charts the beacon's fixed location; the accompanying magenta teardrop flare helps distinguish the beacon from buoys or other navigation aids. The characteristics of the beacon are printed next to the symbol, indicating the light pattern, color, height, and usually the visible range. The light pattern is often flashing ("FL"). The repetition interval of the flashes is identified by the number of seconds, such as "4s." If the light has a color, it is indicated by "R" for red, "G" for green, "Y" for yellow, "W" for white, although most white lights are not labeled. Thus, "FL R 4s" denotes a red light flashing at 4-second intervals.

There are prescribed light patterns for certain navigation aids. For example, a lighted center channel (or safe water) buoy will flash a Morse code "A" (short-long) pattern with a white light. A junction buoy will flash a two short plus one short (2 + 1) pattern in the color of the top band (either red or green). *(continued on page 41)*

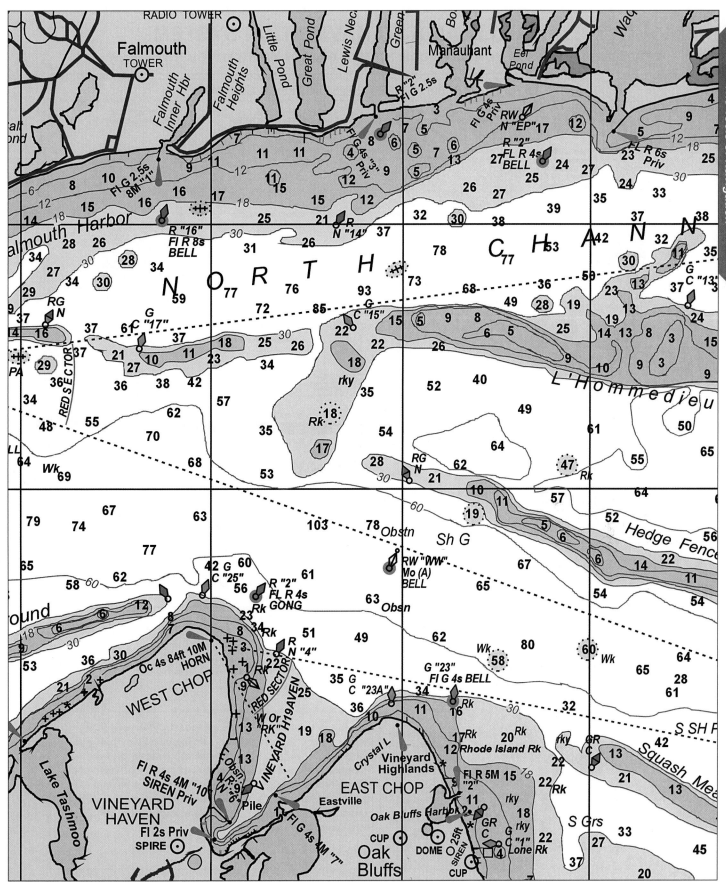

FIGURE 4-14. *The chart section shown in Figure 2-7 is shown here with the symbols for navigation aids added.*

The Tools of Navigation

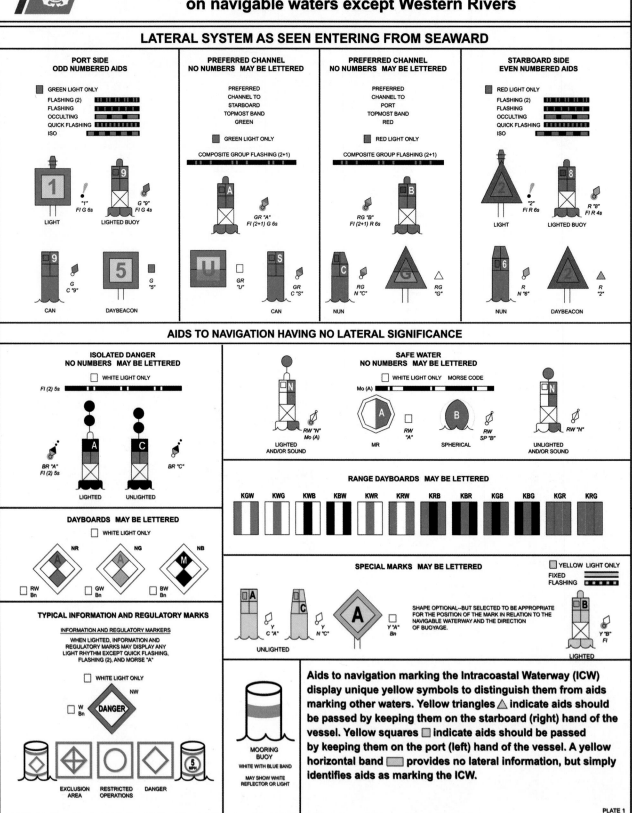

U.S. AIDS TO NAVIGATION SYSTEM
on navigable waters except Western Rivers

LATERAL SYSTEM AS SEEN ENTERING FROM SEAWARD

PORT SIDE
ODD NUMBERED AIDS

GREEN LIGHT ONLY
FLASHING (2)
FLASHING
OCCULTING
QUICK FLASHING
ISO

"1"
Fl G 6s
LIGHT

G "9"
Fl G 4s
LIGHTED BUOY

G C "9"
9
CAN

G "5"
5
DAYBEACON

PREFERRED CHANNEL
NO NUMBERS MAY BE LETTERED

PREFERRED CHANNEL TO STARBOARD TOPMOST BAND GREEN

GREEN LIGHT ONLY

COMPOSITE GROUP FLASHING (2+1)

GR "A"
Fl (2+1) G 6s

GR "U"
U
CAN

GR C "S"
S

PREFERRED CHANNEL
NO NUMBERS MAY BE LETTERED

PREFERRED CHANNEL TO PORT TOPMOST BAND RED

RED LIGHT ONLY

COMPOSITE GROUP FLASHING (2+1)

RG "B"
Fl (2+1) R 6s

RG N "C"
C
NUN

RG "G"
G

STARBOARD SIDE
EVEN NUMBERED AIDS

RED LIGHT ONLY
FLASHING (2)
FLASHING
OCCULTING
QUICK FLASHING
ISO

"2"
Fl R 6s
LIGHT

R "8"
Fl R 4s
LIGHTED BUOY

R N "6"
6
NUN

R "2"
2
DAYBEACON

AIDS TO NAVIGATION HAVING NO LATERAL SIGNIFICANCE

ISOLATED DANGER
NO NUMBERS MAY BE LETTERED

WHITE LIGHT ONLY
Fl (2) 5s

BR "A"
Fl (2) 5s
A
LIGHTED

C
BR "C"
UNLIGHTED

SAFE WATER
NO NUMBERS MAY BE LETTERED

WHITE LIGHT ONLY   MORSE CODE
Mo (A)

N
RW "N"
Mo (A)
LIGHTED AND/OR SOUND

A
RW "A"
MR

B
RW SP "B"
SPHERICAL

N
RW "N"
UNLIGHTED AND/OR SOUND

RANGE DAYBOARDS MAY BE LETTERED

KGW KWG KWB KBW KWR KRW KRB KBR KGB KBG KGR KRG

DAYBOARDS MAY BE LETTERED

WHITE LIGHT ONLY

NR
A
RW Bn

NG
A
GW Bn

NB
M
BW Bn

SPECIAL MARKS MAY BE LETTERED

YELLOW LIGHT ONLY
FIXED
FLASHING

A
Y C "A"

C
Y N "C"
UNLIGHTED

A
Y "A" Bn

SHAPE OPTIONAL--BUT SELECTED TO BE APPROPRIATE FOR THE POSITION OF THE MARK IN RELATION TO THE NAVIGABLE WATERWAY AND THE DIRECTION OF BUOYAGE.

B
Y "B" Fl
LIGHTED

TYPICAL INFORMATION AND REGULATORY MARKS

INFORMATION AND REGULATORY MARKERS

WHEN LIGHTED, INFORMATION AND REGULATORY MARKS MAY DISPLAY ANY LIGHT RHYTHM EXCEPT QUICK FLASHING, FLASHING (2), AND MORSE "A"

WHITE LIGHT ONLY

NW
W Bn
DANGER

EXCLUSION AREA

RESTRICTED OPERATIONS

DANGER

5 MPH

MOORING BUOY
WHITE WITH BLUE BAND
MAY SHOW WHITE REFLECTOR OR LIGHT

Aids to navigation marking the Intracoastal Waterway (ICW) display unique yellow symbols to distinguish them from aids marking other waters. Yellow triangles △ indicate aids should be passed by keeping them on the starboard (right) hand of the vessel. Yellow squares ☐ indicate aids should be passed by keeping them on the port (left) hand of the vessel. A yellow horizontal band provides no lateral information, but simply identifies aids as marking the ICW.

PLATE 1

FIGURE 4-15A. *The U.S. Coast Guard standard symbols for navigation aids are shown on this and the next three pages. Above: The U.S. Aids to Navigation System follows the IALA (International Association of Lighthouse Authorities) -B system, which is also used in Canada, Mexico, South America, Japan, Korea, the Philippines, and the Caribbean. In the IALA-A system used elsewhere in the world, the colors of lateral buoys are reversed—i.e., green buoys mark the right side of the channel, red the left.*

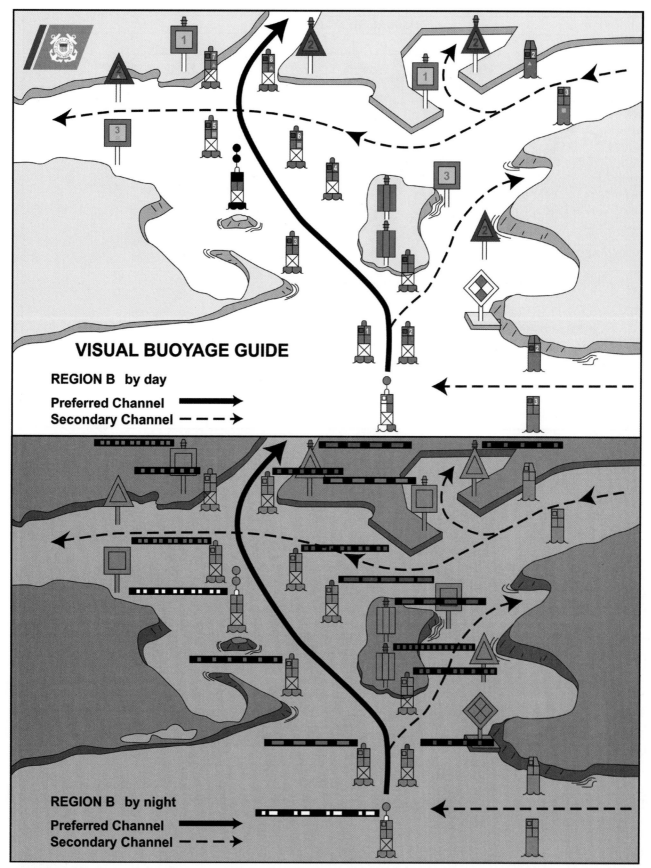

VISUAL BUOYAGE GUIDE

REGION B by day

Preferred Channel ➡
Secondary Channel ⇢

REGION B by night

Preferred Channel ➡
Secondary Channel ⇢

FIGURE 4-15B. *The lateral-system nav aids from Figure 4-15A are shown here in idealized fashion as they might appear by day and by night.*

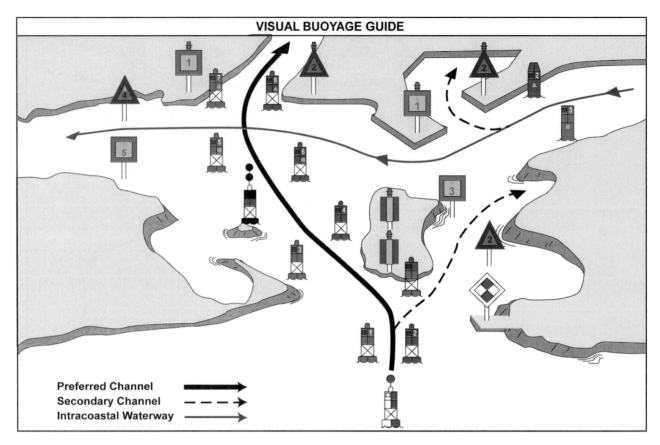

VISUAL BUOYAGE GUIDE

Preferred Channel
Secondary Channel
Intracoastal Waterway

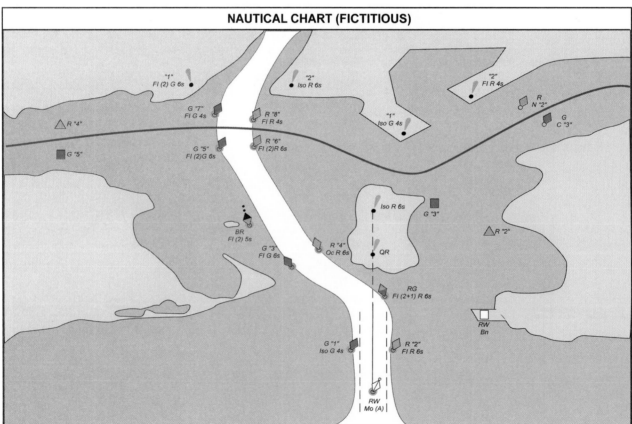

NAUTICAL CHART (FICTITIOUS)

FIGURE 4-15C. *Here we see a visual buoyage guide as in Figure 4-15B, this time with a corresponding idealized chart segment.*

U.S. AIDS TO NAVIGATION SYSTEM
on the Western River System

AS SEEN ENTERING FROM SEAWARD

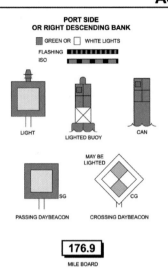

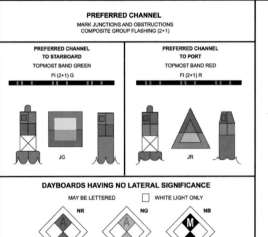

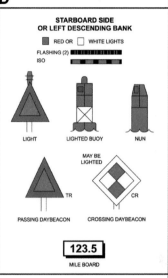

UNIFORM STATE WATERWAY MARKING SYSTEM (USWMS)

Note: The USWMS is presently merging with the U.S. Aids to Navigation System and will be discontinued on December 31, 2003. Vessel operators may encounter both types of systems during this transitional period.

STATE WATERS AND DESIGNATED STATE WATERS FOR PRIVATE AIDS TO NAVIGATION

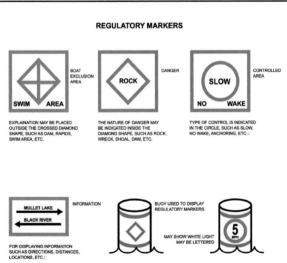

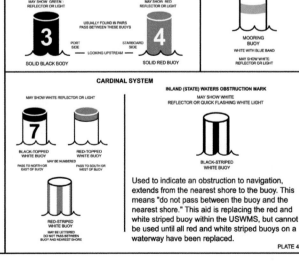

PLATE 4

FIGURE 4-15D. *The Western River System of nav aids used on the Mississippi River and its tributaries differs from the U.S. coastal IALA-B system in several respects, among which are that the nav aids are not numbered. The Uniform State Waterway Marking System used on lakes and inland waterways that are not covered by nautical charts, as well as some that are, has been discontinued in favor of the IALA-B system but may still be encountered here or there.*

SOURCES OF CHARTS

Charts and maps are generally compiled by government bodies that have the resources to collect and process the huge magnitude of data required. Collectively, these organizations are referred to as hydrographic institutions.

UNITED STATES

In the United States, marine charts come from a branch of NOAA called the National Ocean Service (NOS). The U.S. Coast Guard has the responsibility for siting and maintaining navigation aids. They publish the Local Notices to Mariners, reflecting week-by-week changes in key navigation information. These changes are accumulated and annotated on charts for updated publications.

The U.S. Army Corps of Engineers (USACOE) is responsible for navigable inland waterways such as canals, channels, rivers, and the Intracoastal Waterway (ICW). They provide data (and in some cases complete maps or charts) for these regions. The National Imagery and Mapping Agency (NIMA), now the National Geospatial-Intelligence Agency (NGA), is the military source for global maps and charts used for defense. NGA data are often used in the preparation of charts and maps for public applications.

Maps for coastal and inland areas are provided in topographic form by the U.S. Geological Survey (USGS). These "topo maps" show land features, not underwater details, and are popular with hikers. Still, many boaters use USGS or derivative maps for boating if no charts are available for their area. The USGS uses an unusual form of projection called Universal Transverse Mercator (UTM). This format derives from army artillery maps wherein all grid squares are the same size as calibrated in meters. (This makes it easier for the army to plan artillery shots.) These maps use UTM coordinates, which are different from latitude and longitude. If you use the UTM coordinates, you will need to change the setup in your GPS from latitude and longitude to UTM. Many of these maps have been translated by commercial companies into latitude and longitude for other uses. It is imperative that you use the latest charts and information available as many changes are made to charts each year.

INTERNATIONAL

The United Kingdom Hydrographic Office, within the British Admiralty, produces the high-quality British Admiralty Charts used in large parts of the world. Canada and Australia both have national hydrographic offices as well. The unifying body for chart and map standards is the International Hydrographic Organization (IHO). Most nations work to IHO standards, providing a good degree of commonality across international charts.

COMMERCIAL

Today, an ever-increasing percentage of charts and maps come to us from commercial suppliers. These companies usually start with the official masters from national hydrographic institutions and layer them with additional information. In this way, the liability for the fundamental accuracy of the data falls on the government bodies rather than the companies. In fact, the issue of potential liability prevents many of these companies from providing more refined information even when they have access to it.

Usually, they will add other useful information such as marine services, details of marinas, and fishing data. They may also alter charts to clean up details. For example, because most boaters no longer navigate by loran, companies such as Maptech have removed loran lines from older charts, and instead provide one-minute latitude and longitude grid lines to make plotting easier.

Commercial sources also present their charts and maps in a variety of convenient formats. Paper charts are giving way to waterproof charts, which are more suitable for use in the wet cockpits and confined spaces of small boats. These waterproof charts come in books or are prefolded for ease of use and storage. Often, their scales have been modified to create a more convenient size.

A number of commercial companies present chart and map data as digital charts that can be displayed and worked on via computer. This format permits a variety of projections to be geo-referenced to the same latitude/longitude grid, including photographic charts. Having different views of the same waters arrayed side by side is a great convenience to the recreational boater.

A number of companies produce charts or maps only for a particular locale, sometimes providing the sole primary source of information for an inland lake or river. Usually, these maps start with government sources or even road maps and are updated and enriched using local information to make them useful to boaters.

OUTLETS

Charts and maps are available from a wide range of retail outlets. Most marine stores carry charts for local waters. Other outdoor recreational outlets provide maps and charts for their respective regions that are usually tailored to fishing, hunting, or canoeing. Nautical charts are also available from OceanGrafix (licensed by NOAA), which provides "print on demand" versions of charts annotated with the most recent Local Notices to Mariners. Ship chandleries and large nautical bookstores far and wide sell charts and maps, and what they don't have in stock can be ordered to your needs. You may have a choice of competing charts from multiple international sources, particularly if you plan to go offshore. For example, both the British Admiralty and NOAA compile charts for Caribbean waters.

Digital charts and software are available from most marine stores. The most convenient format allows you to purchase a portfolio of digital charts covering a large region on a single CD-ROM or a removable data chip.

(continued from page 34)

Buoys on NOAA charts are indicated by a small, open, black circle indicating the approximate position and a diamond flare (♦). The color of the diamond corresponds to the color of the buoy. If the buoy is lighted, the circle will be surrounded by a magenta-shaded circle. (Outside the United States, lighted buoys are denoted with a flare just as lighted beacons are, but the approximate buoy location is marked by a small hollow rather than a diamond.) The color of the buoy is also given in the label, such as "R" for red, "G" for green, or "RW" for vertical red/white. On the water, the buoy's shape and color are significant. Unlighted conical red buoys are called *nuns* (shown as "*N*" on the chart). Unlighted cylindrical green buoys are called *cans* (shown as "*C*" on the chart). Lighted buoys are often conical or cylindrical as well, but they may also be a bell buoy, gong, or other *pillar* shape (generally a lattice tower on a flat base), and they have a wider range of colors. In addition to red and green, lighted buoys may be painted red/white, black, or yellow. Their lights are red, green, or white, and the light color and pattern are shown on the chart. White lights are used on center channel buoys (red/white) as mentioned above. Buoy sounds are labeled as BELL, HORN, or SIREN if present.

Plotting Tools

Now that you know more about charts, let's look at the tools that are used with them. Although this book focuses on using electronics to navigate, you still need to get charted information into your GPS, and you should verify electronic positions by nonelectronic means from time to time. For that, you need the time-honored tools of piloting.

Dividers

Dividers are used to measure distances and latitude and longitude coordinates on a chart. In its basic form, a pair of dividers comprises two arms ending in points, the distance between which can be adjusted by means of a friction pivot. Friction pivots are quick and easy to adjust but can be inadvertently altered on a moving, bouncing boat. Other pivots use an adjustment screw to fine-tune the position, but setting these can be arduous. The best designs have quick-set capability in addition to an adjustment screw. With these dividers you can quickly open the arms to the approximate setting you want, then turn the screw to fine-tune and lock in the setting.

In addition to a pair of dividers, many mariners like to carry a *drawing compass*, in which a pencil replaces one of the points of a divider. A drawing compass, no doubt familiar to you from school days, is handy for plotting points at specified distances or tracing arcs of specified radii.

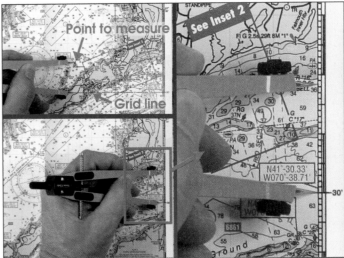

FIGURE 4-16. *Dividers are used to make measurements on your chart. In this example, the latitude of an object or a location is being measured. In the upper-left panel, one point of the dividers is placed on the object and the other point is opened to the closest grid line. Then that second point is traced along the grid line until it reaches the latitude scale on the side of the chart. Now you can read the corresponding value of latitude. In this example, the latitude of our object is 40° 31.84 N.*

DETERMINING COORDINATES To determine the latitude of a spot on the chart, you simply place one point of the dividers on the spot of interest, then adjust the arms to place the other point on the nearest line of latitude. Once this gap is set, move the dividers along the line of latitude to the latitude scale in either margin. Now one point lies on the latitude line and the other marks the latitude measurement for your desired location. In the Northern Hemisphere, the value of latitude increases upward and is read as degrees, minutes, and tenths of minutes north (N).

Longitude is similarly measured by placing one point on the desired location and the other point on the nearest meridian line. You then transfer this setting to the scale in the top or bottom margin of the chart and read the longitude. In North America longitude is read as degrees, minutes, and tenths of minutes west (W), with values increasing to the left.

MEASURING DISTANCE Distance is measured using the two points of the dividers, one point placed on each end of the distance to be measured. While maintaining that setting, move the dividers to the distance scale on the chart, put one point on zero, and read the distance to the second point. Alternatively, you can use the latitude scale and count the number of minutes (nautical miles) and tenths of minutes between the divider's points. *Note: Most charts have distance scales in nautical miles, statute miles, and kilometers. On the water it makes sense to use nautical miles due to the natural relationship with latitude.*

If the distance you wish to measure is greater than the dividers can span, you will need to draw a line be-

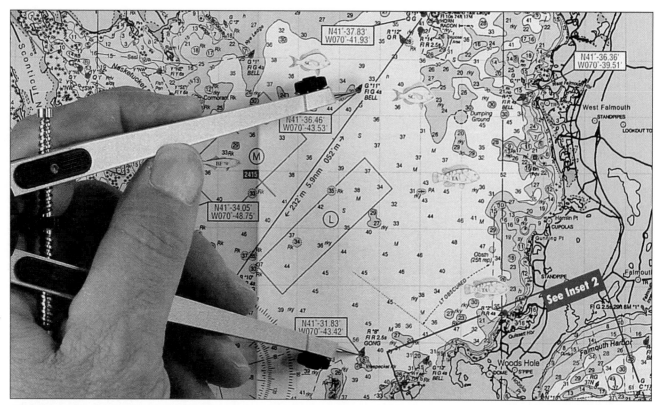

FIGURE 4-17A. To measure the distance between two locations, place one point of the dividers on the first location and the second point on the other location.

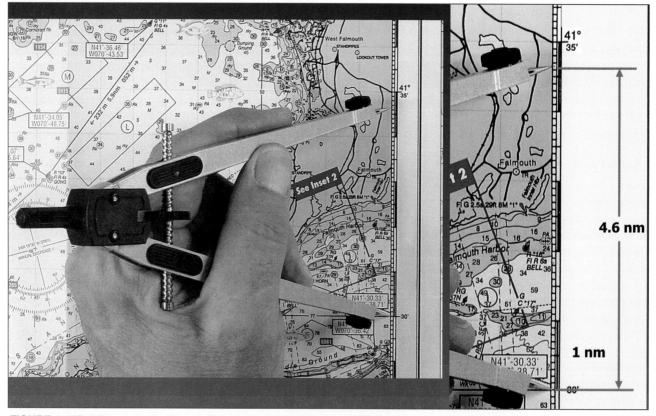

FIGURE 4-17B. Without altering that setting, transfer the dividers to the distance scale on the chart or to the latitude scale on the side. One minute of latitude (not longitude) is exactly equal to one nautical mile, so you can use the latitude scale as a distance scale.

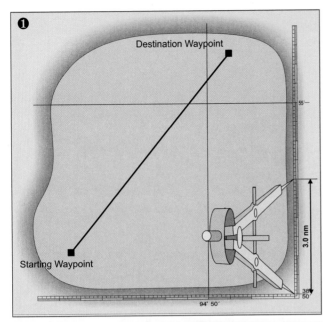

❶

Destination Waypoint

Starting Waypoint

3.0 nm

94° 50′

55°

38° 50′

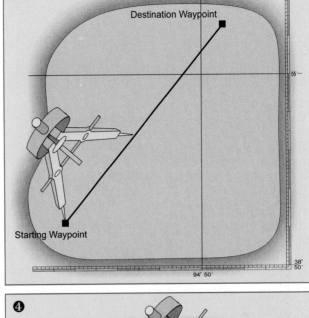

❷

Destination Waypoint

Starting Waypoint

94° 50′

55°

38° 50′

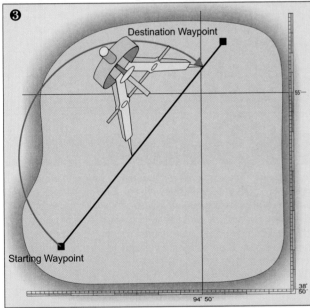

❸

Destination Waypoint

Starting Waypoint

94° 50′

55°

38° 50′

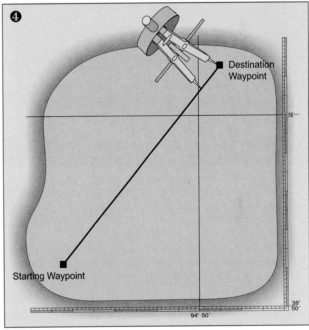

❹

Destination Waypoint

Starting Waypoint

94° 50′

55°

38° 50′

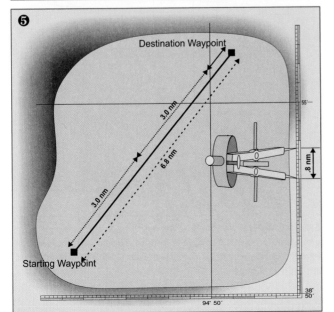

❺

Destination Waypoint

Starting Waypoint

3.0 nm

6.8 nm

3.0 nm

.8 nm

94° 50′

55°

38° 50′

FIGURE 4-17C. *If the distance you want to measure is too large for your dividers to span, draw a line between the locations. Next, set the dividers to a convenient distance, such as 3 nm, using the latitude scale. Walk the dividers from one location toward the other, counting the number of 3 nm increments until the last increment is less than the divider preset distance. Now, set the dividers to measure that final increment, and go to the latitude scale to read that final distance. Add all the increments to get the total distance.*

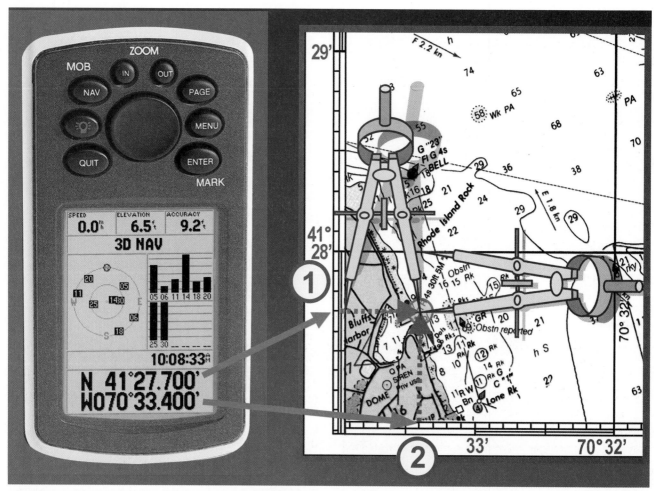

FIGURE 4-18. *When you use a GPS, it will provide values for your current latitude and longitude. To determine where you are on the chart, you must plot these values. This process is similar to what was shown in Figure 4-16, only this time it's done in reverse. In the last example, we transferred chart information to the scales, but here we'll use the same basic techniques to transfer scale information onto the chart. First, place one of the divider points on the scale mark that corresponds with the GPS-derived latitude value. Then open the dividers so that the second point rests on the nearest grid line. Then drag the open dividers across the chart, stopping when you reach your approximate longitude. ("Eyeball" this location.) Draw a short pencil mark at this point.Then repeat this process to transfer the longitude value. Your location is where the two pencil marks meet.*

tween the two locations. Now you can use the distance scale or the latitude scale to preset the dividers to a convenient distance—for example, 5 nautical miles. Next, set one point of the dividers on one end of the line and *walk* the dividers along the line by advancing from point to point, counting the number of preset segments as you do so. Let's say that you've set the dividers to 5 miles and are measuring the distance between two buoys that are 12 miles apart. You count off two divider spans for 10 miles, then see that the remaining distance is less than the gap between the divider points. So you close the divider points until they precisely span the remaining distance, then read that distance on the chart scale: 2 miles. Add this distance to the sum of the fixed intervals you just counted, and you get the answer: 12.

Some charts for locations such as the Great Lakes and major rivers use latitude and longitude scales calibrated in degrees, minutes, and seconds, whereas most nautical charts

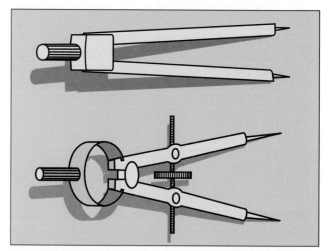

FIGURE 4-19. *Dividers come in several styles. The top pair uses a friction pivot to hold the setting. The bottom pair uses a wheel to adjust the arms. This wheel also helps eliminate errors by firmly holding the setting in place.*

use degrees, minutes, and tenths of minutes. Because minutes and tenths of minutes correspond well with nautical miles and tenths, you may wish to convert any charts that use the more cumbersome seconds. To do so, simply divide the number of seconds by 60 to get tenths of minutes.

PLOTTING COORDINATES ON A CHART Your GPS continually provides the latitude and longitude coordinates for your position, but until you plot this position on a chart, it doesn't mean much. To do this, locate your GPS latitude on the appropriate chart's latitude scale and place one point of the dividers on that spot. Then adjust the dividers so that the second point rests on the nearest latitude line. Now move the dividers along the latitude line to your approximate location (by visually approximating the longitude) and make a small horizontal pencil mark. Then do the same for the longitude. Your current position is at the intersection of the pencil marks (see Figure 4-18).

Parallel Rules

Perhaps the simplest tool for plotting is a set of *parallel rules*. This device comprises a pair of rules that are joined together by two or more swinging hinges. The rules serve as straightedges for plotting courses. The hinges allow you to expand or collapse the distance between the two rules while keeping the rules exactly parallel to each other. This is an easy and accurate way to transfer a plotted bearing line across a chart to the compass rose for measurement, or to transfer a measured bearing (say, the bearing to a nearby lighthouse measured on deck with a hand bearing compass, as described below) from the printed compass rose across the chart for plotting. These operations are explained in Chapter 5. The mechanics of the process are simple. You

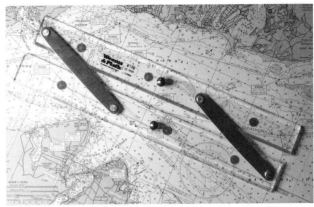

FIGURE 4-20. *Plotting on a chart often involves transferring a course line to a compass rose, or vice versa. In doing so, it's crucial that the second line is drawn perfectly parallel to the first. Parallel rules are popular for this purpose.*

merely press down on one rule while swinging the other outward, then press down on the lead rule while you swing the trailing rule after it. Repeat as necessary, thus *walking* the rules across the chart without altering the bearing. This time-honored device is practical for working on charts at home or at sea. With a little experience, the parallel rules can be walked either across the chart or up or down on it to align with the region of interest. And because the compass roses printed on nautical charts allow you to measure directions relative to either true or magnetic north, using parallel rules obviates the necessity for converting from *true* to *magnetic bearings* and back, with its attendant risk of error (see Chapter 5).

A more modern variation of the parallel rules is the *rolling parallel rule*. This device has only one straightedge and moves across the chart on a long roller, which preserves

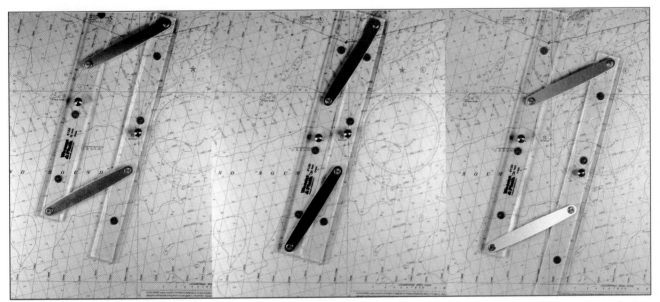

FIGURE 4-21. *If you need to transfer that parallel line to a location beyond the reach of the parallel rules, simply walk them to the location by extending, contracting, and reextending the rules.*

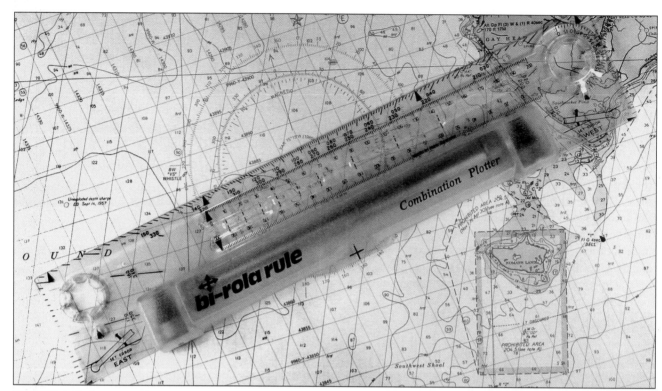

FIGURE 4-22. *A more modern approach uses a rolling bar to move the plotter across the chart. However, this tool requires a smooth surface such as a chart table, and it doesn't work as well on a small boat.*

the proper orientation. What the device gains in simplicity, it loses in versatility. It can go only forward and backward, not side to side. A special variation called the *Bi-Rola* has rollers that are perpendicular to each other. By pressing on one or the other, you can move across or up and down to reach any spot on the chart and still maintain an accurate bearing. These devices work well on a chart table but may slip or shift on less uniform surfaces or in rough seas.

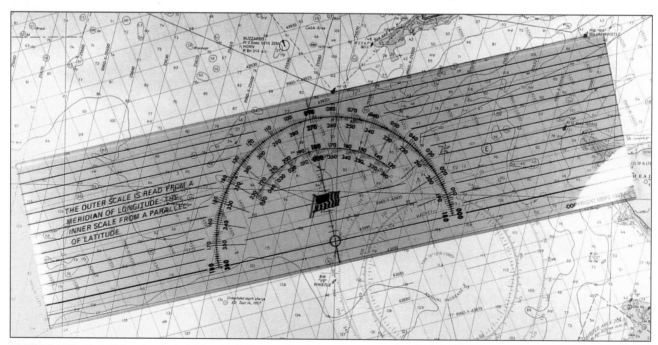

FIGURE 4-23. *One of the simplest plotting tools has no moving parts. The rectangular plotting tool is imprinted with a series of parallel lines. You can move the tool across the chart by drawing intermediate lines, moving the plotter, and realigning one of the printed parallel lines with the plotted line of the chart.*

Protractor Plotting Tool

A *protractor plotting tool* is often included among the materials for basic piloting courses. These tools are inexpensive and reliable. If you're in cramped quarters or on a small charting table, protractors can be less cumbersome than parallel rules. Plus, because a protractor scale is printed directly on the plotting tool, you won't need to access the compass rose for angles. This added flexibility is especially helpful when lack of space forces you to do your plotting on a folded chart. Murphy's Law being what it is, the nearest compass rose is always folded underneath and therefore inaccessible. Chapter 5 discusses a two-piece protractor plotting tool with a swinging arm. For now, however, let's focus on the one-piece *rectangular plotting tool*. This simple, rectangular, see-through-plastic template was designed by the United States Power Squadrons. Two protractor scales and parallel lines are printed on the template, with one for use with latitude lines and the other (printed in reverse order) for use with longitude lines.

To plot a course, align the course's starting point (whether a navigation buoy or simply a waypoint) on the plotter edge, orient the plotter's bull's-eye on a latitude or longitude line as appropriate, and read a direction in degrees true from one of the protractor's scales. This device takes some practice in order to avoid reading or using the wrong scale, and it requires those pesky conversions between true and magnetic bearings and courses, which you can avoid by using parallel rules. Nevertheless, these plotting tools are the least expensive and among the easiest to use once you are comfortable with the conversion between true and magnetic, as discussed in Chapter 5.

Tool Kit

You should put together an onboard kit of tools to support your navigation tasks. In addition to plotting tools and dividers, consider including a drawing compass, a calculator,

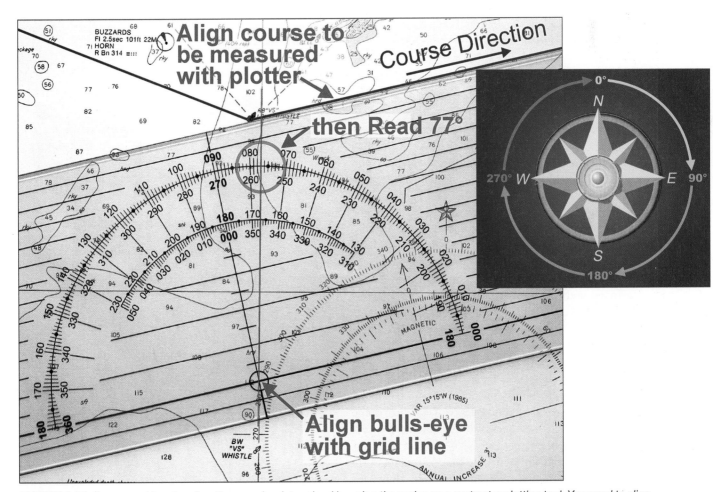

FIGURE 4-24. *Course and bearing directions can be determined by using the scales on a protractor plotting tool. You need to align the bull's-eye with a grid line while you have the plotter aligned with the course line. You can align the top of the plotter or any of the printed parallel lines with the course line. Finally, you read the course direction from the appropriate protractor scale. Which scale to use? Use common sense. This simplistic compass rose (upper right) provides you with a sense of direction. Any course or bearing toward the top right of the chart will be between 0° and 90°. By the same token, any course or bearing toward the bottom right will be between 90° and 180°. Toward the lower left will be between 180° and 270°. Finally, toward the upper left will be between 270° and 360° (0°).*

The Tools of Navigation

a notebook for keeping waypoint information and calculations, a collection of fine-tip pencils and erasers, and waterproof sleeves for charts.

Other Navigation Tools

Now that you have the tools to plot your bearings and courses, you'll need tools to measure and steer them. The most fundamental of these, invaluable to mariners since it was developed in China in the 1300s, is the magnetic compass, and we begin this discussion with it. Next we consider GPS, which is almost as useful as a compass. Then we merely mention (for now) some other electronic tools. The costs of electronic navigation equipment have dropped significantly over the past five years while their performance has improved. Many are designed with smaller boats in mind. Even quite small boats can be equipped with such electronic devices as *chartplotters, digital depth sounders, sonars, radio, autopilots, digital compasses,* and *radar.* Throughout the book, as we discuss their associated navigation techniques, these tools will be explained in greater detail.

Ship's Compass

No boat should be without a magnetic steering compass. Even if you use GPS to set and monitor your courses, you will find it easier to steer and hold a course using the steering compass, and it serves as an essential backup when all else fails. It is a wise investment to get the best compass you can afford. Generally, larger is better. The best have a spherical chamber containing a flat or dished card.

All steering compasses are dampened to counteract the quick motions of a boat, but compasses designed for sailboats are dampened differently from those used on powerboats. In addition, many sailboat compasses provide an additional scale indicating the degree of heel for the boat.

To be useful, your compass probably needs to be compensated. Nearby metallic objects on a boat influence the way the Earth's magnetic field affects a compass. These effects are different for each heading, because a change in heading alters the relative alignment of the metallic objects between the compass and the Earth's magnetic field. Most compasses incorporate built-in magnets that can be rotated to compensate for onboard influences. Usually, there is one magnet for north-south compensation and another for east-west. By running known courses, it is possible to adjust these magnets iteratively until the compass readings are quite accurate. Although compensation can counteract most effects, there is always some residual error. Usually, however, you can reduce this error to 2 degrees or less, depending on the heading, at which point you may choose simply to ignore it. If the residual errors are larger, you can construct a deviation table that provides the difference between the compass reading and the actual magnetic course

FIGURE 4-25A. *The magnetic compass is the most fundamental and important navigation instrument on your boat. Shown here are two powerboat compasses. The compass card is suspended in a liquid-filled bowl of oil and pivots on a fine point. This allows the card to stay level as the boat pitches and rolls. On the left is a front-reading compass. The card is read on its front surface against a lubber's line etched in the glass. This style is a little more difficult to use. A top-reading compass card (right) is more intuitive, because its orientation matches directions around you and those of a chart's compass rose. The top-reading card also gains an advantage of some magnification from the fluid-filled bowl. The cards in powerboat compasses are dampened (intentionally slowed) to counteract the dynamic motions of fast boating and thus improve readabilty.*

FIGURE 4-25B. *Sailboat compasses are a bit different from powerboat compasses in that they are dampened less and are designed to perform under greater angles of heel. The version on the right is designed for a bulkhead mount and provides a scale of heel as well as compass heading. (Courtesy: Ritchie Navigation)*

FIGURE 4-25C. *Large ship compasses are designed for larger boats. They are larger to enhance accuracy and ease of reading. The compass on the right is designed for steel-hull boats, where magnetic interference is significant. The steel balls on either side of the compass help adjust for deviation. (Courtesy: Danforth)*

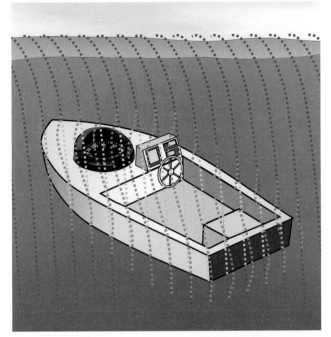

FIGURE 4-26. *The ideal compass responds perfectly to the Earth's local magnetic field (as depicted by the dark dotted lines in the graphic) and always returns to the same reading for the same heading. However, local influences on the boat, such as metallic objects (engines, structure, et cetera), electric motors, or wires can alter the local magnetic field, as depicted by the light dotted lines. This leads to erroneous readings. These effects vary with the heading of the boat, because the aspect angle to the offending object changes as the boat turns. Compasses have built-in compensating magnets that can be used to counteract these effects (one for east-west and the other for north-south). It is recommended that you employ a professional compass adjuster to compensate your compass. You can determine its error (deviation) by using the techniques described in Chapter 29.*

for each direction of the boat. Then you can apply these corrections whenever you steer a compass course by adding or subtracting the deviation as appropriate (see Chapter 5). Compensation to within a degree or two is obviously the more practical solution. (Chapter 29 explains how to use your GPS to measure compass error—or *deviation*—for each boat heading.) Although you can adjust your compass yourself with careful measurements and a lot of patience, this is a challenging task best left to a professional.

Typically, magnetic compass cards are marked in 5-degree increments. This seemingly wide margin between hash marks is okay, because the boat's natural motion makes it difficult to hold a reading to better than a degree or two. The longer hash marks—marking 10-degree increments—are painted to a width of 1 degree, making an "eyeball" estimate of your heading easier. In most marine compasses, the card sits suspended in a thick liquid such as mineral oil, the viscosity of which helps dampen the motion of the boat so that the reading appears relatively steady.

Most compasses present a heading in one of two ways.

You can read your heading either against the *lubber line* on the front edge of the compass card (front reading), or across the top of the card against a pointer on the far side (top reading). The latter is preferable because the numbers will increase clockwise, just as the numbers on a compass rose do. The front- or direct-reading card displays numbers in a counterclockwise progression, which can lead to confusion.

Hand Bearing Compass

From time to time you'll want to take visual bearings in order to fix your location, determine your speed, or measure the relative course of a nearby vessel. At such times it pays to have a *hand bearing compass*, which is nothing more than a handheld magnetic compass with a built-in sight. Simply aim the sight at the other boat or charted object and read its bearing off the compass. Hand bearing compasses come in a variety of configurations and cost as little as $25. Some marine binoculars contain an integral compass, which is displayed as you view a distant object; most such units have crosshairs for accurate sighting.

Hand bearing compasses are subject to onboard magnetic disturbances, just as your ship's compass is. These influences may be different at different locations on the boat. Therefore, you should always use the hand bearing compass from a single spot near the helm. (Also, be sure not to brace the compass against any wire shrouds or metal fittings.) To quickly check the deviation of a hand bearing compass,

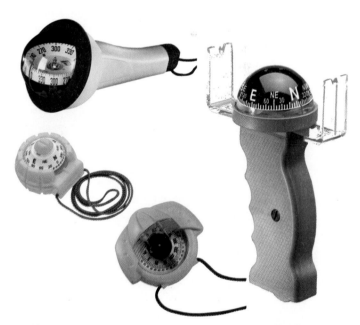

FIGURE 4-27. *A hand bearing compass is essential equipment on your boat. Taking bearings on landmarks and navigation aids with this device is quick and easy. Clockwise from upper left: a Plastimo hand bearing compass that can be fixed-mounted as well; a Davis hand bearing compass that provides accurate readings at an attractive price; a Plastimo "hockey puck" compass; and a Ritchie small-boat "hockey puck" hand bearing compass.*

FIGURE 4-28. *As an alternative to the hand bearing compass, many marine binoculars offer a built-in compass that projects in the bottom of the magnified image (right). Crosshairs in the field of view identify the object being sighted. These devices offer image magnification and quality dampened compasses to make reading accurate bearings an easy task. (Courtesy: Steiner)*

point it at the bow and compare its reading with that of the ship's compass. If they are close, you are in good shape. If they differ (and you know that your steering compass is accurate), apply that difference to any reading you take with the hand bearing compass while on that heading. If the ship's compass reads 5° lower, for example, you need to subtract 5° from each reading of the hand bearing compass. Keep in mind that this deviation will change for every new boat heading. Although the deviation is usually not significant and can probably be ignored, you should check it on all headings to be sure.

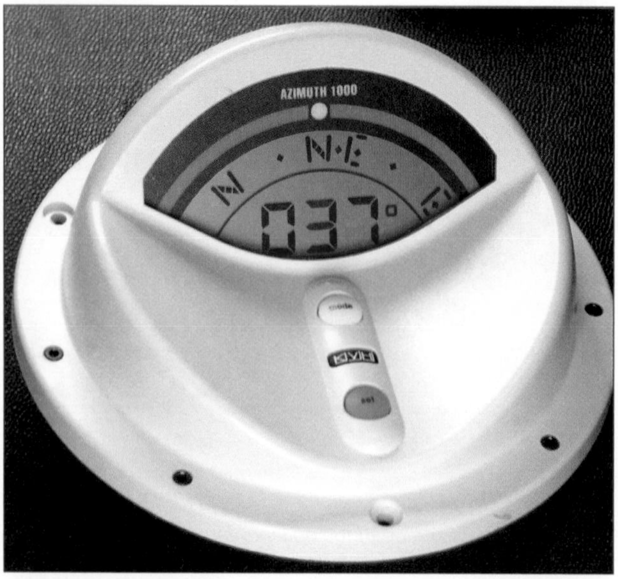

GPS

By far the most popular electronic navigation system is the Global Positioning System, or GPS. The low cost and superb performance of a handheld GPS receiver make it a near-essential tool to have on a boat. GPS uses multiple satellites as artificial stars to provide precise position fixes. To be effective, a GPS receiver must have a clear view of the sky above the boat and be able to simultaneously receive signals from four or more satellites. The resultant three-dimensional fix provides precise north-south and east-west coordinates (typically expressed as a latitude and longitude), a nominal altitude (meaningless to the boater, though not to a pilot or mountain climber), and a precise time. GPS references your fix to a horizontal datum; you must be sure the datum selected corresponds to that used on your nautical chart.

By means of its built-in navigation computer, a GPS receiver can provide other useful information in addition to your position. By comparing your current position with one from a few seconds earlier, the GPS receiver can determine your boat's direction and speed. And by comparing your position with the coordinates of a selected waypoint, the GPS receiver can provide the bearing and distance to that waypoint, plot a course to it, provide a continuous indication of how close you are to that course line, and calculate a time of arrival from your present speed.

Some GPS receivers are hardwired to the boat's power supply. If yours is not, be sure to stow extra batteries or a cigarette lighter–type adapter aboard. As with any elec-

FIGURE 4-29. *Electronic compasses offer many advantages over conventional magnetic compasses. They are extremely accurate (typically less than 1° error), and they are self-compensating. They also provide digital outputs to other instruments and can display both magnetic and true headings.*

MEET YOUR GPS

All GPS recievers offer similar functions. The generic layout shown here is typical. Use your GPS manual to identify any differences in detail.

latitude and longitude of your current position and the precise time. (In this example, Satellite and Position appear on one screen; other models present them separately.) The Map Screen shows your current position with respect to other objects (waypoints) stored in your GPS, and the active course line. The Highway Screen shows a 3-D representation of your active course with your current position in the foreground and your next waypoint in the background. This is likely to be the most valuable screen to keep you on course.

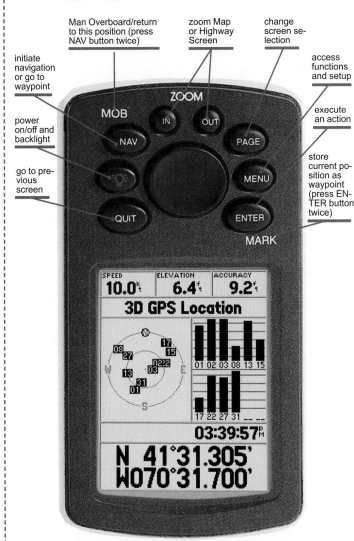

- initiate navigation or go to waypoint
- power on/off and backlight
- go to previous screen
- Man Overboard/return to this position (press NAV button twice)
- zoom Map or Highway Screen
- change screen selection
- access functions and setup
- execute an action
- store current position as waypoint (press ENTER button twice)

Satellite/Position Screen

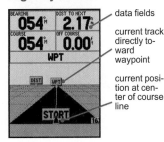

- estimated accuracy
- fix quality
- signal strengths
- satellite positions
- position coordinates

Map Screen

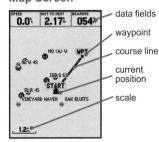

- data fields
- waypoint
- course line
- current position
- scale

Highway Screen

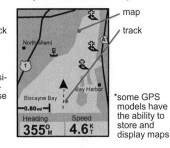

- data fields
- current track directly toward waypoint
- current position at center of course line

Map Screen with Map*

- map
- track

*some GPS models have the ability to store and display maps

MENUS

Use menus to program the GPS, to initiate and control navigation, and to select display format. Most menus are accessed via the Main Menu using the MENU (or ENTER) button, or by paging to find the Main Menu Screen. In addition, most GPS sets offer screen-dependent menus that control how data are displayed on an individual screen. Access these from the current screen by pressing the MENU (or ENTER) button.

BUTTONS

The many GPS functions are controlled by a set of buttons, restricted in number by the space available. Most of the buttons control how the GPS processes and displays information. The button labeled NAV or GOTO controls navigation functions. Press the ENTER button to execute actions. Press the QUIT or ESC button to revert to a prior screen instead of executing an action. The labels may vary slightly by model, but the general approach is always the same.

SCREENS

You can select screens as needed. The Satellite Screen indicates the quality of the GPS position and tells you if part of the sky is blocked to the GPS antenna. The Position Screen indicates the

Move cursor to highlight:

Points: Enter/edit waypoints; view list of programmed waypoints
Routes: List/create waypoint sequences, each called a "route"
Proximity Waypoints: List/enter programmed danger coordinates
Tracks: Control/review recorded paths taken by GPS
Trip Computer: Set/review recorded times, distances, average speed, etc.

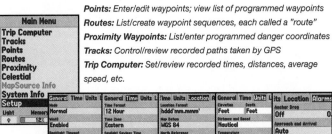

FIGURE 4-30. *GPS has become the primary position sensor for most boaters. They are offered in both handheld and fixed models. The fixed models typically include built-in digital charts, making them into chartplotters.*

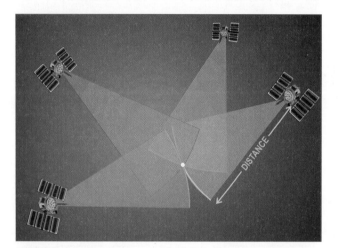

FIGURE 4-31. *The purpose of GPS is to provide a precise position. Basically, it provides a 3-D position in space. Each satellite transmits information about its identity and location, and a time signal. The receiver analyzes the time that the signal is received to determine how far the signal traveled. With signals from four or more satellites, the receiver can deduce position and precise time.*

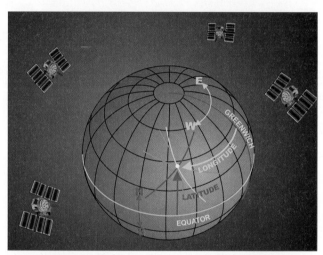

The default grid is latitude and longitude based on a horizontal reference datum called World Geodetic System 1984 (WGS-84).

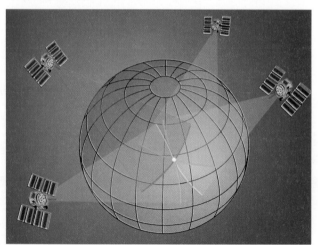

What we really want is a location on the Earth. The GPS uses a mathematical model of the Earth's shape to provide a reference grid.

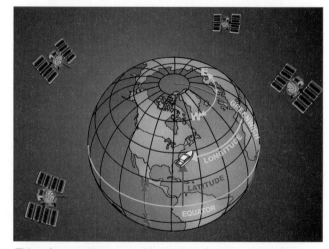

This reference datum provides surface features of the Earth that relate your position to charts.

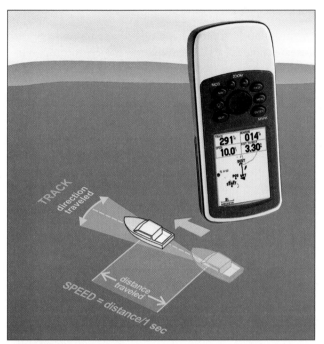

FIGURE 4-32. *Track and speed are computed within your GPS receiver. It compares your current position against your position from a second earlier to determine your direction and speed.*

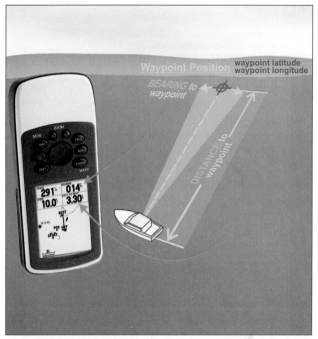

FIGURE 4-33. *Bearing and distance to other objects (waypoints) are computed within your GPS receiver by comparing your current coordinates with those of the waypoint.*

tronic device, a GPS receiver is quite reliable but not infallible. If you use it as your primary position sensor, it's a good idea to carry a backup GPS just in case. If all else fails, you will need to get out your plotting tools and limber up your chart-and-compass piloting skills. And remember, a GPS position is just an abstraction until you plot it on a chart. Your GPS receiver has no inherent knowledge of the shorelines, ledges, or other hazards arrayed around your boat (unless you've programmed a few avoidance waypoints into its memory, as described in Chapter 5). There's just no substitute for a chart's-eye view of your surroundings.

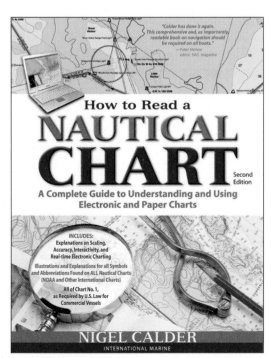

FIGURE 4-34. *The premier book on nautical charts and their symbols is a handy reference as well as an interesting read.*

FIGURE 4-35. The Weekend Navigator *focuses on navigating with electronics. For more about GPS and how to operate your receiver, you can refer to* GPS for Mariners.

Other Electronics

Part VI of *The Weekend Navigator* will discuss each of the following electronic navigation devices in greater detail. In the meantime, however, here's a brief overview of what's available for recreational boaters.

In the competition for the next electronic navigation device to consider after GPS, radar and a digital depth sounder run neck and neck. Although not essential for most boaters, *radar* is a powerful and versatile tool for fixing your position by means of bearings and ranges on surrounding nav aids and landmasses, and it's the *only* electronic device that allows you to track the presence and movements of other boats (and even rain squalls!) in conditions of poor visibility. See Chapters 15 and 25 for discussions of radar.

Some navigators question the usefulness of a *depth sounder*, and they make a strong case. After all, the sounder tells you the depth of water directly beneath your boat. If it says you don't have enough water under your hull, it's likely that you've already run aground. But the depth sounder is actually a very useful navigation tool. By comparing the sounder's reported depth against chart soundings, you can better interpret and confirm your current position. Also, when all else fails, a sounder can help you to navigate by following a depth contour or monitoring the depth trend. Chapter 16 explores this in greater depth—no pun intended.

A *fluxgate compass* uses electronics to sense the Earth's magnetic field, thus eliminating potential errors caused by the friction of a compass card in a standard compass. Fluxgate compasses are also self-compensated to a high degree of accuracy—typically within one degree or better—and many can automatically correct for local magnetic variation to display true north instead of magnetic when desired. Because it is electronic, a fluxgate compass also has the ability to provide digital output to other devices, such as an autopilot or radar. Chapter 18 offers more details on fluxgate compasses. (Large ships may use a gyrocompass instead, but these are larger and a lot more expensive and have found no place thus far on recreational boats.)

An *autopilot* is actually a mechanical (not electronic) device that controls a boat's rudder in response to signals from its control unit. It needs a signal from an electronic compass (fluxgate or gyro) or a GPS to provide a direction reference. You set a heading on the control unit, and the autopilot adjusts the rudder to maintain that course until it has been shut off or altered by the crew.

Though not usually considered a navigation device, a VHF radio is a truly valuable tool—particularly in an emergency. By regulation, all new fixed VHF radios must include a function called digital selective calling (DSC). If the radio is connected to a GPS, your position is automatically radioed whenever a DSC call is made. In an emergency, all DSC-equipped radios within your immediate area will sound an alarm and automatically switch to the distress channel (16) to listen to your call. If the receiving DSC radio is connected to an appropriate chartplotter, your position will be plotted on the screen. This function helps the Coast Guard (and other nearby vessels) locate you.

Even without DSC, the Coast Guard can take a radio bearing on your VHF distress signal. Cross bearings from two or more direction finders can locate your boat within a small search area.

VHF radios also are equipped with receive-only channels that provide weather information. More than 800 transmitters cover all 50 states in the United States. The Canadian Communications Directorate provides similar transmissions in Canada, and similar services exist over much of the maritime world. Marine and standard weather reports are repeated continuously, with hourly updates.

PREVOYAGE PLANNING

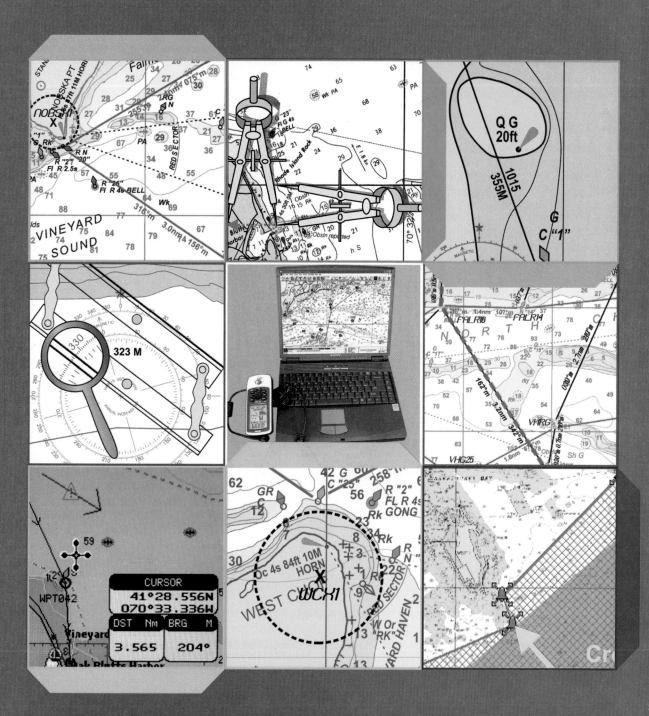

Planning with GPS and Paper Charts

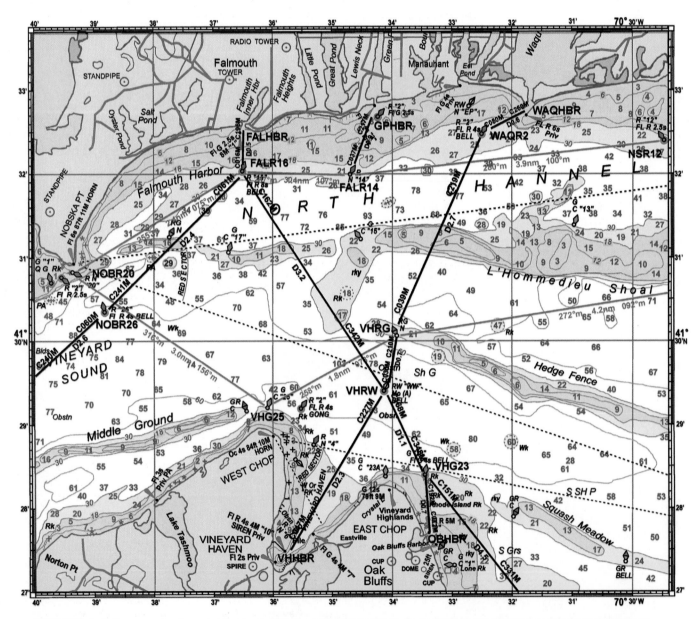

FIGURE 5-1. *At the core of safe navigation is preplanning legs on your chart. Once the legs are planned and their attendant way-points stored in your GPS, you can navigate along those legs with complete confidence. The commercial publisher of this chart provided the preplotted course legs shown in red. To those, you can add your own preplotted courses.*

As described in Chapter 2, the process of navigation can be thought of in three stages—planning, navigating underway, and periodically double-checking your courses, positions, and chartwork. The planning stage—the topic of this and the following two chapters—is essential to ensure your safety. You need to select your courses, check them for hazards, and adjust them to avoid obstacles. Even if you normally boat in an area you know well, it's possible to be caught at sea under adverse conditions with restricted visibility. Careful planning can help you avert discomfort or even disaster in a situation such as this.

The simplest preplanning method involves working with paper charts and pushing buttons on your GPS receiver. Another method, described later in this chapter, eases some of the button pushing by using a computer to upload waypoints and routes into your GPS. A third method, planning directly on digital charts, is presented in the following chapter. Whatever method you choose, preplanning is a good off-the-boat activity that can be done in the evenings or during the off-season.

Planning and Paper Charts

The chart is your security blanket and the navigator's most essential tool. It provides the key information you'll need to plan and enjoy safe boating. Of course, local knowledge and personal observations will enhance your navigation, because charts are not infallible and cannot show everything. You may know from prior experience or the advice of a

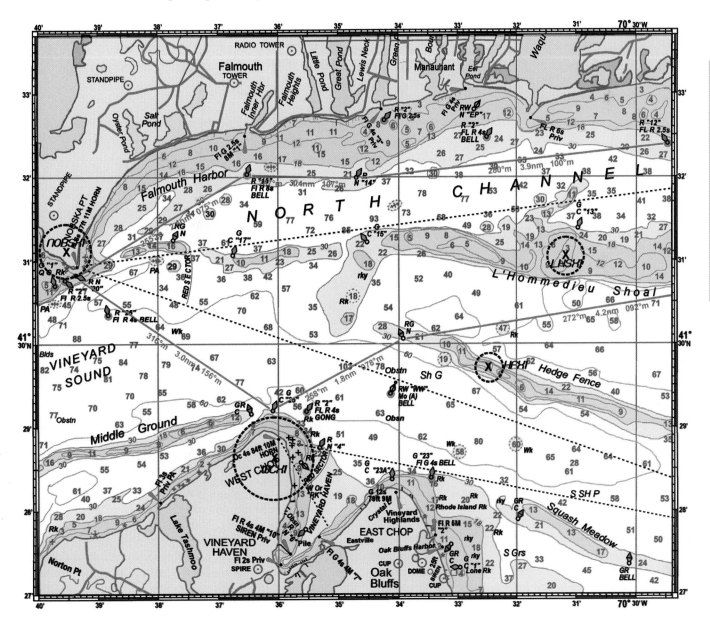

FIGURE 5-2. *As an alternative or a supplement to preplotted legs, you can mark isolated hazards and locations that you must avoid while you are on the water.*

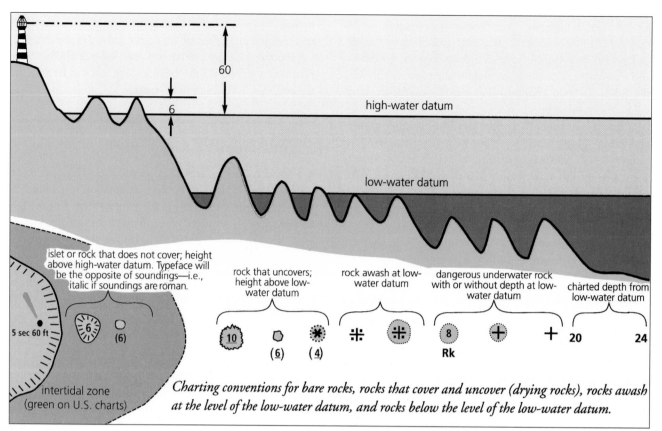

islet or rock that does not cover; height above high-water datum. Typeface will be the opposite of soundings—i.e., italic if soundings are roman.

rock that uncovers; height above low-water datum

rock awash at low-water datum

dangerous underwater rock with or without depth at low-water datum

charted depth from low-water datum

5 sec 60 ft

intertidal zone (green on U.S. charts)

Charting conventions for bare rocks, rocks that cover and uncover (drying rocks), rocks awash at the level of the low-water datum, and rocks below the level of the low-water datum.

FIGURE 5-3. *Rocks and land are hazardous to your boat. To avoid danger, it's essential that you understand the basic chart symbols. (Graphic adapted from* How to Read a Nautical Chart.*)*

local fisherman that aligning a particular red barn in front of a particular white church steeple puts you on the best course through your harbor inlet, but you won't find the barn on your chart (though the steeple might be noted). Nevertheless, it's amazing how much information *is* on a chart, and how seldom it's wrong. It's essential that you have the latest version of the charts for your area. (See Chapter 4 for more on chart descriptions, scales, and sources.)

Criteria for a Safe Course

The fundamental premise when using GPS is that you will first prequalify safe paths, then follow those paths when you're proceeding from one place to another on the water. The same principles apply to prequalifying an area in which to meander without fear of encountering unseen hazards. So, what is considered safe?

DETERMINING SAFE DEPTHS Obviously, you won't go far if your boat has run aground. Thus, adequate depth is the first feature you'll look for to prequalify a safe path. But what is adequate? The answer depends on two factors: the characteristics of your boat, and the characteristics of the seabed.

Each sounding shown on a chart represents a measurement of the bottom depth at a particular location. When enough soundings are assembled, a contour line of

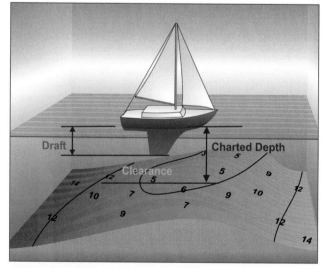

FIGURE 5-4. *The chart provides soundings that represent spot depths at low tide datum. You need to factor in the draft of your boat to determine your clearance. More on tides is provided in Chapter 14.*

constant depth can be drawn using the soundings as a reference. All soundings are referenced to a standard datum, which for most NOAA charts is mean lower low water (MLLW; see Chapter 4). This means that each sounding printed on a chart represents nearly the shallowest water you can expect to find at that location.

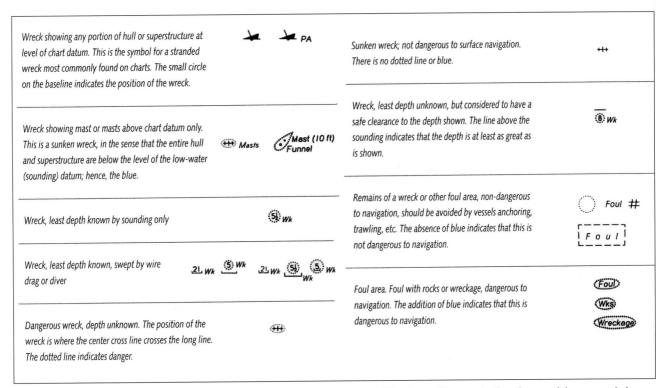

FIGURE 5-5. *Wrecks also can present hazards to navigation. The symbols differ depending on whether the wreck is exposed above high water datum, or below it. (Graphic from* How to Read a Nautical Chart.*)*

The *draft* of a boat is a measure of how far its keel and/or drive unit extend below the waterline. This measurement is usually provided by the manufacturer in feet and inches (though you might want to add a couple of inches to this nominal figure once you've filled every on-board locker and cubbyhole with a few years' accumulation of gear, tools, and belongings). If not, you can measure the draft while the boat is out of the water. When looking for a safe depth, you will need to accommodate the draft plus a margin of a few feet. Determining an adequate safety margin depends on three factors. First, be aware of the seabed. A rocky bottom is far less forgiving than sand or mud. If you run aground on rocks, you can expect boat damage. If you run aground on mud, you may suffer only inconvenience. Second, consider the likely sea conditions. Even in a moderate sea, the troughs of waves may be 1 to 2 feet below the charted water height. Third, consider the characteristics and vulnerabilities of your boat. Sailboats with a retractable centerboard provide greater flexibility than fixed-keel boats. The deepest part of a powerboat is often expensive running gear, such as an outboard lower unit(s) or a propeller(s). Damage to these components can put a boat out of commission or result in costly repairs.

Generally, it is prudent to plan legs of a safe passage that you can use at all times, not just at higher tides when the sea is calm. Try to steer clear of areas where the draft of your boat nears the chart soundings. Where tidal ranges are large, however, you may have occasion to cross waters that would be too shallow at low tide. To do this, you'll need to determine the depth for the present tidal height and plan your transit accordingly (see Chapter 14).

ISOLATED HAZARDS Isolated hazards can be natural or man-made. Outlying rocks are a common example of the former. If you drained all the water from a bay, its underly-

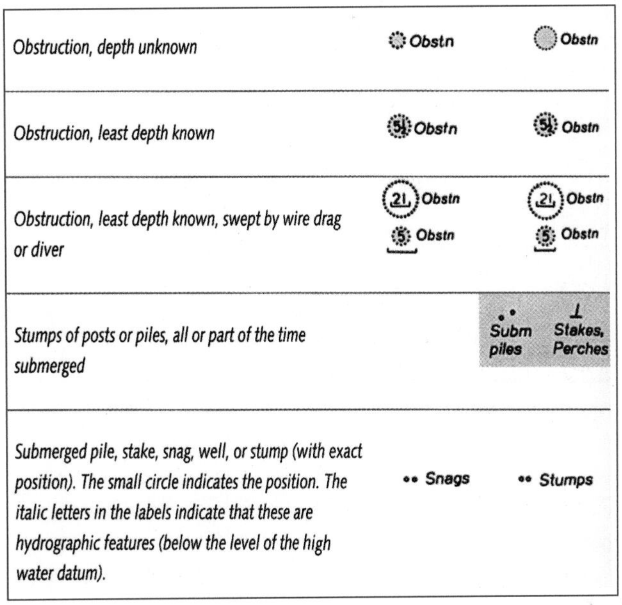

FIGURE 5-6. *Other obstructions, such as pilings, tree stumps, or underwater structures, also present hazards to navigation. Typical obstruction symbols are shown in this figure. (Graphic from* How to Read a Nautical Chart.*)*

59

ing topography would look much like that of the surrounding land, with hills, valleys, and rocky outcrops whose peaks might protrude above the surface or lurk just below for the unwary boater. As with wrecks and other man-made hazards, rocks are classified as exposed, covered, and covering.

In addition to wrecks, man-made hazards include old pilings. These, in fact, represent one of the greatest hazards to boats, because they can easily penetrate a hull.

SHOALS Shoals, or circumscribed shallow areas, are in effect the tops of underwater hills. Often, shoals lie along a line, not unlike the spine of a miniature mountain range. Sometimes, though not always, they are rocky. Main channels frequently run parallel with shoals. Often, the shortest path between two points lies across intervening shoals. Before attempting such a path, take special care to ensure adequate water depth.

HORIZONTAL CLEARANCE Just as you need a safe margin between your keel or running gear and the seabed, you need to plot courses that maintain a safe horizontal margin. You need ample room to steer around obstacles. Wind and waves can cause small deviations from course, so your paths should be wide enough to allow for this. Also, typical GPS accuracy is within 50 feet of your true position. When planning, check along your intended path to ensure safe waters a little more than ten times wider than that GPS error to either side. To make planning easy, look at the latitude scale. Because one minute of latitude is a nautical mile (about 6,076 feet), one-tenth of a minute (the smallest tick mark) is roughly 600 feet. Using this handy reference for perspective, you can scan your projected path on the chart and

confirm that the horizontal clearance on either side of the course is at least as wide as the smallest increment on the latitude scale.

Of course, this assumes that, when underway, you will periodically plot your GPS positions. Plan to plot your GPS position about once every hour, or more frequently if you're traveling fast or in foul weather. While you're at it, try to verify your GPS-derived position through independent means. In the event of a failure, this may be the only information you have.

CLEARANCE OVERHEAD The final consideration for pre-qualifying safe paths is vertical clearance. Will your boat fit under bridges and overhead cables? Generally, one of the manufacturer's specifications for your boat is *bridge clearance*. Remember, this measurement is taken from the waterline to the highest part of the boat's structure *as it leaves the factory*. You have likely added antennas, radar, outrigger poles, and so on. You will need to consider the additional heights of these objects when planning your passage. If they can be lowered, make a note on your chart as a reminder.

The clearance printed on the charts is generally referenced to *mean high water* (MHW), or occasionally *mean higher high water* (MHHW). Check your chart legend for the datum used. Just like timing a passage over shallow water, you might be able to pass beneath a low bridge by using the tides to your advantage. Chapter 14 discusses techniques for predicting tidal heights.

In some waters—on the Intracoastal Waterway along the U.S. East Coast, for example—you will encounter bridges that can be raised or drawn or swung open to provide clear passage. Generally, their heights when closed are shown on the bridge itself as well as on your chart. You also

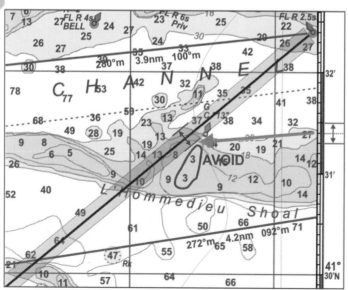

FIGURE 5-7. Just because a course line narrowly misses a hazard doesn't mean your boat will. When plotting, you must ensure that either side of the path has clearance of at least ¹/₁₀th of a nautical mile (about 600 feet or 185 meters).

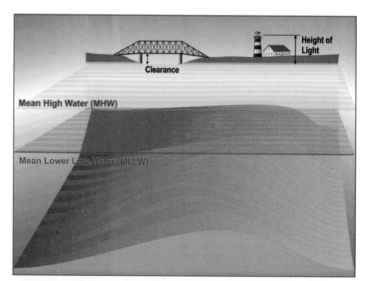

FIGURE 5-8. The charted clearances of bridges or other above-water obstructions, and the heights of lights and towers, are usually expressed in feet above mean high water (MHW).

FIGURE 5-9. *NOAA and other hydrographic offices provide official charts. These are typically large in size and may not work well on recreational boats. However, companies such as Maptech offer more options. The charts are available in convenient sizes and packages, and some are printed on waterproof paper.*

may find a depth of water scale on a bridge abutment. You should be certain of your boat's actual bridge clearance and plan carefully so as not to unnecessarily cause the operator to open the bridge or, even worse, attempt a passage you can't clear.

When you consider vertical clearance, don't forget about overhead cables, especially on inland waterways. Often, these may be low enough to present a hazard, and many carry high voltages.

Steps in Prevoyage Planning on a Chart

It bears repeating: before you do anything, you need a set of charts for your boating area. Chapter 4 discusses various chart formats and sources. With charts in hand, study them in the comfort of your home. Preplanning waypoints, legs, routes, and avoidance waypoints will vastly simplify your navigation underway. Here are the recommended steps for programming waypoints:

- First, locate your home port and other ports you wish to visit. Buoys around these ports will become waypoints.

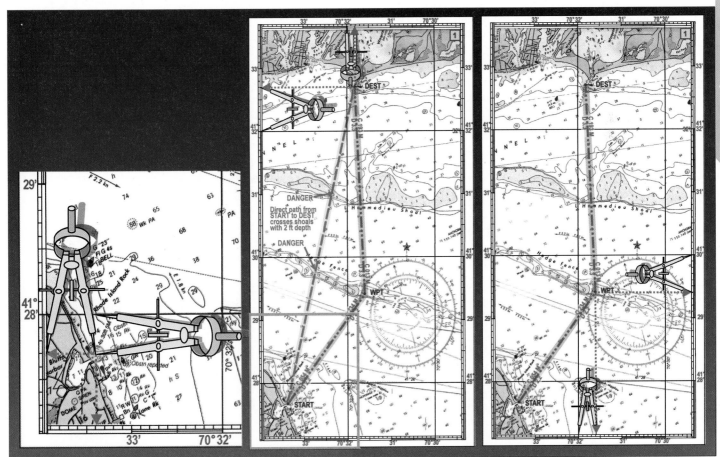

FIGURE 5-10. *Planning on a chart involves plotting lines between your starting point and your destination. You need to measure the coordinates of these end points to enter them as waypoints. A scan along the line indicates the potential for hazards. If potential dangers are identified, you must create intermediate waypoints to build a route that avoids the obstacles.*

- Second, locate hazards—places where the water may be too shallow and must be avoided. This information will help you prepare safe routes or avoidance waypoints.

- Third, plot a sequence of straight-line paths on your chart that will take you from your home port to other points of interest. For safe and confident navigation, these paths will ideally begin and end at prominent navigation aids—preferably ones that emit noise and/or light and are surrounded by safe water. Alternatively, you can plot waypoints just offshore from prominent landmarks fronted by safe water. Given a dearth of likely looking nav aids and landmarks, you'll have to rely more heavily on latitude/longitude waypoints in featureless waters.

- Next, invent short names for each of the connecting waypoints.

- Then note any landmarks you'll be able to use for visual reference while running between waypoints. Charted towers, standpipes, tall buildings, and lighthouses can help you verify your position or guide you to safety if your GPS fails.

- Now, using your plotting tools (as described in Chapter 4), measure the coordinates of each identified waypoint. Be sure to double-check each set of coordinates to avoid mistakes. To keep track of these coordinates and other useful information, create a written table with columns for waypoint name, latitude, longitude, and comments.

- Finally, once the waypoint table is complete, enter the data into your GPS. This can be done manually on the GPS or by using a computer. We discuss both approaches later in the chapter.

Waypoint Table
Martha's Vineyard to Cape South Shore

Waypoint Name	Latitude	Longitude	Comments
FALHRB	41° 32.528 N	70° 36.507 W	Entrance to Falmouth Harbor
FALHR16	41° 32.047 N	70° 36.490 W	Lt R approach to Falmouth Harbor - R16
FALHR14	41° 32.015 N	70° 34.672 W	R N approach to Great Pond - R14
GPHBR	41° 32.649 N	70° 34.811 W	Entrance to Great Pond
WAQR2	41° 32.479 N	70° 32.509 W	R lt approach to Waquoit Bay - R2
WAQHBR	41° 32.726 N	70° 31.805 W	Entrance to Waquoit Bay
NSR12	41° 32.409 N	70° 29.431 W	Lt R Succonnesset Point - R12
NOBR20	41° 30.824 N	70° 39.290 W	R N Nobska Light - R20
NOBR26	41° 32.324 N	70° 38.714 W	R N Woods Hole East Entrance - R26
VHG25	41° 29.205 N	70° 36.034 W	G C Off West Chop - G25
VHRG	41° 30.043 N	70° 33.915 W	RG N off Vineyard Haven
VHRW	41° 29.401 N	70° 34.412 W	Lt RW Entrance to Vineyard Haven - "NW"
VHG23	41° 28.394 N	70° 33.440 W	Lt G Off East Chop - G23
OBHBR	41° 27.655 N	70° 33.398 W	Entrance to Oak Bluffs Harbor

FIGURE 5-11. *Record your waypoints on a tablet or in a logbook. Waypoints should be named to reflect their location and features. The latitude and longitude for each should be recorded along with summarized details. Always double-check the accuracy of your coordinates. A simple slip of a digit can place you in peril.*

NAMING WAYPOINTS

GPS receivers usually allow you to enter six to nine characters for each waypoint's name along with an accompanying symbol. You should develop a naming and symbol convention that works for you. Because there are many buoys labeled R "2" or G "1," you will need to distinguish among them. Generally, you'll find it easier to locate waypoints in your GPS memory if you develop regionally based nomenclature. Let's say you're plotting the waters around Newport, Rhode Island. You could name each waypoint with the prefix "NPT" followed by an identifier such as "R2" for red buoy number "2"; hence "NPTR2." Most GPS sets alphabetize the waypoint names, so using regional prefixes will ease the task of finding waypoints later by grouping those for a particular area. Avoid beginning a waypoint name with a number. Most GPS receivers assign numbers to newly marked waypoints, and you'll want a way to clearly distinguish your established waypoints from more transitory ones.

Next, you may wish to mark danger areas such as isolated rocks or wrecks. Use the same regional prefix ("NPT") for these locations, but also add another character, such as "D," for danger. (With the "D" in place, your danger waypoints will also be alphabetically grouped within their region.) Then add identifying abbreviations such as "RKS" for rocks or "WRK" for wrecks (hence "NPTDRKS" or "NPTDWRK."). If there is more than one rock to mark near Newport, simply add a number ("NPTDRKS2").

Also, on most GPS receivers, you can mark locations on the Map Screen by choosing from a number of different symbols. Use these symbols to clearly differentiate between hazards and navigation aids. For instance, most GPS units offer icons such as a skull and crossbones. This sober image is perfect for marking hazards. Use a distinctly different set of symbols to mark land-based objects such as towers or buildings.

For regions of shallow water, you can add imaginary buoys at key locations if real buoys are lacking. By labeling them "R" or "G" (for "red" or "green"), you will know on which side of them you need to stay. Append with something such as "I" for imaginary before any identifiers or numbers of your choice ("NPTIR3"). Mark and label these points on your chart.

ROUTE NAMING

Many GPS models will automatically assign a route name in this construction:

name of the starting waypoint *[hyphen]* name of the ending waypoint.

This makes the route name clear and unambiguous. As a further convenience, many of these same GPS models can even reverse the order of the waypoints if you opt to take the route in reverse order.

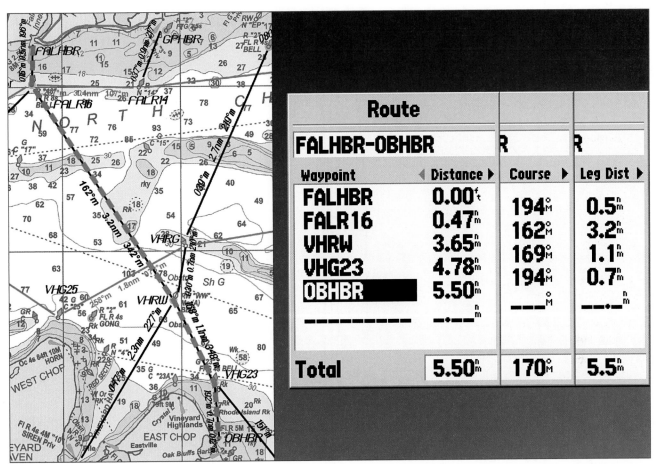

FIGURE 5-12. *Your GPS can execute a route—a preplanned sequence of legs. To build a route, select the New Route Screen and begin by entering the departure waypoint. Then, enter each subsequent waypoint. The GPS computes the course for each leg and its distance.*

CREATING ROUTES To ease your tasks on the water, it makes sense to create routes or route segments using your newly entered waypoints. By accessing the route function within your GPS, you can select waypoints in a desired sequence and thus build a route. Most GPS sets allow you to enter roughly twenty waypoints for each route and can store as many as fifty routes. Usually, the GPS automatically names the route by using the first and last waypoint names. Unless you have a strong reason for changing it, the default naming scheme is preferred.

Now you have created a personal waypoint logbook for your boating area with the information stored in your GPS. By identifying and programming a substantial number of waypoints, you have constructed a frame of reference to compare with visible objects and hazards while on the water.

Plotting on a Chart

Because we are using paper charts in this chapter, it's important to be comfortable with techniques for plotting courses and bearings on a chart. The basic tools are discussed in Chapter 4.

It's wise to thoroughly annotate your paper charts with the information stored in your GPS. This includes labeling the waypoints in the same manner. By the way, another advantage of waterproof charts (other than the obvious) is that they usually can be written on, erased, and annotated at will without damaging the chart.

Summary of Plotting Lines

Chapter 2 describes several types of lines that you will plot on your charts—some in advance and some while you go. Here's a quick summary:

Ahead of Time

Course—a solid line representing your intended path on the water, labeled with the direction and distance of the leg.

Range—a dashed line between two charted objects—generally ashore or in shoal water—that is then extended over navigable waters, where it switches from dashed to solid. A range is labeled with its bearing. Government-established ranges are preplotted on charts; you can add your own ranges as desired.

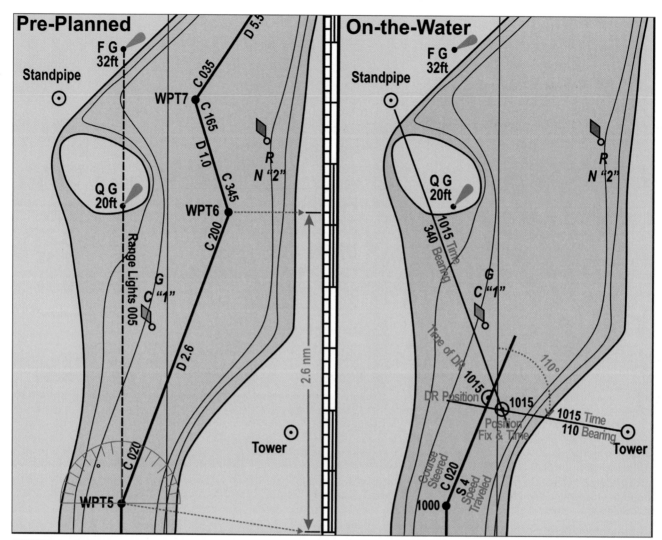

FIGURE 5-13. *Plotting falls into two main categories: prevoyage plotting and plotting that's done underway. Intended courses (legs, waypoints, routes) are preplotted. Ranges are preplotted. On the water, you plot bearings to match your observations, and a DR (dead reckoning) plot to back up your electronic navigation. These courses and bearings have been measured in degrees true using the chart grid for reference.*

While Underway

DR—a solid line representing your estimated progress on the water. A DR is based on the course steered; its length is the distance traveled as estimated from speed and time of travel.

Bearing—a solid line representing your observation of a landmark or navigation aid labeled with the time of the observation and the bearing direction in degrees.

Plotting a Course

In the "Planning and Paper Charts" section of this chapter, we drew straight-line segments on the chart along prequalified paths that avoid obstacles. We then measured the coordinates of the end points of each such leg and programmed these into the GPS as named waypoints. Finally, we programmed routes by calling up waypoints in a desired sequence.

Once a route is entered, most GPS sets provide you with the courses and distances between each of the waypoints in sequence in that route. You'll find it helpful to label the legs of the routes plotted on your chart with these values. To be consistent with navigation conventions, name the leg with the following elements: start with "C" for course, then add the three-digit direction, then finish with the letter "M" for magnetic (assuming you are using magnetic headings in your GPS). For instance, a course of 3° should be labeled "C 003 M." Place this label near the beginning waypoint above the course line. To note the distance of a leg, start with the letter "D," then add the GPS-derived number (usually expressed in nautical miles and tenths). This label should be placed under the course line, ideally near the center of the leg. As you add these labels, verify their accuracy with your plotting tools. Why do this if the GPS computes courses and distances for you? Well, this is another check on the accuracy of your entry for each way-

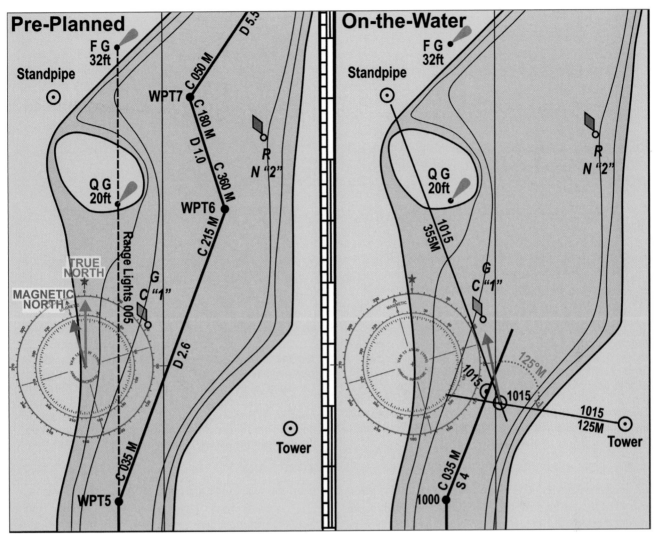

FIGURE 5-14. *Most recreational boaters will want to label their plots with magnetic courses and bearings, as here. This enables them to relate to their compasses without further correction for variation. Directions labeled in magnetic should be annotated with an "M" suffix for clarity.*

point. By comparing your measured course direction and distance with that computed by the GPS, you gain confidence that you've measured, entered, and selected waypoints properly. (You'll be amazed how many times you pick up an error in an entered waypoint by doing this.) Again, waypoint coordinates are just numbers until they're plotted on a chart.

If you have a Maptech or other commercial chart book, you may find that some routes and legs are already labeled, along with waypoint coordinates. Most such books use magnetic headings and nautical miles. You will note that the *reciprocal* course heading is labeled at the other end of each line. The reciprocal is the course you steer from the opposite direction.

To determine a reciprocal, either add 180° to a course of less than 180°, or subtract 180° from a course of more than 180°. You can also use your GPS receiver to determine a reciprocal course simply by selecting the *invert* feature from its menu. Doing so will save you from entering your return trip as a separate route. Once inverted, the route will list the reciprocal course directions for each leg. Invert again to restore the original sequence.

Yet another way to find a reciprocal course is to place your parallel rules over the original course on the compass rose, then read the reciprocal from the other side of the rose.

For the most part, you probably will be working in magnetic rather than true. The language of the boat is magnetic; the language of the chart is true. You need to be comfortable with the conversion—which can be done mathematically by adding or subtracting local variation—or graphically (and more simply) using the compass rose. Let's look at the latter first.

USING THE COMPASS ROSE As described in Chapter 4, the compass rose (which is printed in multiple locations on your chart) provides the chart's fundamental reference for magnetic directions. It is printed in a magenta ink that is

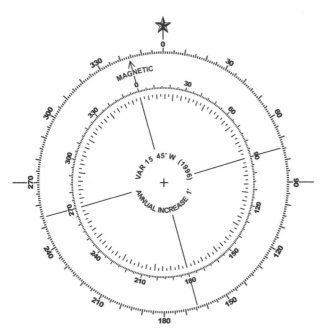

FIGURE 5-15. *Charts are printed with one or more compass roses. The compass rose has two rings. The outer ring is aligned with the chart grid and true north. The inner ring is aligned with magnetic north. A legend at the center of the rose provides the local variation and its annual change. The compass rose simplifies the labeling of courses and bearings and provides instant reference between true and magnetic north.*

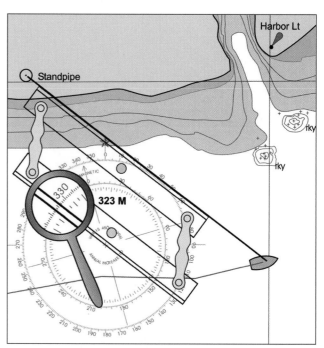

FIGURE 5-16. *The compass rose can be used to measure or plot magnetic direction. With parallel rules, you can align one rule along the bearing to be measured and extend the other rule to align with the center of the compass rose. A magnetic bearing can be read directly on the inner scale. If the distance between the compass rose and the bearing line is too great, you can walk the parallel rules as shown in Figure 4-21.*

distinctive when viewed with red light at night. (Navigators use a red light at night for illuminating charts and instruments, because this color has minimal effect on night vision, which is essential for keeping watch.)

The compass rose has two rings. The outer ring aligns with the chart grid of latitude and longitude lines—that is, with true north; the inner ring aligns with magnetic north. Within the inner ring is a legend that notes the local variation used for the chart. The variation describes both the magnitude of the difference in degrees and minutes between true and magnetic north for the charted location, and the direction of that offset, either east or west. (Magnetic north is moving, albeit slowly, so variation needs to be adjusted for this movement.) In addition, the legend identifies the date used for the variation and the amount by which it will change each year, east or west. You will need to adjust the variation accordingly if your chart is several years old and the annual change is significant.

Many mariners use the compass rose for laying out or measuring a course or bearing. Because the rose is rarely if ever located where you want to plot or measure a course, devices such as parallel rules are used to transfer the direction to or from the rose, as described in Chapter 4 and shown in Figure 5-16. Make sure you read your direction from the compass rose going the right way—that is, by imagining your boat at the center and reading to-

ward the rose in the direction of the course or bearing.

Another type of parallel rule uses a roller (Figure 5-17) to pick up a desired direction from the compass rose and transfer it across the chart to where you are plotting, as described in Chapter 4. Typically, you will need a flat, stable surface for this device to work.

Using your parallel rules, confirm the GPS calculation of course direction for each preplotted leg on your chart as follows: align one rule with the plotted leg, then walk the rules across the chart to the nearest compass rose and read the course in degrees magnetic from the inner ring. Does the result agree with what your GPS is telling you? If so, the course direction calculated by the GPS is correct, and the plot can be so labeled. Now check the distance of the leg by walking it off with a pair of dividers, as described previously. Does the result agree with your GPS calculation? Good; add the label and turn to the next leg of the preplotted route.

Are these courses now ready to steer? Yes, provided your steering compass doesn't exhibit significant deviation errors that you can't get rid of. See "Correcting for Deviation" later in this chapter for more on this topic.

USING THE CHART GRID AND A PROTRACTOR PLOTTING TOOL Measuring and plotting courses and bearings in degrees magnetic, as described above, is simpler than

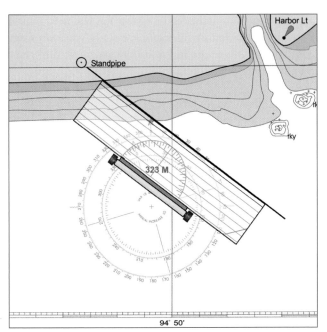

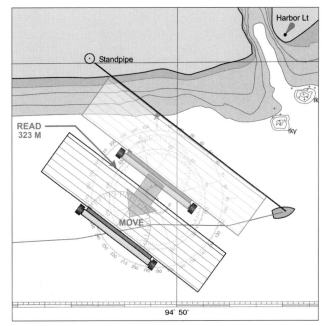

FIGURE 5-17. *An alternative tool uses a roller instead of two rules. The roller allows the rule to glide across the chart without changing its orientation. In the left panel, the parallel rule is aligned with a bearing. In the right panel, the parallel rule has been rolled so that the straightedge aligns with the compass rose for reading the bearing.*

piloting by degrees true. When you confine yourself to the language of the compass, you sidestep the potential for translation errors. The other approach, as mentioned, is to measure and plot courses and bearings in degrees true, then steer or sight their magnetic equivalents after adding or subtracting local variation (always) and onboard deviation (if necessary), as described below.

But why do things this harder way when it's simpler to work in degrees magnetic using the inner ring of a compass rose? The short answer is that most small-craft navigators don't. Nevertheless, the concept of converting back and forth between true and magnetic directions is one you should understand, even if only to recognize when the difference is about to affect your navigation.

And there are practical reasons for knowing how to measure and plot courses and bearings from a chart's grid of latitude and longitude lines. For one thing, the grid covers the entire chart and is always available to you, whereas the nearest compass rose is often folded underneath and therefore not conveniently accessible when you're working on a small surface. Second, those who navigate this way all the time swear that it becomes so second nature as to be faster than using a compass rose. Well, maybe . . .

Finally, if your ship's compass carries deviation on some headings, as described in Chapter 4, you'll have to add or subtract these values from your magnetic courses no matter how you obtain them, in order to get courses to steer (see next page). Because the technique for doing this is just like adding or subtracting variation to get from true to magnetic or back, you might as well learn it now.

If you're still not convinced, think of it like iodine on a cut—painful but good for you.

So let's return to the routes you have preplotted on your local chart or charts in anticipation of a wonderful boating season, this time assuming that you've initialized

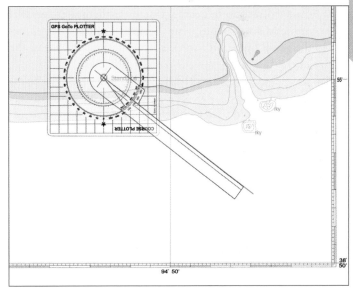

FIGURE 5-18. *A very useful plotting tool has a protractor scale and a pivoting arm. Parallel lines are printed along with the protractor on the fixed part. This is aligned with the grid lines on the chart, with the center of the plotting tool on your current location or the object being sighted. The arm can then be rotated to a selected angle so the line can be measured or drawn. Because the protractor is aligned with the grid, the direction provided is in degrees true.*

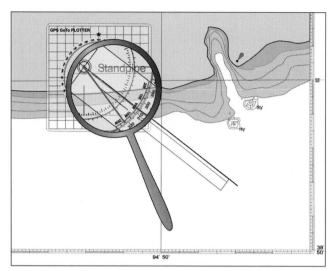

FIGURE 5-19. *In order to allow the plotting tool to be used directly with magnetic directions, the rotating scale is imprinted with a variation scale. Instead of aligning the "0" mark when reading an angle, you incorporate an offset for local variation. The plotting arm is then aligned with local magnetic direction.*

your GPS receiver to calculate course directions in degrees true. As you call up each leg of a route in sequence, the GPS tells you its course direction and distance. As before, double-check these numbers with plotting tools before labeling each leg. To do this, align one of the protractor plotting tools, described in Chapter 4 (see, for example, Figures 4-23 and 4-24), with the plotted leg, then read its course direction in degrees true from the nearest parallel or meridian, as appropriate (Chapter 4 shows how). Does the result agree with the GPS calculation? If so, add the label.

One kind of protractor plotting tool employs a pivoting arm (Figure 5-18). The protractor is aligned with the grid lines on the chart, and the arm is set to the desired angle. Some of these plotters have an extra scale on the movable arm that allows you to adjust for the local variation between true and magnetic, as shown in Figure 5-19, making this a truly versatile tool. For the moment, however, let's assume you're plotting in degrees true.

ADDING OR SUBTRACTING LOCAL VARIATION You've preplotted routes on your chart and calculated the course direction for each leg in degrees true. But before you can steer that course on the water, you'll have to convert it to degrees magnetic, which is the language of your ship's compass. Remember, local variation is the same for all boats in an area and on all headings. Your chart will tell you what the variation was at the time the chart was created. Assuming your chart is the most recent edition (as it should be), you can safely use the charted value of variation. This is an

angular correction either east or west. You will need to add a westerly variation or subtract an easterly variation from each true course to get its equivalent magnetic direction. Summarizing, the formula is:

$$\text{True} \frac{+ \text{ W Variation}}{- \text{ E Variation}} = \text{Magnetic}$$

Suppose, for example, your local variation is 15° W and you want to convert a course of 175° true to its magnetic equivalent. You add 15 to 175 and find that the magnetic course is 190°. If your local variation is 15° E, a course of 175° T would translate to 160° M. Westerly variation is added to a true course; easterly is subtracted. Some navigators find the expression "West is best; east is least" to be a helpful memory aid.

While correcting for local variation, you should correct for compass deviation too; indeed, the latter correction will apply even when your magnetic course has come from a GPS calculation or from a reading off a chart's compass rose. Putting it all together, we get the formula TVMDC, which is the universal technique used to convert between true, magnetic, and compass directions. The initials stand for:

T True direction

V Local variation

M Magnetic direction

D Deviation of the compass (for the heading of the boat)

C Compass direction

Refer to Figure 5-20. As you can see, how these corrections are applied depends upon whether you are going up or down on the TVMDC diagram. In each case, you will add west going down (remember "West is best"). If you remember TVMDC and that one direction, you can figure out the rest. Here are the details.

1. Converting from true to magnetic
   Add westerly variation (going down); subtract easterly

2. Converting from magnetic to true
   Add easterly variation (going up); subtract westerly

3. Converting from magnetic to compass
   Add westerly deviation (going down); subtract easterly

4. Converting from compass to magnetic
   Add easterly deviation (going up); subtract westerly

For plotting, you will use only true or magnetic directions; most navigators choose magnetic for reasons already explained. Compass courses are steered but not plotted.

CORRECTING FOR DEVIATION

Virtually every compass has some deviation error caused by the aggregate influences of onboard metallic objects or electrical wires on the local magnetic field. Because the nature of that influence relative to the Earth's magnetic field changes as a boat turns, the magnitude and direction of deviation is dependent upon the boat's heading.

As indicated in Chapter 4, you should have your compass professionally compensated (corrected) to minimize deviation errors, or do it yourself. (This task requires patience; Chapter 29 describes how to do it using your GPS.) It is reasonable to expect a deviation of 2° or less on every heading from a properly compensated compass, as demonstrated by the sample deviation table below for a real boat that previously had a 35° deviation when on an east-west heading. When the residual deviation can be reduced to 2° or less, it is reasonable to ignore it when steering courses, because 2° is within the margin of error for small-boat course-keeping ability. However, it pays to recheck your compass each time you add or remove a ferrous object or an electrical device, particularly if the change is close to the com-pass. Electronics can play havoc with compasses, so it is recommended that you test your compass with various pieces of equipment turned on and off. Do your compensation with the equipment that you intend to use turned on. One piece of equipment that can affect a compass is a windshield wiper. Even if it is used infrequently, double-check the compass when using it for any additional error.

If your compass's deviation after compensation remains greater than 2° or 3° on some headings, you will want to adjust accordingly when steering these headings. As with variation, you must add westerly deviations and subtract easterly deviations when correcting from magnetic to compass courses. When converting compass courses back to magnetic, subtract a westerly deviation or add an easterly one.

Note that it doesn't matter how you derive a magnetic course: by direct measurement from a compass rose, by reference to your GPS receiver, or by converting from a true course by adding or subtracting local variation. You must still compensate for any significant deviation.

SAMPLE DEVIATION TABLE*

Magnetic	Deviation	Compass	Magnetic	Deviation	Compass
000°	1°W	001°	180°	0°	180°
045°	2°W	047°	225°	2°E	223°
090°	2°W	092°	270°	1°E	269°
135°	1°W	136°	315°	1°E	314°

*For headings between those listed, use the closest listed deviation.

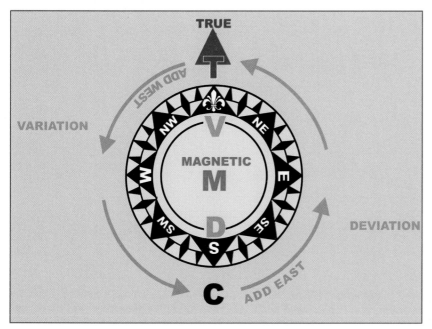

FIGURE 5-20. Often, it is easier to correct the direction between true and magnetic mathematically. To do this, you need to add westerly variation—remember, "West is best." By the same token, if your compass has residual deviation, to go from magnetic direction to what you would read on the compass, you will add westerly deviation. In other words, going down (T to M to C), you add west. Conversely going up (C to M to T) you add east. This diagram provides an easy way to remember this—you always add counterclockwise. On the "west" side of the diagram, you add west (either V or D). On the "east" side you add east.

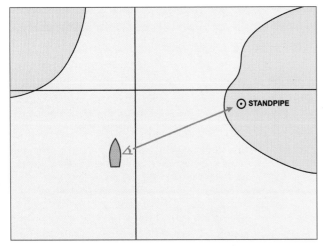

FIGURE 5-21A. *Bearings represent a fundamental way to plot and check your position on the water by sighting on charted objects. You can observe landmarks and other charted objects and measure the bearing to them using a hand bearing compass. The direction is as sighted from the boat to the object.*

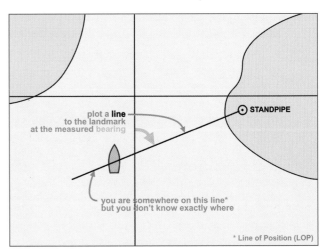

FIGURE 5-21B. *Given the bearing, you can plot it on the chart, either using the compass rose to align its direction (magnetic) on the chart, or the chart grid (convert to true). Remember that the direction is from the boat to the landmark, even though you are aligning the plotting tool with the landmark and drawing a line in open water in the vicinity of the boat. Your position lies somewhere on that line.*

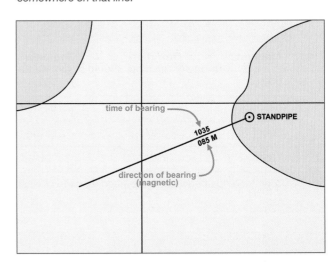

FIGURE 5-21C. *You should label the time of the bearing on top of the line, and the direction below the line.*

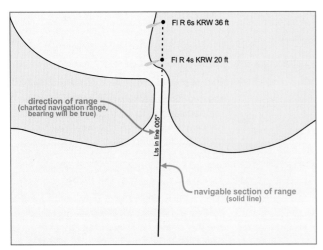

FIGURE 5-21D. *A range represents a special case of a bearing that is preplotted on the chart. A range uses two visible, charted landmarks to define the bearing direction.*

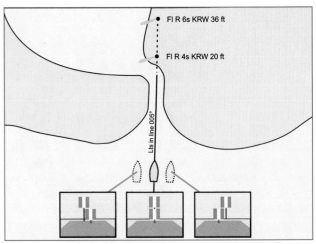

FIGURE 5-21E. *On the water, you simply observe the relative positions of the two objects. If they are aligned, you are on the preplotted bearing. If the rear landmark lies to the left, you are to the left of the range line.*

Plotting a Bearing

While on the water, you will have occasion to take visual bearings on charted objects to help you determine your position. We discussed bearings in Chapters 2 and 4 and return to their use on the water in later chapters, so here we merely discuss briefly how to plot them. Remember, a bearing is considered to be a line of position and as such represents a line on which your boat is located. Because the observed object is charted and your boat is not, you will need to plot the line using the object as the reference point. Still, the line is drawn *toward* the object, in the direction of the bearing, from the estimated location of your boat. It is labeled with the time of the bearing in four digits (24-hour clock) above the line and the direction of the bearing in three digits below the line. These labeling conventions are the same as for courses. See Figure 5-21 for details on sighting and labeling bearings, and Figures 5-13 and 5-14 for examples of labeling in degrees true and magnetic.

Plotting a Range

Ranges are plotted as straight dashed lines between charted objects with the line extending into the intended area of navigation. The portion of the range that is navigable is denoted by a solid line. The bearing of the range should be labeled on top of the line for ready reference on the water. If the range is charted, generally the bearing will be true, as shown in Figure 5-21D. If you plot the range yourself, you can do so in degrees magnetic; just follow the bearing with the letter *M*. Generally, the landmark to the rear will be taller, and the sight picture will be as indicated in Figure 5-21E. If you are "on" the range, the two objects will align. If you are to the left, the rear landmark will appear to the left of the one in the foreground. Plotting and labeling for true and magnetic directions are shown in Figures 5-13 and 5-14. *Any* charted object can be used in a range: a water tower, a church spire, a daybeacon, a bold bluff on one end of an island. With this in mind, you can plot strategically located ranges on your local chart while cruise planning. They'll come in handy.

Entering Waypoints into Your GPS

As we saw earlier in this chapter, cruise planning includes a process of plotting a network of safe legs on charts covering the area in which you intend to boat. These safe legs start and end at waypoints. In turn, each waypoint is referenced by a set of coordinates, specifically a latitude and a longitude. Getting all of that into your GPS can appear to be somewhat tedious, but it's worth the effort. This is the information that makes your GPS so useful.

You've learned how to measure waypoints and construct a waypoint table of latitudes and longitudes. Using this table to manually enter waypoints into the GPS is per-

haps the most straightforward method; however, there are alternatives. All of the methods are summarized below and in the accompanying sidebar.

Manual Entry

Enter coordinates manually by accessing the New Waypoint Screen. Using the cursor button, scroll down until the coordinates field is highlighted, and press ENTER. You will be presented with a single highlighted character. Use the cursor to scroll up or down to change the character (number) until it corresponds to your desired entry. Then use the cursor to scroll right or left to change the values of other characters. When you're satisfied with the entered values for latitude and longitude, press ENTER to accept. Scroll to OK or Save and press ENTER. Your GPS will assign a number in the *name* field. You can change the name (or the symbol displayed with the waypoint) in this field in the same manner as entering values into the coordinates field.

Scroll

An easier way to store coordinates in your GPS is to scroll the cursor on the Map Screen. The cursor's coordinates are shown on the screen. Press MARK to access and edit the New Waypoint Screen, then save. On some GPS models, this is the method by which you access the New Waypoint Screen. Usually, it is quicker and easier to scroll to the general area of the desired waypoint, press MARK, edit the details of the coordinates until you're satisfied, then save.

Bearing and Distance

As indicated earlier in this chapter, it is wise to plot your course on a paper chart and label each leg with its course directions and distances. Now you can put that information to good use. With this technique you can accurately enter all the waypoints into your GPS without entering the coordinates for each one.

Start at one of the intersections for a group of legs and enter the waypoint coordinates for just that intersection.

Many newer GPS models provide a bearing and distance readout of the cursor position in addition to its coordinates, as described above. Akin to the scroll method, you can use those readouts to enter other waypoints, as follows.

Set the current location of the GPS in the simulator mode (usually found in the menu). Select the newly entered waypoint as your simulated position. Now, using the cursor on the Map Screen, scroll until the displayed values for cursor bearing and distance correspond with the course direction and distance of the desired leg. Press MARK and proceed with your naming. Repeat this step for any other legs that emanate from that starting point, or reset your simulated position to another intersection and continue from there.

GPS BUTTONS

You communicate with your GPS via buttons. Like any electronic device, GPS uses a relatively sparse array of buttons to perform a wide range of functions. To do this, it employs subordinate menus and submenus from which you select the action you want to take. This section gives an overview of a typical GPS keyboard. Hand-held units tend to have fewer and less-intuitive buttons than those on fixed, chartplotter models.

POWER/LIGHT

Most GPS models have a button that turns on the unit and can activate the backlight for nighttime or dimly lit conditions. Typically, you turn on the unit by pressing this button for a second or so; you turn it off by pressing the button for about three seconds while the unit powers down. Pressing the button while the unit is active usually lets you access the backlight and perhaps the contrast function.

ENTER

This key is fundamental to any action you take. It operates much like the ENTER key on a computer to activate an action.

ESC OR QUIT

This key is used to go back a step; it operates much like the ESC (escape) key on a computer keyboard.

GOTO

Traditionally, GPS models have used the GoTo button to select a waypoint for navigation. Pressing this button usually brings up a list of the waypoints stored in the GPS, from which you select the one of interest and activate it by using the ENTER button. On some newer models, the GoTo function appears in a menu that is accessed by pressing a button called NAV.

MENU

Most GPS models provide a button to access menus. Pressing this button usually offers you options that relate specifically to the screen you are viewing. If that's the case, pressing it again brings you to a main menu, from which you can select to work with waypoints, routes, get celestial data, and set up, or initialize, the GPS receiver. Some models don't have this button. On these, you access menus by scrolling through the available screens until you get to the Main Menu Screen.

There are two types of menus: screen dependent and general. Screen-dependent menus are used to set up the format of the particular screen you are viewing—data field selection and layout, map features, and so forth. General menus provide access to your waypoint and route functions.

Setup menus are very important, because they control how your GPS operates. There are several critical settings to understand. Specifically, you need to make sure that the location format matches the grid on your chart. You generally will use latitude and longitude, but you have a choice of degrees, minutes, and tenths of minutes, or degrees, minutes, and seconds (see Chapter 6). Select the one that matches your chart. The other critical setting is chart datum. This refers to the horizontal reference frame used to place objects on your chart, as discussed in Chapter 4. Make sure it matches your chart; otherwise, the latitudes and longitudes could be in error. Generally, you will use WGS-84.

The other settings are for your convenience. For example, you can use statute, nautical, or metric units. You can set the GPS to report directions as true or magnetic. Most GPS models provide a selection of alarms that can alert you to important events: arriving at a waypoint, straying off course, nearing a danger waypoint, or dragging your anchor. You can usually choose the distance or limit that triggers these alarms.

Last, the setup function allows you to control how the GPS communicates with other electronic equipment.

PAGE

This button is used to scroll through the various screens on many GPS models. Successive pressings of the button move you from screen to screen. Other models use a button labeled NAV to perform a similar function or offer the screen selection option under a menu.

ZOOM (IN-OUT)

Most GPS models offer a pair of buttons that allows you to zoom in or out on the Map Screen, and usually the Highway Screen too. This allows for a more detailed view of a smaller area on the map, or a wider view of what is around the "highway."

CURSOR

Usually this button takes the form of a four-way rocker switch that allows you to move up-down or left-right. It is used to scroll through the menu to highlight the function of choice prior to selecting it with the ENTER button. On the Map Screen, it moves a cursor away from your displayed current position to measure a distance and bearing or nearby coordinates, or select a waypoint, or simply look around.

MARK

This often shares a button with the ENTER key. Pressing it while underway and monitoring the Map Screen usually brings up a New Waypoint Screen with the current coordinates already filled in. Accepting this screen "marks" the current position as a waypoint. Usually, the GPS selects a number for the waypoint name, which you can edit to whatever you wish.

MOB

The man overboard function is a valuable tool on your GPS. Most models incorporate this capability but often share it with another button, such as the GoTo. In the latter case, pressing this key twice activates a special type of waypoint that marks your current location and immediately interrupts any ongoing navigation to provide directions back to that spot to effect a rescue.

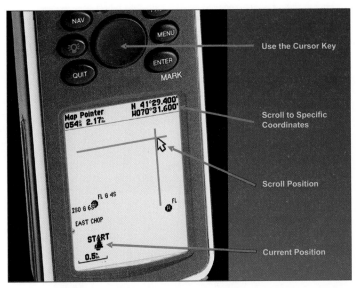

Use the Cursor Key

Scroll to Specific Coordinates

Scroll Position

Current Position

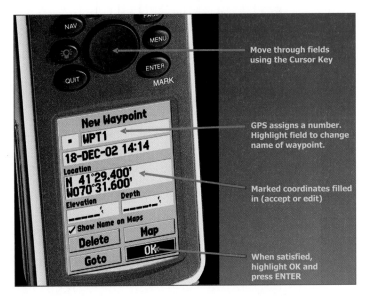

Move through fields using the Cursor Key

GPS assigns a number. Highlight field to change name of waypoint.

Marked coordinates filled in (accept or edit)

When satisfied, highlight OK and press ENTER

FIGURE 5-22. Left: *On many models of GPS, you can scroll across the Map Screen to a set of coordinates. When the cursor coordinates correspond with the desired location, press the MARK button to create a new waypoint. This is a task that you can do at home.* Right: *After pressing MARK, the GPS displays the New Waypoint Screen with the cursor's coordinates already filled in. You can edit the symbol, the name, and even the details of the coordinates before saving this as a waypoint.*

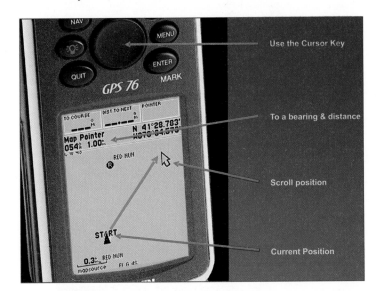

Use the Cursor Key

To a bearing & distance

Scroll position

Current Position

FIGURE 5-23. *The bearing and distance from your current location to the cursor position are also displayed on some GPS models. This information can be used as a shortcut to entering waypoints by their coordinates. As long as you have already entered one waypoint into the GPS, and you know the bearings and distances to the next waypoints in your route, you can simply scroll to the desired location. Once the bearing and the distance information equals the bearing and distance to your desired location, press MARK to create a new waypoint.*

FIGURE 5-24. *A free program, called G7ToWin, is used to enter waypoints, then upload them into the GPS. The waypoints and routes can also be downloaded from the GPS, edited, then uploaded back into the GPS.*

Using a Computer

Manually entering information into the GPS can be a tedious task. Instead, you can use a computer keyboard to enter waypoint names and coordinates, then upload them from the computer into the GPS. Alternatively, you will likely mark waypoints into your GPS while you are on the water (as described below). The software (discussed below)

will enable you to download those waypoints into your computer to manage or rename them.

In addition to managing waypoint names and coordinates, some software programs help you create and manage routes.

Also, by using the computer you are backing up your

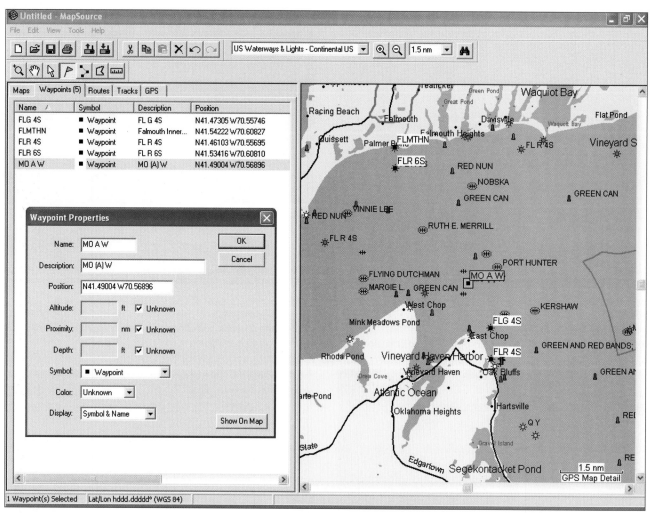

FIGURE 5-25. *Each of the major GPS manufacturers has its own proprietary software to work with its units. This program, called MapSource, is offered by Garmin. It basically does the same task as the freeware, but it includes a crude map to put the waypoints in perspective.*

data. In the event that your GPS unit loses its memory, or you choose to use another GPS, you will be able to upload the same waypoints into the GPS.

GPS sets can be connected to a computer via a custom cable available from the GPS manufacturer. You will need software to work with the GPS. There are a number of freeware and shareware programs that work with the more popular GPS brands and models (see Appendix 3).

Mark

While underway, you can enter a waypoint while passing over a point of interest. Simply press MARK, and the GPS will create a waypoint at your current location. The GPS will also automatically name the new waypoint with a unique number. You can edit the name immediately, although pushing all those buttons while simultaneously operating your boat could be cumbersome. Instead, make note of the waypoint's number and characteristics, then edit the name while at home or at anchor.

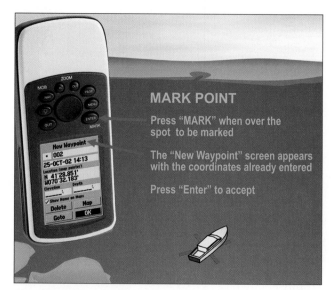

MARK POINT

Press "MARK" when over the spot to be marked

The "New Waypoint" screen appears with the coordinates already entered

Press "Enter" to accept

FIGURE 5-26. *On the water, you can mark any location by pressing the MARK button. It brings up the New Waypoint Screen with the coordinates already filled in.*

Planning with Digital Charts

If you own digital charts for your boating area, you can perform your cruise planning directly on your computer or chartplotter. When you plan on digital charts, you are far less likely to make errors. This is a distinct advantage over the manual approach, which gives you two opportunities to make a mistake: when you read the coordinates from the chart, and when you enter the coordinates into the GPS.

Using digital charts displayed on a computer screen, you can plot routes, mark waypoints, and annotate the charts by simply pointing and clicking while the computer automatically provides the latitude and longitude of each waypoint, the course and distance of each leg, and other useful information. This greatly facilitates planning, adjusting, and storing waypoints and routes for upload into a GPS.

Similar techniques can be used with a chartplotter, but a computer offers unique advantages, particularly for planning. Once you generate waypoints and routes with charting software on a computer, they can be uploaded into virtually any GPS. Then, on the water, even without the chart itself displayed on a computer screen, you can use your GPS for live navigation because you will be following the prequalified paths you generated on a digital chart. This popular approach makes navigation vastly easier for those of us who have a nonmapping handheld GPS receiver. In fact, many boaters who have a chartplotter plan their voyages on a computer at home, then upload the resulting waypoints and routes into their chartplotter.

A desktop or laptop computer with charting software and digital charts offers significant computing power, storage capacity, and a relatively large screen. The screen is smaller than an actual nautical chart, so you will need to zoom in and out and scroll up-down and left-right to see the entire chart. Offsetting this inconvenience is the ability to move from chart to chart or use charts of different scales that are automatically referenced to your current location.

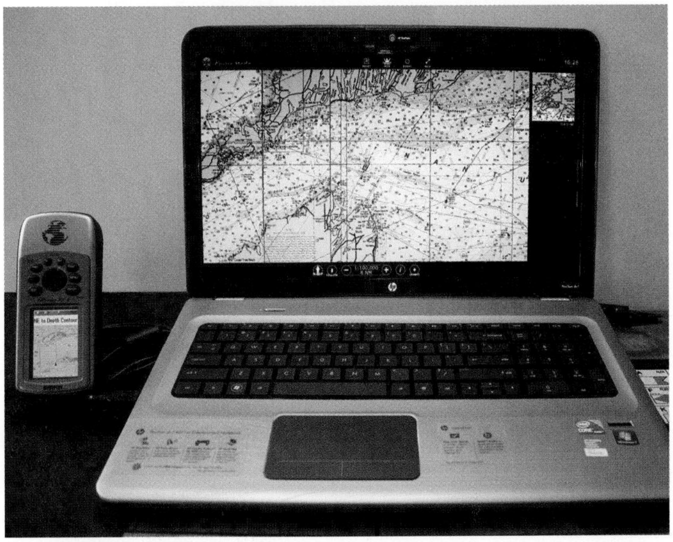

FIGURE 6-1. *You can plan on your computer using charts that replicate paper charts. You need a computer, the appropriate software, and digital charts for your boating region.*

Digital Charts

As stated in Chapter 5, nautical charts are your security blanket, digital charts no less so than paper. Indeed, digital charts display all the same information. Although you don't have easy access to the latitude and longitude scales on the edges of the chart, you have something even better: the latitude and longitude coordinates of your cursor are displayed digitally at all times on the screen.

Because you can see only a limited piece of a digital chart at a time, you scroll across the chart or zoom in and out to get a broader view. Unfortunately, when you zoom out, it's like moving away from the chart—you get a wider view but lose detail. This calls for some techniques that are described later in this chapter.

There are two types of digital charts; which one you use probably will depend on whether you are displaying it on a computer or on a chartplotter. The latter, which may

RASTER versus VECTOR CHARTS

RASTER CHARTS

Raster charts are preferred by many mariners because they look like traditional charts. This is no coincidence; printed charts are created from the same digital masters. Raster charts make it easier to annotate your paper charts with the routes and waypoint names programmed into your GPS. Indeed, the raster charts displayed on your computer clearly identify their corresponding paper chart numbers, thus further facilitating a comparison with the identical paper chart on which you have marked your information. Examples of typical raster charts are shown in Figure 6-2.

Raster charts provide greater detail, more features, and richer imagery than vector charts. For example, the water towers, steeples, and other landmarks printed on paper and raster charts may not be shown on the corresponding vector chart. In addition, new forms of raster cartography are gaining popularity. Using satellite and aerial photometric data, companies such as Maptech, Jeppesen, and Navionics have created scaled photo charts that can be presented on a computer screen next to traditional charts. Other raster chart formats such as topographic maps can be displayed along with their abundant information about land features. These can be useful for identifying prominent features to aid your navigation planning.

When you zoom out for a wider view on a raster chart, the details and labels diminish in size and may become unreadable. On the other hand, zooming way in magnifies the picture, although not the detail. However, a typical suite of raster charts includes larger-scale charts for many harbors and channels. Most popular charting programs allow you to switch to a more detailed chart when you scroll over that region.

Another type of raster chart that is gaining in popularity is the bathymetric chart, which shows seabed contours. One of these charts, when tiled side by side with a navigation chart, helps you identify harbor and channel features. Several companies offer bathymetric charts in two- and three-dimensional formats for limited areas, and coverage is expanding.

VECTOR CHARTS

Chartplotters tend to have a smaller memory than computers, and the CD-ROM format is not cost effective for the exposed conditions often experienced by a chartplotter. Vector charts, which can be stored on a chip and inserted into a special slot on a chartplotter, address this problem.

In concept, a vector chart is "traced" from the original paper chart so as to preserve key features, and the traced lines are stored as vectors. Each vector starts at a specific location (coordinates) and ends at another—not unlike the legs of a planned route. Shorelines and depth contours are nothing more than a sequence of short vectors. Soundings are stored as numbers, each with a location. The same holds true for navigation aids, hazards, wrecks, rocks, and prominent terrain features. Information in this format is extremely compact compared with that on a raster image, which is analogous to a photograph.

Colors are added to depict land and shallow water, emulating some of the look of the paper chart originals. The accuracy of a vector chart is based on and therefore similar to the paper chart from which it was created. Symbols for features such as navigation aids are stored and repeated where necessary on the chart. Some users complain about the somewhat mechanical look of vector charts, because they tend not to depict as much detail as their paper sources. The companies that make them seek to gain efficiency by tracing only key navigation information; features that could be useful as landmarks are often not included.

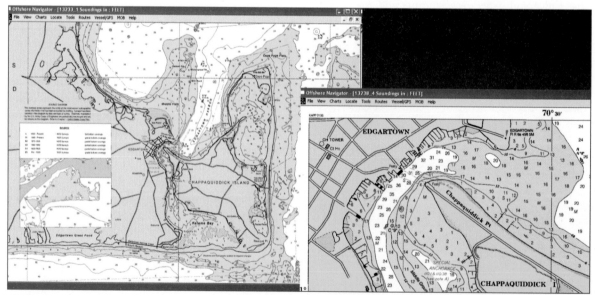

FIGURE 6-2. Digital charts used on computers generally are raster format. Because they are scanned from master paper charts, they look like the original charts.

Planning with Digital Charts

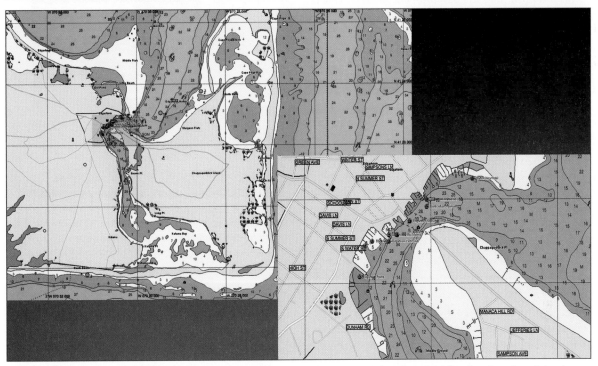

FIGURE 6-3. *Vector charts are created by "tracing" the paper charts as a series of straight-line "vectors," each beginning and ending at a particular set of coordinates. Vector charts have a more mechanical look but are as accurate as the masters and, many believe, easier to read on the water.*

On the water, however, a vector chart has advantages. Its somewhat cleaner presentation is less cluttered and easier to view from the helm under many circumstances. In addition, because the soundings and navigation aids are stored as symbols and numbers by location, they can be seen even when the display is zoomed out. The cartographers are able to select which data to show and which to hide, so the display does not become cluttered with too much information.

Another advantage of a vector chart is that the stored data can be accessed for other uses. For example, using a straightforward look-ahead technique, chartplotter programmers can scan the depths in front of the boat to see whether there is a risk of running aground. For planning purposes, it is possible to let a computer working with vector charts make decisions about routes. In fact, these techniques are finding their way into commercial systems that plan and monitor navigation for large ships.

The latest wrinkle in vector charts is a new class of Electronic Navigation Charts (or ENCs) being prepared by NOAA and other hydrographic offices. These vector charts cover commercial shipping lanes and ports with a greater degree of precision than has previously been available. The charts are updated weekly using the Local Notices to Mariners and other publications to ensure their accuracy. These updates are sent to users, where they are automatically applied, making the charts used on the bridges of these ships the latest available.

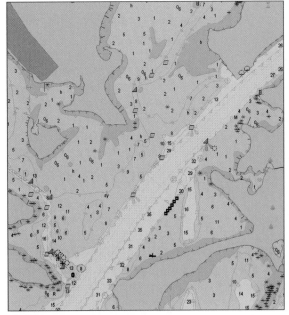

FIGURE 6-4. *As part of an international move to digital charts as the sole charts aboard commercial ships, the International Hydrographic Organization (IHO) created a standard called S-57 for vector charts. The resulting electronic navigation charts (ENCs) for U.S. waters are offered free of charge on the Web by NOAA. However, you need to find charting software that works with them.*

have smaller memory, may need charts in a more compact form. This has prompted the development of *vector charts* on custom chips. Computers generally can store more data and run CDs or DVDs, so they usually use scanned versions of paper charts in what is called *raster format*. Vector and *raster charts* look different but come from the same source data.

Cruise-Planning Software

You will need the appropriate software and digital charts to do navigation planning on a computer. Planning software is offered by a number of companies and may be sold for a nominal cost and sometimes bundled with digital charts. In the U.S., digital charts are available at no cost in both raster (RNC) and vector (ENC) format directly from NOAA. These charts are continuously updated. However, you may find it more convenient to get these charts from a third party or with the planning software to avoid the timely task of downloading them. Charts for regions outside of the U.S. are available from various suppliers. Commercial providers also include extra features such as photo charts, topo maps, and tide and current information supporting the value as well as convenience of the purchase. All of the chart formats are geo-referenced to a common grid—namely latitude and longitude. The various chart formats can even be aligned side by side so you can work simultaneously with, say, a nautical chart and a photographic version of the same area. More about these products can be found in Appendix 3.

Software also is offered by a number of companies for live navigation on a computer connected to your GPS. This software usually does not come with digital charts, which are a separate expense. This software is described in the discussion of live navigation in Chapter 8, but you can use it for planning as well. The material included in this chapter applies to navigation software used for planning as well as to dedicated planning software.

Because not every boater wants to use a computer for live navigation, it's nice not to have to buy full-featured navigation software for planning. As described in Chapter 5, many GPS hardware manufacturers offer proprietary software for uploading and downloading data into or from their GPS receivers. Some of these manufacturers also offer charts that can be viewed on a computer screen and in some cases selectively uploaded into the GPS, although each such chart is compatible only with that brand of GPS. The amount of cartography a GPS will store is limited, though some models offer add-on memory cards to expand the coverage area.

If you have a chartplotter, you may prefer to do your planning on a computer using the same chips that you use in your chartplotter. Jeppesen C-Map, for one, offers a soft-

FIGURE 6-5. *Digital chart producers have developed software and readers so that chips can be used as the digital chart reference for planning on a computer. This Jeppesen (C-Map) reader accepts removable chart chips and links the data to the computer.*

ware package called PC Planner, which comes with a chip reader. All you need to do is insert your chip or chips in the reader, and you can plan on your computer screen. Jeppeson C-Map offers writable chips that can be used to transfer your routes and waypoints to your chartplotter. Garmin offers similar features, and other companies are following.

The planning software that comes with these kits is usually special viewer versions of navigation software and may not perform live navigation, although some offer upgrade packages. Some will permit uploading of waypoints and routes *into* your GPS as well as downloading marks and tracks *from* your GPS. This software also offers a host of editing features. It makes waypoint and route management easy. The major difference from the software described in Chapter 5 is the added ability to display and work with real charts.

Usually, the digital charts used on computers are delivered on CDs or DVDs. Here we describe the Rose Point Coastal Express Viewer program (available for free download through www.weekendnavigator.net; links to other viewers are available as well). Almost all computer-based navigation and planning software accepts BSB-format raster charts available free from NOAA or for a fee for Canadian charts and other areas from various sources. Sample charts for exercises shown in this book and links to NOAA are available at www.weekendnavigator.net as well.

Chart-Planning Software Features

Because the main features of planning firmware and software are quite similar, the tasks described in this section can be performed on either a computer or a chartplotter. As you plot your waypoints and routes on the digital charts, you should annotate the corresponding information on your paper charts for backup reference on the boat. In addition,

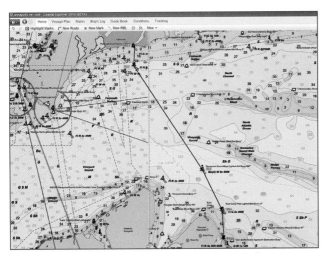

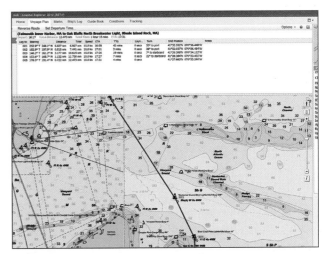

FIGURE 6-6. *Route planning on a computer is easy and accurate. You can point and click along the desired path to create the route. Each click represents a waypoint that will be saved and uploaded along with the route into your GPS. The route can be edited by adding, deleting, or moving any waypoint.*

FIGURE 6-7. *Once the route is complete, you can bring up a route plan that provides the coordinates of each waypoint, the course for each leg, the leg distance, and total distance. You can also use the software to estimate the travel times and fuel consumption for each leg and the overall route.*

you may discover that while plotting the same courses on paper charts you'll find an occasional better or safer path that is not as easy to recognize on the smaller chartplotter or computer screen. As an alternative, many digital chart-planning programs provide a means of printing your own charts annotated with your routes.

The host of features at your disposal will typically include the following.

Waypoint Mark—You can scroll your cursor across the screen and mark a waypoint to be stored. From a computer, this waypoint is uploaded into your GPS receiver. On a chartplotter, this waypoint is stored directly.

Route Development—You can build a route by moving your cursor from point to point of the route on the screen. The computer automatically creates waypoints at each mouse click, as do most chartplotters. Some chartplotters may require you to enter the waypoints first.

Edit Waypoints—You can click on any waypoint on a computer screen and move it to a new location on the chart. Using a chartplotter, you may need to go to the waypoint menu to move it.

Edit Routes—You can move waypoints on a computer screen or create new ones (at the beginning, end, or middle of a route) by scrolling over the selected spot of the route on the screen, selecting a menu item, and clicking on the screen. On a chartplotter, you may need to access a special menu and select MOVE.

Measure Distances and Bearings—Most programs provide a feature to create a bearing or line from any one selected point to any other point. This permits making measurements of distance between the two points and the direction from one point to the other, and usually the reciprocal direction (back to the first point from the second point). This line has no effect on any route, waypoint, or ongoing

navigation. It is simply a handy measurement tool. Multiples of such lines are typically possible, more so with navigation software than with a chartplotter. This is useful for checking distances or bearings on screen.

Route Plan—You can view the elements of a planned route to display leg course, leg distance, and total route distance. In addition, many programs permit entering an intended speed for each leg and an anticipated start time to get ETA and ETE (estimated time of arrival and estimated time en route) for each leg and the total route. Some programs permit entering a fuel consumption rate as well (GPH) and calculate total fuel consumed by leg and route.

Chart Management—You can view various charts at a given location. With a chartplotter, you can zoom to a larger scale to view greater detail. With a computer, you can view any of the nautical charts that cover a given location, or, alternatively, view photo charts, topographic maps, or

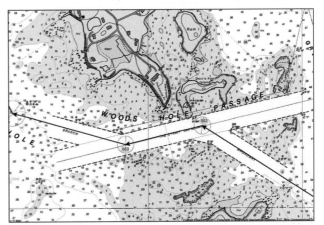

FIGURE 6-8. *Once you have planned on your charts at home using your computer, you can print the charts for use on the boat.*

FIGURE 6-9. *Chart-planning software provides a wide array of options. You can select directions as true or magnetic, distance units, and the level of symbols and information that will show on the chart.*

bathymetric charts. Many programs allow you to select which specific charts can be viewed.

Navigating the Screen: A Quick-Start Guide

Typical software provides a row of icons along the top of the screen that can be used to access most of the software functions. Usually, there are two other ways to access these functions: use the right-click button on your mouse to get a drop-down menu, or use the drop-down menus at the very top of the screen. These options are familiar to any user of word-processing or spreadsheet software, and the choice is a matter of personal preference.

CURSOR The usual way of navigating the screen is with a cursor icon, typically a small hand or an arrow. In addition, you can move the chart across the screen by pressing and holding the left mouse button while you move the mouse. Alternatively, if you move to a corner or side of the chart, the chart may scroll to reveal what lies in that direction. On a chartplotter, you will be able to scroll across the visible portion of the chart until you reach the edges of the screen. Once there, the chart itself will scroll from under your cursor. To stop the chart from scrolling, simply move the cur-

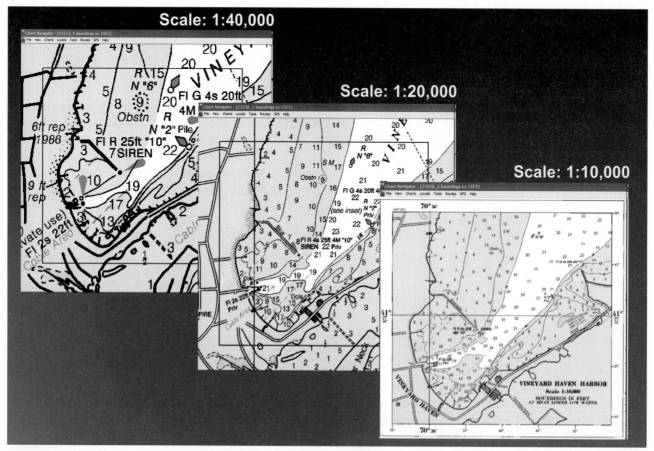

FIGURE 6-10. *When you're planning with digital charts, the software usually searches for larger-scale charts stored on your computer as you zoom in. Each successive chart shows you in your current location, but with greater surrounding detail. In these examples, each showing the same area in the chart window, the 1:40,000 chart shows far less detail than is found in the 1:20,000 chart to its right, and even less detail than in the 1:10,000 chart on the far right.*

sor away from the screen's edge. Then you can move the cursor across the visible portion of the chart to mark a point or read the pop-up features. By pressing ESC or QUIT, you will be returned to the original presentation showing the boat.

SETUP You should go to the drop-down menus at the top of the screen and look for Setup or Options. This helps you to set up the chart planning for your personal preferences. On a chartplotter, setup can be found under the Setup Menu option.

Bearings—You can choose to have the bearings reported as magnetic or true. Generally, you will find magnetic—the language of your compass—more convenient.

Distance Units—You can set the distance units to nautical (recommended for coastal charts), statute miles (Great Lakes), or kilometers.

Lat/Lon Format—You can set latitude and longitude coordinates to read in degrees, minutes, and tenths (recommended for coastal charts); degrees, minutes, and seconds (Great Lakes); and other formats.

TOOLS The chart-planning tools or modes we use here are accessed either by icons on the top row or from drop-down menus, mentioned above. Typical options include the following.

Cursor—For navigating around the chart and scrolling.

Chart Portfolio—To see a list of available charts stored on the computer.

Charts Here—This tool will list all the available chart scales and formats that cover the cursor coordinates or the chart area on the screen.

Scale or Zoom—Usually a pair of tools—one for zooming in and one for zooming out. These change the presentation of how much chart is shown on the screen and its relative magnification. As you move in, usually the chart becomes magnified (simply a magnified view of the previous screen) until the software detects a larger-scale chart to be more appropriate. At that point, the source chart changes, which may alter the presentation but will provide you with a more accurate chart of this smaller area. Moving out accomplishes the opposite, showing progressively larger areas, but at lesser detail. (A larger scale means more detail for a smaller area; see Chapter 4 for a discussion of chart scales.)

Quilting—If quilting is an option included in the software, when selected it will coordinate and mesh the edges and scales of the best available charts to present an apparently seamless, continuous single chart on the screen. When quilting is off, you see only the present chart on the screen until you scroll across a boundary, which usually brings up an adjacent chart.

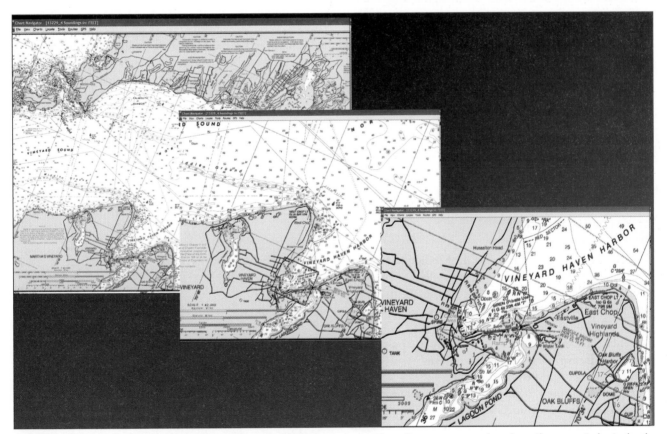

FIGURE 6-11. *If you have no larger-scale charts stored on your computer, the software can zoom in only on the current chart, simply magnifying the view within your display window. Zooming in this fashion provides no new information nor any greater accuracy. Here we see a 1:40,000 scale chart at three different zoom levels.*

Range/Bearing Line (RBL)—With this tool you can measure distances and bearings without impacting any navigation tasks that also appear on the screen. (See "Working with Digital Charts," below.)

New Route—This tool is used to create a route on the chart. (See "Working with Digital Charts.")

New Mark—This is useful when you want to mark a spot that is uncharted. (See "Working with Digital Charts.")

Annotation—Many planning programs allow you to annotate your digital charts with notes. This information is not uploaded into your GPS but provides a ready reference whenever you bring up your digital charts. Many programs also allow you to print out these annotated charts to take aboard.

Chart Display—There are usually several ways to display charts. First, you can select the type of chart to display. The selection may be raster, vector, photo, or topo. You may have the option of letting the software select the best chart for the region from raster or vector. Next, you can select the color scheme for the display if using vector charts. Third, you can select other layers or information to display, such as tides and currents. Next, you may be able to control the text size (applies to vector charts). And last, you may be able to array multiple charts side by side, or even create three or four panes on the display, each with different information.

Working with Digital Charts

The real power of digital charts lies in the flexibility to create and adjust courses to suit your needs, then upload that information directly into your GPS for navigation. The principal digital chart-plotting techniques include:

RBL—point-to-point measurements

Mark—waypoints for navigation

Route—routes for navigation

Let's look at each in turn.

RBL

RBL (range/bearing line) is one of the handiest navigation tools available on the software or chartplotter. This is a planning technique that is used for measurements rather than creating waypoints. The RBL marks are not uploaded into a GPS but reside on the planning software screen for reference. This tool temporarily marks any two points and provides information about the location and relative position of each with respect to the other (bearing and distance). It can be used to quickly measure a distance or establish a bearing. Move the cursor to the location of the first point, and left-click on the mouse. Now move the cursor again, and you'll draw a line from point A like a spider trailing a thread. Many programs provide the coordinates of the cursor and the bearing and distance from the point to the cursor location. When you are satisfied with the cursor location, left-click again to plant the second point. Now you can access a screen or window that provides details about the line you just created. Usually, this screen provides distance between them and the bearings from the first point to the second point, and a means of reversing them. You can add notes explaining what the line represents and name it for future reference. This is particularly useful in checking a visual bearing or just checking the distance and direction to a point of interest. You can also measure the bearing of an impromptu range on the chart—that is, any two charted landmarks whose alignment can be used as a visual reference line on the water. With this software it's easy to create a portfolio of ranges in nearby waters—your personal library of local knowledge. Many programs impose no upper limit on the number of RBLs you can use on your chart.

Mark

A mark is any convenient reference point you place on a chart, perhaps a wreck you've discovered or a favorite fishing spot. The mark tool permits you to name this mark and upload it into your GPS, choosing an appropriate symbol. This is a handy means of annotating a chart (and your GPS receiver) with features or hazards that are not otherwise charted. Each mark is shown on the chart and stored in a Mark List by name and location. You can use the mark feature to annotate your charts with updates found in the U.S. Coast Guard's *Notices to Mariners* and from similar organizations throughout the world. This will keep your digital charts and your GPS information current. Many systems use Mark, Point, and Waypoint interchangeably as in each case it represents a set of coordinates, a name, and often some notes.

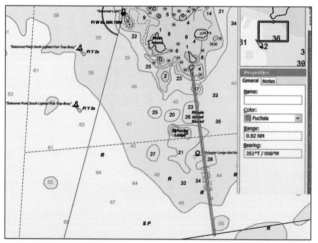

FIGURE 6-12. *The Range/Bearing mode can provide key information about any two points of your choosing. With just a few mouse clicks, you can learn the distance and bearing from one point to another. You also can reverse the bearing from the second point to the first.*

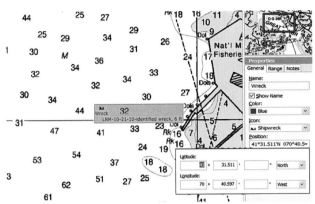

FIGURE 6-13. *Often, you'll need to annotate your charts with the latest information from the Local Notices to Mariners, or add a new buoy or an uncharted feature. You can insert notes and symbols using the mark feature.*

Route

The route tool is the most powerful tool available on digital charts. This enables you to plan your paths on the water from point to point, avoiding obstacles and moving toward and back from various destinations. When the route is complete, it consists of a sequence of waypoints representing each turn between straight-line route segments, or legs. The planning software computes the course and distance for each leg and the total route distance. These waypoints and the route can be uploaded into your GPS and subsequently accessed by name. Once selected, the route will direct you through the preplanned sequence of waypoints.

You can move any of the waypoints in a route by clicking on the waypoint and dragging it to a new location, or lock it so that it cannot be altered without first unlocking it. You can also add waypoints at the beginning of the route, at its end, or at some intermediate point. When you are finished, the route can be saved. By accessing the list of stored routes, you can review each route's details or edit the route with your keyboard by manually changing the waypoint coordinates. You can also assign names and symbols and provide notes relevant to the waypoints. The "short" name is usually uploaded into your GPS and appears as the waypoint name on your GPS.

Search or Locate

Many programs help you find key information, including:

Place-name, Marine Facilities—These menus provide lists of all place names and marine facilities available with the charts.

Conditions

Conditions may cover such topics as weather, tides, or currents. Weather data is often available via e-mail alerts, NAVTEX, or satellite service. The information may be displayed as text messages, graphically, or both.

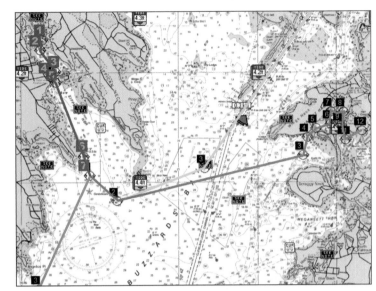

FIGURE 6-14. *Most GPS models limit the number of waypoints per route. An efficient technique for route development is to break a total route into segments. For example, the detailed route from your slip to the main channel or mouth of the harbor is common to most routes (shown in red). So, make that one segment and begin the remainder of your routes from there.*

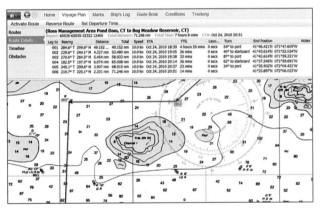

FIGURE 6-15. *Most boaters develop a route leg by leg, starting at the beginning and working to the end of the route. Usually, you will use reasonably large-scale charts, to provide adequate details about channels and hazards. You may need to work across several charts of different scales to complete your route.*

Log or Track

A log or track function may be available to present a track history of your positions and enable you to store various notes about your voyage.

AIS

Automatic identification system information may be available in both data format and plotted, showing the locations, courses, speeds, closest point of approach to you, and other data about each other vessel transmitting messages via automatic identification system beacons.

Guide

This feature may be available to provide cruising information such as local harbors, facilities, medical services, and information relevant to your cruising locale.

Cursor

The coordinates of the current cursor location are displayed in a window, usually in a panel at the top or bottom of the screen. The bearing and distance of the cursor from the boat may also shown.

ROUTE-PLANNING STRATEGY Quite often it makes sense to build route segments rather than complete routes from a common starting point to each of several frequent destinations. For example, you may need to get from your mooring or slip to some mark outside the harbor before proceeding to any of a number of destinations. This would make a logical route segment. Then the paths to each of the

divergent destinations can be built as route segments from that outer mark. Because most chartplotters limit the number of waypoints per route, creating route segments rather than complete end-to-end routes enables you to build more complexity into each segment. The downside is the need to sequentially call up segments as you make progress along your route. This briefly takes your attention from the helm, so you should begin and end your segments at nonchallenging locations. There are two common ways to plan a route. Each is described below.

Linear Planning—This technique is similar to planning on paper charts with pencil and plotting tools, as discussed in Chapter 5. You start at a given spot and plot the route leg by leg and point by point from one end to the other. You generally will use the largest-scale chart that shows both ends of a given leg, zooming in or out as necessary. You determine the best path for each leg as you go, setting waypoints accordingly. This approach is analogous to how you will navigate the course, one leg at a time.

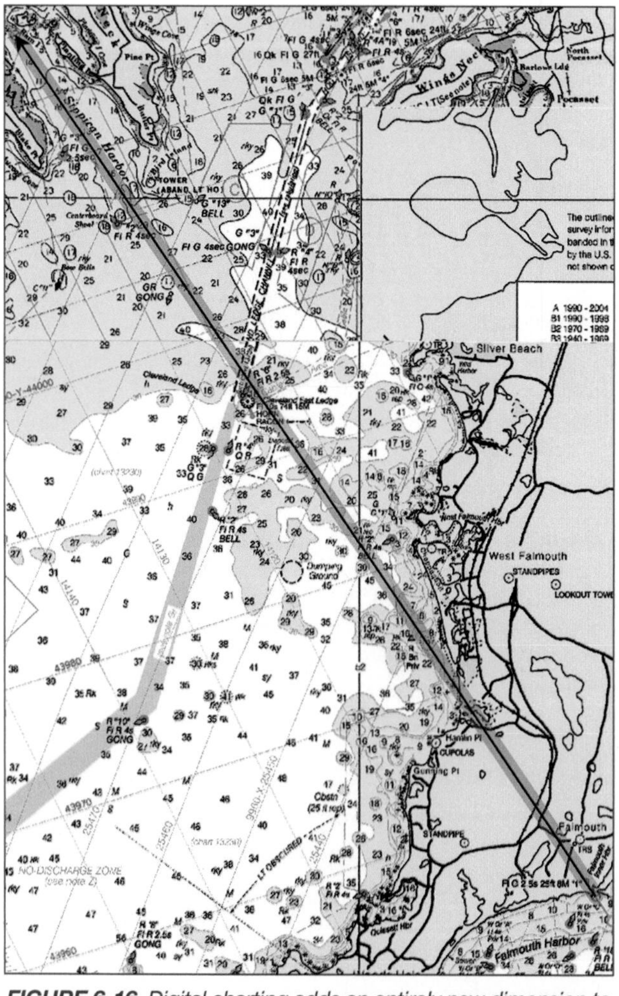

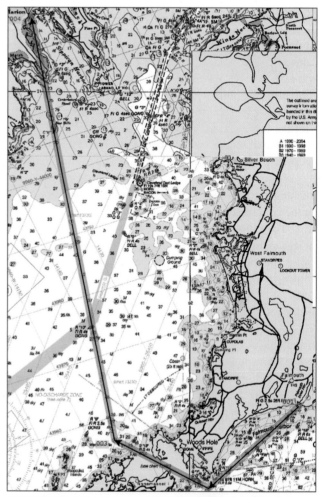

FIGURE 6-16. Digital charting adds an entirely new dimension to route planning. It allows a technique called quick planning. You start by displaying a chart scale that lets you mark both your starting point and destination as a two-point route. This is a straight line between these two points, which clearly is the shortest path. However, there likely are obstacles along the path.

FIGURE 6-17. Next, you can add intermediate waypoints to modify the route around major obstacles or landmasses along the way. Most digital charting programs allow you to create the routes by pointing and clicking while it generates the waypoints for you. When you add or move the waypoints, they are adjusted automatically.

Quick Planning—This alternative (and preferred) technique is rendered practical by the ease of editing afforded by digital charting. It uses the power of zooming and chart-scale selection to its full advantage. You initiate your planning on a chart that shows both the starting and end points of a route. Selecting these two points, you create a single leg (straight-line path) between them, disregarding for the moment what lies along the path.

Next, you modify this path to an acceptable level of safety by adding waypoints as necessary to avoid obstacles. By scaling in and out between harbor charts (1:10,000 or 1:20,000 scale), local charts (1:40,000), and coastal planning charts (1:80,000 or smaller scale), for example, you can address and fine-tune your route through the starting harbor, intermediate channels, and destination harbor. Finally, you should review your entire new route at the largest scale possible for a final tuning of your paths. Virtually all software permits creating and moving points at will, typically by scrolling your cursor over the waypoint shown on the screen, pressing and holding the mouse button, and moving the waypoint to a new location. This, combined with the ability to zoom and scale in or out on an area of interest, makes this task quick and easy. When you start with a straight line representing the shortest distance for your trip and modify it as needed, you will likely get the most efficient route between those two original points. Quick planning is faster and easier than the linear approach because modifying a route is actually easier than creating one. In addition, most computer software permits displaying side-by-side screens at different scales so you can view both at the same time with your route plotted on both.

Route, Waypoint, and Mark Lists

Each route, waypoint, and mark can be reviewed and edited in a list or tabular format. These lists provide extensive information about your routes that is handy for review and planning purposes. Usually, you can access this information by placing the cursor over a route on the screen and right-clicking to get a menu with something like Route Plan. Alternatively, you can use the drop-down menu at the top of the screen under a heading such as Routes.

ROUTE PLAN The route plan shows all the legs of the selected route, beginning with the first waypoint. The coordinates of each waypoint are shown in the same format that you selected in the setup. The following information usually can be found in the route plan:

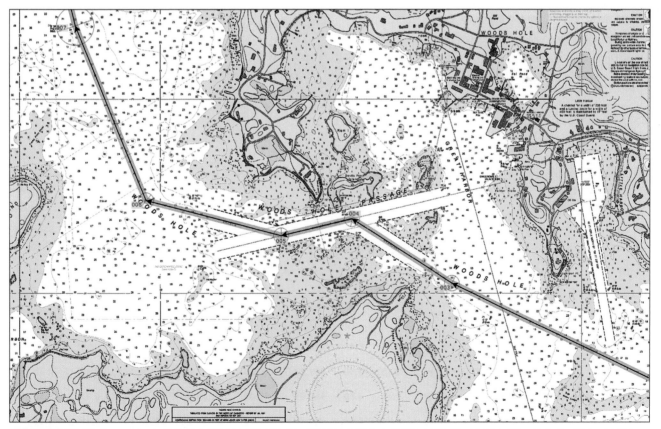

FIGURE 6-18. *Then you can switch to a larger-scale chart and/or zoom in for a better view of a section of your route. Because the quick route is a nearly straight line, you can be sure that the route segment that shows on your screen is close to optimum with respect to distance. With the more refined view, you can adjust the route by adding or moving waypoints to avoid obstacles. You can scroll the screen along the route and fine-tune each segment from beginning to end.*

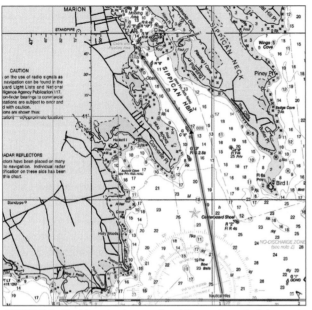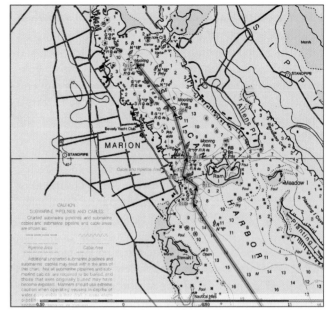

FIGURE 6-19. *After you have refined the main part of the route, you can use the largest-scale charts to tackle the harbors—where precision is most important.*

Starting and ending waypoint coordinates

Leg distance

Cumulative route distance

Course for each leg

Speed (you can enter values for this for each leg)

Time (leg time will be computed using speed)

Time sum (cumulative time for the route will be computed)

The route can be presented in the forward or reverse sequence. It can be printed for reference, and completed routes can be uploaded into the GPS.

MARKS A list of your marks by name and coordinates usually can be found under a drop-down menu. Marks, too, can be uploaded into the GPS.

EDITING Plotting routes using digital charts is easy, and editing them is even easier. Any point that is placed on a digital chart can be moved, and points can be added at the beginning, end, or middle of an existing route by simple mouse clicks. The edited route can be uploaded into your GPS for navigation.

MOVING WAYPOINTS, MARKS, AND RBLs To move any waypoint or mark on the screen, simply move the cursor to the spot, hold down the button on the mouse, and drag the waypoint or mark where you will. To move the RBL points in a RBL plot, do exactly the same thing. All associated information is automatically updated.

ADDING OR DELETING WAYPOINTS IN A ROUTE This is easy. Usually, you do it by placing the cursor over the route line or one of the waypoints of the route,

ROUTE PLAN – FALMOUTH HARBOR to OAK BLUFFS HARBOR									
WPT	**WPT COORDINATES**	**DIST (NM)**	**DIST SUM**	**BEARING**	**SPEED**	**TIME**	**TIME SUM**	**FUEL (GAL)**	**FUEL SUM**
1 FALHBR	41° 32.528′ N 070° 36.507′ W				10.00	00:00:00	00:00:00		
2 FALR16	41° 32.047′ N 070° 36.490′ W	0.48	0.48	194.11	10.00	00:02:52	00:02:52	0.10	0.10
3 VHRW	41° 29.401′ N 070° 34.142′ W	3.18	3.66	161.98	10.00	00:19:04	00:21:57	0.64	0.73
4 VHG23	41° 28.394′ N 070° 33.440′ W	1.14	4.80	168.01	10.00	00:06:50	00:28:48	0.23	0.96
5 OBHBR	41° 27.655′ N 070° 33.398′ W	0.74	5.54	193.15	10.00	00:04:26	00:33:14	0.15	1.11

FIGURE 6-20. *Once you have completed your route, you can access and print a tabular route plan. This plan provides waypoint coordinates, course direction for each leg, leg distance, and cumulative distance. Some programs can even estimate travel times and fuel consumption.*

then accessing a menu by a right click of the mouse. Typical menu choices include:

Insert Waypoint at Beginning (of Route)—Self-explanatory.

Insert Waypoint at End—Ditto.

Insert Waypoint in Line—Simply place the cursor over the route segment where you want to add a waypoint, and click. Usually, a new waypoint is created at this point; it can be moved at will by dragging and dropping. This is particularly useful for adjusting a route around obstacles, and is the key to quick route planning.

Chartplotters

A chartplotter superimposes GPS information directly on a displayed digital chart. Most chartplotters include an integral GPS receiver, but some use the input from a remote GPS receiver. Because the chartplotter is designed for mounting at the helm, most contain a display that can be seen in direct sunlight. Digital chips contain the charts.

The limited size of most chartplotter screens makes planning a little more tedious than when using a computer, but a chartplotter is a powerful tool that can be used to plan while you are on the move. Naturally, this extra capability comes with a price, and chartplotters are generally somewhat more expensive than noncharting handheld GPS units. The cost of the digital chart chips is usually on a par with the cost of a digital chart package for a PC.

Both chartplotters and computers use programs to perform their intended functions. A chartplotter comes with built-in "firmware" designed to perform specific navigation tasks and controlled by the buttons on the unit. Chartplotters generally have a limited amount of processor capability and memory. They are designed primarily for live navigation; when you use one for planning, you generally do so aboard, though it is possible to buy or make interconnecting cables and power supplies so you can remove the chartplotter and work with it at home.

Using a Chartplotter to Plan a Route

A chartplotter lacks a keyboard and mouse to speed various tasks. Because it has fewer buttons, many of its features may not be as obvious or as easy to access as when planning on a computer. Routes is usually a main menu selection, with a submenu selection for New Route.

After selecting this function, you are likely to find an associated menu that provides two ways to enter a route. One option allows you to select named waypoints already stored in your chartplotter/GPS, as described in Chapter 5. The other option permits you to plan your route directly on the map or chart, much as you can with a computer. After selecting this option, you are presented with a Map

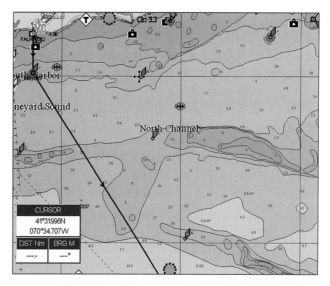

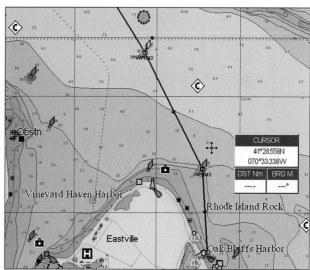

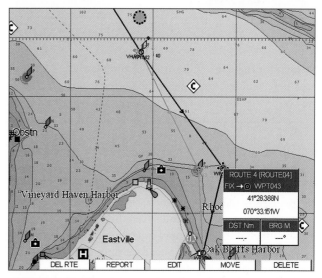

FIGURE 6-21. *Planning on a chartplotter is fundamentally the same as working on a computer. It may not be quite as easy, because the chartplotter lacks a mouse and usually has a smaller screen. But you can perform most of the same functions with the cursor key.*

Screen centered on your current position (or the last active position in the absence of live GPS data). Now you can scroll to your desired route starting point and use the chartplotter's mark feature to make a waypoint, then move sequentially from point to point to build a route. As you do so, the route course line is drawn on the chart, enabling you to scan the path for safety as you go. Once you have completed the route segment, it will be saved for future use. Generally, the chartplotter uses the first and last waypoints of the route as the route name. Once entered, the route can be edited.

Cell Phones and Tablet Computers

Cell phones have supplanted personal digital assistants (PDAs) by merging telephone capability with many other services and functions. Tablet computers (e.g., iPads) have migrated from laptops to truly portable touch-screen workhorses, many of which incorporate broadband connectivity for real-time communications. These are among the latest platforms for navigation software and digital charts. The cell phone's mandated 911 service has driven the GPS market to create highly sensitive receivers that can develop position fixes even within the confines of many buildings. By integrating the internal GPS of these devices with the powerful processors contained within the phones and modern operating systems, a number of software suppliers have developed navigation applications. While most of these apps are for land navigation, an increasing number are oriented toward marine navigation.

Software has been created that can read digital charts and provide many of the features of full-fledged navigation software. Most of these programs had initially been written for smartphone (Microsoft) or Palm operating systems; however, because of the popularity of iPhone and Android phones and iPad computers, navigation apps have been written for these operating systems as well. Marine navigation apps will continue to expand and follow the technology of the rapidly expanding intelligent phone market.

The cell phone navigator is similar to a handheld GPS in terms of its capabilities and utility. Users need to buy the software, which may come with charts, and then possibly subscribe to a service to obtain usable navigation charts or updates. With the cost of cell phones largely underwritten by the service carriers, these devices are remarkably competitive, with features extending far beyond a typical handheld GPS. The rapid expansion of cell phone and tablet markets with their attendant apps is driving costs down and features up, and these devices may largely supplant handheld GPS units as backup devices. The basic programmability of cell phones means updates are easy to access and are constantly improving, whereas handheld GPS units tend to have a limited ability to be updated.

A few words of caution are in order, however. Most cell phones and tablet computers are not marinized or waterproof the way a typical handheld GPS is. And they tend not to provide documented specifications for their GPS accuracy, as most handheld unit manufacturers do. In addition, most are not set up to interface with other electronics such as your VHF radio in order to provide position information contained in a DSC transmission. However, the cell phone or tablet computer makes an ideal backup and supplement. This is a rapidly expanding technology and certainly becoming a mainstream component in marine navigation.

In addition, most people upgrade their cell phones on a regular basis, perhaps every few years as technology expands. This is economical because the cell phone provider service fees help offset the true cost of the hardware, and the production quantities are astronomical. In this way, many users will continue to have the latest technology in GPS, processors, and displays. At the same time, cellular phone systems provide increasing access to a myriad of services, such as weather, tides, and marine facilities that integrate well with your navigation tasks and software.

Cell phones offer an advantage of access to external resources for updates and supplemental information; however, regarding cell phone navigators, you need to remain aware of the limited range of the phone services for real-time applications. Also, charts are provided through various companies and organizations that repackage actual hydrographic data. This may lead to out-of-date or inaccurate charts that could pose a danger on the water. These phones are generally not designed for the environment, meaning it is up to the user to protect the device, and their small screens are as challenging to use as those on handheld GPS units, without being as well protected.

Typical cell phone navigators are shown in Chapter 9.

Planning for Sailing

Preplanning for sailing is like preplanning for a passage under power, with one significant exception—tacking into the wind. When you tack, you are zigzagging across rather than following the direct path, or *rhumb line*, between waypoints. Consequently, you need to ensure that an entire band, centered on the rhumb line, is prequalified, then constrain your tacks within that band's limits to avoid having to pull out the charts. To some extent you can prequalify an area or a region, as explained in the next chapter, but you may not be able to predict which legs will be into the wind, so you need to plan while you navigate. This is discussed in Chapter 21.

Planning to Avoid Danger

There will be days on the water when your desire is not to proceed directly from point A to point B but to wander here and there, exploring coves and bays, poking among islands, and generally enjoying a summer day. After all, freedom from goals and restraints is one of the great attractions of boating. Furthermore, sailors often need to tack back and forth into the wind rather than sailing from point to point. At times such as these, you may be more interested in knowing where you do *not* want to go than where you do. Now it's time to draw on a family of avoidance techniques using GPS with paper or digital charts.

Define the Area

First, figure out how large an area you wish to prequalify, and the characteristics of the hazards within that area. When an entire bay contains only a moderate number of hazards, you may be able to flag all of them in your GPS receiver's memory. But if the waters in question are liberally sprinkled with ledges and other obstacles, you may be able to prequalify only a small swath across one section.

The idea is to clearly mark the hazards on your chart, then use the techniques below to enter this information into your GPS.

Mark the Obstacles

Obstacles come in various flavors, some more isolated than others. A wreck lurking just below the surface is an isolated hazard, much like an isolated rock. An outcropping of shallow rocks or a series of sandbars covers a broader area. A tightly circumscribed area is naturally easier to delimit. Shoals typically extend some distance and cover even larger areas than outcrops, requiring their own avoidance techniques and navigation tools.

Isolated Hazards

Wrecks, submerged pilings, rocks, and other isolated obstacles are easy to identify and mark. Each of these hazards represents a point on your chart. You can measure the coordinates for each, then enter them as waypoints into your GPS. You need to set a criterion as to how far you want to stay away from any of these isolated marks. Generally, a radius of 1/10th of a nautical mile (about 600 feet) is practical. If the hazard is marked with a navigation aid, you can use that as a supplement when you are on the water; if the object is not marked, 600 feet is a good rule of thumb. If you need to mark only a few isolated hazards, you can save them as avoidance waypoints and set an alarm at the danger radius (see below). But your GPS permits only a few avoidance waypoints; when there are many hazards to mark, you'll have to save them as ordinary waypoints (see page 59 for naming conventions) and, when on the water, monitor their proximities using your chart and the GPS Map Screen.

Hazardous Regions

Outcroppings of rocks are common, often occurring over a definable region; unlike isolated hazards, they cannot be adequately reduced to a single waypoint. In this case you need to draw a circle (or other boundary) that encompasses the rocks. If you're working with a paper chart, measure across the hazardous area at its broadest extent and set your drawing compass to half that distance. Now place the point of the compass in the center of the area and lightly swing a circle. If the circle encompasses all the hazards, make the circle darker and note the coordinates of its center, which you can mark with an X. You may need to adjust the center until you find the best fit. Measure the radius of the circle by taking your drawing compass over to the latitude or distance scale, and note this value. (All this can be done just as easily—in fact more easily—on a digital chart, designating the

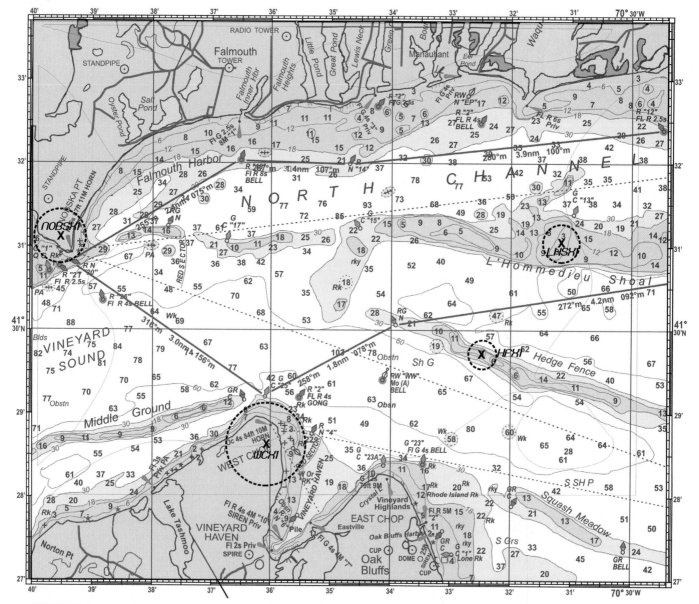

FIGURE 7-1. As an alternative to point-to-point navigation, you can boat more freely within an area by identifying areas to avoid.

center of the hazard as a mark and finding its radius with a RBL. See Chapter 6.)

Now you can enter the center point coordinates into your GPS as an avoidance waypoint. This is a special form of waypoint that allows you to set an alarm if you wander within a preset radius. When you set up the waypoint, enter both its coordinates and the alarm radius. Make sure the alarm is on and you can hear it.

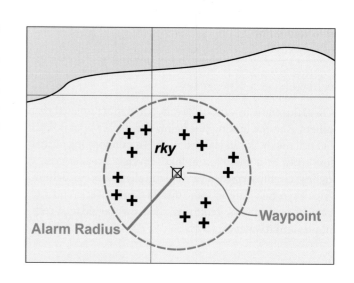

FIGURE 7-2. An avoidance waypoint allows you to set an alarm radius around isolated hazards or hazardous areas. Once set, the GPS will sound an alarm if you've entered the danger circle.

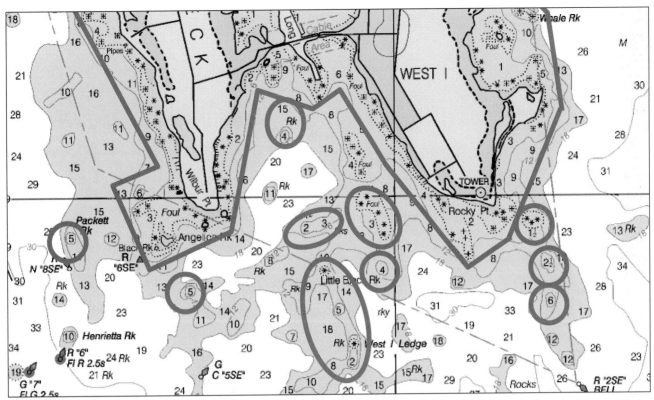

FIGURE 7-3. *Your first task is to identify what constitutes a potential hazard for your boating area. This somewhat extreme example is taken from a prominent point on Buzzards Bay. The entire area is a maze of hazards. Many boats have run aground in these waters.*

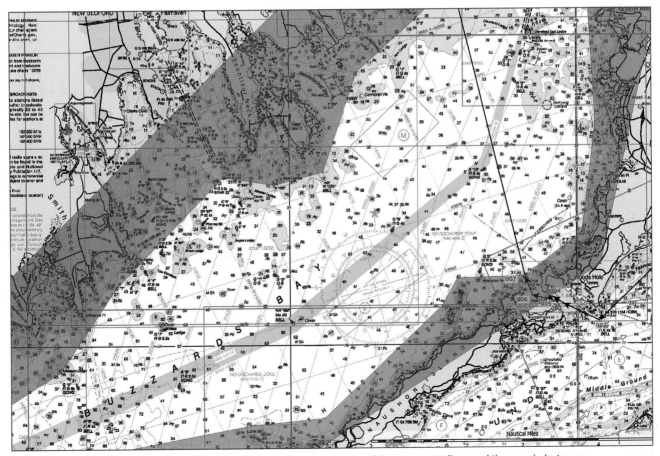

FIGURE 7-4. *By marking dangerous boundaries (shown in red) you can safely maneuver all around the area in between.*

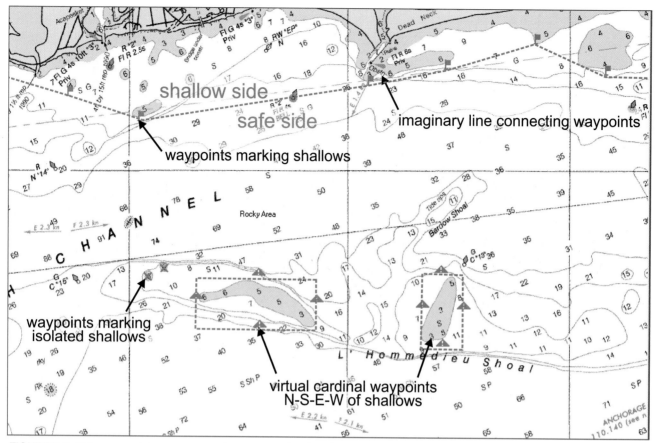

FIGURE 7-5. *Using waypoints, you can create your own virtual navigation aids along the coastline that match your safe depth. A string of these waypoints makes a convenient reference. For hazardous areas, you can use a cardinal waypoint system. Place a virtual waypoint at each cardinal point marking the perimeter of the area (N-S-E-W). Make sure that you do not venture within the box. (Your GPS Map Screen will help with this.) Isolated hazards can be marked with avoidance waypoints or any standard waypoint.*

As an alternative, you can mark several points that bound the region. This is analogous to the cardinal system of buoyage used in many places around the globe. Using this approach, buoys are placed at the cardinal points (north, south, east, and west) marking the edges of the hazardous area. Each buoy is distinguished by a unique pattern of black and yellow bands based on its location. You avoid the area by noting the cardinal point marked by each buoy and staying outside the imaginary boundary defined by that buoy. For example, the north buoy defines an imaginary east-west line and indicates that you should stay north of it. The net effect is an imaginary box around the hazard.

You can do the same thing using waypoints stored in your GPS. Note the location of each waypoint on the chart and the name you will assign to it. For example, HAZ1 might note the hazard, and the four waypoints would be named HAZ1N, HAZ1S, HAZ1E, and HAZ1W, respectively. Measure the coordinates of each entry into your GPS, then you can monitor the hazard box on your GPS Map Screen.

Shoals

Shoals are likely to be far more extensive than the two categories of hazard noted above. The characteristics of a shoal determine its degree of danger. You may experience little more than aggravation if you run aground in soft mud, whereas a rocky bottom can sink your boat.

Channel edges are usually marked by buoys. Most bays and larger bodies of water are also delimited by lateral buoys to mark deeper water. If these navigation aids are available, you may wish to enter their coordinates into your GPS.

Often these buoys mark the edges of very deep channels for big ships. Recreational boaters can and do navigate closer to shore and in shallower water, cutting inside these buoys in part to stay out of ship channels. These lateral buoys may thus be of little value to you, in which case you can always create imaginary lateral buoys to mark your chosen limits. These virtual buoys will exist only in your GPS (and on your annotated chart) as waypoints to help guide you on the water. Assign them names that correspond to a buoy convention, note the names on your chart, and enter them into your GPS.

You should note your depth criterion on your chart near the line of virtual buoys. You will want to use your depth sounder along with your GPS to stay safe on the water.

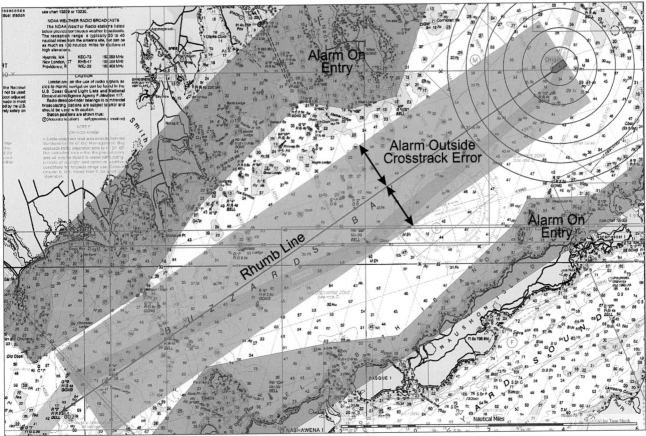

FIGURE 7-6. *Returning to the prequalified Buzzards Bay area, here is a simple technique that uses another feature on your GPS. Once you've identified a band of clear area along the bay, you can make a route down the middle of it. Then note the distance from the route center to the edge of the clear area on the chart. When you are on the water, activate the route segment and set the crosstrack error alarm to that measured value. You will be able to maneuver throughout the bay area within the limits of the crosstrack error and avoid the hazards that lie beyond.*

Bands of Clear Area

Sometimes the techniques outlined above would lead you to define a very large number of waypoints, cluttering your GPS display and leading to confusion rather than helping. Instead, consider using other features of your GPS such as *crosstrack error* to help define a safe area for boating.

Crosstrack error indicates the distance left or right of your current position from an active course line. Crosstrack error can be associated with an alarm that indicates when you have wandered more than a preset distance off course. In effect, this creates a band of chosen width centered on an active course line between two waypoints.

To use the crosstrack error effectively as an avoidance technique, look for a band of open water crossing your region of interest. The band you want will have two parallel edges defining the limits of safe water, placed to avoid lateral hazards. You need to determine the centerline halfway between these edges, define that as the leg of an imaginary course, and use the GPS crosstrack error data field. Your choice of width for the band is virtually unlimited. This technique works for a narrow passage, for defining lateral limits for tacking a sailboat into the wind,

or for outlining the safe area of an entire bay for a day of fishing.

You need to enter the waypoints of each end of the imaginary course leg. It makes sense also to enter as another waypoint your point of entry into this area, thus creating a three-point route beginning with that point. Plot the course leg on the chart and draw the edges of the safe band as dashed lines. Measure the distance from the course line to each edge; this becomes the crosstrack error limit, which you should mark on the dashed lines. You will want to set the GPS's crosstrack error alarm when you boat in this region.

Mark Landmarks

Not all the waypoints you use to define safe areas need be on the water. You can also use visible, charted landmarks to help guide you in a number of ways.

Using Ranges (or Clearing Lines)

You have learned how useful a range can be in keeping you in the center of a channel. A variation of a range, called a

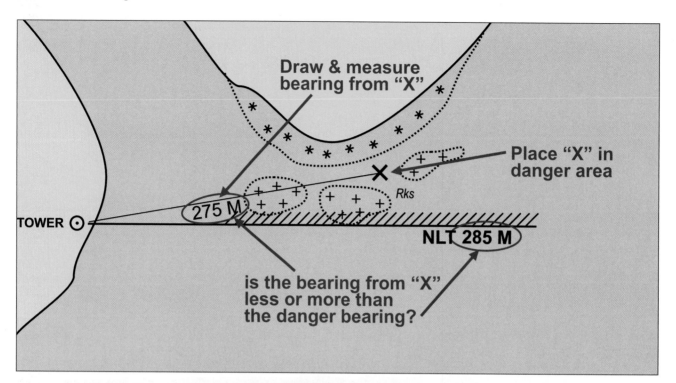

Draw & measure bearing from "X"

Place "X" in danger area

Rks

275 M

TOWER

NLT 285 M

is the bearing from "X" less or more than the danger bearing?

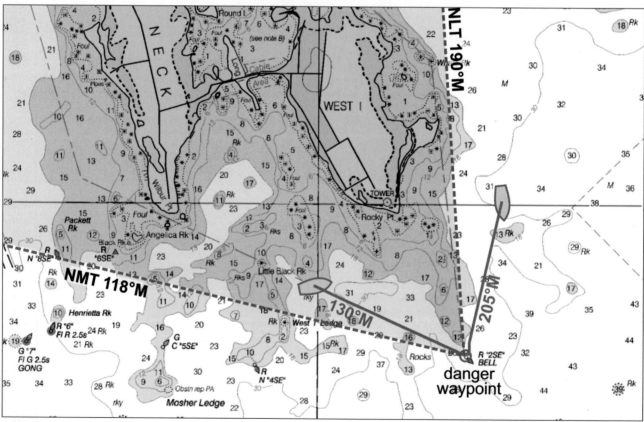

FIGURE 7-7. Top: *A danger bearing is planned using a danger waypoint (in this case a charted landmark). A bearing line is drawn from that point across the edge of the hazardous area, then it's measured. Once you've drawn and labeled the danger bearing with its measurement, add crosshatches or shading to the hazardous side of the danger bearing. Then draw an "X" anywhere on the hazardous side of the line. Is the bearing to the danger waypoint from "X" greater or less than the danger bearing? If it is greater, mark the danger bearing as NMT (not more than); if it is less, mark the bearing NLT (not less than). On the water, you will monitor the bearings visually to ensure that you never violate the noted values. You can do the same thing with a GPS. Below: Here, two danger bearings have been drawn to exclude an entire dangerous region. West of the danger waypoint, do not let your bearing to it exceed 118° M. When north of it, do not let your bearing to it fall below 190° M.*

clearing line, can help define limits. The clearing line uses two charted objects, just as with a range, the primary difference being that the clearing line defines an edge rather than the center of a channel. On the water, you want to stay on the appropriate side of the clearing line. When the two landmarks are perfectly aligned, you are on the edge of safe water. Create clearing lines for places where no navigation aids are deployed to mark edges or limits, and label each clearing line with a bearing.

Using Danger Bearings

A variation of the same technique uses only one visible charted landmark, or nav aid, from which a line is drawn across the safe side of a hazardous area you wish to avoid. Measure the direction of that bearing as seen from the water and mark it on the line. To highlight the danger bearing, crosshatch the dangerous side.

On the water, you can monitor the bearing to that landmark with a hand bearing compass or your GPS to ensure that you do not venture onto the hazardous side. For most boaters, the real challenge in this technique is determining whether the bearing on the safe side needs to be less than or more than the danger bearing. Figure this out in advance and label the danger bearing line as NMT or NLT (for "not more than" or "not less than"). To make this determination, simply imagine that you are on the dangerous

side. Is your bearing to the danger waypoint more or less than the danger bearing? If it is more, label the danger bearing as NMT, and vice versa.

Using Danger Circles

By now you're familiar with the concept of a line of position (LOP), which results from a visual bearing on a charted landmark or buoy, from a range, from a radar bearing, and so forth. A *circle of position* (COP) is similar; all you need to know to plot one is your distance from a charted object.

You will discover in Chapter 15 that radar can be used to define a COP as well as an LOP. You can also use your GPS to define a COP by observing the distance to a nearby landmark that is stored in the GPS as a waypoint. By plotting an arc around that waypoint that you want to avoid, you can use your GPS to stay outside a hazardous area. All you need to do is measure the radius of the arc and note that on your chart, then stay outside that radius when you're on the water. The manufacturers of GPS receivers have recognized the power of this approach and, as mentioned, have included avoidance (or proximity) waypoints that can be stored along with a danger radius set to trigger an alarm. You can use a COP to avoid dangerous areas even if your GPS does not have this feature, but it will require vigilance on the water.

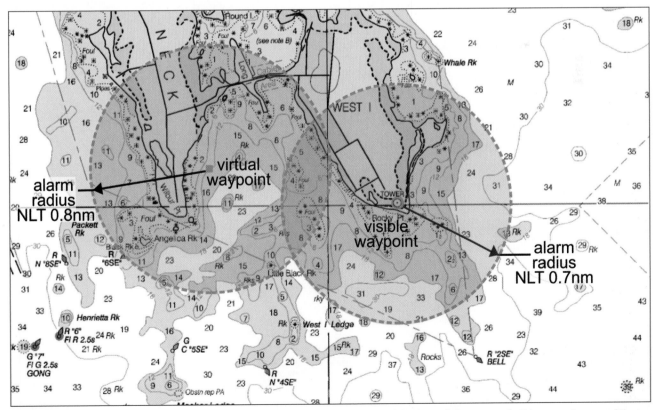

FIGURE 7-8. *The avoidance waypoint technique can be used to isolate most of the hazards in an area. In this example, one of the avoidance waypoints uses a charted landmark, and the other uses a virtual waypoint. The locations of the waypoints are optimized to encompass as many of the hazards as possible.*

NAVIGATING UNDERWAY

Underway with GPS and Paper Charts

In Part II we discussed navigation planning. By prequalifying courses and routes in your boating area, you have established paths that are free of underwater obstacles and identified areas to avoid. Now it's time to get underway.

Steps in Waypoint Navigation

Chapter 2 introduced the concept of navigating to a GPS waypoint. The process is quite simple. Here are the steps.

1. Select and activate the waypoint.

Use the GoTo function of your GPS receiver:

This function is accessed via the buttons. Some GPS models have a button labeled GoTo. Others place the GoTo function on a submenu accessed via another button such as Nav.

Scan until you find the desired waypoint from the stored list.

Select and activate that waypoint.

The GPS receiver:

Calculates the bearing and distance to the activated waypoint

Plots the course line on the Map Screen from your current position to the waypoint

Draws a highway on the Highway Screen from your current position to the waypoint

Let's say you are starting a cruise from the entrance to Oak Bluffs Harbor on Martha's Vineyard. Your ultimate destination is Waquoit Bay, across Nantucket Sound on the mainland of Cape Cod. You previously have created an intermediate waypoint, which you have stored in your GPS as "WPT." So, to get started, you use the GoTo function on your GPS and scroll through the waypoint list until you find WPT. Pressing ENTER brings up the corresponding waypoint screen for this selection. It's the correct one, so you select OK. Your GPS computes the course and distance and puts a highway on your Highway Screen, which you are planning to use for this cruise.

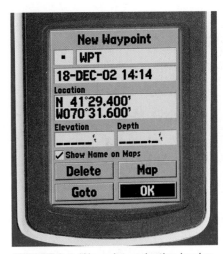

FIGURE 8-1. *Waypoint navigation begins by selecting and activating the first waypoint. The GPS provides a course from your current location to that waypoint.*

2. Double-check that this is a prequalified path.

Are you following a prequalified path—that is, one that you have plotted on your chart and used to define the starting and destination waypoints you are using for this leg of your route?

If not, plot your current position (as reported by the GPS) on a chart and draw the course line from there to the active waypoint. Is it safe?

Just to make sure, you decide to pull out your chart and plot the course from Oak Bluffs to WPT before you set out on the first leg of your cruise. All looks good, so let's go.

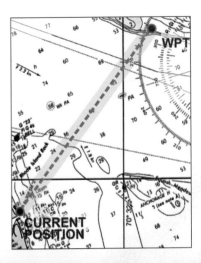

FIGURE 8-2. *It is your responsibility to ensure that the path to the waypoint is clear of obstructions. You should plot your current position and the waypoint, then draw the course line between them. Scan the intended course for hazards.*

3. Steer to the bearing direction indicated on the GPS.

Note the "Bearing to Waypoint" reported by the GPS.

Steer a heading corresponding to that initial bearing. (The initial bearing will be the same as the course, but the bearing will change if your actual track deviates from the rhumb-line course, whereas the course between the two waypoints in question is a fixed value in GPS memory. Some GPS models offer a "course" readout that presents the course direction corresponding to the line plotted on the Map Screen.)

Be sure that the initial track matches the bearing to waypoint.

Look at your compass. It, too, matches the initial GPS bearing within the accuracy of the compass, assuming you've set up the GPS to report courses and bearings in degrees magnetic.

Your GPS indicates that the bearing from Oak Bluffs Harbor to WPT is 054° magnetic (which is the same as your course to steer), and the distance is 2.17 nautical miles. Because your ship's compass has been properly compensated, you will steer to 054° M on your compass. You're underway.

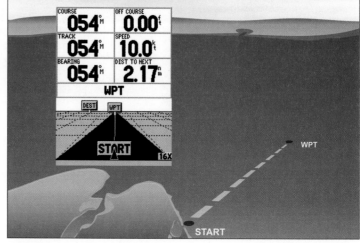

FIGURE 8-3. *You can use the Highway Screen to navigate to your next waypoint. The course field provides the desired course to steer. When you start, the bearing to the waypoint is the same as the course. Steer the boat until the highway extends straight ahead to the waypoint, as shown.*

4. Monitor your progress.

Monitor distance to waypoint.

Monitor track (the direction of your progress "over the ground") and compare it with the bearing. If your track does not match the active course from the waypoint you just left to the one ahead, it will not match the present bearing to the active waypoint either—a sign that you are getting off course.

The bearing is continually updated from your current position. If you're off course, the bearing will diverge from the original course line.

Monitor your Map and Highway Screens.

Are you on the original course line? Monitor your crosstrack error and observe your Map Screen or, preferably, your Highway Screen; your boat will appear to be on the original course line on the Map Screen if you are still on course. You will also appear to be in the center of the highway on the Highway Screen, and the highway will be extended straight ahead to the active waypoint.

Does the bearing to the waypoint match your track? If yes, you are on course. If no, you are off course. If you are close to the original course line, make adjustments to return. If you have wandered significantly from the course line (by more than your prequalified path width), plot your current position (as reported by the GPS) on your chart, and plot a line directly from your location to the active waypoint. Is it safe?

If yes, proceed. If not, plot a safe path back to your original course line.

As you proceed from Oak Bluffs toward WPT, you're operating under the principle "make your plan, follow your plan." You want to stay on course. You're in the middle of the highway, and WPT is dead ahead. You can use the Off-Course data window on your GPS for more refined details. That's what this model uses for crosstrack error. You're now only 1.38 nm from the destination, and you are off course by only 26.3 feet to the left, which is very close. So far, so good.

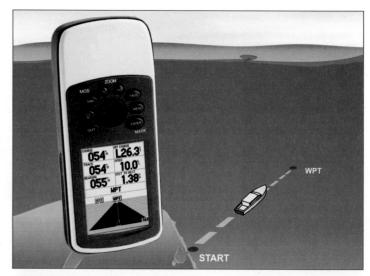

FIGURE 8-4. *As you proceed along the course, check to make sure that you are still in the center of the highway, with the highway pointing straight up. Note that the distance to the waypoint continues to diminish as you progress. When you started, you were 2.17 nm from the waypoint. In this example, you are now only 1.38 nm away.*

5. Be alert as you approach your destination.

Many GPS receivers sound an arrival alarm when you are approaching the active waypoint.

Prepare your next step before you arrive.

As you approach WPT, an alarm sounds and an information box pops up to say you are "Arriving at Destination." This is your cue to get ready to enter the next waypoint. You're still on plan.

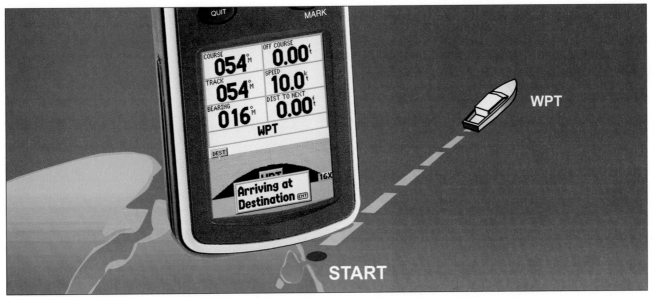

FIGURE 8-5. *As you approach your waypoint, most GPS models sound an arrival alarm and display a message.*

6. Select and activate the next waypoint (as appropriate).

If you are planning to go to another waypoint immediately, initiate a GoTo and select the next active waypoint, repeating the steps above.

Now it's time to enter the next waypoint, called "DEST," repeating all the steps that successfully got you to WPT. As soon as DEST is entered and activated, your GPS indicates your new bearing and course to be 013° and the new distance as 3.31 nm. You steer in that direction and get underway.

FIGURE 8-6. *To complete this cruise, activate the next waypoint and repeat the process.*

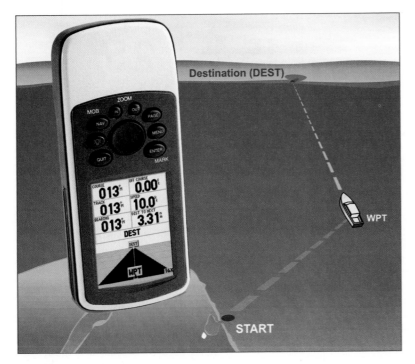

SATELLITE SCREEN

When you first turn on your GPS, it acquires satellites. The number and orientation of the received satellites determine the quality and accuracy of the position fix displayed on the GPS. The Satellite Screen is your window into what the receiver is doing.

A text field on the Satellite Screen tells you what is happening. Initially it says something like "acquiring satellites." After it has acquired three, it says "2-D fix." After acquiring four or more, it says "3-D fix." If the antenna becomes blocked, it may indicate "weak GPS signal" or "lost GPS signal."

The GPS receiver computes a quality index based on the geometry and quality of the satellite signals. Usually, this is displayed as EPE (estimated precision error). It's the GPS's best estimate of the actual accuracy of the fix in feet. On some models, this is displayed as a circle on the Map Screen to give you a sense of what that error means geographically. (Some GPS models have this data field on the Position Screen instead.)

POSITION SCREEN

The Position Screen presents your coordinates, usually expressed as a latitude and longitude. It also may provide other data fields, such as heading, track, speed, and bearing to waypoint. On some models, the position is provided on the Satellite Screen, and there is no separate Position Screen.

MAP SCREEN

The Map Screen provides a two-dimensional plan view of the area, usually with your current position indicated by an arrow or similar symbol near the center. Usually, the display is oriented with north at the top of the screen (North-Up), so the direction of the arrow provides a sense of your heading. North, to the GPS, can be either true north or magnetic north, whichever you select in the setup menus.

Any waypoints you have stored within the current field of view of the Map Screen will be shown in their respective positions. The Map Screen can be zoomed in or out to provide a more detailed or broader view of the area. In the absence of a chart on the screen, the Map Screen can be quite vacant of information. Obviously, the more waypoints you have entered, the more meaningful the display will be. Some GPS models come programmed with a marine database that includes significant buoys and beacons. These, too, will be shown, adding more meaning to the display.

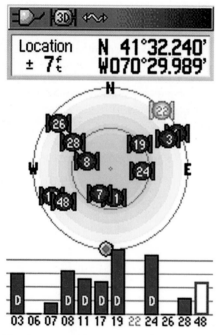

FIGURE 8-7. The Satellite Screen provides information about the quality of the signals and the resultant position fix. It indicates that the receiver is receiving signals from eight satellites. The height of the bars indicates the received signal strength. The circular "skyview" display shows the relative locations of these satellites. This GPS is processing a "3-D Differential" fix with an approximate accuracy of seven feet. If a portion of the sky is blank, it's likely that you're blocking the antenna. In this example, we might question whether the antenna is blocked to the north.

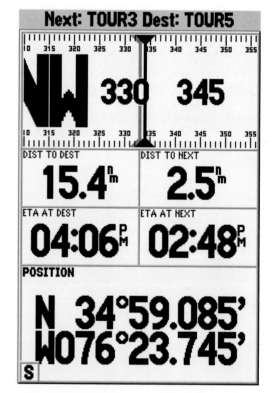

FIGURE 8-8. Most GPS models provide a separate Position Screen. This screen provides your coordinates along with other useful data fields. The display at the top of this screen looks like a compass. It is not. The light bar indicates your direction of motion; the dark bar indicates the direction to the waypoint.

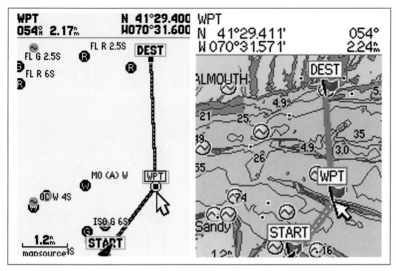

FIGURE 8-9. *When you activate a waypoint, the GPS draws a course line on the Map Screen. In the example on the left, a route has been activated and both legs are drawn simultaneously. Your location is indicated by a black arrow. In this example, the cursor (hollow arrow) is used to highlight "WPT." The bearing and distance from your current location to the cursor are shown at the top of the screen alongside the cursor's coordinates. A distance scale is provided at the bottom.*

The screen on the right comes from a GPS with built-in mapping (charting) capability. It represents a companion screenshot to that on the left. On this screen you see depths, depth contours, and navigation aids. This is basically a chartplotter screen. By zooming in, you will be presented with greater detail and information about navigation aids in view.

Whenever you activate a waypoint, an intended course line is drawn on the Map Screen from the place where you activated it to the selected waypoint itself. This line will stay on the screen, independent of your location, until you subsequently activate another waypoint. If you select a route (described below), the entire route will be displayed on the Map Screen.

Your current position will be displayed on the Map Screen as you advance toward your waypoint. If you wander from the course line, it will be indicated by the position arrow moving away from that line. If you elect to use the track feature in the GPS setup menu, your actual track (historical path) will be shown on the Map Screen, usually as a dotted line.

HIGHWAY SCREEN

The Highway Screen is an artificial three-dimensional representation of a highway to the active waypoint from your location when you selected it. Your present position is indicated at the center on the bottom of the screen (proximal end of the highway). Your heading (or track) is toward the top center of the screen. If you are on course, you will be in the center of the highway and the highway will extend directly toward the middle near the top of the display.

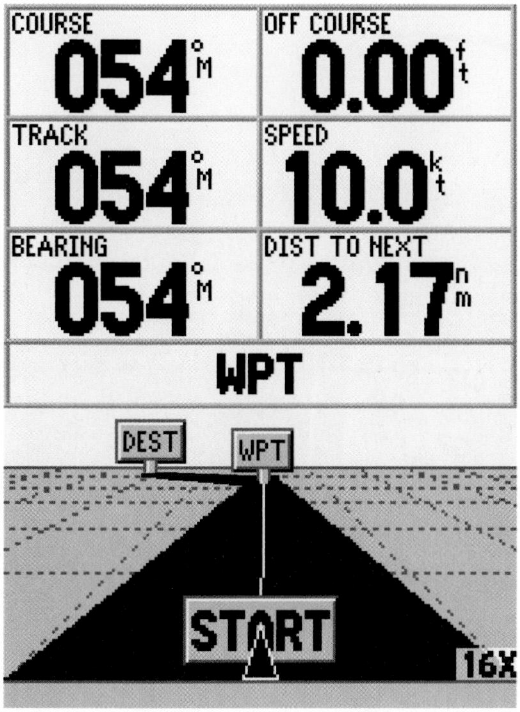

FIGURE 8-10. *The Highway Screen is possibly the most valuable screen on a handheld GPS. At a glance, you can tell whether you are on your intended course line and are headed in the proper direction. The screen depicts a 3-D view of a virtual highway. In this example, you are on the center of the highway, and thus on the center of your course line. You are heading directly toward your active waypoint. A route has been activated, so you see not only the active leg but the next leg as well. The data fields are user-selectable. In this case, you have chosen course, off course, track, speed, bearing, and distance as your data fields. Course is the direction of the active leg (what you intended). Off Course is your current distance from the center of the highway. Track is the direction of your actual motion over ground. Speed is your speed over ground. Bearing is the direction to the active waypoint, and distance is your current distance from it. You can change the perspective of this screen by zooming out (it currently is shown at maximum zoom). The name of the active waypoint is indicated in a data field.*

(continued on next page)

GPS SCREENS (CONTINUED)

If you have not selected an active waypoint, there will be no highway on this screen. As soon as you activate a waypoint, the highway is drawn. It stays on the screen, providing you with a frame of reference to your originally selected course, until you activate another waypoint. If you select a route, all legs of the route will be shown on the Highway Screen sequentially, with the appropriate turns between each leg.

The "highway" is what you would expect to see from a vantage point above your boat, looking in the direction you are moving. You steer to stay in the center. If you get off the highway, you steer to get back on it.

Newer GPS models have sufficient resolution on their displays that other waypoints can also be displayed relative to the highway, and you can zoom in or out to get a more or less detailed view.

In the absence of a chart on your Map Screen, the Highway Screen is perhaps the most useful screen on your GPS.

COMPASS SCREEN

The Compass Screen shows a circular representation of a compass card. Your current heading is at the top. Usually, the bearing to your active waypoint is shown by a separate indicator, and you steer to line up the two. The Compass Screen is more useful for hiking than boating. The Highway Screen presents more useful information.

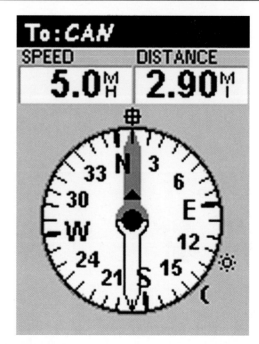

FIGURE 8-11. *The Compass Screen is not as useful for marine navigation. Remember, this is not a compass. The light bar at the top indicates your direction of motion. The black arrow indicates the direction to your waypoint. This GPS also shows the bearings of the sun and the moon to provide additional visual references.*

Staying On Course

If you wander from your intended course line, you need to get out the charts, plot your present position, and decide on a new path from there to your destination waypoint. It is better, obviously, to stay on the original course line, but there are a number of reasons why you may get off course: (1) steering to avoid visible obstacles, (2) a crosswind, (3) a crosscurrent, (4) your boat yawing in waves, or (5) inattention to the helm.

Recovering from Off Course

If the waters you've strayed into are relatively free of obstacles, you may be able to approximate your position, see that the path from your current location directly to the waypoint is clear, then simply steer to the bearing of the waypoint as shown on your GPS. Be aware that whatever environmental influence moved you off course (often a tidal current) is still likely to be operating on you, so compensate.

If there are hazards nearby, however, take the time to plot your position on the chart and prequalify the direct path to the waypoint. You may well find that you should return to your original course line, still showing on your Map

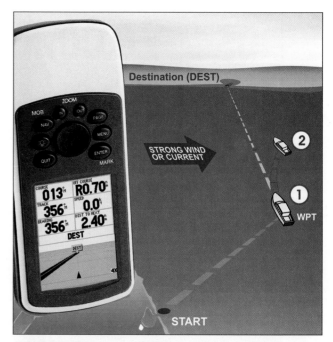

FIGURE 8-12. *Even with GPS, you may find yourself off your intended course line. You began the leg steering toward your destination (1), but some time later you find that you no longer are on the intended course line (2). Now you'll need to consult the chart (see Figure 8-13).*

MONITORING GPS DATA

Most GPS units offer a wide variety of data windows that you can monitor. Typical data available include the following:

Bearing—True or magnetic direction to the active waypoint from your current location

Distance—Direct-line distance to the active waypoint from your current position, usually in nautical miles

Course—The intended course for the active leg, extending from the location where the waypoint was activated or from the last turn in a route—shown as a line on the Map Screen and as a highway on the Highway Screen (this will remain fixed until you enter another GoTo to activate a waypoint)

Track—(also course over ground, or COG) expressed as true or magnetic (according to your setup choice); actual motion of the boat with respect to the Earth

Speed—(also speed over ground, or SOG) usually in knots (nautical miles per hour), indicating the actual speed of the boat with respect to the Earth

Position—Coordinates, usually latitude and longitude, in degrees, minutes, and tenths of minutes

Time—Universal time (UT, which is the time referenced to Greenwich, England) or adjusted to local time using the proper offset in the setup menu

Accuracy—(sometimes GDOP, for geometrical dilution of precision) an indication of the potential error of the GPS based on the geometry of the received satellites

Elevation—GPS elevation accuracy is only a hundred feet or so. An elevation error does not mean your horizontal coordinates are wrong. Short of a disaster, your elevation is irrelevant.

You may have the option to either replace one of the above data fields or insert user-selectable choices in extra data fields. The most useful of these optional data fields are as follows:

Off Course—(also crosstrack error, XTE, or XTK) the distance (in feet or nautical miles) of your current position from the center of the course line that was set when you initiated navigation to the active waypoint—often associated with an "L" or "R" for left or right

VMG—(velocity made good, or speed made good) your actual speed of closure toward the selected waypoint, even if your course is not directly toward the waypoint

Time to Next—(also ETE, estimated time en route) the time it will take to reach the active waypoint at your present speed

Time at Next—(also ETA, estimated time of arrival) the actual expected time of arrival at the active waypoint at your present speed

The optional data fields Off Course and VMG are probably the most useful for boaters. For example, if you use the Highway Screen to keep you on course, the off-course data field will show exactly how far you are from the centerline of the course. Using the graphic and the data readout, you can more easily tune your steering to stay on course. If you do get off course, you will know just how far you are from the course line. VMG monitors your progress toward your active waypoint. This is useful if you must deviate from the straight-line course because of wind or waves but still intend to reach that waypoint. This field also helps sailors determine when to tack if sailing upwind (see Chapter 21).

Note that there is no GPS data readout for your heading, which is the compass course you are steering. GPS doesn't know or care where your boat is pointing—only where it's actually going.

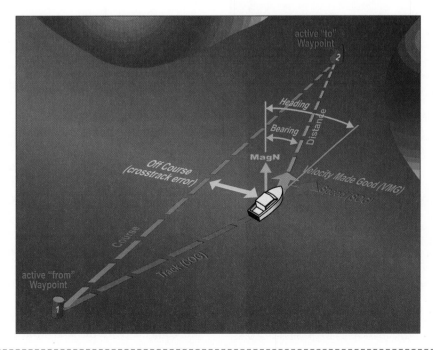

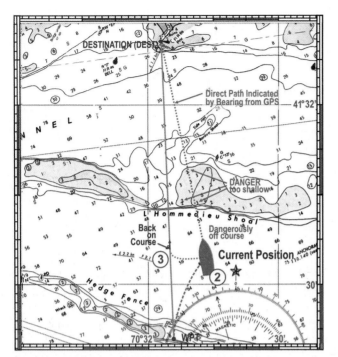

FIGURE 8-13. *As soon as you discover that you're off course, you need to plot your current position (2) on a chart and draw the direct path to your destination waypoint to determine whether it is safe to proceed. In this example, it is clear that you are facing dangerous shoals. Your best choice is to plan a direct path back to your intended course line (3), then proceed from there.*

FIGURE 8-14. *In this example, you have returned to the original course line and aligned yourself so your position is in the center of the highway and the destination waypoint is straight ahead.*

and Highway Screens, before turning toward the waypoint. Just be sure that the path you take back to the course line also is clear of obstacles.

HOW CAN I TELL WHERE I AM WITH A GPS? If you have a handheld GPS without built-in charts, you probably will need to pinpoint your location on a paper chart using plotting tools. GPS units provide all the information you need to do that. There are two approaches: (1) latitude and longitude coordinates, and (2) bearing and distance to a waypoint.

PLOTTING LATITUDE AND LONGITUDE Plot your GPS latitude and longitude coordinates on the chart as described in Chapter 4 to get your current position. This sounds simple and straightforward, and in principle it is; however, it may not be so easy to perform on a moving, bouncing boat at sea.

TIP—A quick way to plot an approximate latitude and longitude is to slide a rectangular plotting tool across the chart by eye. First, align the tool with the chart grid and slide it so the top is next to the latitude scale at the latitude shown on the GPS screen. Next, slide it over so the left (or right) side is close to the longitude shown on the GPS, and mark the latitude with a pencil. Now slide the tool to the longitude scale and align it more carefully with the GPS longitude, then slide it back to complete the mark. This is a quick way to check your position, but it is not precise. If it places you near charted hazards, get out the dividers or use the technique below.

PLOTTING BEARING AND DISTANCE A better approach uses the bearing and distance to a waypoint that is shown on the GPS and plotted on your chart. This information is continuously updated and available on the GPS screen for the active waypoint (though any other waypoint can be selected; see below). Using parallel rules (and assuming you're working in degrees magnetic), transfer the magnetic bearing from the inner (magnetic) ring of the chart's compass rose to the charted location of the active waypoint, then draw the bearing line from your approximate location to the waypoint.

Next, using the GPS distance to that waypoint, mark off this distance from the waypoint along the bearing line you have just drawn, as described in Chapter 4. This is your current location.

This approach works well when your chart is folded. You only need to see a compass rose and the charted waypoint (which is probably a navigation buoy) and have access to the distance scale or one of the latitude scales. More important, this plot has physical significance because it is the bearing and distance to your active waypoint. The bearing line coincides with the straight-line path from where you are to where you want to go.

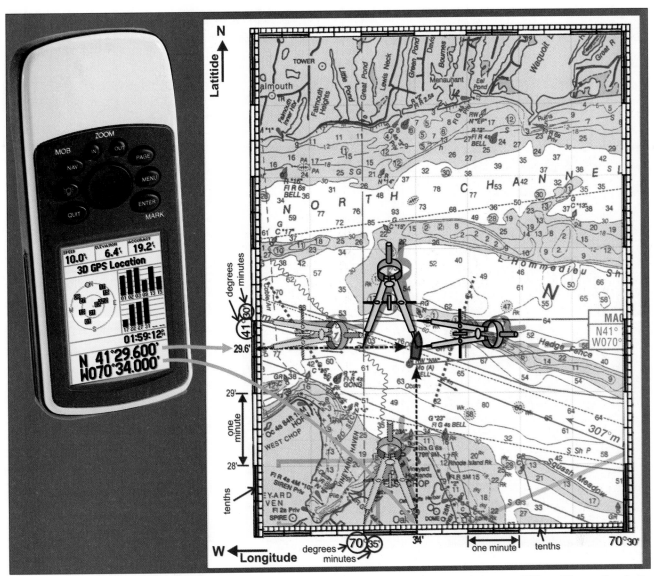

FIGURE 8-15. *Whenever your location relative to preplanned courses is in question, you should plot your GPS position on the chart.*

Suppose you find that you are off course. If you used your active waypoint as the reference, the bearing line you have just drawn is also the direct path to the waypoint. Look along the path for obstacles. If it is clear, you can steer directly to the waypoint. Just remember that the wind or tidal current that pushed you off course in the first place may continue to act on the boat, moving you even farther off.

The original course line will stay on the GPS map and Highway Screens. If you prefer to restart navigation from your present location, simply use the GPS GoTo function again, selecting the same active waypoint. The original course line will disappear, and a new line from your present position to the waypoint will replace it.

If the new direct path is not free of obstructions, however, you will need to find a safe path back to the original course line before proceeding to the active waypoint.

TIP—If you don't have or can't use parallel rules conveniently on your boat, you can try a quick technique to transfer the angle. Align your plotting tool correctly on the compass rose, then slide it across the chart so it aligns with your waypoint. Even working freehand, you generally can transfer a direction to within a few degrees using this technique. But it is approximate, so if you are near hazards, use the more precise approach.

USE ANOTHER WAYPOINT FOR BEARING AND DISTANCE You are not limited to using the active waypoint for these measurements. Often, another waypoint is closer or more convenient. Any nearby waypoint will do, provided it is charted. Using the Map Screen, you will see all the stored waypoints that lie within the current zoom level of the display.

On many GPS models, you can determine the bear-

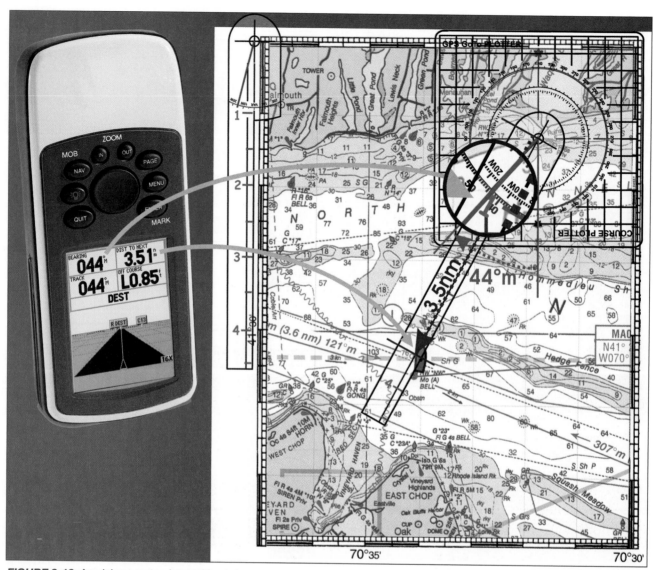

FIGURE 8-16. *A quicker way to plot position is to use a protractor plotting tool with a pivoting arm to locate your position by bearing and distance. You align the bearing of 44° M opposite 15° W on the variation scale (see Figure 5-19). (Remember to read 44° on the reciprocal scale or turn the protractor upside-down. Then measure out 3.5 nm along the arm to mark your current position.)*

ing and distance to any waypoint by simply scrolling the cursor over that waypoint until it is highlighted. The GPS usually indicates the corresponding bearing and distance in a data window. You don't want to navigate to this waypoint, just sample its bearing and distance, so use the QUIT or ESC buttons to return to the original GPS display. Your active navigation will not be interrupted.

Alternatively, you can go to the Waypoints or Nearest Waypoints menu and call up the desired waypoint there. The Waypoint Screen will provide the current bearing and distance to the desired waypoint. (Use QUIT or ESC to go back without causing the GPS to consider this the new active waypoint.) Using this bearing and distance, plot your position as above. If you find that you are off course, however, you will need to draw a line from your plotted location to the active waypoint before attempting to steer to its bearing.

Waypoints off to one side of your course often provide greater precision and convenience for this bearing-and-distance measurement. You can get a quick sense of whether you are off course simply by looking at the distance from the reference waypoint.

TIP—Your chart has several built-in bearing protractors—namely, its compass roses. Simply enter the center point of each printed compass rose as a waypoint in your GPS. Anytime on the water, look up the bearing and distance of a given compass rose, then plot that bearing using the rose without a protractor. All you need to mark your position is a straightedge and some means of measuring the distance. Just remember either to use the reciprocal of the bearing or to plot using the angle on the far side of the rose from the center point. That's because the bearing your GPS gives you is from your boat to the rose, not from the rose to you.

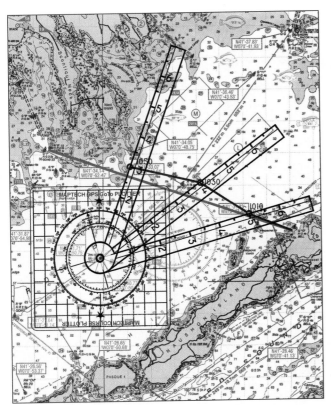

FIGURE 8-17. *It's possible that your destination waypoint is some distance away, or another waypoint may simply be more convenient. In this example, a waypoint to the side of the intended course line has been used for bearing-and-distance plots at 1010, 1030, and 1050 hours. Each plot was done as shown in Figure 8-16.*

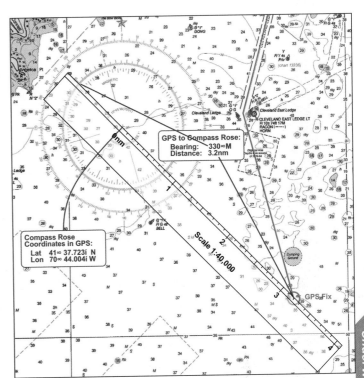

FIGURE 8-18. *Another tip is to use the center of the chart's compass rose as a virtual waypoint. If you do this, you don't even need a protractor scale; the compass rose provides that for you. All you need is a straightedge calibrated to distance. Enter the compass rose coordinates as a waypoint, then call up that waypoint to determine its bearing and distance from your current position. Mark the bearing directly using the inner ring of the rose for magnetic direction. Remember that you are reading the bearing from you to the rose, so read the bearing on the far side of the compass rose center.*

TIP—As an alternative to plotting a bearing from a compass rose, you can place a protractor plotting tool over the waypoint to which you wish to plot a bearing and distance. Some plotting tools come with distance scales already printed on the straightedge. But because the scales of today's commercial charts may not be standard, it is recommended that you first align the straightedge with the latitude scale and mark the nautical miles (minutes of latitude) and half miles directly on the straightedge using a pencil. Now align the straightedge with the bearing using the protractor and read outward to the distance provided by the GPS. This is your current location. This approach is ideal for a folded chart, because you do not need access to either the latitude/longitude scales or the compass rose to mark your position.

There is one complication: because the plotting tool aligns with the chart's latitude/longitude grid instead of magnetic directions, you will need to correct for variation if your GPS is set to magnetic headings. Some tools provide a correcting scale on the straightedge (as shown in Figure 8-16). Otherwise, you will need to convert mathematically (see Chapter 5).

If you want to monitor your progress along a route, you can use a single waypoint along the side of your route and periodically plot successive bearings and distances, as shown in Figure 8-17. Also note that this technique will work with a standard protractor if you don't have a protractor plotting tool at hand, but it should be placed with 180° pointed north, so the scale reads the reciprocal course. This is harder to describe than to do; if you try it, you'll see.

Effects of Wind or Current

It's natural to head your boat directly toward your next waypoint, but in the presence of an oblique tidal current or a strong crosswind, which will push you away from your planned course line, it's a mistake. As you're pushed off course, your GPS shows a new bearing to the waypoint. If you then steer to that new bearing, you will be pushed even farther off course. Finally, you will approach the waypoint not from your direction of origin but from the side. The result is called a *hooked course*—a curved path instead of the intended straight line to your waypoint. When a hooked track takes you far enough off your intended course, you can easily encounter hazards that you had planned to give a

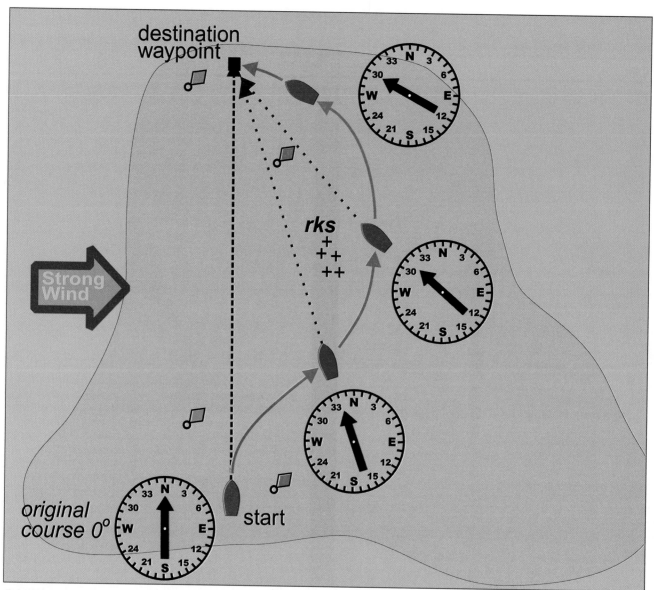

FIGURE 8-19. *A natural tendency while boating is to head toward your destination or waypoint. This is fine when you start, but it's not so good if you've been pushed off course by wind or current. In this example, you have adjusted your heading to correct for the bearing to the waypoint at several points along your path. Instead of heading directly to the waypoint, you will reach it from the side. Unfortunately, hazards lurk to the side of the intended course line.*

wide berth. Clearly, steering to a waypoint without checking your position relative to the course line can be dangerous. (Chapter 14 provides more information about winds and currents.)

This is the same thing that happens when you visually steer directly toward the next buoy in a tight channel with a crosscurrent. By focusing on the buoy and not your course line, you can be pushed out of the channel.

This occurs on a regular basis in Woods Hole, Massachusetts, for example, even to experienced mariners. The "Hole," as it is called, has a shortcut called "Broadway," which takes boaters through a narrow channel between two substantial outcroppings of shallow rocks. Adding insult to injury, at certain phases of the tide, very strong crosscurrents

develop in Woods Hole as Buzzards Bay empties into Nantucket Sound. This current cuts across Broadway. Those who steer by eye to the next buoy may find that the resultant hooked course has taken them onto the rocks, as shown in Figure 8-20.

Figure 8-21 shows graphically what happens. You steer directly toward your destination, but the wind or current pushes you to the right. You still are pointed in the original heading, but your position is shifted to the right. Your actual track is at an angle downwind or "downcurrent."

The solution is to steer into the wind or current as shown in Figure 8-22. Your heading is upwind or "upcurrent" of your destination, but the actual track of your boat is along your intended course line. In effect you are pro-

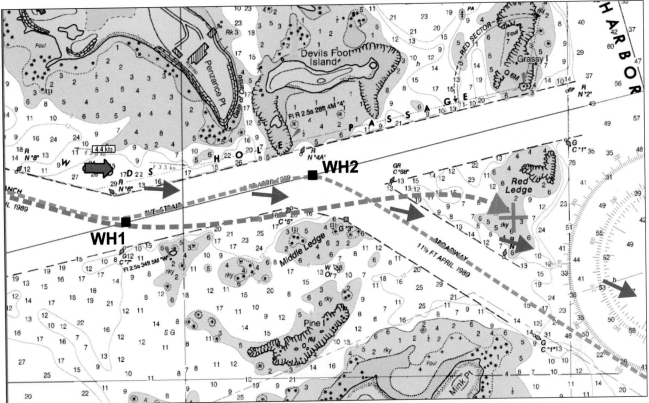

FIGURE 8-20. *A real example of the danger of the hooked course is illustrated using Woods Hole Passage in Massachusetts. This is a narrow passage with rocks on both sides. Many boats have foundered on these rocks. A strong tidal current (red arrows) can push you from your intended course line (green), first onto the rocks to starboard, then later to port. (This is shown as the orange path ending in a grounding.)*

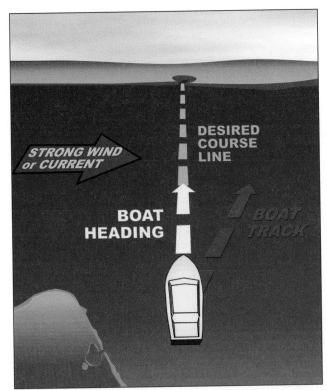

FIGURE 8-21. *In this example, you have steered directly toward your waypoint along the desired course line. The actual boat track is a line off to the right, as shown.*

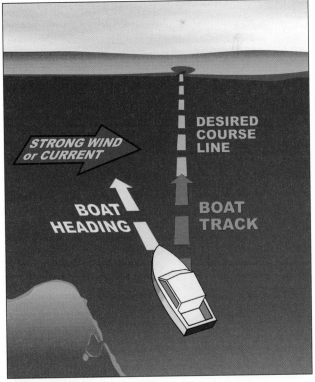

FIGURE 8-22. *You can adjust your heading such that your track aligns directly with the desired course line.*

FIGURE 8-23. *You can use the Highway Screen on your GPS to determine the course to steer. Adjust your heading in small increments until the off-course data field becomes stable and stops increasing. If you are still away from the center of the course line, temporarily overcompensate until you have returned to the center. When properly aligned, you will find that your boat heading does not match your course direction or your actual motion (track). You can still use your compass to steer. Simply maintain the heading shown on the compass, in this case about 340°.*

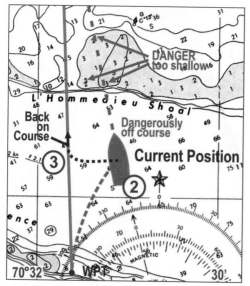

FIGURE 8-24. *In this example, you found your location to be off course (2) and decided to return to the original course line (3), because going directly to your destination would have put you in danger. You can see on the Map Screen that your location is somewhat to the right of the intended course line. However, there is no way to tell from the GPS Map Screen of the potential peril along the path. The Highway Screen (see Figure 8-25) will show the highway off to the left, but you are pointed toward your destination.*

ceeding "crabwise" along your course line. The big question is, how much to compensate—how far do you have to turn into the wind or current? GPS provides a ready answer.

The Highway Screen, as shown in Figure 8-23, provides the ideal solution. All you need to do is stay in the center of the highway with the highway extending straight up in the center of the display. This is the position that represents an on-course orientation.

Initially, you will head the boat directly toward the active waypoint. In a crosswind or current, however, you may soon notice that you are moving to one side of the highway or the other, a signal that you need to adjust your course into the wind or current. To get back on course, you need to "oversteer" a bit to return to the centerline, which means that the highway shown on the screen will be at a slight angle. You will be heading temporarily toward the center of the highway rather than the waypoint.

Once back in the center of the highway, by adjusting your course into the wind or cur-

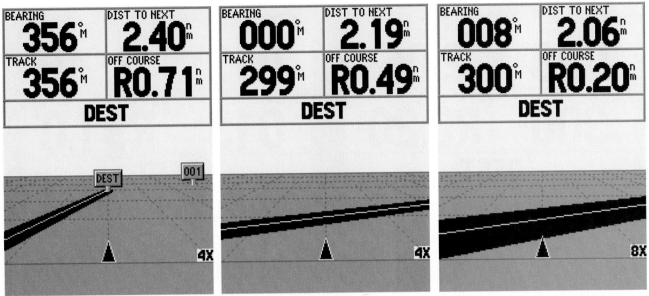

FIGURE 8-25A. *Although somewhat intuitive, the Highway Screen may take a little experience to use it effectively. Going back to the example shown in Figure 8-24, these screens provide a step-by-step view of how to return to the original course line. Left: Your highway view from Position 2 in Figure 8-24. Middle: You have decided to head back to the original course line. Now the highway appears to cut across your screen. Your destination waypoint no longer appears within the field of view. In the real world, this is the view that you would have returning to a roadway. Note that the off-course data field has been reduced to 0.49 nm from 0.71 nm. Right: You are closer to the highway. Note that off course is now down to 0.20 nm.*

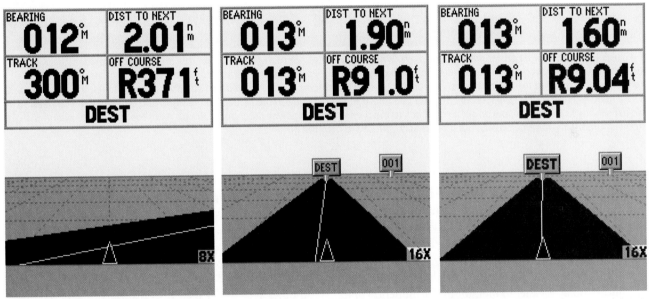

FIGURE 8-25B. *Left: Off course is now only 371 feet. Time to begin your turn toward your destination. Middle: Now you are nearly aligned with your destination waypoint. Off course is down to 91 feet. Right: You continue to close on the centerline by small steering increments. The off course is now down to 9 feet (on course). Because the wind or current that moved you away from your intended course may still be acting on you, your heading may not correspond with your boat's track. You will continue to adjust the steering until the off-course indicator remains steady. If you are close to the center of the highway, simply maintain this heading.*

rent in small increments you will find the steering angle that keeps you in the middle of the display with the highway extending straight ahead toward the active waypoint. This is the steering angle to maintain until such time as the wind or current change, necessitating a further adjustment. As an alternative, display the course and track data windows on your GPS and steer to keep these values equal to each other. This is easier if you begin when you are on course, simply adjusting your steering so that they match. If you are already off course by some distance, using these two data fields can be more confusing than simply observing the highway.

If your GPS does not display the intended course as a data field, you can use the bearing data field instead. You

111

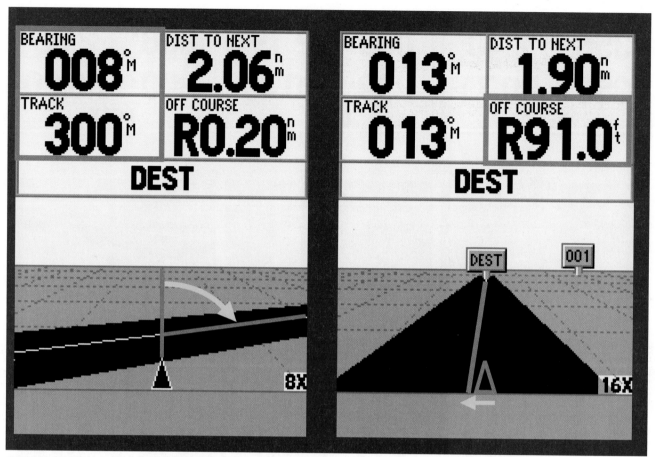

FIGURE 8-26. *Most of us prefer graphical displays, which the Highway Screen provides. But this display also provides data fields that can be used to accomplish the same tasks. With only a glance, you can tell whether you are on course and determine your direction with respect to the waypoint and intended course. In the screen on the left, you can see that, in order to reach your waypoint, you'll need to steer to the right (yellow arrow) as you return to the highway. In the screen on the right, you can see that you need to adjust slightly to the left (yellow arrow) to get back to the center of the highway (intended course). All of the same information is shown numerically (orange boxes), but it's less straightforward than the graphics.*

will need to make a note of the intended course when you first activate the waypoint. The bearing from that spot is exactly the same as your intended course. Just make sure that the bearing does not change from that value as you move toward your waypoint, and be sure the bearing and track readouts continue to match.

But again, studies and experience have shown that a graphical display is easier to monitor than a numerical one. With even a quick glance at the Highway Screen, you can tell if you are on course as shown in Figure 8-26.

If you use the ship's compass to steer, all you need to do is note the compass reading for the heading that keeps you on course and stay on that heading. As shown in Figure 8-23, you will see that the compass heading and the boat's track, or course over ground, no longer match. The difference is the amount by which you have had to "crab" the boat into the wind or current to compensate for leeway or set. Remember, by holding your position in the center of the highway with the highway straight ahead toward your destination waypoint, you guarantee that your track

will follow the planned course line. The GPS track readout is an accurate reflection of your true motion over ground, whereas the compass shows the boat's heading through the water.

Crosstrack Error

Another very useful data field displayed on the Highway Screen is crosstrack error (sometimes labeled as "XTE," "XTK," or "off course"). Crosstrack error is the distance that you are off course, either L (to port) or R (to starboard). When you are close to your intended course line, the distance is usually presented in feet. If you venture farther from your course line, the distance is usually presented in nautical miles (assuming you have your GPS set up in nautical units). Whether you're off course due to wind, tide, or simple inattention, crosstrack error tells you by how much. You can program your GPS to sound an alarm at a preset distance in case it's needed to bring your attention back to navigating.

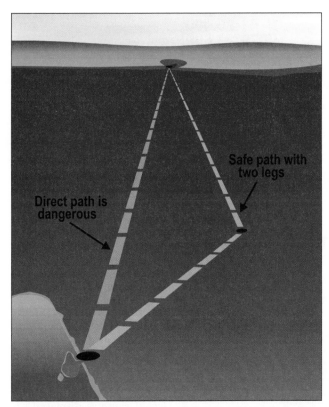

FIGURE 8-27. *Navigating from point to point is the most common form of GPS navigation, even by experienced boaters. In this example, the direct path is unsafe, so an intermediate waypoint was added. The GPS offers a route function that sequentially navigates to selected waypoints. This two-leg path can be conveniently automated.*

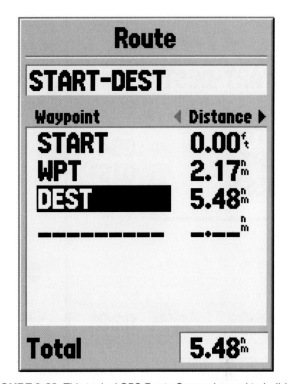

FIGURE 8-28. *This typical GPS Route Screen is used to build a route. In this example, you access the field with the cursor and scroll through your stored waypoints until you find "START." Next, you do the same for "WPT," then "DEST." (If you intended to add another waypoint, you would highlight the dashed data field at the bottom and select another waypoint.) Note that the total distance for the route is displayed on the screen. By scrolling to the right, you will find the course and distance for each leg. In this example, the route name has been provided by the GPS. The default mode will name the route using the names of the first and last waypoints in the sequence. This is easy to use and easy to remember.*

Navigating a Route with GPS

Manually navigating your route from waypoint to waypoint is simple, but you'll need to activate the next waypoint as you complete each leg. Unfortunately, this usually occurs at the same time your attention is needed to execute a course change. The GPS route function simplifies the process by automatically activating the next leg as soon as you reach a waypoint. As explained in Chapter 2 and elsewhere, a route is a sequence of legs defined by starting and ending waypoints. Your GPS navigates each leg using the beginning waypoint as the "active from" waypoint and the leg destination as the "active to" waypoint, and calculates the intended leg course, distance, and other functions such as time or fuel consumption.

FIGURE 8-29. *There are a few cautions to consider when you use a route. When you activate a route, most GPS receivers compute the course from your current location to the second waypoint (in this case, WPT). The GPS assumes that you are starting at the first waypoint on the route list. If you are not, as shown in the figure, you need to plot your position and a safe course to the waypoint.*

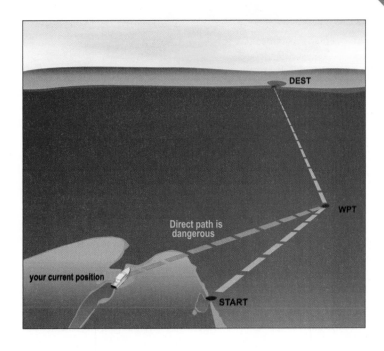

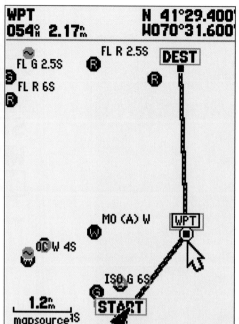

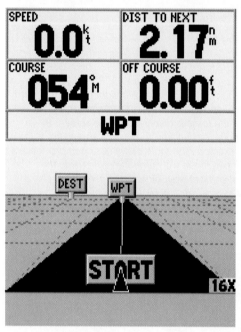

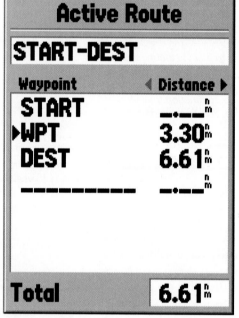

FIGURE 8-30. As soon as you select and activate the route, your Route Screen indicates the active leg and waypoint (see arrow on Active Route Screen). Your GPS can now also display a corresponding highway on the Highway Screen and a course on the Map Screen. Note that the entire route is displayed on both screens.

Selecting a Route

Routes should be preplanned, at least in segments; you activate the desired route from the Routes menu. Most GPS units automatically store route names in a format that lists the first and last waypoint names of each route. This is the preferred naming convention, though you can name routes as you choose. Just make absolutely certain you are activating the correct route. On the water, when there are other boats to avoid, passengers to watch and converse with,

weather to observe, waves, and countless other stimuli clamoring for your attention, it is easy to make a mistake even with a simple task. This is where the first and last waypoint names help, and one of the reasons why you should clearly label your waypoints during the planning process in a way that makes it easy to distinguish one from another. These same labels should appear on the charts that you carry with you.

Using the carpenter's maxim "Measure twice, cut once," you need to double-check your selection. In addition to checking the name twice, you should look at the bearing and direction to the initial waypoint of the selected route as displayed on your GPS to make sure it makes sense.

Your choices when you select a route are to activate, invert, or edit. Activating the route starts the navigation process from your current location, which may or may not correspond with the first waypoint on the route list.

If it doesn't, you must ensure that your path to the newly active waypoint is safe, which means pulling out your chart, locating your current position on the chart, and establishing the safety of the direct path to the route's starting point.

Alternatively, you may be at the route destination and wish to return to the initial waypoint. In this event you will select "invert" from the Routes menu, which reverses the order of the waypoints. Often, the route name will invert as well.

Following a Route

On the GPS Highway Screen, the imaginary highway of the route you've selected extends not only from your starting point to the active waypoint, but to all the subsequent

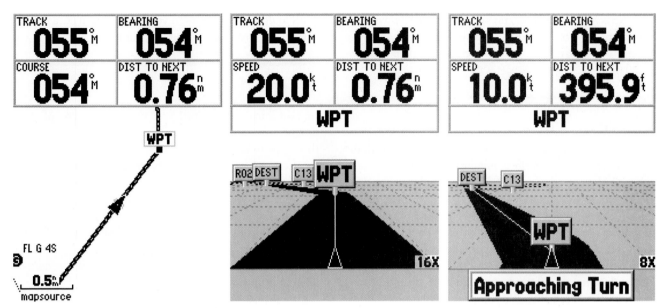

FIGURE 8-31. *Underway, you can monitor your progress on the Map and Highway Screens. The black arrow shows your position on the map. Your position is also shown on the highway. As you approach your first waypoint, an alarm and message indicate that you're "Approaching Turn." As you get within an arrival radius of the first waypoint, the GPS activates the next waypoint and provides the course and bearing to that waypoint. You need to steer in that new direction and monitor your progress.*

waypoints as well. In addition, most GPS models display all other waypoints within the field of view, including those that are not part of the active route. Danger waypoints will appear relative to the highway, to alert you as you approach them. Seeing the entire route plotted also helps you to prepare in advance for each turn.

The Map Screen also is useful, but unless you have a chartplotter it may appear rather vacant of detail. Your position will be indicated by a symbol, typically a triangle that points in the direction of your boat's motion (usually with a few seconds' lag). Also shown are the route's course line and all programmed waypoints within the field of view at the selected zoom level. A track line showing where you have been will be displayed if you activate that feature. You can monitor your track or position relative to the intended course line as you navigate, but to use this display to stay on course, you may need to zoom well in, at which point you will see only a small segment of the route. Monitoring your position using the Map Screen takes quite a bit more visual attention than using the more intuitive Highway Screen. Most GPS models also let you select which data readouts are displayed on the Map Screen.

Entering a Route at a Midway Point

You may wish to enter a route at some midway point, as opposed to one of its ends. Simply activate the route, and some GPS models give you the bearing and distance to the nearest waypoint in that route. Others point you to the route's initial waypoint, but assuming you have checked your planned action on a chart, you can set out toward the place where you wish to join the route. Most GPS models

interpret this move and switch to the next logical waypoint so you can join the route from there.

Navigating in a Region

Chapter 7 describes methods for preplanning a cruise in a region, avoiding obstacles and hazards marked in your GPS. Having identified critical hazards, you can meander more or less freely around the region in question, as long as you regularly monitor your GPS to make sure you are not encroaching upon any of the danger areas. Danger or proximity waypoints and crosstrack error are useful functions for this, because they are associated with an audible alarm. You may not hear the alarm, however; most handheld GPS units have limited audio volume.

Generally, you will find it convenient to use the Map Screen when you navigate casually in a region. By monitoring the screen, you can see when you are encroaching on one of the hazard areas. You will need to set the zoom level to correspond with your speed. If you are fishing or puttering, you can zoom in; when moving fast, you will need to zoom out far enough see the entire area of operation. Recognize that at high speeds, it is possible to "outrun" your GPS. That is, your reported position will be behind you. Also, you may find that setting the GPS screen to its Course-Up option helps with your orientation. In this mode the track of your boat is always up, so your visual surroundings match the GPS screen.

You will not need to select an active waypoint. Rather, the display will show all waypoints within your

Map Screen's field of view. Having selected special symbols for hazard waypoints during the planning process, such as a skull and crossbones, you will know which points to avoid.

Marking Objects

On the water, you will inevitably find objects whose locations you want to record. Locally maintained buoys are often not listed on charts, and you may find clusters of lobster pots or uncharted hazards you want to add to your GPS memory.

Usually, you can mark a location on a handheld GPS simply by pressing the designated button, often twice. The GPS will store the waypoint coordinates with a number rather than a name. Jot the number on your chart or a notepad with a notation of its significance; then you can create a name for the new waypoint and edit its information later, on your mooring or at home.

You may also see landmarks that can be useful for position finding or for checking the GPS, including potential ranges. You may not be able to mark these at the time, but you should identify them on your chart and make a note to enter them into your GPS upon your return home.

Keeping Track

In traditional navigation, you maintain a plot of your progress on your chart using dead reckoning, then verify this "guesstimate" of your current position with a position fix (from a navigation aid, crossed bearings, et cetera) at every opportunity. By telling you your precise coordinates, GPS obviates the need for dead reckoning. But what do you do if the GPS quits? As you will see in Chapter 12, you will need to resort to dead reckoning based on your last known position. But if you didn't plot it, you won't know what it was. Then, if you don't have charted navigation aids or landmarks in view, you're lost—literally.

The solution is simple: plot your GPS position on your chart from time to time. On an extended cruise in open waters, an hourly interval is okay. At high speed, in dangerous waters, or in poor weather, consider doing so more frequently. We'll revisit this in Chapters 10 and 12.

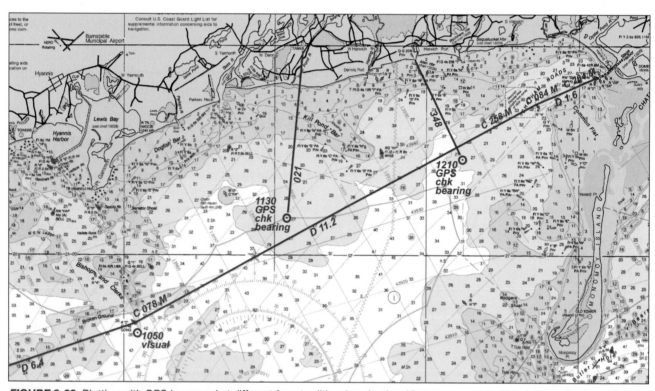

FIGURE 8-32. *Plotting with GPS is somewhat different from traditional navigation. You are encouraged to plot your GPS position at intervals nominally an hour apart (depending upon the area and type of boat). Each time you plot your GPS position, you should make an attempt to verify its accuracy by taking a bearing and comparing it with the GPS. In this example, the GPS fixes have been plotted more frequently. They are close to the planned course line but deviate a bit to port or starboard. This could be due to winds or currents or just inattention at the helm.*

Underway with Digital Charts

There is no question that displaying GPS information directly on a Chart Screen is ideal for ease of use and safety. You are freed from the tedious task and potential errors associated with transferring positions back and forth between your GPS and paper charts. This ideal in no way diminishes the effectiveness of a nonmapping handheld GPS, a paper chart, and the techniques described in the previous chapters. Digital charts are just easier, though somewhat more expensive. Most boaters start with a handheld GPS and gravitate toward using a computer with the GPS at home for planning. The next step in the progression is usually either a chartplotter or an onboard computer for live navigation.

A chartplotter is specifically tailored to navigation tasks, whereas a general-purpose computer can be used with navigation software to do the same things and potentially more. Where and how you plan to use the equipment and how much you care to spend on it are the primary considerations.

At some point in the near future, the differences between chartplotters and onboard computers will blur. With improving performance and lower costs, chartplotters are already finding their way onto smaller boats, which is actually where they belong. These self-contained units are ideal for an 18-foot boat that has little room in which to lay out a paper chart.

Meanwhile, advances in onboard computer hardware and software are giving computers increasing application on the water. Today, most oceangoing commercial ships are moving to totally computerized electronic navigation suites. The power and versatility of computer-based navigation is attractive to anyone who cruises. As previously noted, many boaters use both chartplotters and computers. The computer shines for planning; for navigating longer, more complex routes; and for use in an enclosed helm station. The chartplotter, with its marinized, waterproof construction and simplified keyboard, is a better choice for an open helm. In the future, most chartplotters may in fact be general-purpose computers in custom enclosures with large, touch-screen color displays. Later in this chapter, we'll glimpse into the future by taking a look at one of the high-end systems offered today.

Using a Chartplotter Underway

In essence, a chartplotter is a custom display and processing unit that is programmed to present live position information on a digital representation of a chart. It may include a GPS with a built-in antenna or a remote external antenna, or it may accept input from an external GPS receiver.

Most chartplotters are tailored to the marine environment, including some degree of waterproofing for use at open helm stations. Their grayscale displays are bright enough to be seen in sunlight, with color displays becoming more common but still somewhat more expensive as of this writing. Color adds an extra dimension that helps cue the helmsman, and the charts appear in their natural colors.

Most chartplotters use vector charts, as described in Chapter 6. The charts are sold on chips that can be inserted into the plotter, each chip holding a substantial portfolio of charts for a particular region. Several companies provide cartography on chartplotter chips, and manufacturers design their chartplotters to be compatible with a particular chip configuration. Chips are interchangeable among units using the same cartography, but not more broadly.

Regardless of chip configuration, all chartplotters display your current position superimposed on a chart, your active route or leg, and all stored waypoints within the field of view of the current zoom level on the display.

There is usually a much greater amount of information available than could be displayed on the screen without overly cluttering it. When you scroll the cursor over the object in question, a pop-up box usually provides further details. It is important to note that the accuracy of the chart is limited to the accuracy of the source chart at its original scale. Overzooming can give you a false sense of security if

FIGURE 9-1. *Chartplotters display your GPS position overlaid on a digital representation of a chart. Typically, chartplotters are designed with 5- to 10-inch screens. Because these devices are designed for use on the water, they usually are sealed. To provide a more waterproof interface and compact data, the digital charts typically are provided on removable chips in vector format. Chartplotters may have a built-in GPS or use an external GPS. Often, they can display depth sounder and radar information. (Courtesy: Raymarine, Garmin)*

you seem to be clear of charted objects. Actually, the locations of these objects may be charted in error, which is only exaggerated by the increased zoom. Some digital chartmakers such as C-Map prevent significant overzooming for this very reason.

Many chartplotters permit the user to select the amount of detail that will be displayed at a given level of zoom. Although seeing more details may appear to be an advantage, particularly for planning, details often are a distraction on the water. Underway, a simpler display is better, because you may not be able to devote a high degree of attention to the chartplotter and man the helm at the same time. This is one of the clear advantages of vector charts. They are simpler, clearer, and the chart data are sized to the

▶ ● CHARTPLOTTER SETUP FOR NAVIGATION

Just as you would in preparing to pilot an airplane, you need to go through a preflight check of your chartplotter. Here are a few things to do:

1. *Fire up the chartplotter at the dock and check that it's reporting your docked location accurately both on the chart and in the digital readout.*
2. *Look into the setup menu to ensure that the chart datum matches the chart chip installed in the unit. Also, double-check other settings such as "Auto Magnetic" for heading, "Nautical" for units, and "DDD MMM.MMM" for coordinates (if boating in coastal or offshore regions).*
3. *Make sure you have up-to-date chart chips for the regions you intend to navigate. While you're at it, check that you have corresponding paper charts.*
4. *Check under the Routes menu to make sure you have stored the appropriate planned routes (and corresponding waypoints) in the unit.*
5. *On a chart, check the intended path from your current location to the first waypoint you intend to use. Plan this first "pre-leg" before departure.*
6. *Make sure you have your backup strategies and equipment in place. Typically, a handheld GPS with the same waypoints and routes is a good idea, and paper charts are always an important backup.*
7. *As you fire up other equipment and the engine(s) on the boat, recheck the GPS to ensure that nothing has changed regarding your reported position before departure. It's a good idea to turn off the GPS (and other programmed electronics) before starting the engine to avoid any current surge, which could scramble settings.*
8. *Select your first waypoint or route.*

This predeparture check will take just minutes and will add to your confidence, safety, and comfort underway. Remember, navigation is but one of your tasks at the helm, so you want it to be easy.

Underway with Digital Charts

level of zoom. Chartplotters can be operated in two modes: planning and navigation. You need to preplan how you want to set up and use your chartplotter while navigating.

Many chartplotters are fixed-mounted and cannot readily be removed from the boat for planning. This is one of the reasons why many chartplotter users also use planning software on a computer at home. The resultant routes and waypoints can be uploaded from a laptop computer into the chartplotter using the standard NMEA (National Marine Electronics Association) 0183 protocol (see later in this chapter). You may need to have a cable made if your chartplotter manufacturer does not provide one as an option. With that cable, you can connect directly to the chartplotter from the serial port on your computer.

Become familiar with the buttons and functions of your chartplotter while in port, so you can change modes quickly on the water without diverting attention from the helm. The large screen and easy-to-access buttons of a typical fixed-mount chartplotter make navigation a great deal easier than with a handheld GPS.

As with GPS, the two screens you will find most useful underway are the Map (Chart) Screen (which, unlike handheld GPS models, contains an actual chart) and the Highway Screen.

Chart Screen

Typically, you will use the Chart Screen while getting into position for a leg, while in harbors or channels, or near obstacles. When departing, you can zoom in to view the details of a channel and the approaches to your boating waters.

LOCAL CHANNELS AND HARBORS Harbors are likely to show the least amount of preprinted chart detail. For these areas, you should annotate your charts with waypoints marking hazards or cues that you will use to navigate safely.

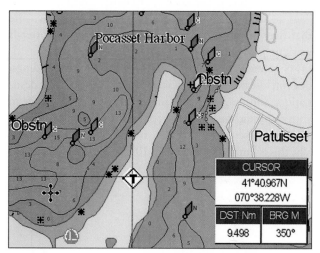

FIGURE 9-3. *You can look ahead using the cursor (cross symbol). This harbor is 9.5 nm at a bearing of 350° from your current location. You can set the chartplotter to "GoTo" this location. This will result in a course line and highway being drawn on their respective screens.*

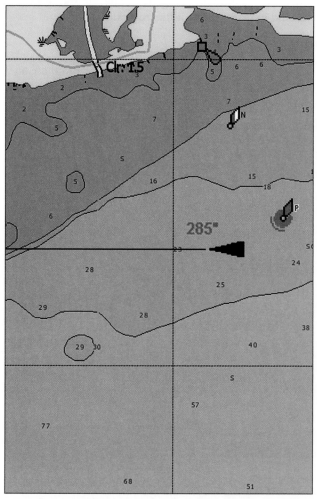

FIGURE 9-2. *The boat position is indicated by the black arrow symbol on the chart. The vector chart shows navigation aids, shorelines, depth contours, and soundings.*

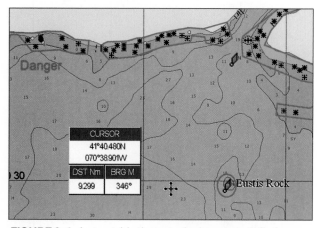

FIGURE 9-4. *Just outside the same harbor, you will find a number of circled potential hazards. (The highlighting is not a feature on the chartplotter.) Having the chart on the screen helps you to stay clear of the hazards.*

Mark them when the weather is fair, keeping in mind what references you will need when visibility is impaired. The Chart Screen provides a rich trove of information. Just remember that if you overzoom, you may be lulled into believing that the chart is more accurate than it really is. Don't rely on the placement of navigation aids that comes with the chart data; mark your own where maneuvering is tight and accuracy is critical. Most chartplotters today offer WAAS GPS, which can give your position to within ten feet of accuracy. In fact, your WAAS-plotted position is likely the most accurate feature on the chart.

OPEN WATER In open water the Chart Screen is useful to check for hazards and to stay on planned courses. You will be able to see depth contours and soundings in addition to wrecks, rocks, and other obstacles. Your boat will be represented by a symbol that shows its position and direction of travel. You should compare your chartplotter screen with your depth sounder, visible landmarks, and radar to ensure that they match. Then you know that the chartplotter is working properly.

Zooming in, you will see details of your surroundings, but you lose perspective on your progress toward your destination. Zooming out, you can see your position relative to your route and land features. Some chartplotters permit displaying two screens side by side or one over the other. Usually, this is limited to units with 10-inch or larger screens.

About every hour, or more frequently depending on boat speed and weather and sea conditions, you should plot your position and the time on a paper chart. This is in case the chartplotter or other electronics fail or start providing suspect information. Then you can go back to the last known plotted point and estimate your current position from there using dead reckoning. When you use dead reckoning, try to verify the accuracy of your estimated positions by using other tools and your eyes to obtain fixes whenever possible.

PLANNING ON THE FLY A chartplotter is invaluable when you need to plan or replan on the fly. Many chartplotters provide a point-to-point measuring feature that allows for planning without disrupting ongoing active navigation.

During replanning, your primary mission is to plot your new intended course on a chart and scan along that line for potential obstacles. You can zoom out to locate your new destination. Scroll the cursor to the intended destination, then zoom in to fine-tune the location of the new waypoint. Then you can scroll along the course line to make sure it is clear, and you can add waypoints to adjust the course around any obstacles along the way, much as you did in planning the initial routes.

Highway Screen

A chartplotter provides several screens similar to those on a GPS. Generally, however, the chartplotter screens are more

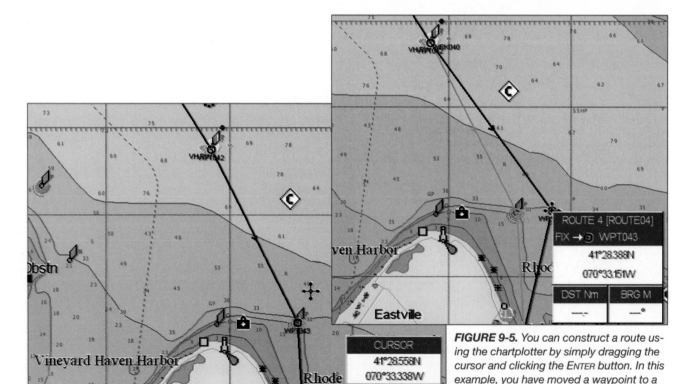

FIGURE 9-5. You can construct a route using the chartplotter by simply dragging the cursor and clicking the ENTER button. In this example, you have moved a waypoint to a new location (cursor position).

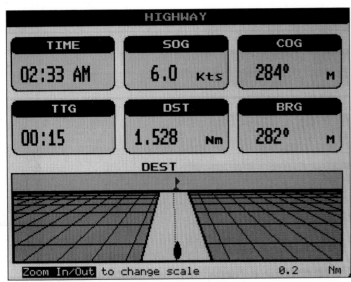

FIGURE 9-6. *Most chartplotters also offer the Highway Screen as an option. Because the display is larger and has higher resolution, more data can be shown.*

FIGURE 9-7. *Using the full size of the larger display, many chartplotters offer large numeral data displays, which can be read from some distance. Here, one of the windows shows the readout from an interfaced depth sounder.*

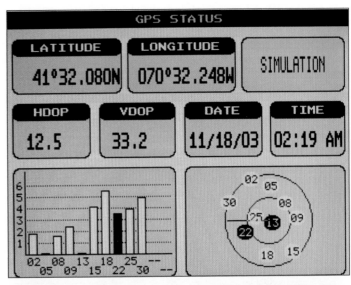

FIGURE 9-8. *Top: The Satellite Screen on a chartplotter is very similar to that found on a handheld GPS. Above: The Navigation Position Screen is similar to the Position Screen on a handheld GPS. Given the larger display size, more data fields can be presented.*

feature-rich than those on a handheld GPS owing to the higher resolution and larger screen size.

The Highway Screen is preferable to the Chart Screen while running a leg because it is easier to navigate with less attention to the screen. The use of the GPS Highway Screen is described in Chapters 7 and 8; the techniques are the same with a chartplotter. But the Highway Screen on a typical chartplotter has a great deal of detail and higher definition, thanks to the larger screen. Moreover, the larger screen usually allows you to add more data windows and possibly a compass band to help with your navigation.

Staying on course using the Highway Screen takes only a glance from time to time. This allows you to concentrate most of your attention on other duties.

Under normal circumstances underway, you can concentrate on the Highway Screen and stay in the center of the highway with the active waypoint straight ahead. Periodically, you will want to switch to the chart display to observe details of what is around you. Many helmsmen prefer to use the large digital readouts for navigating. Either way, if you've preplanned your routes, your navigation on the water is rather simple.

Celestial and Tide Data

Most new chartplotters provide access to the rising and setting times of the moon and sun and the times of high and low tide at the location of the cursor. Usually, tide and

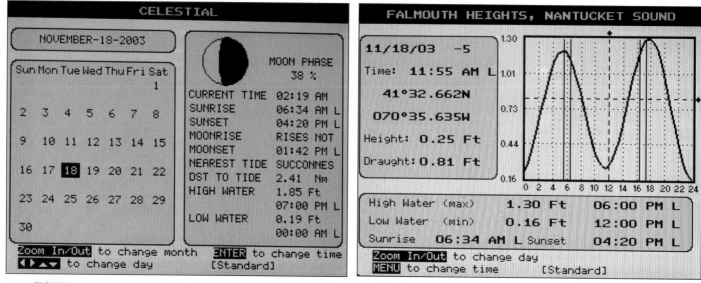

FIGURE 9-9. Left: *Typical chartplotters provide a great deal of information, such as sunrise, sunset, moonrise, nearest tide station, and times of high and low water. This display provides a handy calendar for looking ahead to other dates. All of this information is stored on the chart chips that you use with the chartplotter.* Right: *Tide charts can be displayed on the chartplotter to indicate the present tide height and the times of high and low water. You can look forward or backward to determine the predicted tide level at any time for this station. You can also select other stations.*

tidal current stations are identified as icons on the display. By scrolling over a nearby icon, you can bring up a tide chart.

Using a Computer and GPS Underway

With appropriate software, you can use a computer for on-board navigation and as an excellent planning tool. Indeed, a navigation computer offers far more capability than can be achieved with a typical chartplotter. Over time, this trend toward computer-based navigation will find its way onto progressively smaller boats, and chartplotting in higher-end networked systems is typically computer based.

Offshore sailors have been using computer-based navigation for years to help solve complex weather-routing problems. The major issue with using a computer onboard is the hostile marine environment. When the computer is on, it generates heat, and the air inside the case expands. When it cools and the air contracts, salt-laden air can be drawn into the computer case, where it will condense its

FIGURE 9-10. *Modern commercial ships and yachts use extensive electronic navigation tools. Typically, redundant systems are used for reliability. (Courtesy: Westport Yachts)*

FIGURE 9-11. *The U.S. Navy makes extensive use of laptops and onboard computers to ease navigation tasks.*

capability to keep up with the usual changes along the way. A computer is far more versatile for that task, and many navigation programs can access updated and expanded information about weather and cruising conditions using the Internet when within range, as well as updating charts and sharing data with other mariners.

Several marine electronics manufacturers, such as Raymarine and Furuno, offer networked solutions, which include onboard computers to do the processing. This enables Furuno to use the very popular MaxSea software as an integral part of its NavNet 3D system. Raymarine uses RayTech Navigator System software as part of its network, and its G Series is computer driven. These are described at the end of the chapter in the section "The Future of Onboard Computers." The ultimate flexibility of a PC platform means that the device can be reprogrammed and updated to stay current. It also is an ideal solution for an integrated helm station.

Many boaters use both a computer *and* a chartplotter, with the latter mounted at the helm, the former belowdecks, and the two in communication. The computer is used more for planning and routing; the chartplotter is used for steering. Ultimately, as boating technology continues to improve, there will be no discernable difference between a chartplotter and a computer.

corrosive salts on circuit boards and components. A number of computers have been suitably marinized for use on a boat: they are adequately sealed to prevent salt-air intrusions and have extra protective coating on internal circuits to combat corrosion. They use sealed cases with external heat sinks for cooling as opposed to circulating outside air. Marinized computers are surprisingly reasonable in price, and the prices for marinized displays are coming down.

Most recreational boaters use laptop computers onboard, then take them home after a day's sail. Laptops are convenient to handle and require only limited battery power to operate. They can be recharged onboard through inverters. Additional protection onboard can be provided by storing the laptop in a sealed container when not in use, or purchasing a ruggedized laptop.

A significant issue is the display. Although chartplotters typically offer sunlight-readable displays, there are fewer options for a laptop screen. Typically, laptops are not used above decks. Special sunlight-readable, high-brightness, marinized LCD displays are available from a number of companies, with options for touch screens. Belowdecks or in the pilothouse, the display brightness is not a major issue.

Computers gain favor with those who cruise considerable distances. Unlike most chartplotters, computer-based navigation software does not limit the number of waypoints in a route or, for that matter, the number of routes. Also, mariners on extended cruises need more onboard planning

Navigation Software

Computer navigation software generally is far more versatile than are the fixed programs of a traditional chartplotter. In addition to a much larger number of waypoints and routes, navigation software offers many useful tools, and its memory can be substantial. You can plan even while navigating on a route. Some software provides *range rings* (circles of given radius, as on a radar screen), a compass rose around the plotted location of your boat on the chart screen, and multiple user-selected range/bearing lines so you get a better sense of your surroundings.

Computer screens tend to be larger than those on chartplotters, so you can make use of such features as side-by-side displays or even four displays on a single screen. For example, you can place a smaller-scale chart on one side and a larger-scale chart on the other. Your position is displayed on both screens, and both will scroll as you move.

Another two-screen combination is a nautical chart with its corresponding photo chart. The photo chart helps identify land features and gives you a visual sense of surrounding waters. Your position is indicated on the photo chart, too, because it is geo-referenced to the same set of coordinates as your chart.

Alternatively, you can use topo maps derived by third parties such as Maptech from such sources as the U.S. Geological Survey (USGS). These maps provide land contours and other land features, such as buildings, that are missing

FIGURE 9-12. *Many navigation software packages are available for live navigation using an onboard computer. Rose Point Navigation offers Coastal Explorer (shown on screen) and Coastal Express. NavSim offers BoatCruiser. Nobeltec offers Admiral and Visual Navigation Suite. The CAPN is a traditional package, and Raymarine offers RayTech RNS, which interoperates with its onboard systems.*

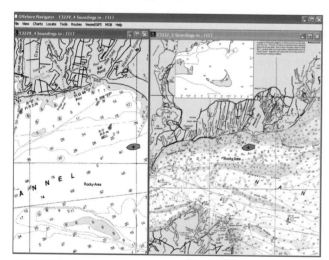

FIGURE 9-13. *A computer offers a much greater degree of flexibility for displaying information. This example shows two side-by-side displays of the same area at two different scales. The larger scale, on the left, provides more detailed soundings and navigation information. The smaller scale, on the right, shows a wider area. The boat symbols on both are synchronized. Typically, the digital charts displayed on computers are raster charts, which are scanned from the paper chart masters. Thus, they look like their paper chart equivalents.*

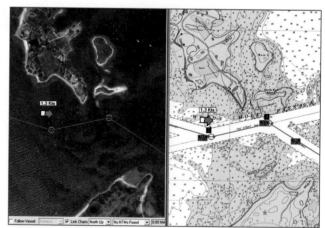

FIGURE 9-14. *It is also possible to array a nautical chart and a photo chart for the same area side by side. The photo chart is geo-referenced to the same coordinate system. Photo charts, derived from aerial photographs used for mapmaking, more dramatically and visually demonstrate shoals and hazards.*

or heavily curtailed on nautical charts. The maps can be useful when you are attempting to orient yourself with respect to nearby topographic features such as hills.

NAVIGATION SOFTWARE VERSUS PLANNING SOFTWARE

The major difference between digital chart planning software (see Chapter 6) and navigation software is the latter's ability to accept and plot GPS positions on the screen. Most such programs will work with a host of different GPS models. Many offer a menu from which you select a GPS model; the software takes care of the rest. Beyond that, virtually all GPS receivers output key information in a standard format called NMEA 0183 and some in another format called NMEA 2000 (both are explained in Chapter 27). The National Marine Electronics Association (NMEA) created these protocols to share specific coded information. Many GPS receivers also offer a standard USB connection that will work directly with a computer.

The navigation software receives and interprets this coded information to plot your position. Generally, most of the other computations performed within the GPS are not used by the software. Instead, these computations are performed in the computer independently. For example, you select waypoints and routes for navigation in your computer, and it computes your course, bearing, and distance to the active waypoint. You can, of course, select the same waypoint in the GPS for active navigation and it, too, computes the course, bearing, and distance—independently. The GPS processor and the computer are working in parallel, doing the same thing using position

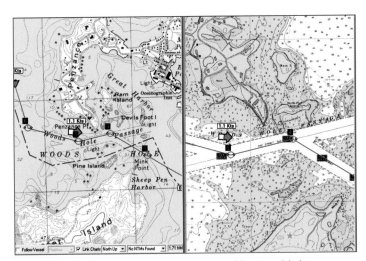

FIGURE 9-15. *You can also place a topographic map side by side with a nautical chart. The advantage of the topo map is its rich representation of land features, handy for identifying shorelines, hills, etc., for nativagtion.*

information from the GPS. This is the way you are likely to navigate with a chartplotter at the helm and a computer belowdecks.

Navigation Computer Display Information

The heart of a computer navigation display is the nautical chart. When you're using raster charts, these appear virtually identical to the paper charts you carry. The higher-resolution, larger display of a computer can be used to its full advantage. Some computers are designed to work with

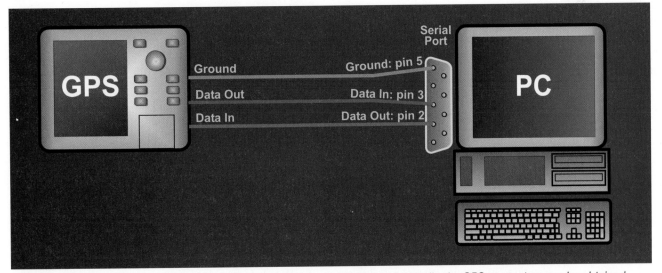

FIGURE 9-16. *Connecting a GPS to a computer is reasonably straightforward. Usually, the GPS connectors can be obtained from the manufacturer. The connector for the PC is usually a standard 9-pin serial port connector. Most marine electronics equipment offers NMEA 0183 interfaces. That means there is one pin for data out of the GPS, one pin for data in, and a ground pin. By the same token, the serial port on the computer has one pin for data in, one for data out, and a ground pin. The units connect much like a DVD player and a TV set. Unfortunately, most new notebook computers are delivered without a serial port. There are a variety of USB adapters on the market, but not all software has been updated to deal with the virtual serial port created by these adapters.*

touch screens, so your interface becomes the display rather than a keyboard and mouse. But even if you do not have a touch screen, a keyboard and mouse are far easier to use than the limited number of buttons and the joystick cursor control of a typical chartplotter.

Data windows are typically large and clear, and you can position them at will so they won't interfere with tracking your boat's progress across the chart. In addition, you have a wide choice of data to display in these boxes, and you can select data at will without any interruption of ongoing navigation. It's easy to switch to a full-screen chart display for a better look, for example. Often, an inset display is available to show a wider or more detailed area.

Typical data fields (digital readouts) include the following:

VESSEL	Course over ground (Track)	Speed over ground
WAYPOINT	Bearing	Distance
CURSOR	Bearing	Distance
CHART ROSE	True	Magnetic
STEERING	Crosstrack error	
CHART INFO	Chart number, Name	Scale, Soundings (feet, fathoms, meters), Datum (match to GPS)
GPS INFO	GPS status	
CONTROLS	Zoom	Chart scale
		Track
		Mark
		GoTo
		Plan
		Measure
CHART INFO	Tide (height)	Current (set and drift)
Other	ETA, ETE to next waypoint, to destination	
	Bearing, Distance from last waypoint	
	Heading, Speed (through water, using current set and drift calculations)	

If the navigation software is supplemented with depth contour data, the display can be set up to show a depth contour in front of the boat.

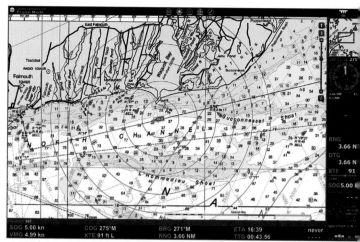

FIGURE 9-17. Most navigation software has special screens for on-the-water use. This screen provides large data fields that are easy to read at the helm. In addition, a small window shows the area covered, and a set of instruments helps with navigation tasks. This program provides voice indications of shallow water and hazards that lie along your path. Range rings provide a convenient frame of reference.

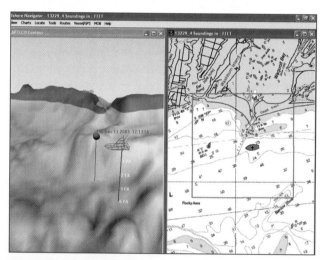

FIGURE 9-18. Bathymetric (contour) charts provide a view below the surface of the water. In this split view, the image on the left shows the boat and the depth below it. A vertical red line shows the depth in fathoms below the boat. A red ball indicates the location of a nearby red beacon. The image on the right shows the corresponding chart. The box around the boat on the chart shows the area displayed in the contour plot.

MONITORING AND PLANNING WITH NAVIGATION SOFTWARE Your present boat position will be displayed directly on the chart along with the current active course and track, if selected. If you choose to array chart windows side by side, your boat's position will be shown on all open windows to facilitate comparisons between chart scales and between a nautical chart and a photo chart.

Using navigation software, you will be able to call upon a wide range of alarms that can be set in advance or adjusted. These include anchor alarms, waypoint vicinity

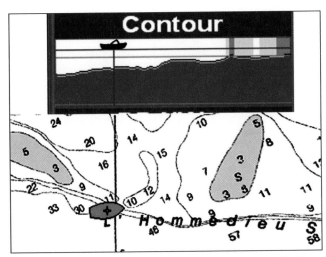

FIGURE 9-19. *The depth contour (top) shows the variation in charted depth based on bathymetric data. An alarm can be set to a particular level; those areas are highlighted in the contour to indicate potential hazards. The corresponding chart image is shown below the contour.*

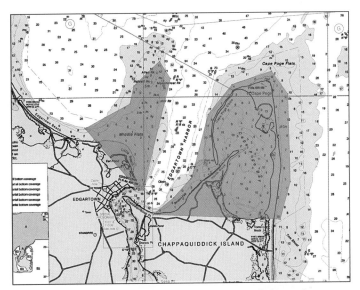

FIGURE 9-20. *Navigation software offers a range of alarms. In this example, polygonal shapes have been placed over areas to avoid. An alarm will sound if you enter either area.*

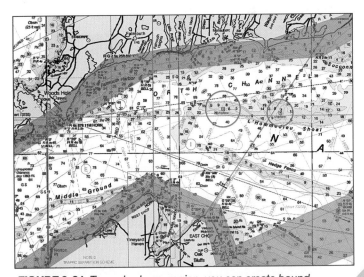

FIGURE 9-21. *To mark a larger region, you can create boundaries, as shown in Chapter 7, and add danger circles for any additional hazards within the remaining area, as shown by the two circles in the figure. These are set to sound an alarm upon entry within their respective boundaries.*

and arrival alarms, avoidance area alarms, fishing area boundary alarms, and crosstrack or off-course alarms. Unlike most chartplotters, the alarm boundaries are flexible, including custom shapes. Alarms can be audible, visual, or both, and can be set up to go off if you enter or, alternatively, if you leave a selected area.

The software can support planning on the fly even while plotting the present path and monitoring your navigation. You will be able to use the complete suite of tools described in Chapter 6. This includes the ability to plot unlimited range/bearing lines to measure distances and bearings. New routes can be constructed or current routes can be modified in real time.

You can add notes on a digital chart for future reference. Most CD or DVD chart packages include notes on marine facilities, local regulations, coast pilot information, light lists, and other tools to provide key information at your fingertips.

If your GPS receiver quits or starts to provide inaccurate information, it is possible to use the navigation software to continue in dead-reckoning mode (but read the cautionary tale from the *Royal Majesty* in Chapter 2). You will be able to plot bearing lines from your observations and create fixes. Once a fix is identified, you will be able to reposition the boat symbol over that spot to continue the dead-reckoning navigation.

A Man Overboard (MOB) feature, available on most packages, immediately marks the accident location and plots a return path to effect a rescue.

Most navigation software programs output instructions to an autopilot in NMEA 0183 sentences. The software provides a host of information in addition to the intended course and track. Steering information and crosstrack error are provided to let the autopilot return to a planned course line.

Waypoint proximity and arrival information are also provided, in addition to advance information on changes in course.

Cell Phones and Tablet PCs

As mentioned in Chapter 6, cellular phones and tablet PCs can be equipped for live navigation. Most cell phones have internal GPS, many with very high sensitivity receivers. Those with Palm-based operating systems have a diminishing advantage of a choice of software and charts, as software for the iPhone and Android operating systems

are emerging. Microsoft continues to upgrade its operating system as well. Standalone PDAs have virtually disappeared, as their functionality has been incorporated into cell phones, which gain further advantage through direct access to services and downloads. Some tablet PCs include GPS and may serve as navigators. Others will need an accessory GPS that can be connected to the unit either wired or wirelessly.

All of these devices are essentially programmable computers that use GPS and digital charts for live navigation. They demonstrate the convergent evolution of computers and chartplotters. Planning can be done directly on the cell phone, tablet PC, or on a home computer, and operated as a live navigator or uploaded to another device.

One distinct advantage of these devices is the touch screen, which makes working with charts quite easy and eliminates the need for buttons. Handheld GPS models and chartplotters are evolving to use touch screens as well. Most cell phones are not designed for the marine environment, so they need to be suitably protected while on board. Also, they generally do not have screens that can be viewed in direct sunlight. Ultimately, we'll see specialized units designed for the marine environment. In the meantime, if you use one of the existing units available on the market, consider keeping it in a clear, waterproof pouch to protect it from the environment. These small handheld units have sharp color displays that present clear charts. The small size of the screen, however, makes navigation tasks somewhat more difficult than their larger counterparts because you can see only a small part of the chart at a time. The other challenge is power. Typically, cell phone devices are designed for intermittent use to conserve battery power. As a result, they typically do not present constant views of on-screen data. On-board power connections are possible, and will help.

A competitive advantage to cell phone–based naviga-

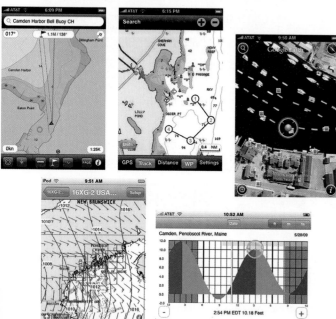

FIGURE 9-22. *Cell phones and their companion tablet computers are rapidly finding applications for navigation. With their bright color touch screens, these devices are portable and convenient. Top: An Android cell phone with navigation app. Bottom: Sample screens for navigation, weather, and tides are shown on an iPhone, but similar applications are available for almost all cell phone and tablet operating systems. (Courtesy: Ben Ellison, www.panbo.com)*

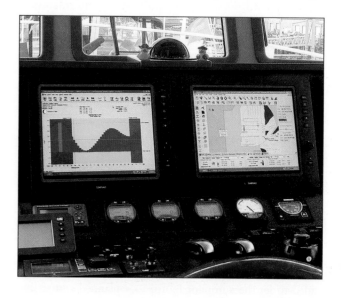

FIGURE 9-23A. *Onboard computers and their software offer a variety of information options, as shown. Marinized displays and self-contained units such as this make these screens readable even in bright sunlight. (Courtesy: Maptech)*

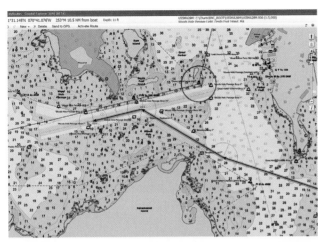
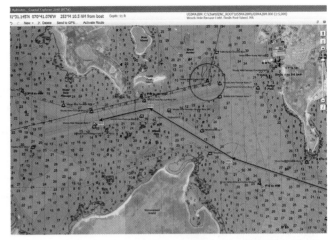

FIGURE 9-23B. Left: *A NOAA vector chart is shown with plotted route.* Right: *A corresponding photo chart is overlaid by the chart. The chart transparency can be controlled by the user for reference. (Courtesy: Rose Point Navigation)*

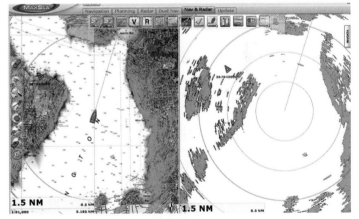

FIGURE 9-23C. Left: *Aerial images can be manipulated and merged with chart information in this perspective view. (Courtesy: Furuno)* Right: *Radar images can be presented overlaid on photo/charts and by themselves. (Courtesy: Furuno/MaxSea)*

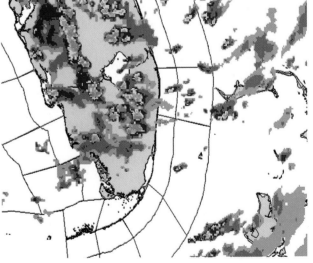

FIGURE 9-23D. Left: *3-D bathymetric and contour images can be annotated with boat position, course, and other charted objects.* Right: *Weather services add remote sensing in this example of weather radar showing storms over Florida. (Courtesy: RayTech RNS)*

FIGURE 9-24. *Onboard computer systems are becoming very popular, especially with larger boats. These marinized components are essential for fixed-mount applications and exposed bridge installations. Right: Marinized displays. Below: Marinized computer. (Courtesy: Argonaut and MarinePC)*

tion is the use of common, open-architecture operating systems. This leads to competition for both navigation software applications as well as charts. The downside to the evolving number of choices is keeping up with the quality of both software and charts. It becomes very important to monitor reviews, as errors in either can cause "oopses" when you rely upon them for navigation.

Cell phones also offer additional live services that can be of great assistance with your navigation tasks. For example, Google Earth provides outstanding photo imagery that can be plotted and merged with your navigation. Weather data and weather radar images can be received and processed to help you avoid squalls and storms. Facility information and reviews are readily available. However, cellular services have limited range, so you can't count on having these services at all of your boating locations.

Look for similar devices with larger displays and waterproofing as the ultimate alternative to the chartplotter. As this is an evolving technology, it's a good idea to keep in touch by visiting www.panbo.com, a marine electronics blog hosted by Ben Ellison, author of many marine electronics articles in boating magazines. See Figure 9-22 for examples of cell phones used as chartplotters.

The Future of Onboard Computers

The future of navigation is here today. Historically, chartplotters designed for the marine environment have been custom devices with limited memory and fixed functional-

ity. Today, a number of high-end chartplotters are in fact computer-based marine units, many with touch-screen displays. These units have the flexibility to run tailored navigation software and can be upgraded and expanded much like any onboard computer-based system. Look for this trend to continue and expand. This means you may not need to replace your chartplotter when new features emerge on the market. A software upgrade may be able to do the trick.

Meanwhile, marinized computers and displays have become more available and reasonable in cost. A truly marinized computer is likely to be one that is sealed to the environment, relying upon conductive cooling to keep the unit at a reasonable operating temperature.

An increasing selection of displays are on the market, some designed for an open helm with its exposed environment and sunlight-readable display. Many of these displays can be acquired with touch-screen capability. This facilitates operation even without a keyboard or mouse. However, most computer-based installations have displays in an enclosed pilothouse.

The component approach to on-board computers permits great flexibility and supports the use of displays that are larger than found in typical chartplotters. In addition, these systems can run your choice of navigation software.

Whichever approach you take, the computer-based chartplotter or components, you will be able to interconnect a host of electronics and even electronic engine controls. In this way, you can manage most of the ship's systems on screen. Many of the newer instruments and controls are electronic and designed to interface using the

NMEA 2000 bus protocol explained in Chapter 27.

Some examples of display screens available today are shown in Figure 9-23. Laptops are quite affordable and suitable for interior pilothouse navigation. However, marinized computers and displays are becoming more popular and within the price range of many boaters. Some samples are shown in Figure 9-24. While these systems may be currently out of the price range for many recreational boaters, as with all new technologies, that will eventually change. At this point, most of us can just dream.

DOUBLE-CHECKING YOUR NAVIGATION

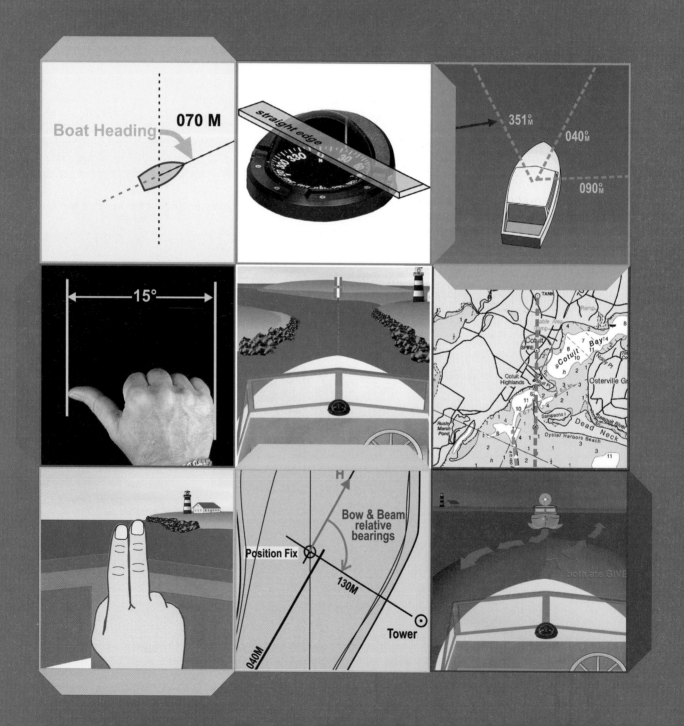

Double-Checking Using Instruments

In Part II of this book we did our navigation planning, and in Part III we put the plan into action on the water. But what if we made plotting or measuring errors while planning, or what if our GPS receiver is feeding us unreliable data on the water? We might not be where we think, and that could be dangerous.

As a matter of safe practice, you never should rely on a single device or technique while navigating. We've talked throughout about double-checking and verifying your navigation. This and the next two chapters explore this—the third phase of navigation—in greater depth.

Maintaining a sense of your environment and the world around you is the key to safe navigation. In coastal waters with good visibility, this is simply a matter of comparing your visual observations with the charts. The GPS can give you precise bearings on charted objects, such as navigation aids and landmarks, with which to compare your visual bearings. In order to do this, you need to have the positions of these landmarks stored in your GPS. This is done during your planning before you go out on the water. Although it is possible to add landmarks into the GPS while underway, doing so can be a distraction.

Objects of interest stored as waypoints in the GPS should be designated so as to be easily and quickly recognizable on the water, and their names annotated on your charts as mentioned in Chapters 3 and 8.

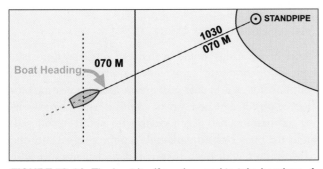

FIGURE 10-1A. *The boat itself can be used to take bearings. A bearing over your bow corresponds with your heading. In this case, the magnetic bearing to the standpipe is 70°M.*

Quick Observations

Bearings Using the Boat as a Reference

You should habitually identify navigation aids and landmarks as they become visible, often just with a simple reference to their bearings relative to your heading. Bow bearings (45° off the bow) and beam bearings (90° off the bow) are particularly easy to sight and can be reasonably accurate, especially when a buoy or landmark is not far away and can

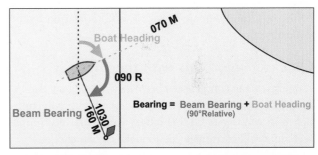

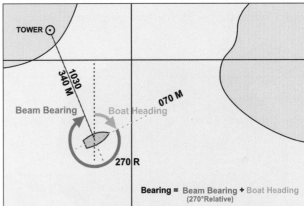

FIGURE 10-1B. Top: *Beam bearings are easy to see and can be reasonably accurate. To determine a bearing off your starboard beam, simply add 90° to your compass reading. In this case, the bearing to the buoy is 160°. Bottom: To determine the magnetic bearing to an object off your port beam, you will need to add 270° to the ship's compass reading. The magnetic bearing to the tower is 340°.*

be positively identified by buoy number or other means. Alternatively, you can sight over a protractor or plotting tool aligned with the centerline of the boat to estimate a relative bearing. Many boaters note angles as sighted across various features on a boat, such as a stanchion or one edge of a window. Some boaters even place marks on rails or other prominent vantage points at intermediate relative angles, such as 45°, as viewed from the helm.

Remember, any relative bearing must be converted to a magnetic or true bearing before you can compare it with your GPS or plot it on a chart. Add the heading of your boat (usually magnetic) to the relative bearing as measured clockwise from the bow. If the result is greater than 360°, simply subtract 360° to get a magnetic bearing you can plot.

Bearings Using the Ship's Compass

This technique is a bit more precise and easier to compare with corresponding GPS bearings. This time, you sight the bearings, particularly forward of the helm, using your steering compass as a guide. You just sight across the top of a flat or dished-card compass and note the approximate direction to the buoy or landmark as indicated on the compass card. To help, you can lay a plastic (not metal!) plotting tool across the top of the compass as a sighting guide. The result is a magnetic bearing, assuming compass deviation is negligible. In other words, this is an absolute bearing, not relative, and doesn't need to be added to your boat's heading before you can compare it with the GPS bearing to the same object.

Quick Comparisons with the GPS

A quick comparison of visual bearings with their corresponding GPS bearings isn't precise, but it will give you confidence in what your GPS is telling you. This very simple technique will encourage you to make regular checks.

Your GPS Map Screen displays nearby landmarks and buoys whose waypoints you have programmed into your

FIGURE 10-2. *You can sight bearings using your ship's compass. Place a nonmetallic straightedge across the compass to take readings. This technique is not precise if used on a domed compass.*

unit. You may need to zoom out to bring them into the field of view, and you need to get yourself oriented. Generally, you will be using a North-Up display on the GPS, and your direction of travel will be indicated by the orientation of the boat symbol (usually a sharp triangle). If you are sighting quick relative bearings, such as a beam bearing, simply look to see whether the chosen landmark appears to be abeam of the symbol on the screen. If the GPS has truly failed, it is unlikely that the two will agree; if the two agree, it is unlikely that the GPS has failed. If you are still uncertain, take some more precise bearings for comparisons.

If you've sighted a bearing across the compass, you need a numeric GPS bearing to compare it with. Using the cursor key on a newer model GPS, scroll to that buoy or landmark on the Map Screen; when it is highlighted, the GPS will show its bearing in a data window. (If your GPS receiver doesn't have this Map Screen feature, see "Ways to Access a Waypoint Bearing" below.) Simply compare the GPS reported bearing with your visual observation. Assuming you set up your GPS to magnetic direction, no conversion is required. If the GPS bearing and your observation match, at least within about three to five degrees, your GPS appears to be working properly.

If any of your quick observations do not match, it's time for a more detailed approach.

Comparing Your Bearings with a Chart

Even if the GPS appears to be working, it's a good idea to periodically plot your quick bearings on a chart to get a better idea of where you are along your course line. This also gives you a sense of what's around you.

To do this, simply take the magnetic bearing from your observation and align that direction on the inner ring of the compass rose with your course plotter. Make sure you use the far side of the rose rather than the one closest to you, because the bearing is from you to the buoy or landmark, not the other way around. Next, slide your plotting tool so it lines up with the buoy or landmark and trace the reciprocal bearing back to intersect your course line. Note how this compares with your progress along your course line as reported by GPS.

More Accurate Bearings

Quick observations should be frequent, and they don't take long. But periodically, or whenever a question arises about your position, you should take a more accurate bearing on a charted object. The best way to do this is with a hand bearing compass or a pair of binoculars with a built-in compass. Sight the buoy or landmark and read the compass bearing to within a few degrees, then compare that number with the GPS bearing. Again, the landmark or navigation aid will need to have been stored in the GPS memory for this

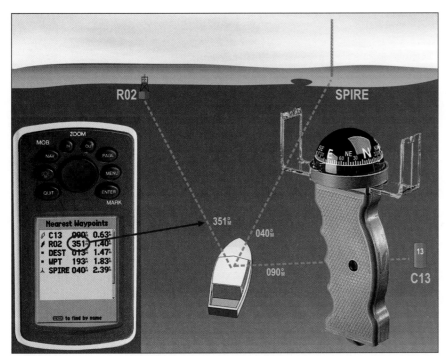

FIGURE 10-3. *You can confirm the accuracy of your GPS by comparing its bearings to charted landmarks or buoys against your own visual bearings. A hand bearing compass provides the easiest comparison. The charted landmarks need to have been stored as waypoints in your GPS in order to make the comparison. Checking just one bearing should give you confidence that the GPS is accurate.*

to be useful. If the bearings match, you are probably in good shape. A single bearing does not provide a position fix, but it is unlikely that even a single bearing would match if the GPS were malfunctioning.

Remember, you need to be sure that the hand bearing compass or compass binoculars are not influenced by nearby metallic objects or wiring. The quick way to check for this is to briefly sight dead ahead with your hand bearing compass and compare that reading with the ship's compass. If they match, you are good to go. If they don't, consider sighting from a different location on the boat; otherwise, you will need to correct your bearing for deviation.

Ways to Access a Waypoint Bearing

This section may be useful if you are unfamiliar with accessing a waypoint bearing from your GPS.

SCROLL Many GPS models, particularly newer ones, provide a bearing and distance readout on the Map Screen when you scroll the cursor. Simply use the cursor key to move the cursor over the landmark. Usually, you will know that you are on that stored waypoint when the name field is highlighted (often with a box around the name on the screen). Simply read the bearing in the data window on the screen.

WAYPOINT SCREEN Another way to get a bearing from your GPS is to use the Nearest Waypoints Screen. Some

GPS models provide a menu selection for nearest waypoints, generally a screen showing the closest waypoints from your current location, ranked by distance, along with their respective bearings. On some GPS models, you may need to go to the Waypoints (or Points) menu item. When the list of waypoints pops up, scroll to the waypoint you want. The Waypoint Screen usually presents the bearing and distance from your current location to that waypoint. Now make your comparison. When you're done, use QUIT or ESC rather than ENTER to back up to your original screen; otherwise, you might reset the active waypoint.

REFRESHER—CONVERTING BETWEEN TRUE AND MAGNETIC Remember, your hand bearing compass provides a reference to magnetic north. Your GPS needs to be set up in magnetic mode to match; otherwise, you need to convert observed bearings between magnetic and true degrees. The easiest way to do that is to use a nearby magenta compass rose on the chart. The inner ring is oriented with magnetic north. The outer ring is oriented with true north. Draw a line through the center of the rose over the hand bearing compass reading on the inner ring, and read the equivalent true bearing where the line crosses the outer ring.

To be sure that your hand bearing compass does not have deviation error, sight a bearing over the bow with it and compare the reading with the heading shown on your ship's compass. If they match, you're in good shape. If they differ, apply that same difference to any bearing taken with the hand bearing compass from that same location on the boat while on that same heading. If your ship's compass itself has significant deviation, you need to factor that into the comparison.

TAKING MORE THAN ONE BEARING If you feel at all uncertain about the match between a single visual bearing and the GPS, or just want to make sure, take a second bearing or even a third. Try to select bearings that are separated by at least thirty degrees from one another. If these readings also do not match, your GPS is suspect. Plot your position based on the visual bearings, and proceed with manual navigation from there.

Eye of the Mariner

Safe navigation requires constant awareness of what's around you, as noted in Chapter 10, and your eyes are fundamental to this. Over the centuries, mariners have honed a set of skills referred to collectively as the "seaman's eye." This chapter summarizes these essential and enjoyable techniques. (For further reading, try *Boat Navigation for the Rest of Us*, an excellent book with dozens of practical, everyday tips and techniques compiled by career U.S. Coast Guardsman, Captain Bill Brogdon.)

Headings

Fundamental to navigation is maintaining a heading, preferably one that has been planned. "Coursekeeping," it's called. From Odysseus on down, a helmsman or -woman who can hold a course has always been a valued member of the crew. Steering by compass can be tedious, because it requires close

FIGURE 11-1. *Steering can be a tiring process, particularly if you are using your compass. The seas naturally cause the boat to yaw, so you frequently swing back and forth across your compass course. Using a horizon landmark is far easier. Sight on some distant feature that lies along the bow, and steer toward it. Focusing on a solid point of reference lessens fatigue.*

attention that tires your eyes and takes them off what is around you. Also, in a seaway, your heading varies continuously back and forth as your boat reacts to passing waves or swells. A skilled helmsman can reduce this yawing to a minimum by anticipating each motion and steering to "meet it," but you can't reduce it to nothing. Steering by compass requires you to perform continuous mental averaging to keep your course centered where you want it.

Whenever possible, steer toward an object on or above the horizon along your intended heading, checking the compass only periodically rather than continuously. As your bow oscillates back and forth across or under this distant spot, you can evaluate whether the swings "average" the course toward your objective. If your distance object is a star or the moon, remember that the object itself is in motion across the sky. You can hitch your wagon to it for ten to fifteen minutes, but then you'll have to jump off that star and find yourself another one.

Offset from Direct Heading

What if you can't find a suitable landmark that lines up with your heading to help you steer your course? It happens all the time. Perhaps there's one offset a bit to either side; you can use that instead.

You'll need to determine the angular difference between your heading and the bearing to the object. You can approximate it, or you can determine it more precisely with a chart, provided the object in question is charted. Simply mark your current location, plot your course, and plot a line from your position toward that object. Then measure the angular difference between the two with a protractor.

Alternatively, you can use your GPS to determine that bow angle, though you will need to have stored the object as a waypoint for reference. Call up the waypoint, note its bearing, and subtract that from your heading (or vice versa) to get the angular difference.

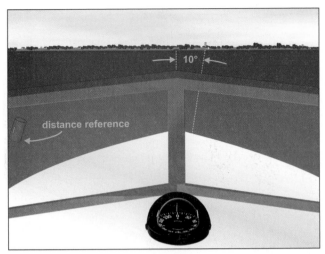

FIGURE 11-2. *Often, there is no prominent feature off the bow; however, there may be one near the bow. You can steer to the left or right of the feature. At a particular distance, that feature may have a convenient angular separation from the intended heading—for example, 10°. You can use your compass to sight 10° and still use the landmark. Just remember that the angle widens as you get closer, so you need to update the separation angle from time to time.*

Now you can use that angle to help you steer, at least for a while. As you approach the object, however, its angle off your bow is constantly widening, so be prepared to do a periodic update.

IT'S ALL IN THE HANDS To make this technique even more convenient, all you need is an instant means to approximate that angular difference. It turns out that your hands can provide that reference. If you hold up a single finger at arm's length, its width will span about two degrees of angle. Two fingers side by side will mark four degrees,

and so on. A closed fist is good for about twelve degrees, and with a fully extended thumb about fifteen degrees. See Figure 11-3.

Ranges

One of the most useful and certainly the most accurate line of position is a range. As described earlier, a range is a plotted line through two visually prominent charted objects, which are usually on land but may be fixed in shallow water. The extension of that line into navigable waters (where, by convention, it changes from dashed to solid on the chart) is a fixed, immutable line of position. When you see the two objects in line from your viewing point, you are somewhere on that charted line—no two ways about it. Cross it with another line of position, and you've got a good, solid fix.

As mentioned in Chapter 5, you should look for opportunities to plot ranges wherever you might need some extra help navigating a channel, running an inlet, or checking your position. All you need is two charted and easily identifiable objects. This technique is particularly useful for identifying and entering your home harbor, in which case the objects don't even have to be charted. If that flagpole directly in front of that tall oak tree guided you down the middle of the approach channel yesterday, it will do the same tomorrow.

Ranges are often, though not always, established navigation aids. Visually aligning the two visible marks, as in Figure 11-4, will keep you in the middle of the channel. If the marks are misaligned, you are either too far to port or to starboard.

Because a range provides a highly accurate and con-

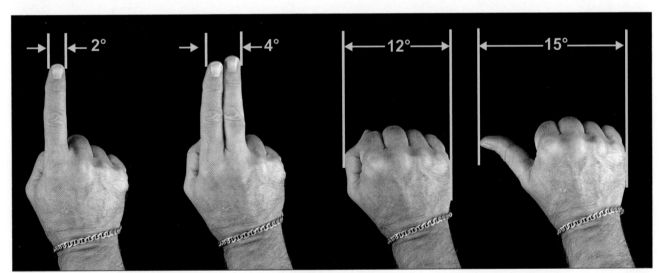

FIGURE 11-3. *Use your hands to make quick angle measurements. A single finger held up at arm's length marks about two degrees; two fingers mark about four degrees, and so on. A closed fist marks about twelve degrees; a closed fist with an extended thumb marks about fifteen degrees.*

FIGURE 11-4 (left). In many locations, a navigation range is deployed to help you navigate a narrow channel. Two visual navigation aids are spaced some distance apart, with the one in back taller. Both share the same pattern, often a three-bar color pattern. If you are located in the center of the range, the two aids line up. If you are off the range, the aids separate. If the taller of the two is to the right, you are to the right of the centerline. If it's to the left, then you are too. Usually, these ranges are maintained much like other navigation aids and are preplotted on the chart for your convenience. They are labeled with the bearing along the line that goes through both aids. **FIGURE 11-5 (right).** You can create your own ranges and plot them on your charts. In this example, the water tower is aligned with the left side of the building. As long as you maintain this view, you will be on the centerline of the range. This can help you locate and navigate this channel.

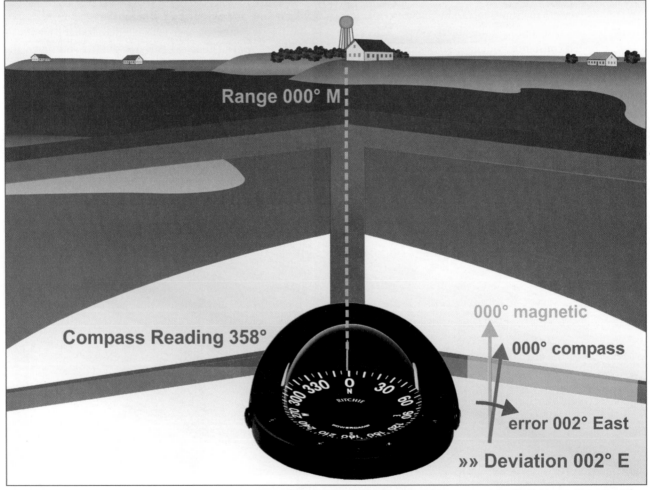

FIGURE 11-6. A range can be used to help check your compass. In this example, the plotted bearing of the range is 000° magnetic. However, your compass reads 358° when you are along the range. This means that the compass has an error and needs to be corrected 2° east for this heading—although you may reasonably choose to ignore a deviation of less than 3°.

Eye of the Mariner

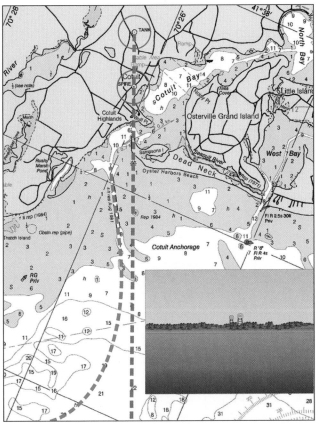

FIGURE 11-7. Left: *You can use prominent features near your harbor to help you locate the harbor and align yourself to enter the channel. In this example, two water towers are nearly aligned, with the one in back to the left. By maintaining this view and adapting as you get closer, you can use the towers to help line up for the harbor entrance. Seldom will you find two objects that align perfectly for your harbor, so you will more often use a technique like this one. In this case, you want to stay to the left, otherwise you could hit one of the two isolated rocks shown on the chart.* Right:*You can use your hands to measure specific angles by which you need to clear landmarks to stay in safe water.*

venient bearing, it can be a valuable tool for quickly checking your GPS. And if you take a bearing on another visible landmark or buoy at the same time using your hand bearing compass, you will be able to quickly plot a fix. After all, one of the bearing lines already is plotted for you.

Finally, a range is valuable for checking your compass and determining its deviation. In fact, this is one of the most common ways to check and compensate a compass. Simply maneuver your boat onto the range, with the near range marker precisely in front of the far one, then note your compass reading as you point toward the markers. Any difference between the magnetic bearing of the range and what your compass indicates is your deviation for that heading.

Relative Positions of Landmarks

Sometimes you just can't find two landmarks that form the range you need. In such cases, close may be good enough. For example, you may be able to find two aligned towers during the approach to one of your favorite harbors. If you can visibly distinguish which one is in front, you might be able to use them anyway. Just be aware that as you run the

approach channel, the angle between the towers will slowly increase. Adjust accordingly, and you'll find this a useful technique.

Bearings

As you know by now, bearings are lines plotted from your boat to charted objects or other vessels. Bearings are taken and described in two ways: direct and relative. A direct bearing is measured from true or magnetic north, using an instrument such as a hand bearing compass. A relative bearing is taken with reference to the bow of the boat.

Direct Bearings

Using your hand bearing compass, sight on a visible charted object, then plot the magnetic bearing line toward the object on your chart as described in Chapter 4. (Imagine that you are at the center of the compass rose, drawing the line toward the indicated bearing direction on the rose. Your bearing line should be parallel to that.)

Remember, two or more direct bearings that cross

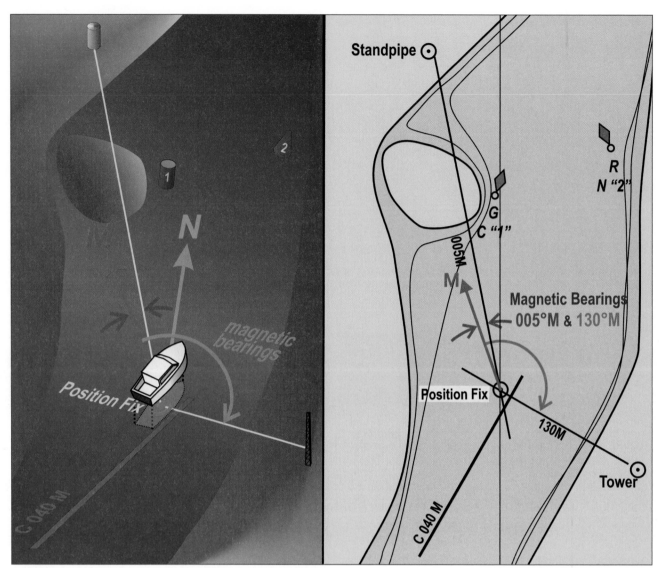

FIGURE 11-8. *GPS is quite accurate and provides a position fix; however, it is essential that you use independent means to check the GPS. Bearings provide the most convenient and comforting means of staying in touch with your surroundings. By taking two reasonably well-separated bearings (typically greater than 30° but less than 150° separation between bearings), you can get a good fix. Using a hand bearing compass, you will be reading magnetic bearings, as shown in the graphic on the left. When you plot these bearings, remember to use the magnetic north reference.*

produce a fix. The greater their angle of crossing (where 90° is optimum), the more accurate your fix is likely to be. When a third bearing verifies that fix, your confidence in it will increase. Most likely the three bearings will intersect not at a precise point but rather in what navigators call a "cocked hat" triangle. Your true position is somewhere within that triangle. The smaller the triangle, the greater your confidence. And remember, you can do this plotting in degrees true if you prefer, as long as you first adjust the bearings from your hand bearing compass for variation.

Relative Bearings

Relative bearings are usually taken by eye. Though approximate, this is substantially more convenient and quicker than using a hand bearing compass. Remember, the relative bearing is referenced to your heading—that is, to your boat's bow. This corresponds to your visual frame of reference on the water, and it is the default frame of reference for radar.

The bow provides one easy point of reference, and the stern another. Beam bearings can be surprisingly easy to sight as well. Simply position yourself with one arm extending toward the bow and the other toward the stern, then sight straight ahead. These are not precise bearings, but they do provide a quick reference for checking your position and your GPS.

To convert a relative bearing into a direct bearing for plotting, simply add your boat's compass heading (adjusted

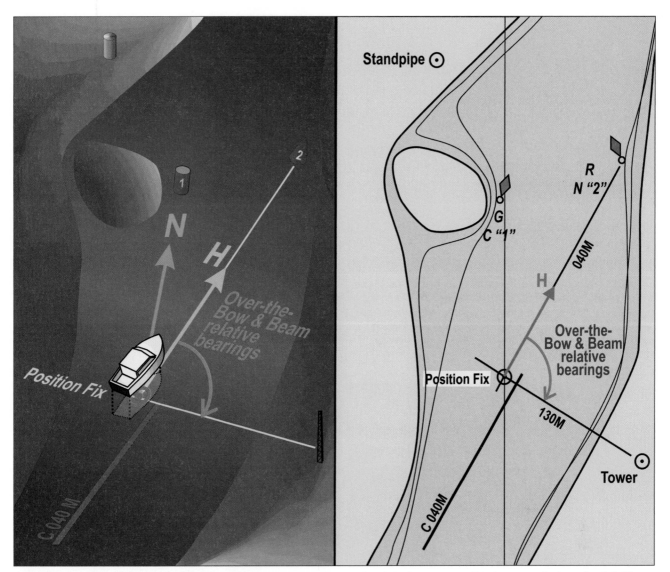

FIGURE 11-9. *Relative bearings are taken with reference to the boat rather than the compass. Bearings over the bow, by definition, will match your heading. Beam bearings are also quick. Although not precise, this technique can quickly and easily confirm your GPS readings. If you choose to plot a relative bearing, you'll need to add the heading of the boat to the relative bearing.*

for deviation if necessary) to the relative bearing (measured clockwise from the bow) to get the equivalent magnetic bearing.

Collision Bearings

You can use relative bearings to anticipate the potential for a collision. Simply sight on another boat that might cross your path and note how its position aligns with some object on your boat. Use a stanchion, a section of windshield—whatever is convenient. Take, for example, the situation shown in Figure 11-11, where the other boat is located some distance away and is approximately aligned with the corner of the windshield on your boat.

Follow the relative progress of the other boat as you both continue along your respective paths. In Figure 11-12, the other boat is closer, but its relative bearing from yours remains unchanged. Finally, in Figure 11-13, you see that the other boat is much closer, but still its relative bearing is unchanged. (Note that your heading must be constant for these sequential observations to be valid.)

If the relative bearing to another boat does not change as it approaches, YOU WILL COLLIDE. That is what is about to happen in this example if neither boat takes evasive action. In this particular example, you are the give-way vessel, as explained in the next section. You should immediately steer hard to starboard to avoid the collision.

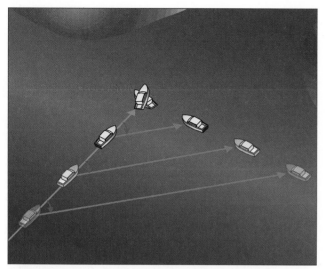

FIGURE 11-10. *One form of relative bearing that is easy to use and essential to your safety is the collision bearing. When you sight another boat on an intersecting course, note where it appears across some nearby object on your boat, such as the windscreen. If that boat maintains its same relative bearing, you are likely to collide.*

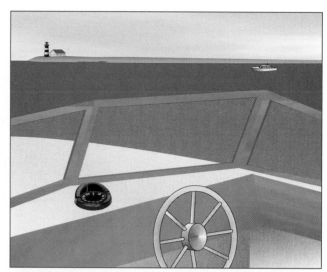

FIGURE 11-11. *A view on the water puts the collision bearing in perspective. When you see another boat crossing from some distance away, note its position relative to some feature on your boat—in this case, the corner of the windscreen.*

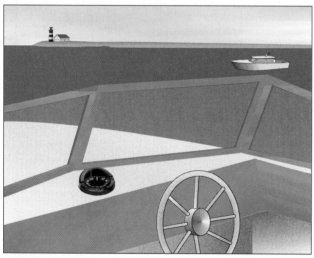

FIGURE 11-12. *Some minutes later, you note that the other boat appears closer and its relative bearing is unchanged. This is a call to take action.*

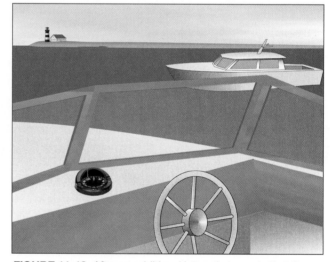

FIGURE 11-13. *After an additional interval, you note that the other boat is closer and its relative position remains unchanged. This means you are in imminent danger of a collision—take immediate action.*

An overhead view of the situation is shown in Figure 11-10. Note that the relative bearing remains unchanged as both boats move ahead. If the relative bearing were to shift more toward your bow as the two boats approach, the other boat would pass ahead of you, as shown in Figure 11-14. If the other boat's relative bearing were to drop back toward your stern, the boat would pass behind you, as illustrated in Figure 11-15.

When a collision seems possible, you have two alternatives. The first is to alter your speed, then note whether the relative bearing to the other boat shifts forward or aft, indicating a miss. The second alternative is to change course,

albeit briefly. After returning to your original course, continue to monitor the relative bearing to the other boat.

This subject arises again in Chapter 15 as a technique to use with your radar.

Obviously, you need to maintain a vigilant lookout, because the other vessel could also change course or speed. This could either help avoid a collision or increase its likelihood. Unfortunately, many boaters do not know the rules of the road and cannot properly handle their boats, so the burden of collision avoidance may fall entirely on you. A brief summary of the rules follows, just in case you could use a refresher.

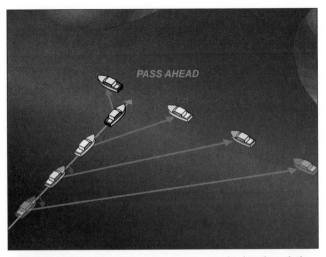

FIGURE 11-14. *In this example, you are monitoring the relative bearing to the other boat and you discover that its position is advancing toward your bow. This is an indication that the other boat will pass ahead of you if both boats maintain course and speed.*

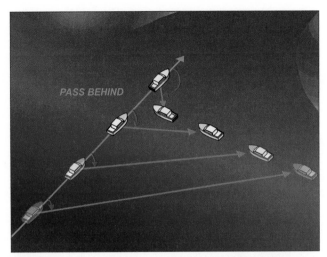

FIGURE 11-15. *In this example, you note that the other boat's relative position is slipping away from your bow. This is an indication that the other boat will pass behind you if both boats maintain course and speed.*

RULES OF THE ROAD—QUICK VERSION

The rules of the nautical road are relatively simple and closely parallel the rules for roadways ashore. Generally, you keep to the right—at least that is preferred. "Roads" at sea lack lines and lanes, so you need to be vigilant. The several conditions of encounter between vessels are summarized below.

RIGHT-OF-WAY

There is no right-of-way on the water. Instead, there are stand-on and give-way vessels. If you are the stand-on vessel, you are required to maintain your current course and speed. Why? Because the other party, the give-way vessel, is required to keep clear of you. To do that, he needs to anticipate what you will do. Do not confuse the situation. Generally speaking, the give-way vessel maneuvers to starboard. But which vessel is stand-on and which is give-way?

PECKING ORDER

In a word, less maneuverable vessels have priority. In an encounter between two vessels, the one higher in the pecking order is the stand-on vessel; the other is the give-way vessel. As a practical matter, tonnage has priority. When in doubt, give way. Large vessels lack your ability to stop or turn, and the same can be said for vessels engaged in towing. Fishing boats come next, then sailing vessels. (A sailing vessel is one that is under sail alone. If it is running an engine—even if the sails are also set—it is considered a power vessel.) Power-driven recreational vessels are near the bottom of the list. That means if yours is a power-driven boat, you give way under most circumstances. Only seaplanes rank lower than powerboats. Rules for meeting, crossing,

and overtaking, as well as some special rules for sailboats, are described below.

POWER-DRIVEN BOATS MEETING

If two power-driven boats meet head-on, neither is a stand-on vessel—both must give way. The preferred action is to pass port

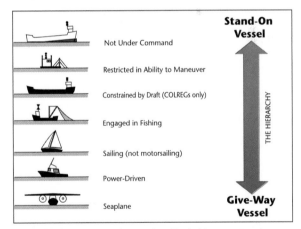

FIGURE 11-16. *Vessels are classified either as stand-on or give-way. The stand-on vessel must maintain current course and speed; the give-way vessel must maneuver to avoid the stand-on vessel (usually to starboard). The pecking order for vessels is based on their maneuverability, or lack of it. The least maneuverable vessels have the most priority as stand-on. (From* The One-Minute Guide to Rules of the Road, *by Charlie Wing)*

(continued on next page)

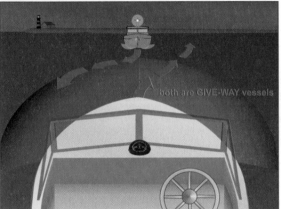

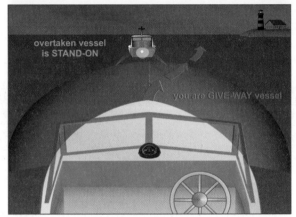

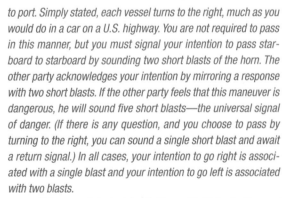

FIGURE 11-17. Top: *When two powerboats meet nearly head-on, both vessels are give-way. Generally, both vessels turn to starboard such that they pass port to port as shown. Any boat under power is considered a powerboat, including a sailboat with engines engaged. Above: At night, the same rule applies. Because you may not be able to see the other boat, you rely upon the other boat's light pattern. You see a green light on his starboard side, a red light on his port side, and a white light above and in the center (the white light tells you that the boat is under power).*

FIGURE 11-18. Top: *When overtaking another vessel, you are the give-way vessel and the overtaken vessel is stand-on. You can pass on either side, but your intention must be clear to the other vessel. You remain the give-way vessel until you have passed the other vessel. Above: At night, the same rules apply. Because you are overtaking, you will not see the red and green sidelights on the other vessel. Only one white light will appear.*

to port. Simply stated, each vessel turns to the right, much as you would do in a car on a U.S. highway. You are not required to pass in this manner, but you must signal your intention to pass starboard to starboard by sounding two short blasts of the horn. The other party acknowledges your intention by mirroring a response with two short blasts. If the other party feels that this maneuver is dangerous, he will sound five short blasts—the universal signal of danger. (If there is any question, and you choose to pass by turning to the right, you can sound a single short blast and await a return signal.) In all cases, your intention to go right is associated with a single blast and your intention to go left is associated with two blasts.

This scenario is depicted in Figure 11-17 for daytime and nighttime conditions.

POWER-DRIVEN BOATS OVERTAKING

If you are the overtaking boat, you are always the give-way vessel, whereas the overtaken boat is the stand-on vessel. If you approach from anywhere within a band of 135° centered on the stern of the overtaken vessel, you are overtaking. This corresponds with the arc of the required stern light of that vessel. If you are overtaking while within this arc, you are the give-way vessel and the overtaken vessel is stand-on. The rules say that, if in doubt, you should assume you are overtaking and react accordingly.

You can pass either to the right or to the left, with right preferred but not mandatory. If you choose to pass to the right, sound a single short blast of your horn. If to the left, sound two short blasts. Listen for an echoing response. Again, five short

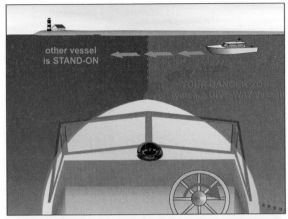

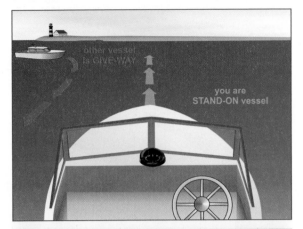

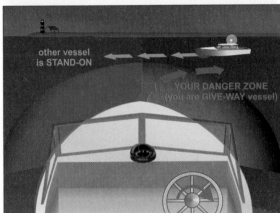

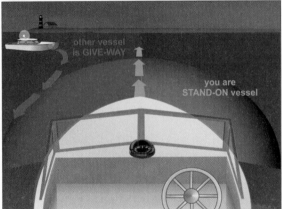

FIGURE 11-19A. *Top: Powerboats crossing represent the most complex situation. Your status is dependent upon the relative location of the other boat. You have what is known as a danger zone, which extends from your bow to 22.5° aft of your starboard beam. Any other vessel within that sector is the stand-on vessel and you are the give-way, as shown here. You must take action to avoid the other boat. In general, that involves turning to starboard. Never turn to port unless it is your only option to avoid a collision. You may also reduce power. Never try to power your way ahead of the other vessel. Above: At night, you are the give-way vessel. You have the other vessel's running lights to help you decide. If you can see his red sidelight (on his port side), you are the give-way vessel. Take the appropriate action.*

FIGURE 11-19B. *Top: If the other vessel is crossing from your port side, he is the give-way vessel and you are the stand-on vessel. Look for him to turn to starboard or reduce power. If that does not appear to be happening, you may need to take evasive action. Turn to starboard, not to port. You cannot run the risk that he might turn to starboard at the last moment, resulting in the two of you colliding. Above: At night, the other boat shows a green sidelight, indicating that you are the stand-on vessel. The same rules apply.*

blasts indicate that your maneuver is dangerous and you must not overtake at this time.

You remain the overtaking vessel until you are clear of the other boat.

POWER-DRIVEN BOATS CROSSING

A third situation involving power-driven boats is crossing. To visualize the circle around your boat, think of the running lights you carry. You show a white light astern at night over a 135° arc, as

mentioned above. Of the two arcs forward, the one that demands most of your attention is the 112.5° arc extending from the bow to just behind your starboard beam (right side). This is your "danger zone"; any boat approaching from this sector is the stand-on vessel and you are the give-way vessel. At night, the side running light on that side of your boat is green, signifying to the other party that he is the stand-on vessel. By the same token, the 112.5° arc extending from your bow to just behind your port beam shows a red sidelight at night. This indicates to the other boat that he is the give-way vessel because you are in his danger zone.

Always pay special attention to vessels in your danger zone, because you may need to take early and decisive action as the give-way vessel. (continued on next page)

FIGURE 11-20. Sailboats under sail alone represent a special case. When two sailboats encounter each other, the boat on the port tack is the give-way vessel. A port tack means that the wind is coming across the port side of the boat. Again, you should turn to starboard.

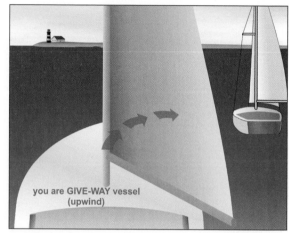

FIGURE 11-21. If two sailboats are on the same tack, the one that is windward (upwind) of the other is the give-way vessel.

SAILBOATS MEETING

A sailboat encountering another sailboat is governed by different rules, because both are limited in their ability to maneuver. The rule states that a sailing vessel on port tack should give way to one on a starboard tack. On a port tack, the wind is coming from the port side of the boat. The sailboat on a starboard tack is the stand-on vessel; the give-way vessel (port tack) will turn to starboard. If you are operating a power-driven boat, you will need to know this if you encounter two sailboats meeting.

SAILBOATS ON THE SAME TACK

When two sailboats on the same tack encounter each other, the one to windward of the other is the give-way vessel. The windward vessel is simply the one closer to the wind. The rationale is that a windward vessel that passes the other may block the wind and cause the other to lose maneuverability.

GOOD ADVICE

When in doubt, act early to avoid the other vessel, particularly if you do not recognize its type. This is especially true when you meet a large ship or one that may be towing.

BOXING THE COMPASS (A "POINT" OF INTEREST)

Those running light arcs described above come from a long-standing set of standards generated over the centuries. Originally, compass cards and the compass roses on charts were subdivided into points rather than degrees. The cardinal directions—north, south, east, and west—defined quadrants, which were subdivided into 45-degree octants by adding the intercardinal points: northeast, southeast, southwest, and northwest. These octants were divided into $22\frac{1}{2}$-degree sextants by adding NNE, ENE, and so forth, which were halved again to form a total of 32 unique directions at $11\frac{1}{4}$-degree intervals. These were called the "points" of the compass, the rationale being that it was easier to divide into halves than any other subdivision. Today, we use degrees to divide our compass into 360 equal parts, but the old points system lives on in the arcs of running lights. The sidelights extend from the bow to 2 points abaft (behind) either beam of the boat, thus 112.5° apiece or 225° in total. The remaining arc of the full circle is the 135° covered by the stern light. Rare is the mariner these days, however, who must learn to "box the compass" by naming all the points in sequence: north, north by east, north northeast, northeast by north, northeast, and so on around the card.

RESPONDING TO CHANGING CONDITIONS

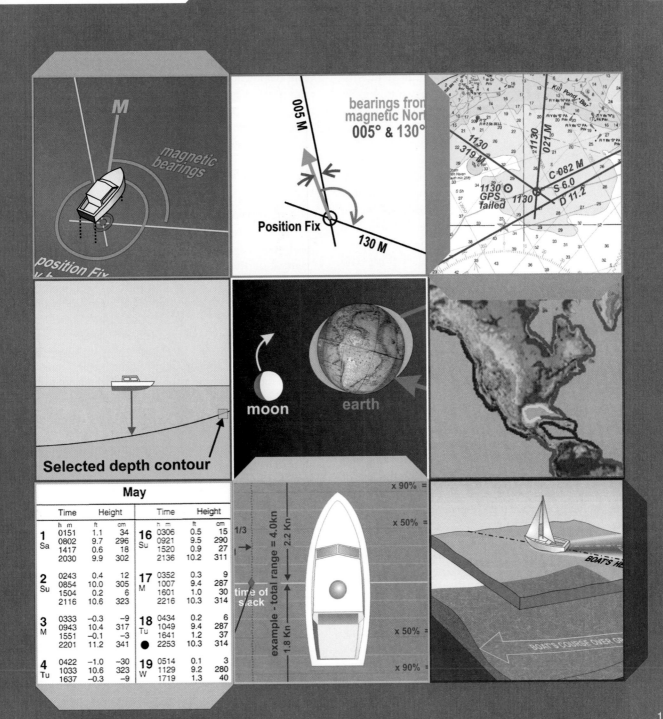

What to Do If the GPS Quits

GPS is a complex system but one that works reliably. Yet you may get bad readings on rare occasions. In an international crisis, the U.S. Department of Defense can degrade the accuracy of civilian GPS satellite signals (called *selective availability*). On a much more mundane and immediate level, however, your receiver might malfunction, a wire might come loose internally, or something on your boat could interfere with incoming signals. It's also possible that you could make an error entering or selecting a waypoint or route. Perhaps most likely of all, the AA batteries in your handheld GPS might simply die, and the replacements you meant to bring are still at home on the kitchen table. At one time or another, a GPS "glitch" happens to all of us—and usually at the least opportune time.

It's then that your planning efforts and practice pay off. You'll be glad you took the time to understand the elements of traditional navigation. If you have honed your skills at taking bearings and have practiced dead reckoning, you'll be ahead of the game. Ideally, you were taking bearings and using them to verify your position when you discovered the GPS malfunction. This increases your chances of knowing when you had your last good fix, which will be the starting point for your dead reckoning (DR) plot.

Chapter 10 showed you how to verify your GPS readings by other means. In the event that this checking and staying in touch with your surroundings using the "eye of the mariner" raised questions about your position, you should immediately undertake the steps outlined in this chapter.

Stop and Regroup

The first thing to do is to stop your boat, assuming you are not blocking other traffic. There is no point in proceeding until you are confident that the path ahead is safe, and you can't know that until you know where you are and plot your location on the chart. If you have any concern about drift-

ing or being blown from your current position, you may consider anchoring. Before proceeding, take a look around and check the water depth beneath you to see how urgent this step may be. Obviously, if you are being pushed toward rocks, you should anchor immediately or hold your position under power.

Find Your Present Location

You need to ascertain your current position. The most obvious starting point is to look around for local landmarks or navigation aids to use as references. If you're close enough to a navigation aid to identify it by number, you can readily locate yourself on the chart. If you're a quarter mile south of the eastern end of Silver Dollar Island (for example), you're in almost as good shape. Or you can try one of the following.

USING A BACKUP GPS In most cases when GPS fails, it's your GPS receiver and not the satellites overhead that's at fault. If you had the foresight to bring along a spare GPS, now is the time to pull it out. If it acquires adequate satellite signals and gives a credible position indication, you can regroup with new data. Then use the same checks that you performed with your primary GPS receiver to reinforce your confidence. To do this smoothly in an emergency, it pays to have preplanned and entered the same waypoints in your backup unit that you stored in your primary GPS. If all check out, plot your reported position on the chart before proceeding. Then, on a chart, check the direct path to your next intended waypoint for safety and proceed accordingly, or plan a safe route around any obstacles.

If the backup GPS receiver's reported position also is suspect, it may be worthwhile to investigate whether you are generating local interference—but don't dwell on this for long. Take a quick look at both units and ascertain that they are receiving adequate signals. On the Satellite Screen, this condition is indicated by solid bars of some height corresponding to four or more satellites. If you note that part of the sky is blocked—as indicated by no signals from satel-

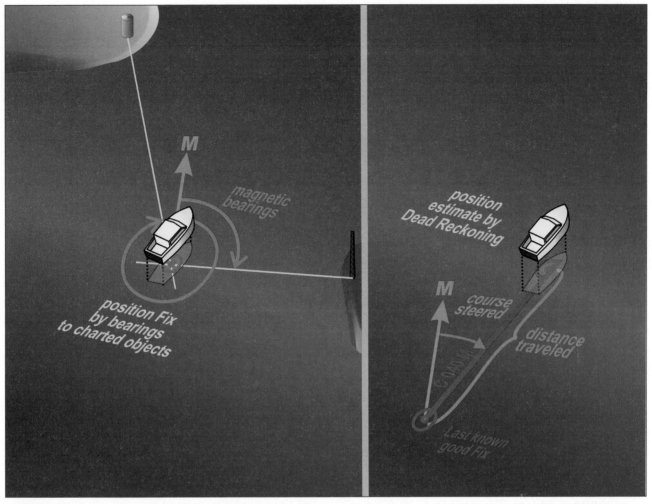

FIGURE 12-1. *If your GPS is suspect, you should stop in a safe spot (out of traffic if possible) and regroup. You'll want to determine and plot your current position before taking any further action.*

lites shown on the skyview display of either unit from a given direction, try moving the backup GPS to another location. As a last quick check, try turning off other electronic and electrical equipment and see whether it results in any change in GPS signal levels or reported position. If it does, you may have been creating self-interference. Double-check the new position and proceed with the other equipment turned off. Some devices, such as some active TV antennas, can cause GPS interference under certain conditions.

USING BEARINGS TO CHARTED OBJECTS If visible landmarks or identifiable buoys are available, you can use them to plot your current position. You need two or more objects that lie at some reasonable angle from one another—between 30° and 150° is good. Using a hand bearing compass, you can sight on these objects and record their magnetic bearings. Remember to sight over your bow to check that your handheld compass is in line with your calibrated ship's compass. In other words, both compasses should match for this direction. (See Chapters 4, 10, and 11.) Then plot each

bearing line, as discussed in Chapters 2 (see Figure 2-11), 10, and 11. Where the lines cross is your fix. If you have three bearings, place your location near the center of the triangle formed by the three intersecting lines. If you have more than three, select the spot where most of the lines converge. If two bearing lines are nearly parallel, they will not cross at a sharply defined spot; this produces a poor fix. If they are nearly perpendicular, your fix will be much better. When visible landmarks are limited, go with what you have.

If you do not have a hand bearing compass (as you surely should), set a nonmetallic straightedge on top of the ship's compass and align it with the sighted object and the center of the compass card. Read the bearing by sighting down to the compass card, or just turn the boat until each landmark is directly ahead and read their bearings as headings on the ship's compass.

If you can find no landmarks or charted and identifiable navigation buoys for bearings, a steep bluff or bold point of land will do. Any feature that is both charted and recognizable is all you need.

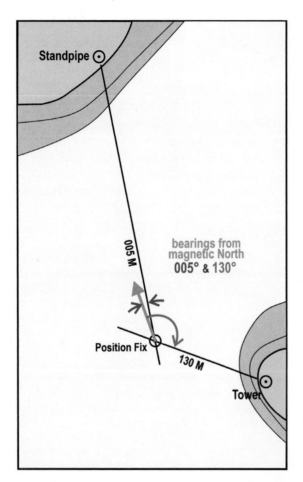

FIGURE 12-2. *The best way to determine your position is to take bearings on two or more charted objects and plot these on your chart. Where they cross is your fix.*

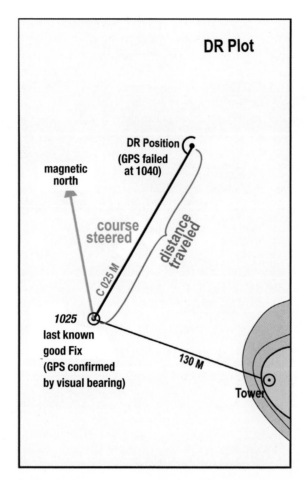

FIGURE 12-3. *In the absence of two or more charted landmarks or identifiable buoys on which you can take bearings to get a fix, you need to use dead reckoning to deduce your position. Go back to your last known good fix. (This is why you should regularly plot your position while everything is working.) From that, plot the course or courses you have steered and the distance you have traveled on each course, multiplying speed traveled by elapsed time. Plot each course and distance in succession. This is your DR position, an estimate of your present location that is uncorrected for leeway or tidal currents. Use it with caution.*

BACKUP ALTERNATIVES TO FIND POSITION In the absence of visible landmarks and a functioning backup GPS receiver, you need to resort to one of the following alternatives, in descending order of preference.

Radar: Use your radar, if you have one, to look for obvious navigation aids or landmarks. Then, using the distance and bearing to each identified radar return, derive and plot your approximate position on your chart as shown in Chapter 15. You need to factor in your boat's heading and the relative bearing from the boat to the identified object to derive the charted heading. Understand that a radar fix may not be precise. The greatest challenge is unquestionably identifying a specific navigation aid or landmark amidst other boats and clutter. Carefully compare your radar screen image with your chart. The most significant advantage of radar is that it presents the real world around you rather than a deduced position. Moreover, because it provides range as well as bearing to a target, all you need is one clearly identifiable object to get a fix.

Backward Dead Reckoning: Locate your last known position on your chart and plot the course that you have

taken from that point. This is the reason you should follow planned legs, so you have a record of what course you steered. It's also why you should have checked and plotted your GPS position from time to time, so you have a good point to go back to. Then you need to estimate how long you traveled along that course and at what average speed. Distance of travel can then be calculated by multiplying the time of travel (in hours) by the speed (in knots) to get nautical miles. Usually, however, it's easier to use minutes; to do this, simply divide the number of minutes by 60. This is why it's a good idea to carry a calculator. Do these calculations on paper rather than in your head. Because this may be the only information you have about your location, do a careful computation. The resultant location is one you've deduced by dead reckoning, as discussed in Chapter 2 and elsewhere. The accuracy of your position estimate is entirely dependent upon how recently you had a solid fix, how far you traveled since then, and the accuracy of your course and speed estimates. Still, this approach gives you some idea of your location.

Depth and Depth Profile: Given a good guess of your position, and depending on the local contour of the bottom, you might be able to refine your estimate to a higher degree. If you have a fishfinder (see Chapter 16), the depth profile over the path you've just taken will still be on the screen. Look for rapid shoaling or drop-offs that can be aligned with the chart. If you have a digital depth sounder rather than a fishfinder, you can still track the depth readouts as you get underway and compare them with those predicted along your charted course from that spot. If they match, your estimate may be good. If they don't, you may wish to scan along the chart for an area that better fits the actual profile, then recalculate your dead-reckoned position.

Plan Before Proceeding

Plot your best position estimate on your chart. If the surrounding region is free from charted hazards, you can live with some error in the estimated position. If hazards lurk nearby, you need to proceed with great caution, striving to skirt a wide path around the hazards.

Take a look at the charted path from your estimated location to your intended waypoint. If it is clear and of reasonable width—enough to accommodate the uncertainty in your current position—plot the course and measure the distance to that waypoint.

If the direct path is not clear, seek an alternative. Remember, you will be proceeding without GPS to maintain a precise course over ground, so leave enough room for errors, and select a path that affords visible landmarks to the greatest possible extent. Measure your new courses and distances.

If there are any clusters of hazards along the newly planned paths, make note of their respective distances off the course line so you can be extra alert when passing them.

Navigating without GPS

Now set your course using your ship's compass and your speed according to the risks. You will proceed by dead reckoning, so pay close attention to your course, speed, and elapsed time, keeping course and speed as close to constant

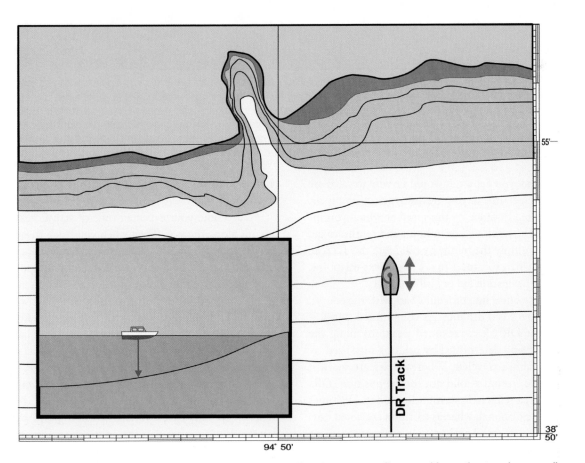

FIGURE 12-4. *Where depth contours increase or decrease uniformly, you can refine a position estimate using soundings.*

FIGURE 12-5. *You have established your position, either by a new fix (shown at 1130 on the left), or by a dead reckoning estimate from your last known fix at 0950 (shown on right). Imagine navigating from both locations without GPS. In either case, you'll begin by plotting and measuring the planned course direction, then carefully steering in that direction. Along the way, you'll need to pay close attention to your speed and the time. Using the formula discussed in Chapter 2, you can use speed and time to plot DR positions. On the left, you're starting from a fix—your position is better defined. On the right, you will commence from a DR position. In this latter case, you will need to leave greater margin around charted obstacles due to the relative uncertainty of your starting position.*

as you can. Before you depart, it would be wise to calculate the estimated travel time to your next waypoint; simply divide the estimated distance by the speed at which you intend to travel. The result will be in hours and tenths; to get minutes, just multiply the tenths by 60. Note this ETA so you will know when to expect to see your next waypoint, assuming it is a navigation aid or visible object.

Draw this course line on your chart with the course, speed, and (if you wish) distance. As you proceed, periodically mark your DR (dead-reckoned position) along the line, each DR being determined by multiplying speed by time to get distance traveled. Whereas fixes are marked with a full circle around a solid dot for the position, DRs are marked with a semicircle surrounding a dot. DR times are noted on the diagonal, whereas fix times are noted horizontally on the chart. Anytime you change course or speed, you need to mark your DR as the point of departure for the new course or speed. Plotting your course on the

chart is your only way of tracking your progress, so do it carefully.

Also note your expected time of arrival near charted hazards along the way. Then when you reach that area, you can use your depth sounder, bearings to landmarks, and extra attention at the helm and on surrounding waters to stay safe.

Recognize that although you can plot a course with great precision, you will be fortunate to steer it within five degrees. And though you try to stay at a steady known speed, you can be off in this estimate too. These factors lead to a cumulative potential error. A strong tidal current can cause even larger errors. Indeed, although a DR plot does not account for the effects of wind or current, your navigation may have to. More on this in Chapter 14. By all means, use your best efforts in planning and navigating courses, but be aware that the only way to wring precision from a dead reckoning plot is to take regular bearings along the way.

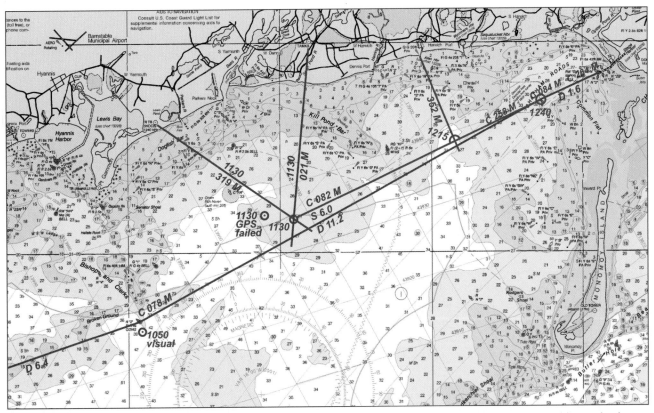

FIGURE 12-6. *This example demonstrates a scenario when the GPS fails. The 1050 GPS fix was verified visually with a navigation buoy. At 1130, two bearings produced a fix that was a mismatch with the GPS fix, so the GPS became suspect. You plotted a new course from the intersection of the bearing lines and proceeded by dead reckoning. At 1215, using speed and time, you plotted your DR position and were able to verify it with a single visual bearing. At 1240, you converged with your original intended course line at a navigation aid, then plotted a course to the anchorage along your original intended course.*

When you reach your first waypoint, follow the same process to the next waypoint. If the waypoint was a buoy or other identifiable object, this becomes a fix. For obvious reasons, using charted objects allows you to adjust your plotting. That's why charted navigation buoys make such popular waypoints. When you're proceeding by DR, especially in poor visibility, you'll prefer those that are surrounded by safe water and broadcast their presence with a bell, gong, whistle, horn, or light. Also, lighted buoys are better, even in daylight, because they typically are larger than non-lighted buoys and easier to see at a distance. In any event, always begin the next leg of the DR plot from the fix. If you cannot rely upon seeing charted objects along the way, recognize that the uncertainty of your DR position increases with the distance traveled. Over a 10-mile run in a boat going about 10 knots, you could miss your waypoint by as much as a mile in any direction. It pays to have intermediate reference points.

UPDATING YOUR POSITION If your chosen path has visible landmarks, plan on taking bearings from time to time to check your position. Because GPS is not available to you, you need charted visible objects to use as references for plotting.

If you have only one bearing, you need to estimate your position. It's a good idea to plot a DR for the same time and compare that with the point where the bearing (line of position, LOP) crosses your course line. If, for example, the DR position is farther along than the intersection of the bearing LOP with your DR line, you are probably not making the speed you estimated—not over the ground, at least. Adjust your calculations accordingly as you proceed.

If you pass reasonably close abeam of an identifiable buoy, you can consider that to be a fix. Just draw a line on your chart perpendicular to your course line that intersects the buoy. Mark that spot on your course line and proceed with your dead reckoning from there.

And remember, you can get a fix from a single bearing if you can also get an accurate range for the sighted buoy or landmark. Radar gives you this; so does a vertical sextant angle, though that's not a technique we cover in this book. With practice you'll become a fairly accurate eyeball distance estimator. Whatever works!

Planning as You Go with GPS

You can't preplan everything. Planning as much as you can will simplify your on-the-water navigation, but inevitably you will want to go somewhere that is not planned or adjust a preplanned route underway. And why not? Your plan is supposed to be an aid, not a straitjacket. The freedom to go where you wish is one of the great appeals of boating.

A constant theme throughout this book is to prequalify safe paths. This is not quite as easy on the go as it is when you can lay out charts and study them at your leisure. Nevertheless, electronic tools provide features that ease the task, and good chartwork gives you confidence in your changing plan.

If you're using a handheld GPS, generally you do not have the advantage of a digital chart display. If you do, skip to the next section; otherwise, read on. The basic steps for planning on the go are:

Find where you are.

Plot a safe path to the new destination.

The trick is to manage the boat and come up with a new plan at the same time. You will find this easier if you have had the foresight to store a sufficient number of waypoints in your GPS.

Find Where You Are

It's always a good idea to keep a chart by the helm, preferably with your stored waypoints and routes marked on it for easy reference. On all but larger boats, which have space to lay out a chart, you'll probably keep the active chart conveniently folded with the active area face up, so you can work with the chart on your lap. Unfortunately, when you do this, the latitude and longitude scales are often hidden from view. The following techniques will help you find your location without using these scales.

Location along an Active Leg

If you are following an active leg of a course or route, determining your position is greatly simplified. You can reasonably assume that you are somewhere along that course line. All you need do to confirm that is to look at your GPS Highway or Map Screen. Then, because stored GPS waypoints are also noted on the chart, even if the route leg itself is not plotted, draw a line from the waypoint you just left to the active waypoint you're headed toward. Now, where are you along that line? Here are some quick tricks to find out:

- **Bearing to a Landmark**—Simply sight on a charted feature to the side of your current course, usually a landmark or a buoy. It is enough to estimate a relative bearing quickly by eye; then, on the chart, align your plotting tool to that relative bearing and move it to intersect the charted feature. See where it intersects your course line? You are there!

- **Using a Grid Line**—Scan along your active course line. Is there a plotted grid line (a line of latitude or longitude) on the course in front of you? If so, you can do your planning from where that grid line intersects your course line. Now all you need to do is proceed along the course line and watch your GPS display until you reach that precise latitude or longitude. You then know where you are.

- **Using a Waypoint**—Obviously, if you wait until you reach your current active waypoint, you will know where you are. Alternatively, you can use another waypoint stored in the GPS or a charted object near your course line. This is a variation on the bearing approach, but here you are looking for a nearby object. The easiest and safest way to do this is with a beam bearing to that object. Plan from that spot, and use your skilled "mariner's eye" to identify when you have reached that location. If you are planning to use a stored waypoint that does not represent a buoy or other visible, charted feature, use the Map Screen to eyeball when this waypoint is abeam of your course. The closer the object is to your course line, the more accurate your established position will be.

Location in Open Water

If you are sailing in open water without following an active course, determining your position is a little more complex. Assuming you have preplanned by identifying regions of hazards, you can steer safely to a particular spot and avoid those hazards.

The spot you select can be a waypoint, a charted object, or the intersection of two grid lines on the chart. In the latter case, you simply steer until those coordinates show on the GPS. Alternatively, you can select any arbitrary spot using two bearings to visible landmarks. Draw the corresponding bearing lines on your chart and determine their magnetic directions. If the landmarks are stored in your GPS, use the Nearest Waypoints Screen to monitor the bearings from your current location to those two waypoints. When the values correspond with your charted bearings, you have arrived. If the landmarks are not stored waypoints, get out your hand bearing compass and sight them visually until the bearings match your plotted values. See also Chapters 8, 10, and 11 for more on locating yourself quickly in open water.

Using Radar

You can use your radar to determine your location, as described in Chapters 15 and 25. By selecting a clearly identifiable charted object that can be seen on radar, you can read the range and bearing to that object directly on the screen. By drawing that bearing line on your chart and using dividers to scale off the range, you can locate your current position. But suppose you cannot see your distance scale without unfolding the chart? Try an alternative. Typical large-scale charts have grid lines at every five minutes of latitude, which corresponds to 5 nautical miles. Set this distance with your dividers. Now sail until the range to that object is 5 miles, and read your bearing from the radar. Plot this location. Alternatively, you can preselect the spot by drawing a bearing and 5-mile mark from the object and sail to that location.

The advantage to selecting a "hopping-off" point for a replanned path is that you can use the time in transit to do your planning.

Plot a Safe Path to the New Destination

Given a planned starting point and a new destination, you can plot a direct path on your chart. Scan along it to ensure that it is free of underwater hazards. If it passes the test, enter the destination waypoint's coordinates into the GPS.

If the path comes too close for comfort to a potential hazard, you have two alternatives: (1) plan legs around the obstacle using one or more intermediate waypoints, whose coordinates you need to enter into the GPS; or (2) consider a different starting point along your active leg—one that provides a clear shot to the destination. The latter approach requires less real-time GPS programming and thereby is probably preferable.

Entering New Waypoints into the GPS

If the new destination and any necessary intermediate waypoints are not already stored in your GPS, now's the time to do it. The direct way of entering a waypoint into your GPS is via its coordinates, but to do so you might need to unfold your chart to get at the latitude and longitude scales. To measure and store waypoint coordinates, see Chapter 5. Unfortunately, this technique is fraught with potential errors both in reading and entering the coordinates when practiced in a moving small boat on the water. It's more compatible with the dining room table at home. A better approach on the water uses other features on your GPS.

BEARING AND DISTANCE This technique is far more intuitive than using coordinates. Once you have identified the starting point for your new course, measure the bearing and distance on your chart from that location to any new intermediate waypoint(s) and to your destination. Then, using the cursor key in your GPS Map Screen, scroll the cursor while looking at the data window, which shows bearing and distance to the cursor. Scroll until the cursor is over the first intermediate waypoint (using bearing and distance), and use the Mark function to store this location. Step and repeat until you have entered all the needed waypoints—with each one referenced as a bearing and distance from your hopping-off point. You needn't take the time to give these waypoints names, just note the sequence of numbers assigned by the GPS. Again, these bearings and distances are all measured from the same point—your starting point. Most GPS models require you to wait until you are at that starting point before using this scroll method.

Tides, Winds, and Currents

In most coastal areas, tidal heights and tidal currents have a significant effect on navigation. Accurately predicting the height of tide can help you avoid a grounding, and accurately anticipating the directions and velocities of tidal currents can help you plan the best time to transit a particular passage. Proper use of GPS can also help you measure and counter the effects of currents and winds, which might otherwise drive you from your chosen course. It pays to understand these effects and be prepared to anticipate them.

Tides can have a profound effect on where you can go and when. At the very lowest of low tides, you will find even less water over shoal areas than charted soundings suggest. You should plan accordingly.

Tides are a coastal phenomenon, imperceptible on the open sea. Boaters on the Great Lakes experience a similar but less predictable rise and fall of nearshore waters called *seiches* (pronounced *sayshes*). This chapter explores both predictable and unpredictable effects of tide, wind, seiches, and ocean currents.

About Tides and Tidal Currents

Many GPS receivers, chartplotters, and navigation software programs provide tidal height and tidal current predictions. Most such tools in the United States use predictive data and algorithms developed by the U.S. Naval Oceanographic Office and enhanced by other parties. The predictions for a substantial number of primary and subordinate tide and tidal current stations are based on extensive data and are reasonably accurate. Subordinate locations are referenced to the primary stations via tables of differences. Even if you don't have electronic tools available, tide and tidal current tables can be used with a few simple rules to predict the tidal height or current for a particular time and location.

What Causes Tides?

Tides and tidal currents are influenced by a number of factors, some of them predictable, some not. The prime mover is the gravitational pull of the moon, which "pulls" the ocean waters toward the moon, causing a bulge on the side of the Earth facing the moon.

A second bulge, which appears on the side of the Earth opposite the moon, is caused by centrifugal force. To see how this happens, we need to discard the traditional notion that the moon orbits around the center of the Earth. The problem with this notion is that it discounts the moon's pull on the Earth, which, though less than the Earth's pull on the moon, still exists. Thus, the Earth and moon actually spin as a pair about a common point—called a *barycenter*—that is located 900 nautical miles inside the surface of the Earth facing the moon. This means that the far side of the Earth is about five thousand nautical miles farther from the barycenter than the side facing the moon. It is this eccentricity that leads to a somewhat greater centrifugal force on the far side of the Earth and thus produces the second tidal bulge. These bulges are about a meter above the global average level of the oceans. Generally, due to friction, these bulges follow a little behind the moon as the Earth turns—one bulge on the side nearest, the other bulge on the side farthest.

But the moon does not act alone to produce tides. The sun also has an effect, though its magnitude is only about 46 percent of the moon's due to the sun's much greater distance from Earth. The Earth orbits the sun once each year, whereas the moon orbits the Earth every $27\frac{1}{3}$ days, so the angular relationships of the sun and moon to the Earth change constantly. In addition, because the moon's orbit around the Earth is elliptical, the moon is closer at some times during each lunar month than others. In fact, this orbital eccentricity is so significant that during the moon's closest approach to the Earth (called the perigee), the moon appears as much as 11 percent larger to an observer on Earth than it does at its farthest remove (called the apogee).

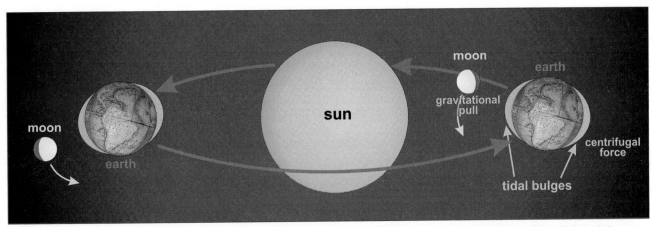

FIGURE 14-1. *Tides are caused primarily by the gravitational pull of the moon and the sun. The sun, though overwhelmingly larger than the moon, is also 370 times more distant, so its gravitational attraction is only some 46 percent that of the moon. The Earth spins about its axis every 24 hours; the high-tide bulges (see text) follow the moon. As a result, along most shorelines on the Earth, there are two high tides per day. In some locations, due to factors including the tilt of the Earth's axis, the angle of the moon's orbital plane, and geographical effects, there may be only one bulge per day.*

The orbit of the Earth around the sun is also elliptical, although not nearly as eccentric as the orbit of the moon. The Earth is closest to the sun around January 3 and farthest from it around July 4, although the specific days change slightly year to year. The tides that result from these complex interactions are themselves complex. It turns out that the astronomical pattern for the sun and the moon repeats every 18.6 years, which is why tide and tidal current tables are different each year.

Imagine that the two high-tide bulges remained relatively fixed as the Earth rotated under them. As your location passed by, the first bulge would produce a local high tide as that one meter of extra water height bunched up along your shore. Then the tide would drop, only to return again when the second bulge passed by about twelve hours later. Because the moon is the primary source of tides, it is not surprising that tides appear to follow the moon. The moon's apparent motion around the Earth takes 24 hours

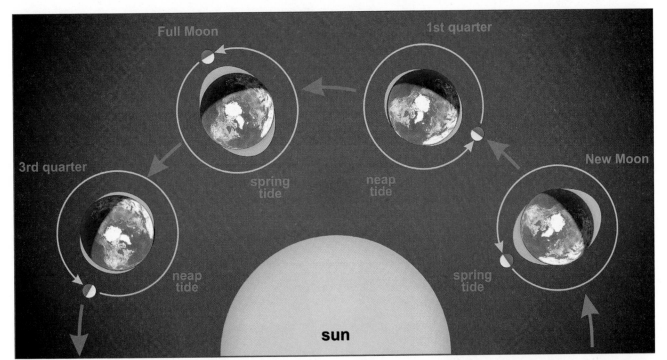

FIGURE 14-2. *At a new moon, the moon and sun are pulling in the same direction. This leads to spring tides, which are higher (and lower) than the average high and low tides. We also get spring tides during a full moon, when the moon and sun are aligned on opposite sides of the Earth. During the first and third quarters, however, the moon's pull is perpendicular to that of the sun, and the resultant neap tides have less than average ranges.*

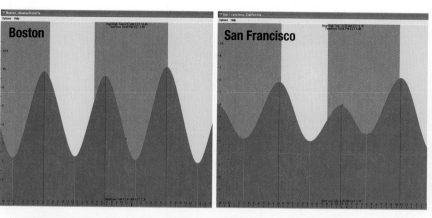

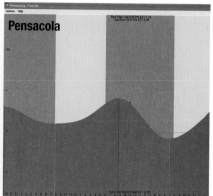

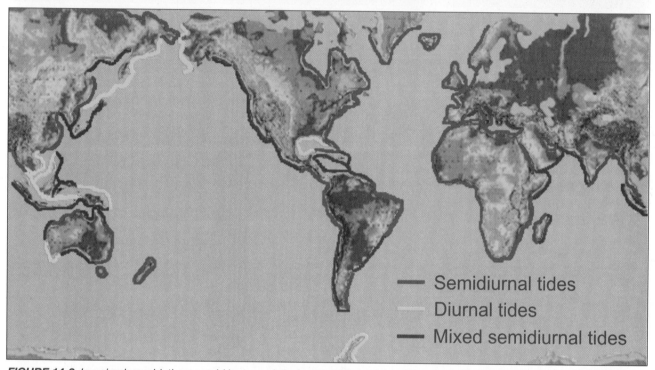

FIGURE 14-3. *In a simple world, there would be two relatively equal tide cycles per day, as shown for Boston at top left; indeed, most of the world experiences something akin to this. Some locations, such as San Francisco, experience mixed tides (top center), in which one of the two daily high tides is significantly greater than the other. Yet other locations, such as Pensacola, Florida, experience only one daily cycle rather than two (top right). NOAA's National Ocean Service prepared the graphic above to depict the locations of various tide patterns throughout the world.*

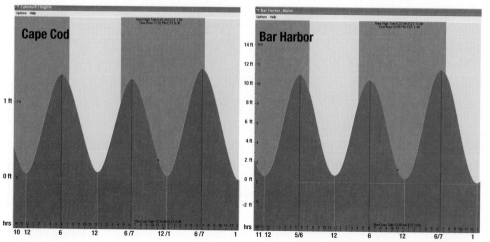

FIGURE 14-4A. *Local basin shapes, bathymetries, and coastline constrictions can either enhance or mute the tidal signal. On the south side of Cape Cod, for example, the tidal range may be only one and a half feet, whereas on the same day at Bar Harbor, Maine, the tidal range can be eleven feet.*

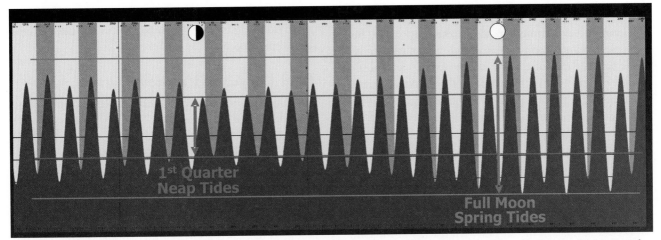

FIGURE 14-4B. *Tidal ranges vary not only by location but also, substantially, in a fixed location over time. Here is the tidal pattern for Boston Harbor over a 15-day period in April 2004. The tidal range reaches a minimum during the quarter moon and a maximum during a full moon, as illustrated in Figure 14-2.*

and 50 minutes. This means that the tides each day are effectively delayed by about fifty minutes from the previous day. If there were no land, the one-meter-high bulges would be quite regular; however, the presence of landmasses causes unique local patterns based on shoreline and seabed shape. Your detection of a bulge depends on whether you are on a coast where the bulge approaches (east) or departs (west). Tidal patterns for a specific location are more or less predictable, though unpredictable effects such as local weather and faraway storms have some effect on the actual tidal heights and currents at any given time.

Tidal Heights versus Tidal Currents

Tides are perceptible only along shorelines. In the middle of the ocean, there is no reference to indicate whether you are on top of a bulge or in the valley between bulges; a shoreline provides that reference. In addition, the heights of tides are accented by near-coastal shoaling. The shape of a shoreline also has significant effects. Near shore, tidal currents are produced by the flooding (incoming) and ebbing (outgoing) of the waters that correspond with the tides. Currents are most significant where there is some restriction to flow, causing the water to accelerate through a passageway or channel.

Imagine, for example, a large bay that communicates with the open sea through a restricted opening. Suppose that bay's waters are, on average, ten feet deeper at high tide than at low. Where does that water come from? The answer is obvious: water must flow in from the sea through that narrow opening, and must flow out again when the tide falls. The time of maximum flood current is somewhere between the times of low water and high water; the time of maximum ebb is somewhere between high water and the following low. We can't be more precise than that without extensive local historical data. Those measurements may tell

us that the greatest range between high and low water is at the very head of the bay, whereas the greatest ebb and flood velocities are at its mouth.

Thus, though tidal currents are caused by tides, the relationship of one to the other is a complex result of local and regional shoreline shape and bathymetry. You can't predict tidal currents from tidal heights; you need tidal current tables for such predictions. Tidal heights generally are computed for harbors, whereas tidal currents are computed for the more constricted areas where current is a dominant factor.

Spring and Neap Tides

Due to the relative motions of the moon and sun, tidal ranges vary by day, month, and year. The Earth's changing distances from these two bodies is one cause of variation, but more important to the height of a particular tide is whether the sun and moon are working together or at cross-purposes (Figure 14-2). Once every $29\frac{1}{2}$ days, the moon's orbit places it between the sun and the Earth. We call this the *new moon*, because the moon's dark side (unlighted by the sun) is entirely toward Earth at this time. Because the sun and moon are aligned at the new moon, their gravitational effects are additive; the resultant larger-than-normal tide ranges are called *spring tides*. (The high tides are higher and the low tides are lower during spring tides.)

Halfway between new moons is the *full moon*, when the moon is on the side of the Earth opposite the sun and thus is fully illuminated. This, too, produces a spring tide. Halfway between new moons and full moons come the first and third *quarters*, at which times the sun and moon pull at right angles to each other. Under these conditions their effects partially cancel; the result is the smaller tidal ranges we call *neap tides*, during which the high tides are not as high nor the low tides as low.

Tidal Patterns

Tides vary in a cycle from high to low, then back again. Because the sun and moon raise two high-tide bulges on opposite sides of the Earth, one might reasonably expect a regular pattern of two high tides daily in coastal areas. Most areas do see two tides, called *semidiurnal* (diurnal means daily; semidiurnal means twice daily). However, the two successive highs and lows are generally not of equal height. If the Earth were a perfect sphere and there were no continents, the tidal pattern would be regular, but the continents block the westward passage of the tidal bulges and cause complex effects in each ocean basin and along each coastline.

For example, in the far northern reaches of the Gulf of Mexico, away from the Atlantic Ocean, the incoming and outgoing tides somewhat counteract each other. The net result is only one high and one low tide each day; the other high and low cancel each other out. These are called *diurnal tides*. Other places on the Earth are north or south of one of the semidiurnal tidal bulges; these places, too, experience only diurnal tides.

In yet other areas, the net effect is two daily tides that are so significantly different from each other as to be called *mixed tides*. Mixed tides are found all along the Pacific coast of North America and parts of the Caribbean, whereas diurnal tides are found in the Gulf of Mexico and along part of the coast of Alaska. The Atlantic coast of North America, most of Europe (except for south-facing coasts on the Mediterranean Sea), and Africa experience semidiurnal tides; South America experiences both semidiurnal and mixed tides. Figure 14-3, from NOAA, shows tide patterns around the globe.

Tidal Ranges and Vertical Datums

The range of a tide is the difference between a high tide and the following or preceding low. Tidal ranges vary by place and over time. A typical tidal range on the south side of Cape Cod is 1.5–3 feet (0.5–1 meter), whereas for the same day in Bar Harbor, Maine, it might be 11 feet (3.3 meters), as shown in Figure 14-4A.

At a given location, such as Boston Harbor (see Figure 14-4B), the tidal range varies with the phase of the moon, as discussed above. In this sample of about fifteen days, you can see a minimum range of about 5.5 feet (1.7 meters) during the first quarter of the moon, versus 12 feet (3.7 meters) at the same location during the full moon only seven days later. This tidal graph depicts April; if you were to look over the entire year, you would find a seasonal effect as well. This highlights the need to know the tides at your location for the day and time of interest. This chapter shows you how to get that information.

Complexities such as these point to the need for reference standards and a common terminology for tides. As described in Chapter 4, charts reference soundings as well as heights of bridges and landmarks to one of several vertical datums, such as mean low water (MLW) or mean lower low water (MLLW). A *mean* is simply the middle value for a collection of readings, usually developed over a complete as-

---

STANDARD TIDAL RANGES AND WATER LEVELS

MEAN LOW WATER (MLW)

Mean low water is simply the average of all the low-tide levels over the analysis period at a particular location. It generally is expressed in feet and tenths. Because it is a mean, you can expect that 50 percent of the time the actual low tide height will be lower than this value.

MEAN LOWER LOW WATER (MLLW)

Mean lower low water is the average of the lower of the two low tides each day. NOAA and its National Ocean Service (NOS) use MLLW as the vertical datum for soundings on most of its charts.

MEAN LOWER LOW WATER SPRINGS (MLLWS)

Because the tidal range is greater during full and new moons, only those lower low tide heights are averaged to obtain mean lower low tide springs.

HIGH WATER (MHW) (MHHW) (MHHWS)

The high-tide equivalents for each of the low-water definitions are MHW, MHHW, and MHHWS. NOAA and NOS use mean high water as the vertical datum for heights of bridges, landmarks, and landmasses on most charts.

MEAN TIDE LEVEL

Mean tide level is the mean depth of the water throughout all tides for all periods over the reporting cycle at a particular location.

MEAN RANGE

Mean range is the local difference between the mean of the highs and the mean of the lows, in feet.

MEAN RANGE SPRINGS

Mean range springs is the local average tide range during full- and new-moon spring tides. It does not represent the most extreme tidal range one could experience locally, because it is based on means, not extremes.

tronomical cycle of 19 years. Each of these mean levels is summarized below and shown in Figure 14-10.

Tide Height and Tidal Current Information

NOS has established a number of primary reference stations for which daily predictions of tides or tidal currents are available. Generally, tide stations are located in harbors or at points along coastlines, whereas tidal current stations are located at points of constricted flow where currents are significant.

A much larger set of subordinate stations has been compiled, the tides or tidal current predictions for which are referenced to a nearby reference station by a time difference and a ratio. All this has been mathematically modeled. NOAA's National Ocean Service (NOS) is one of the dominant providers of this information. These mathematical prediction models have also been made available to the public and have been incorporated by commercial vendors into software and hardware devices.

ELECTRONIC SOURCES Many handheld GPS models, and most chartplotters and navigation software using digital charts, can display tidal data derived from NOS predictive models.

On a handheld GPS, you can access a listing or graph of the tides, usually located via the menu for "celestial" or "other." Many GPS receivers recognize your location and

bring up the nearest tide station. On others, you need to use a drop-down menu and select the station yourself. A Garmin handheld GPS shows a tide graph; see Figure 14-5.

If a graph is displayed on your GPS, it will show the date and time on one axis and the height of the tide on the other. A bar will indicate the current time. You can scroll to a future date and time to look at the tides at that time. Many GPS models also allow you to access the nearest current station, where you can see a similar graph of speed and direction correlated with date and time.

Many digital charts display symbols for tide and current stations. By scrolling the cursor over one of these symbols, you can get the present conditions and access the complete graph. On Maptech digital charts, a current or tide symbol indicates the stage of the tide or current with arrows, as shown in Figure 14-6.

In addition, numerous computer programs display tidal heights and currents using essentially the same computations. One, which is distributed as freeware, is called WX-Tide32; it can be found at www.wxtide32.com and operates on Windows-based systems. Another program, called Tideware and offered by Eldridge, provides detailed tide information and interesting graphics. Users of Palm handheld PDAs can download a free program called Tide Tool, which provides tide graphs.

PRINT AND ONLINE SOURCES If you do not have access to a digital chart or a computer, you can purchase printed tide tables. These tables were formerly published by NOAA but are now printed by International Marine (see Figures 14-7A, B, C, D) and other vendors from data com-

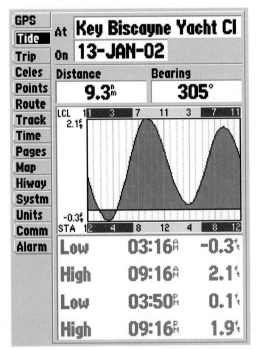

FIGURE 14-5. *Most marine GPS receivers include software to compute tides. Shown here is a Garmin display showing the tidal pattern for a specific location. The current predicted tide for 11 a.m. EDT is about 1.5 ft at the station 9.3 nm and 305° from your current position.*

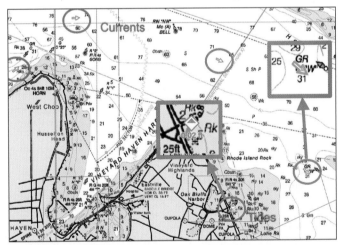

FIGURE 14-6. *Digital charts such as those used in chartplotters and computer-based navigation generally provide symbols for tides and currents. This example from Coastal Explorer shows a tide station and several current vectors. The tide is rising at a present level of 0.2 feet and the current is running to the right (ebb). By clicking on any of these symbols, you will be able to display the complete tide or current plot (see Figures 14-12 and 14-14).*

Boston, Massachusetts, 2004

Times and Heights of High and Low Waters

	April						May						June				
	Time	Height		Time	Height		Time	Height		Time	Height		Time	Height		Time	Height

April

	Time	Height (ft)	Height (cm)		Time	Height (ft)	Height (cm)
1 Th	0135 0751 1413 2029	1.9 9.3 1.0 8.7	58 283 30 265	16 F	0232 0851 1504 2122	0.7 10.0 0.3 9.9	21 305 9 302
2 F	0227 0842 1459 2114	1.3 9.7 0.6 9.3	40 296 18 283	17 Sa	0326 0943 1550 2206	0.3 10.1 0.3 10.2	9 308 9 311
3 Sa	0316 0929 1543 2156	0.7 10.1 0.1 9.9	21 308 3 302	18 Su	0413 1029 1631 2245	0.0 10.1 0.3 10.4	0 308 9 317
4 Su	0402 1015 1626 2237	0.0 10.5 -0.3 10.5	0 320 -9 320	19 M	0456 1111 1710 2322	-0.1 10.0 0.5 10.4	-3 305 15 317

May

	Time	Height (ft)	Height (cm)		Time	Height (ft)	Height (cm)
1 Sa	0151 0802 1417 2030	1.1 9.7 0.6 9.9	34 296 18 302	16 Su	0306 0921 1520 2136	0.5 9.5 0.9 10.2	15 290 27 311
2 Su	0243 0854 1504 2116	0.4 10.0 0.2 10.6	12 305 6 323	17 M	0352 1007 1601 2216	0.3 9.4 1.0 10.3	9 287 30 314
3 M	0333 0943 1551 2201	-0.3 10.4 -0.1 11.2	-9 317 -3 341	18 Tu	0434 1049 1641 2253	0.2 9.4 1.2 10.3	6 287 37 314
4 Tu	0422 1033 1637 2247	-1.0 10.6 -0.3 11.7	-30 323 -9 357	19 W	0514 1129 1719 2330	0.1 9.2 1.3 10.3	3 280 40 314

June

	Time	Height (ft)	Height (cm)		Time	Height (ft)	Height (cm)
1 Tu	0305 0915 1519 2129	-0.6 10.1 0.1 11.6	-18 308 3 354	16 W	0411 1025 1612 2226	0.5 8.8 1.6 10.1	15 268 49 308
2 W	0357 1009 1610 2220	-1.1 10.2 -0.1 12.0	-34 311 -3 366	17 Th	0451 1107 1652 2305	0.4 8.8 1.6 10.1	12 268 49 308
3 Th	0450 1102 1701 2312	-1.5 10.4 -0.2 12.2	-46 317 -6 372	18 F	0531 1146 1733 2344	0.4 8.8 1.7 10.1	12 268 52 308
4 F	0543 1157 1754	-1.7 10.4 -0.1	-52 317 -3	19 Sa	0610 1226 1813	0.4 8.8 1.7	12 268 52

Date
New Moon   Time of Tide   Height of Tide

FIGURE 14-7A. *NOAA's National Ocean Service (NOS) provides annual predictions of tides and currents for most of the world. These can be purchased in book form from International Marine and other publishers. The tables include details for a series of reference stations on a day-to-day basis; a second table provides factors to adjust reference station values to local secondary stations.*

This graphic shows a portion of a reference station tide table for Boston. This table provides the time of each high and low tide for each day of the year, and the height of each tide relative to the vertical datum (usually mean lower low water). A minus value for the low tide indicates that the water level is below the datum by that amount.

TABLE 2 – TIDAL DIFFERENCES AND OTHER CONSTANTS

No.	PLACE	POSITION Latitude	POSITION Longitude	DIFFERENCES Time High Water	Time Low Water	Height High Water	Height Low Water	RANGES Mean	Spring	Mean Tide Level
		North	West	h m	h m	ft	ft	ft	ft	ft
	MASSACHUSETTS, outer coast Time meridian, 75° W					on Portland, p.36				
805	Newburyport, Merrimack River	42° 48.7'	70° 51.9'	+0 31	+1 11	*0.86	*0.86	7.8	9.0	4.2
807	Plum Island Sound (south end)	42° 42.6'	70° 47.3'	+0 12	+0 37	*0.94	*0.94	8.6	9.9	4.6
809	Annisquam	42° 39.3'	70° 40.6'	0 00	-0 07	*0.96	*0.96	8.7	10.1	4.7
						on Boston, p.40				
811	Gloucester Harbor	42° 36.2'	70° 39.9'	-0 01	-0 04	*0.91	*0.91	8.7	10.1	4.6
813	Salem Broad Sound	42° 31.4'	70° 52.5'	+0 04	+0 03	*0.92	*0.92	8.8	10.2	4.7
	Boston Harbor									
815	Boston Light	42° 19.7'	70° 53.5'	+0 02	+0 03	*0.94	*0.94	9.0	10.4	4.8
817	Deer Island (south end)	42° 20.7'	70° 57.5'	+0 01	0 00	*0.97	*0.97	9.3	10.8	4.9
819	BOSTON	42° 21.3'	71° 03.1'	Daily predictions				9.5	10.3	5.1
821	Charlestown, Charles River entrance	42° 22.5'	71° 03.0'	0 00	+0 01	*1.00	*1.00	9.5	11.0	5.0
823	Amelia Earhart Dam, Mystic River	42° 23.7'	71° 04.6'	+0 01	+0 01	*1.01	*1.00	9.6	11.1	5.2
825	Chelsea St. Bridge, Chelsea River	42° 23.2'	71° 01.4'	+0 01	+0 06	*1.01	*1.00	9.6	11.1	5.1
827	Neponset, Neponset River	42° 17.1'	71° 02.4'	-0 02	+0 03	*1.00	*1.00	9.5	11.0	5.0
829	Moon Head	42° 18.3'	70° 59.3'	-0 01	+0 04	*0.99	*0.99	9.4	10.9	5.0
831	Rainsford Island, Nantasket Roads	42° 19'	70° 57'	0 00	+0 02	*0.95	*0.95	9.1	10.6	4.8

Station No.   Location   Time Differences High & Low   Height Ratios High & Low   Ranges   Mean

FIGURE 14-7B. *To simplify the tables, all subordinate tide stations are shown in Table 2. Each station is related to a reference station. Times of high and low water at subordinate stations are listed in the table as hours and minutes before or after the corresponding times at the reference station. The heights of subordinate station high and low tides are usually given as a multiplier (ratio) to apply to the corresponding reference station height.*

Tides, Winds, and Currents

162

Boston Harbor (Deer Island Light), Massachusetts, 2004

F—Flood, Dir. 254° True   E—Ebb, Dir. 111° True

April

Day	Slack (h m)	Maximum (h m)	knots		Day	Slack (h m)	Maximum (h m)	knots
1 Th	0146	0504	1.0F		**16 F**	0228	0005	1.3E
	0729	1158	1.2E			0810	0547	1.0F
	1414	1734	1.1F			1454	1229	1.4E
	2005					2048	1815	1.2F
2 F	0236	0023	1.1E		**17 Sa**	0321	0056	1.4E
	0820	0552	1.1F			0908	0639	1.1F
	1500	1240	1.2E			1542	1318	1.4E
	2053	1818	1.3F			2140	1903	1.3F
3 Sa	0323	0103	1.2E		**18 Su**	0410	0144	1.5E
	0909	0636	1.3F			0959	0726	1.2F
	1544	1315	1.3E			1628	1405	1.4E
	2137	1858	1.4F			2224	1948	1.3F

May

Day	Slack (h m)	Maximum (h m)	knots		Day	Slack (h m)	Maximum (h m)	knots
1 Sa	0159	0503	1.2F		**16 Su**	0302	0034	1.4E
	0742	1148	1.2E			0854	0617	1.1F
	1421	1729	1.3F			1519	1257	1.3E
	2013					2119	1839	1.2F
2 Su	0249	0015	1.3E		**17 M**	0350	0122	1.4E
	0834	0550	1.3F			0943	0704	1.2F
	1509	1222	1.3E			1602	1344	1.3E
	2101	1810	1.4F			2201	1923	1.2F
3 M	0338	0048	1.4E		**18 Tu**	0434	0208	1.5E
	0923	0634	1.4F			1026	0749	1.2F
	1555	1254	1.3E			1645	1429	1.3E
	2148	1848	1.5F			2240	2006	1.2F

June

Day	Slack (h m)	Maximum (h m)	knots		Day	Slack (h m)	Maximum (h m)	knots
1 Tu	0307	0548	1.4F		**16 W**	0410	0145	1.4E
	0851	1215	1.3E			1006	0724	1.1F
	1522	1803	1.5F			1619	1408	1.2E
	2115					2212	1940	1.1F
2 W	0358	0048	1.5E		**17 Th**	0451	0230	1.3E
	0943	0639	1.4F			1043	0808	1.1F
	1612	1305	1.3E			1700	1452	1.1E
	2205	1852	1.5F			2250	2021	1.1F
3 Th	0449	0137	1.5E		**18 F**	0532	0313	1.3E
	1034	0730	1.4F			1121	0849	1.1F
	1703	1358	1.3E			1742	1535	1.1E
	2254	1941	1.5F			2328	2100	1.1F

Annotations: Date · New Moon · Time of Slack · Time of Max · Speed at Max (E or F)

FIGURE 14-7C. *There are also predictive tables for tidal currents. This reference table for Boston Harbor provides the times and speeds of maximum flood and ebb in addition to the times of slack water.*

No.	PLACE	Meter Depth (ft)	Latitude (North)	Longitude (West)	Min. before Flood (h m)	Flood (h m)	Min. before Ebb (h m)	Ebb (h m)	Flood (ratio)	Ebb (ratio)	Min. before Flood (knots)	Min. before Flood Dir.	Max. Flood (knots)	Max. Flood Dir.	Min. before Ebb (knots)	Min. before Ebb Dir.	Max. Ebb (knots)	Max. Ebb Dir.
	MASSACHUSETTS COAST Time meridian, 75° W				on Portsmouth Harbor Entrance, p.12													
956	Gunboat Shoal		43° 01'	70° 42'	+0 05	+0 05	+0 05	+0 05	0.4	0.3	0.0	--	0.5	340°	0.0	--	0.5	160°
961	Isles of Shoals Light, White Island		42° 58'	70° 37'	0 00	0 00	0 00	0 00	0.2	0.2	0.0	--	0.3	020°	0.0	--	0.3	200°
	Reference Station				on Boston Harbor, p.16													
966	Merrimack River entrance		42° 49.1'	70° 48.6'	+1 04	+1 15	+1 13	-0 34	2.0	1.2	0.0	--	2.2	285°	0.0	--	1.4	105°
971	Newburyport, Merrimack River		42° 48.8'	70° 52.1'	+1 28	+1 48	+1 47	+0 35	1.4	1.2	0.0	--	1.5	288°	0.0	--	1.5	098°
976	Plum Island Sound entrance		42° 42.3'	70° 47.3'	+0 36	+0 50	+0 48	-0 07	1.5	1.2	0.0	--	1.6	316°	0.0	--	1.3	013°
981	Annisquam Harbor Light		42° 40.1'	70° 41.1'	+0 42	+0 49	+0 58	+0 03	0.9	1.1	0.0	--	1.0	200°	0.0	--	0.3	195°
986	Gloucester Harbor entrance		42° 34.9'	70° 40.5'	-0 28	+0 01	-0 29	-0 36	0.3	0.2	0.0	--	0.3	340°	0.0	--	0.3	195°
991	Blynman Canal ent., Gloucester Harbor										0.0	--			0.0	--		
996	Marblehead Channel		42° 30'	70° 49'	+1 09	+1 09	+1 09	+1 09	0.4	0.3	0.0	--	0.4	285°	0.0	--	0.4	105°

Annotations: Station No. · Location · Time Differences Slacks, Flood & Ebb · Speed Ratios Flood & Ebb · Ave. Speeds & Directions

FIGURE 14-7D. *As in the tide tables, Table 2 of the current tables provides time and velocity differences for subordinate stations relative to a reference station. In this example, the time differences are in hours and minutes. The speed differences are provided as a ratio of the subordinate station speed to that at the reference station. The directions of maximum flood and maximum ebb are provided as well.*

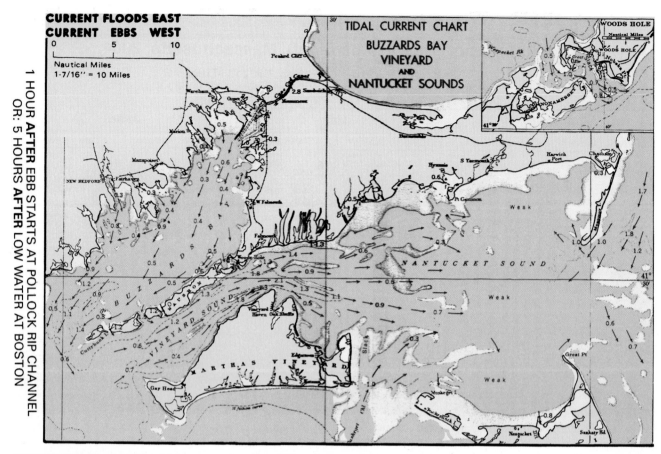

FIGURE 14-8. *Commercial publishers compile regional tide and current tables tailored to the needs of mariners in that region. Typically, these are not as complex or as detailed as the NOS tables. Often, they provide graphic representations of the current patterns in chart form, as here. Usually, these charts are provided for hourly increments based on the time of high tide at a reference station. You can determine the approximate local current by noting your position and computing the number of hours since high tide at the reference station. (Source: Eldridge Tide and Pilot Book)*

FIGURE 14-9. *Many government small-craft charts show printed vectors of maximum flood and ebb currents at various locations. In this example, near Martha's Vineyard, the maximum speeds and directions are shown. You need to consult other sources to determine the time of maximum flood or ebb, but the printed information alerts you to a potentially significant effect if you are crossing these waters.*

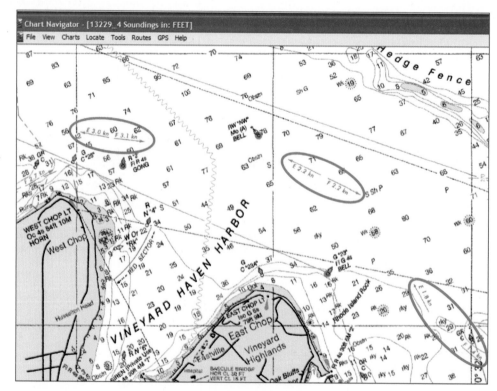

piled by NOAA. These NOS tables cover extensive regions; you need one book for tides and another for currents. Other companies publish abridged or extracted tables for local areas. Typically, these are based on local NOS primary reference stations with corrections for subordinate locations. These tables also provide a listing of currents for respective reference stations. Often, a set of simplified current chart diagrams is shown for various times relative to high tide at a primary tide station, with labeled arrows indicting the current directions (set) and speeds (drift) at that stage of the cycle. Figure 14-8 shows a sample of one of these diagrams.

Eldridge Tide and Pilot Book, which covers the U.S. East Coast with special emphasis on the Northeast, is a good example of commercial coverage for a broader region. This single book provides tide and current tables, current maps, and other useful material. *Reed's Nautical Almanac* offers tide and current tables in addition to coastal pilot information and tutorials on navigation. In its various editions, Reed's covers the North American East and West coasts and the Caribbean.

Tide and current information also can be found on the Web. NOAA provides information on its website: http://co-ops.nos.noaa.gov.

TIDAL CURRENT ARROWS ON NAUTICAL CHARTS

Some paper charts indicate areas of strong current, usually with arrows indicating the directions of flood (incoming) and ebb (outgoing) currents. Usually, a numeric value is provided that indicates the mean of peak currents in each direction. These arrows are printed on many charts in the NOAA small-craft series.

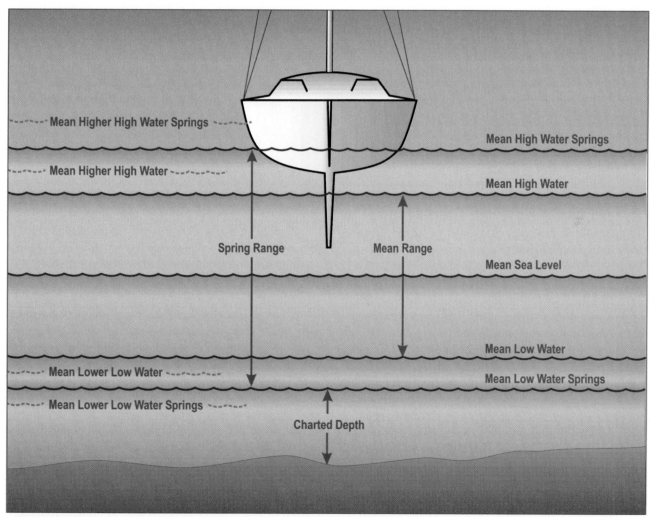

FIGURE 14-10. *Earlier we discussed horizontal chart datum (for example, WGS-84). Charts also employ vertical chart datums. Depth soundings are usually referenced to mean lower low water (MLLW), whereas heights, such as bridge clearances and heights of lights, are referenced to mean high water (MHW). Here is a graphic representation of various vertical levels. Typical NOS tide charts provide the mean tide level (mean of all tides over a nineteen-year cycle), the mean range (difference between MHW and MLW), and the spring range (difference between MHW and MLW for spring tides only).*

Adjusting for Tides and Tidal Currents

Tidal Heights

Your charts indicate soundings and depth contours based on a vertical datum that is printed in each chart's title block. Mean lower low water (MLLW) is frequently used as a datum. MLLW is not the lowest conceivable tide a given location might experience, but using a sounding based on MLLW will rarely get you into trouble. Only during spring tides, when the range is greater, might you find a low-tide height that registers as a negative value (called a *minus tide*) in the tide tables. This indicates that the actual low tide for that day is predicted to be below the tidal datum.

Note that some charts use mean low water (MLW) as a vertical datum. MLW is less conservative than MLLW; proceed accordingly.

Armed with your predicted tide level, you can add the amount indicated to the sounding—minus a foot or two as a margin of error—to determine if you will have enough water under your boat.

You need to recognize that the predictions, although reasonably accurate, are an approximation. Winds, swells, barometric pressure, and other factors can retard or accelerate the tide and even affect its high- and low-water levels in harbors and bays.

Recognize that charted soundings may have been taken years ago; NOAA has limited resources for depth soundings and must focus its efforts on major channels. As a recreational boater, you probably spend most of your time outside these channels. For you, little is available. Updates are provided using local resources; for example, U.S. Power Squadrons members contribute updates under their Cooperative Charting Program with NOAA.

Changes in bottom contours occur continuously in some places, due to silting, storms, tidal current erosion, et cetera. Local knowledge can be invaluable; you can get a great deal of insight from local fishermen and experienced boaters regarding bottom conditions.

A sample from a reference station (Figure 14-7A) shows the predicted times and heights of high and low tides for each day. Annual tide tables provide this information for each day through an entire year. The days of new and full moons also are shown. Unless you're boating near a reference station, you need to use Table 2, which includes a related set of subordinate stations, as shown in Figure 14-7B. Each subordinate station is associated with one reference station.

In Table 2, you identify the station of interest and are provided with a time difference (usually in hours and minutes) to add or subtract from the times of high and low tides at the identified reference station. You are also provided with a factor by which to multiply reference-station heights, to get the heights of high and low tides at the sub-ordinate station. Other information, such as mean tide and mean tidal ranges, is also available.

Using these two tables, you can predict the local height of tide for any time. This example shows how that is done:

1. It makes sense to look at Table 2 first (Figure 14-7B). Locate the tide station closest to your location of interest, then the identity of its associated reference station. Let's select Rainsford Island, Nantasket Roads. The reference station is Boston. Note that the coordinates of this tide station are provided.

2. Looking at the Boston reference station, let's select April 19. We expect to be sailing near Rainsford Island that day, so we'd like to know the times and heights of the high and low tides during the daytime there. Note that at 1111 hours, the height of the tide in Boston is 10.0 feet; at 1710 hours, the height of the tide is 0.5 feet.

3. Now, looking back at Table 2, you note that the time difference for high water is zero and the time difference for low water is +02 minutes (the plus sign means later). The height ratio for both is 0.95.

4. There is no difference in the time of high water, so it will occur at 1111 hours; however, its height is only 95 percent of that in Boston, so 10.0 feet x 0.95 = 9.5 feet at Rainsford Island. The time of low water is 1711 + 0002 = 1713 hours. Its height is 0.5 feet x 0.95, which is still about 0.5 feet.

This process is simple. In this example, the tidal range at Rainsford Island is not much different from that in Boston; however it's not uncommon to find time differences of one to two hours and height ratios of 20 percent. When the time difference is significant, you often need to convert the times of all high and low waters to the local subordinate station to know which one applies to you.

Well, that's interesting and useful, but the tidal range is still 9 feet. You would like to know what the height will be when you pass by. Let's assume you will do that at about 1 p.m. (1300 hours). By the way, all these tables are printed in standard time, so if you're boating in summer, you need to take daylight saving time into account.

A third table included with the tide tables enables you to predict the tide at some intermediate time; here, however, we use a much simpler method called the Rule of Twelfths, which provides similar accuracy for fewer time intervals. This simpler approach is more than adequate for most recreational boaters.

THE RULE OF TWELFTHS The Rule of Twelfths says that the tide level changes in increments of twelfths of its total range in each of six equal time periods. This is depicted in Figure 14-11A. Let's take for an example going from a high tide to a low tide. In the first time period, the tide drops by one-twelfth of its range. During the second time period, it drops by an additional two-twelfths. This is followed by in-

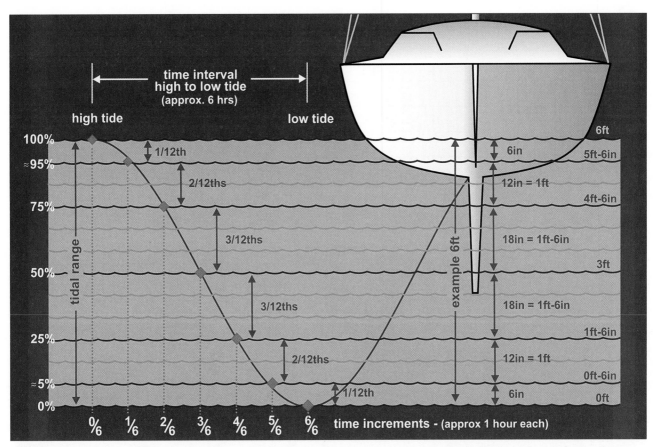

FIGURE 14-11A. *When GPS or computer tidal predictions are not available, you can estimate the height of the tide for any time using the Rule of Twelfths. Divide the present tidal range into twelfths and the time of rise and fall into sixths. Each sixth is about one hour. Noting the time of the most recent high or low, adjust the height of the tide by 1/12th for the first time increment, 2/12ths for the second, 3/12ths for the third, et cetera, as shown in the graphic. As you can see, the tide rises or falls fastest during the middle phase of each cycle. In this phase, the height of the tide will change fastest, and the tidal current is likely to be strongest. Tidal ranges vary from day to day, so a local tide table will help. If not available, take the nominal tidal range and estimate whether you are closer to the spring or neap tide. The difference in tidal range from spring to neap is about 20 percent. The whole idea of using the Rule of Twelfths is to get you somewhere close to the actual tide. Remember, it is an estimate, so you should always add a comfortable safety margin. Note also that this example uses the eastern seaboard, where there is roughly a six-hour interval between high and low tides in coastal areas, which means two high tides and two low tides each day. In these areas the heights of rise and fall are about equal. In the Gulf of Mexico there is only a single high and single low tide each day. The West Coast and the Caribbean tend to have highs and lows of different heights. Make sure you adjust the time interval to one-sixth of the total rise or fall time.*

crements of three-twelfths, three twelfths, two-twelfths, and finally one-twelfth.

Let's look at a typical tide cycle. In most areas, there are two complete tide cycles per day—the semidiurnal pattern. These two cycles nominally take twenty-four hours and fifty minutes to complete (the 24 hours of the Earth's daily rotation plus 50 minutes for a given spot on Earth to once again overtake the moon's orbit). This means that each half cycle (high to low, or low to high) takes about six hours and twelve and a half minutes. For most areas meeting this semidiurnal pattern, you can break this into six equal periods of approximately one hour (actually 1 hour and 4 minutes). This is easy to remember.

Now, armed with periods of about one hour, you can look at how the height actually changes. Take, for example, a 6-foot tide range (180 cm). Dividing that into twelfths, $^1/_{12}$ is 6 inches (15 cm). So, every hour the tide drops or rises by some multiple of 6 inches.

In this example, assume high tide was about 6 feet and low tide (nominally at MLLW—the sounding level) was 0 feet. Remember, at MLLW (0 foot tide) the water depth is what is shown as the sounding on your chart for that location. You can construct the table shown in Figure 14-11B. If you were continuing from low to high, you would do the same thing in reverse. Using this technique, you can develop a mental feel for what the tide level will be at any location at any given time. Clearly, you would expect that three hours after high tide you would be at half tide (half the tidal range); this table gives you a couple of other easy reference points. After two hours (2 hours and 8 minutes), the tide has dropped by only 25 percent, whereas after four hours (4 hours and 16 minutes) it has dropped by 75 percent.

Let's return to our example using Rainsford Island. We already know the times and heights of the local high and low water bracketing the time of interest, which is

HOURS AFTER HIGH TIDE	NUMBER OF TWELFTHS	CHANGE IN HEIGHT	HEIGHT OF TIDE	% RANGE
High Tide	0	0	6 ft (180 cm)	100
1	1	6 in (15 cm)	5 ft 6 in (165 cm)	~90
2	2	1 ft (30 cm)	4 ft 6 in (135 cm)	75
3	3	1 ft 6 in (45 cm)	3 ft (90 cm)	50
4	3	1 ft 6 in (45 cm)	1 ft 6 in (45 cm)	25
5	2	1 ft (30 cm)	0 ft 6 in (15 cm)	~10
6 (Low Tide)	1	6 in (15 cm)	0 ft	0

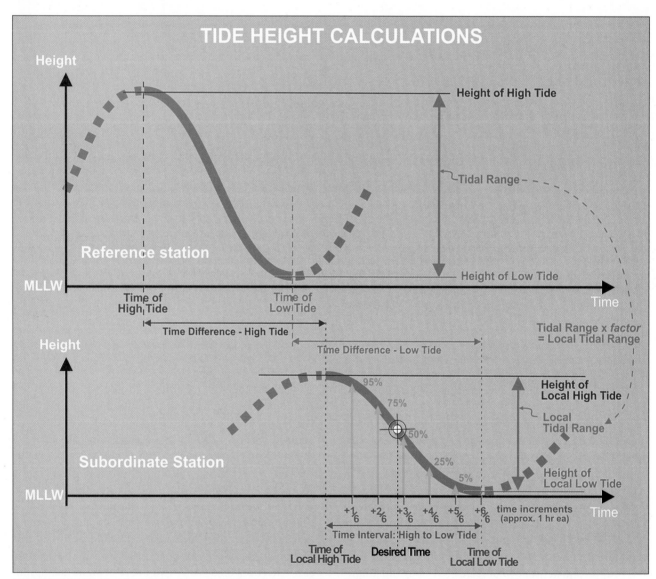

FIGURE 14-11B. *The tide tables shown in Figure 14-7 provide the tide heights and times for reference stations and the relative height and time differences for a much larger number of subordinate stations. Here we see graphically how calculations are performed using the Rule of Twelfths to predict the height of the tide for a specific time of interest (shown by the bull's-eye). In the example shown, you are going from a high to a low tide. Determine the number of hours from the time of high tide to the time of interest (round to the nearest half hour) and apply the Rule of Twelfths. After the first one-sixth time interval (nominally an hour), the tide will have dropped to 95 percent of its range toward low tide; after two intervals (nominally two hours), it will have dropped to 75 percent of its range; after three intervals to 50 percent, and so on, as shown.*

1300 hours standard time. The tide just before was 9.5 feet (290 cm) at 1111 hours. The height of low water was 0.5 feet (15 cm). Therefore, the range is 9 feet (275 cm). For simplicity, we assume the cycle from high to low takes six hours exactly. (Actually, the time difference is 1111 to 1713; that's 6 hours and 2 minutes. Close enough.)

1. You are interested in the height of tide at 1300 hours. That's about two hours after high tide.

2. After two hours, at 1311, the tide will have dropped to 75 percent of the range, or about 6.8 feet (210 cm). That's close enough to use as your answer.

If you are in an area where the tides are diurnal (one cycle per day), the time intervals using the Rule of Twelfths become a little more than two hours each, but the principle is about the same. In the Gulf of Mexico, the diurnal tidal ranges are usually less than a few feet, so the errors should be quite small.

Understand that the Rule of Twelfths is an estimate. You need to leave a reasonable margin to account for the rounding in these estimates, as well as for other influences on the actual tides. For example, wind and weather conditions can significantly alter tide timing and heights from the predicted levels.

There are areas where the tidal flow causes an irregular pattern, with the potential of the time interval from high to low tide, or low to high being substantially greater or less than six hours. In this case your approximation must be based on time intervals of one-sixth of that actual total interval. For example, if the time from high to low is six hours, fifty-four minutes, you will need to use equal intervals of one hour, nine minutes instead of the rounded one hour. If you don't account for those extra minutes, the error will build with each successive increment and can lead to a false assumption of water depth.

USING GPS OR A COMPUTER FOR TIDE LEVEL You can use your GPS or computer to see predicted heights of tide. Not all GPS models offer this feature, but special models designed for the marine market usually contain both tidal data and the locations of buoys. If you have one of these units, you can go to the Celestial function, which provides sunrise and -set, moon phase and moonrise and -set, and tides. Because the GPS knows your present coordinates, it uses the nearest tide station programmed into the unit. Usually, the GPS presents a graph much like that in Figure 14-12. The present time is shown by a vertical line or marker. Where the tidal graph lines up with the time, read across to find the predicted height at this station.

Most newer chartplotters provide this feature, because they are designed solely for marine use. If your GPS or chartplotter does not have this capability, you can find programs that will work on your computer or even your PDA to provide the same information.

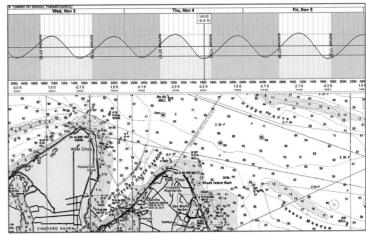

FIGURE 14-12. *Computers and chartplotters usually identify tide stations. By clicking on the station, you can get a graph of the tide pattern. You can change the date or time to look ahead for what the tide height will be for that location at a particular time.*

Many chartplotters and much navigation software place icons on the charts corresponding to tide and tidal current stations. By scrolling over one of these stations, you are presented with the corresponding tide or current graph.

Often you will want to look ahead and anticipate the height of a tide at some future time. Using the GPS celestial modes, tide prediction software, or navigation software, you can scroll to a future date or time, or enter the date, and observe the predicted tide pattern. Usually, these programs plot tide cycles to make it easy to spot the level at any time on any date. Recognize that the same caveats relative to predictions from printed tables apply to electronic predictions as well; the source data are the same, and local environmental conditions can have a significant impact.

Clearance over Your Boat

When noted on your chart, the heights of landmarks and other land features above the water are usually referenced to mean high water (MHW) (see Chapter 5). Usually, bridge clearances also employ that reference. If you have any doubt whether your boat will fit under a bridge, you need to know the boat's vertical clearance, then add a few feet for error. You have probably added antennas, outrigger poles, or other objects to your mast top or superstructure that cause your actual vertical clearance to exceed your manufacturer's specified clearance. Many such appurtenances can be lowered, but fixed items such as a radar antenna or a mast top VHF antenna should be factored in.

Remember that MHW is an average of all high tides over an extended period, and a particular high tide can be higher, thus providing less clearance. Thus, a high-tide transit may require a little more homework. You can find the local height of MHW by looking up mean tide level in the local tide listings and adding one-half of the local mean tidal range. Many paper charts also contain an abbreviated table of tidal data, including MHW, for key locations. Either way, you get MHW in feet above the local datum for soundings, which is usually MLLW. Is the high tide that's of interest to you higher than MHW? If it is, subtract the difference from your expected clearance beneath that bridge you're hoping to pass under.

Predicting Tidal Currents

Tidal currents are driven by the tides and thereby have similar cycles, but the timing of peak currents is offset from their corresponding high and low tides, and their relationships are complex. Incoming currents are called *flood* and outgoing currents are called *ebb*. Each flood and ebb are separated by an interval of zero flow, called *slack water*. This interval is usually brief.

Because tidal currents are most significant where tides fill and depart from bays and rivers, these are the places where reference stations are found. Currents can have a profound effect on your course over ground, especially when crossing a large bay or passage. You may be headed in the proper direction, but your actual track will be diverted, as shown in Figure 14-13A. You need to adjust your heading "upcurrent" to counteract this effect, as described under "Staying on Course" in Chapter 8. Knowing in advance what the current will be makes that task easier and more intuitive.

Currents in narrow channels and rivers tend to flow along the axis of travel, either assisting or retarding a boat's progress, as shown in Figures 14-13B and C. In extreme cases, sailboats under sail or power may not be able to make any forward progress. Usually, special tables are available for such locations (the Cape Cod Canal, for example, where

current tables are prepared by the U.S. Army Corps of Engineers and also are available online). Some areas are bedeviled by *tide rips*—notorious systems of standing waves that look like river rapids—at peak ebb or flood. Certainly, you will want to plan your passage through such waters for a slack or favorable current.

As with tide tables, tidal current tables provide daily predictions for reference stations and offsets for subordinate stations. The format of a current table is a bit different from that of a tide table. For the reference stations, currents are expressed as maximum flood (incoming) and maximum ebb (outgoing). The maximum flood is nominally in the opposite direction from the maximum ebb, so there are two speeds in two different directions to contend with. Between the maximums, the times of slack are predicted (see Figure 14-7C). The subordinate station tables provide the time differences for each slack and each maximum (see Figure 14-7D). The speed ratios for flood and ebb currents are provided as well. In addition, the directions of the flood and ebb currents are provided.

Using a third table, you can interpolate the predicted current for any intermediate time. In this book, however,

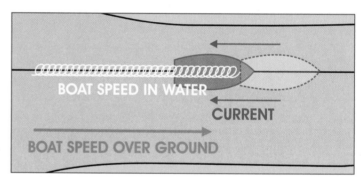

FIGURE 14-13B. In a channel, you are likely to experience currents that flow with or against you. In this case, the current is against you. Your boat speed is the same as in (A), but the current is attempting to push you backward. In this case, your forward motion from your engines exceeds the speed of the current, so you are making forward progress over the ground, albeit more slowly (green arrow).

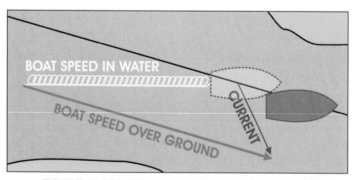

FIGURE 14-13A. When you encounter a crossing current your boat will be pushed from its intended course. To see how this happens, draw a vector along your heading, of a length proportional to your speed, and label it "Boat Speed In Water" as shown. From the end of this vector draw another in the direction of current set, with its length proportional to current speed. Now draw the vector from the point of origin of your boat speed vector to the end point of the current vector. The direction of this vector is your course over ground (unless you change your heading to counter the effects of current), and its length is proportional to your speed over ground. See also Figure 14-16A.

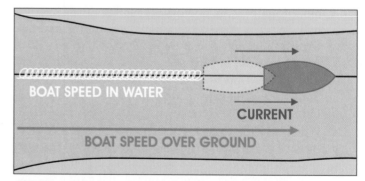

FIGURE 14-13C. Now the current has turned so that it is going with you. In this case, the speed of the current adds to your boat speed to result in a greater speed over ground (green arrow).

we use a simpler technique called the 50-90 Rule, which is just as accurate but provides fewer times.

Tidal current curves are not as regular as tide curves, for several reasons. Usually, the bodies of water on either side of a tidal current station are of irregular shape and uneven in size. This leads to different flows from flood to ebb. The speeds may be different, and their directions often are not directly opposing. As a result, tidal current curves may take on a somewhat irregular shape, so we break the total ebb/flood cycle into four parts and treat each one individually. Each phase begins and ends with a slack water or a maximum current, as follows:

slack to maximum flood

maximum flood to slack

slack to maximum ebb

maximum ebb to slack

Calculations for intermediate current strengths are done separately for each of these four increments. Otherwise, the method is similar to that used for tides.

USING THE 50-90 RULE   Because the four phases are not of equal duration, you cannot calculate intermediate current velocities in one-hour increments using the 50-90 Rule. Instead, you need to determine the actual duration of each phase from the current tables. That time interval (for example, the time between slack and maximum flood) is then divided into equal thirds, and the 50-90 Rule is applied to those thirds. For example, in going from slack to maximum flood, the current increases from zero at slack to 50 percent of maximum after the first third, then to 90 percent after the second, and finally to 100 percent.

Now let's try an example with numbers. Say the maximum flood is 2.2 knots and the time from slack to maximum is 2 hours 30 minutes or 150 minutes. This means that the time increments are 50 minutes each. The next segment from maximum flood to slack is 2 hours 0 minutes, or 120 minutes. This means that the time increments are 40 minutes each. Continuing, the maximum ebb is 1.8 knots, and the elapsed time from slack to maximum ebb is 3 hours 30 minutes, or 210 minutes. This means the time increments are 70 minutes each. Finally, the segment from maximum ebb to slack is 4 hours, or 240 minutes. This means that the time increments are 80 minutes for this segment. You can construct the table as below (+ is flood; – is ebb).

Sometimes you may not have all the data from the NOS tide tables. For example, *Eldridge Tide and Pilot Book* provides times of slack and maximum speeds but not times of maximum ebb and flood. If that is the case, you can apply the 50-90 Rule to the entire period from slack to slack. Divide that cycle into six equal time increments and apply the

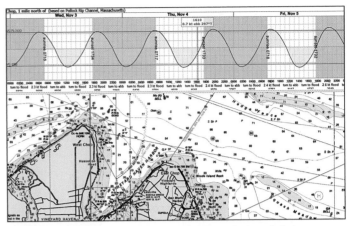

FIGURE 14-14. *Tidal current stations are identified on digital charts as well. By clicking on a station, you can get a graph of the present tidal current strength and direction, or you can look ahead to another date and time to anticipate what the current will be.*

TIME	SPEED RATIO	SPEED
1st Interval		
Slack (00:00)	0%	0 kn
00:50	50%	+ 1.1 kn
01:40	90%	+ 2.0 kn
Max Flood (02:30)	100%	+ 2.2 kn
2nd Interval		
Max Flood (02:30)	100%	+ 2.2 kn
03:10	90%	+2.0 kn
03:50	50%	+1.1 kn
Slack (04:30)	0%	0 kn
3rd Interval		
Slack (04:30)	0%	0 kn
05:40	50%	– 0.9 kn
06:50	90%	– 1.6 kn
Max Ebb (08:00)	100%	– 1.8 kn
4th Interval		
Max Ebb (08:00)	100%	– 1.8 kn
09:20	90%	– 1.6 kn
10:40	50%	– 0.9 kn
Slack (12:00)	0%	0 kn

rule as 0 percent, 50 percent, 90 percent, 100 percent, 90 percent, 50 percent, and 0 percent of the maximum speeds. This assumes that the maximum ebb and flood occur midway between their respective slack waters, which may not be the case in reality. This can lead to some error but should be accurate enough to work with.

Let's try another example using actual current tables.

1. Figure 14-7D shows a section of Table 2 for currents. We'll use Marblehead Channel as our location of interest. This is referenced to Boston Harbor. Note that the time differences for all four conditions is +1:09, which means you add 1 hour and 9 minutes to each maximum and both slacks from the reference station to get the local times. The speed ratios are 0.4 for flood and 0.3 for ebb. The direction of maximum flood is 285°, and the direction of maximum ebb is 105°.

2. In the reference table (Figure 14-7C), you are interested in early afternoon on May 18. These tables are for standard time, so keep that in mind. The time of slack is 1026, and the following maximum ebb is 1429. The speed of the maximum is 1.3 knots.

3. Now, add 1:09 to each. This means that the time of slack in Marblehead is 1135, and the time of maximum ebb is 1538. The speed of the maximum ebb is 0.3 x 1.3 knots = 0.4 knot.

4. Let's assume that you intend to make the passage at 1300 hours EST (1400 EDT). The time interval from slack to maximum is from 1135 to 1538. That's 4 hours and 3 minutes, or 243 minutes. One-third of that is 81 minutes, or about an hour and twenty minutes.

5. Applying the first third, at 1135 plus 1:20, you get 1255, which is very close to 1300 hours. The speed factor is 50 percent of maximum, or 0.5 x 0.4 knot = 0.2 knot at the selected time.

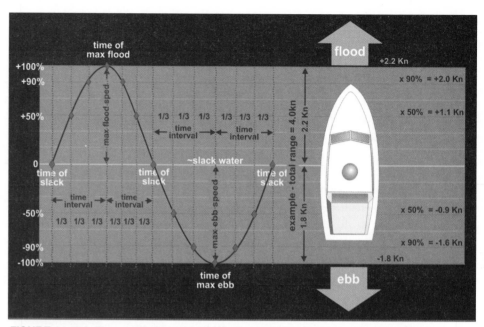

FIGURE 14-15A. *The speed of a current between maximum flood or maximum ebb and slack water can be estimated using the 50-90 Rule, which is a somewhat more complicated variation on the Rule of Twelfths. The time intervals for each quarter cycle are divided into equal thirds, as shown. During the first third from slack to maximum, the current will rise to 50 percent of the maximum. After the second third, the current will rise to 90 percent of the maximum. After the final third, the current is at maximum.*

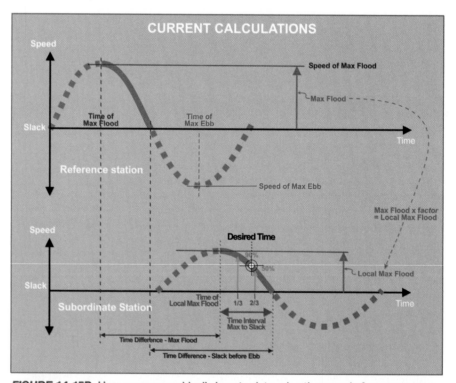

FIGURE 14-15B. *Here we see graphically how to determine the speed of a current at an intermediate time of interest (bull's-eye) between a maximum and a slack current. Note that the currents are treated in quarter-cycles, whereas tidal heights are interpolated through half-cycle increments. Determine the local times of maximum and slack and the speed of the local maximum of interest using the information in Table 2 (Figure 14-7D). After dividing the interval from maximum to slack into thirds, you can estimate the current at an intermediate time using 90 percent of maximum after the first third, then 50 percent for the second third, and finally zero.*

USING A COMPUTER OR GPS FOR TIDAL CURRENT IN-FORMATION Chartplotters and computer digital charts often provide access to tidal current information, often as arrows in selected locations on the chart screen reflecting the present direction and speed of current at those locations. By scrolling your cursor over the arrow, you can usually access a graphical current curve for that location as well. Figure 14-14 shows one example. The pop-up box provides a tidal current curve and numeric data for slacks, floods, and ebbs. The present time is noted with a vertical red dashed line superimposed on the curve. You can advance the presentation to see what the currents will be at some future time. Note the somewhat irregular shapes of the curves and the slightly different maximum currents between flood and ebb. This diagram is for currents in a relatively wide bay. As you look at the data for narrower channels, you may find the curves to be even more irregular, and the differences in maximum flood and ebb more pronounced. As described above, these asymmetries are due to the uneven and unequal shapes of the bodies of water on either side of a narrow channel.

Ocean Currents

The prevailing currents in each ocean basin have nothing to do with tides. In the Northern Hemisphere, the currents tend to circulate clockwise around each ocean basin. In the Southern Hemisphere, they circulate in a counterclockwise fashion. The Gulf Stream is one well-known example. Flowing north from the Gulf of Mexico through the Florida Strait, it skirts the U.S. East Coast before turning northeast near Labrador to become the North Atlantic Current, which bathes the shores of northern Europe with warm water. From there the North Atlantic Current turns southward along Portugal as the Canary Current, ultimately meeting the North Equatorial Current off the coast of Africa, then flowing westward in the trade wind belt to complete the circuit. In the Pacific, the east-flowing North Pacific Current becomes the south-flowing California Current along the West Coast of the United States. The California Current meets the west-flowing North Equatorial Current, which feeds the Kuroshio Current flowing north along the Asian coast. Countercurrents near the poles and the equator flow in opposite directions.

These currents exist throughout the year, although their precise paths and speeds vary seasonally. Charts based on long-term records show the most likely prevailing currents by month and location. Coastal recreational boaters may encounter these prevailing currents if they venture offshore along the coastlines.

An excellent resource for ocean current information can be found in pilot charts. These publications show the prevailing historical currents and winds within 5° latitude by 5° longitude sectors for every month of the year. These pilot charts are prepared by the U.S. National Imagery and Mapping Agency and are available commercially and on the Internet.

Some offshore navigation software takes weather and currents into account in route planning. One such program offered by MaxSea accepts small packets of information that can be received over the Internet via shortwave radio. This information is updated on a daily basis to replan your best route across the ocean, taking winds and currents into consideration. This program was developed for offshore sailboat racing, in which the winning boat is often the one that uses winds and currents to the best advantage.

Wind, Waves, and Other Unpredictable Effects

Weather is the major unpredictable factor. Although it may be possible to make some advance prediction of weather effects, your window for planning is certainly limited.

Winds

Wind—particularly a crosswind—can push a boat off course. The resultant course error depends on the characteristics of the boat both above and below the waterline and is much less predictable than the effect of a tidal or ocean current (see Figures 14-16A and 14-16B). The angle between the intended course and the actual track of the boat over the ground is called *leeway*. Sailboats under sail make more or less leeway depending on wind strength, heel angle, boat speed, and keel lift. Powerboats with a large superstructure make more leeway than those without. You need to know how your boat responds to winds before you can begin to estimate the effect of a crosswind on your course.

TIP—To see whether you are being affected by the wind, look at your wake. If your wake recedes straight behind you in line with your boat's heading, you are making no leeway due to wind. Any angle between your wake and your heading reflects your angle of leeway. (This technique does not work for currents, because the water itself is moving along with the boat.)

You counter the effects of leeway just as you counter a current—by adjusting your heading toward the wind until your GPS track matches your intended course. When both wind and current are present at the same time, they may oppose each other. Still, you use your GPS to adjust your heading until you stay on course. The effect of a wind on wave action and currents is difficult to predict. Again, the solution is to adjust your heading to maintain your intended course over ground, as explained in Chapter 8. (Refer to Figures 8-21 through 8-23.)

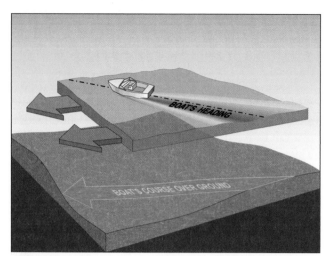

FIGURE 14-16A. *When you operate in a current, it is as if the entire platform on which you are boating moves. Your motion through the water may match your heading, but your motion over the bottom (ground) is deflected by the current, as shown by the green arrow.*

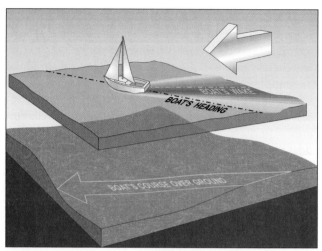

FIGURE 14-16B. *In the presence of a crosswind and no current, you are being pushed sideways through the water. The amount of this leeway depends upon the windage of your boat and its underwater hull form. You can tell whether you are making leeway by looking at your wake. If it extends behind the boat at an angle to your heading, you must account for leeway to know what direction you are moving (the green arrow).*

Waves

When a boat angles across the waves, its bow is pushed away from oncoming waves in a motion called *yaw*. After the crest of a wave passes, the heading turns back in the opposite direction. Thus, steering in seas can be a challenge. Generally you try to center the yawing of the boat around the heading you want. An autopilot can be very useful for this. (See Chapter 19 and refer to Figures 19-2A and 19-2B.)

Swells are caused by winds in distant weather systems, whereas wind waves, or chop, arise locally. Swells travel great distances from their region of origin, at speeds proportional to their *wavelength*—the distance between crests. The greater its wavelength, the faster a wave moves. The *period* of a wave is a measure of how long it takes two successive crests to pass a stationary point.

Wave height is based on the amount of wind operating on the water. Stronger winds make higher waves, but it takes time and space to get waves moving. The distance over which the wind acts on the water, called *fetch*, is of prime importance. If you are at the far end of a large body of water and a moderate wind blows across that entire body before getting to you, the resultant waves can be high. The combination of a strong wind and a long fetch produces even higher waves. Wind and waves can both be magnified when funneled between islands or headlands, as often happens in large bays.

Finally, waves are affected by water depth. A deep-water swell, as it moves toward shore, is retarded by friction with the shoaling seabed. In response, the wave steepens, and the top begins to outrun the bottom. Eventually the wave becomes too high and steep to be stable, and it begins to break. Often, when facing strong chop in a shallow area,

you can find less severe wave action in deeper water.

Locally formed chop tends to have short wavelengths, which means that you will deal with yawing action much more frequently in a chop than in swells.

Variable Currents

Because the wind is somewhat unpredictable, so is its effect on currents. Generally these effects result in distortions of tides and tidal currents. In a constrained bay, channel, or harbor, the wind can either retard or accelerate the flow of tidal waters.

Runoff also can affect currents in rivers and channels, especially after a sustained rainfall or snowmelt. Because the source of the runoff may be some distance inland, the effects on local currents can be delayed by days, then sustained for some time until inland water levels return to normal. Sometimes a riverine current through coastal receiving waters is more or less permanent; local current tables usually account for such influences.

Whether or not a current is predictable, your navigational response is the same: use GPS to maintain your intended course and monitor your progress.

Seiches

A seiche is found within a fully enclosed body of water rather than a coastal area. Dramatic seiches can be caused by seismic action within the Earth; on very large bodies of water, such as the Great Lakes, they can be produced by strong winds. On Lake Superior, seiches can even be produced by differences of atmospheric pressure over various parts of the lake.

The net effect is similar to the back-and-forth sloshing of water in a bathtub. Along a given lakeshore, the rise and fall may look similar to tidal action on the coasts, but seiches are not easily forecast. The atmospheric phenomena that cause them may warn of the potential, but the actual effects are generally unpredictable.

Generally, seiches on the Great Lakes cause water levels to vary by only a foot or so; however, local water levels have been known to rise as much as 10 feet (3 m) under extreme, rare conditions. Lake Michigan is deep, so these effects are nominal. On Lake Erie, which is shallower and aligned with the prevailing winds, seiches can reach 6 feet (2 m) or so, with a repetition period of about fourteen hours.

Seiches build up in strong winds over a period of time. In a similar fashion, they abate slowly when the wind subsides.

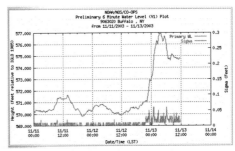

FIGURE 14-17. *The Great Lakes are far removed from ocean tides, but local effects can alter the depth of water. Called seiches, these effects are much like the sloshing of water in a bowl that has been bumped.*

OTHER ELECTRONICS

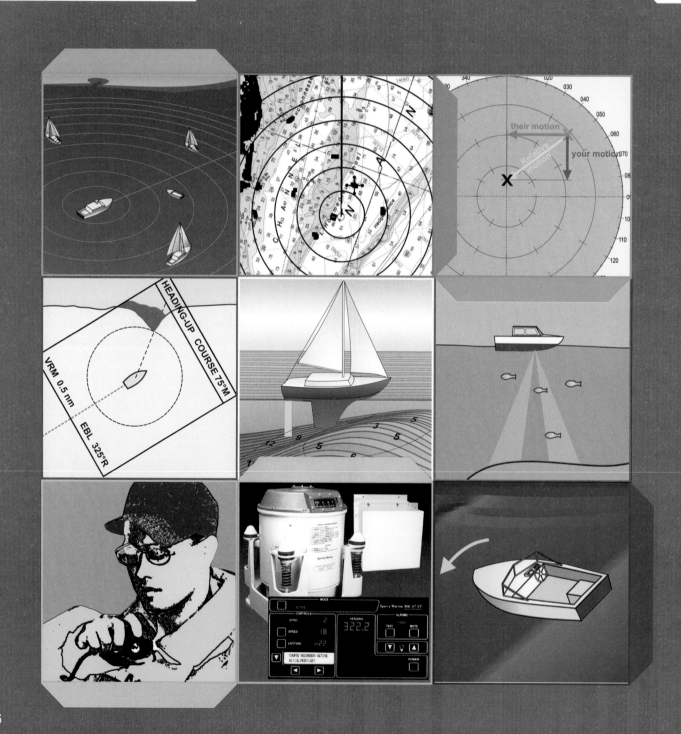

Navigating with Radar

Throughout this book, we've spent a lot of time discussing the power of GPS as a navigation tool. However, although your GPS receiver can pinpoint your location anywhere on Earth, it is utterly blind to your surroundings. It cannot see nearby boats. It cannot detect the presence of incoming squalls. And unless you've uploaded charting software, the GPS cannot indicate your position relative to the shoreline. Radar, on the other hand, can do all these things. This complementary navigation tool penetrates both darkness and thick fog to present a clear picture of all that surrounds you. When it's dark or foggy, radar can help you get home safely. It's an invaluable tool for avoiding collisions with other boats. It can show you nearby shorelines, and it can help you find navigation aids that would otherwise be out of view. Many seasoned boaters navigate by radar. Even in clear weather, radar can alert you to nearby boats that you may have missed.

For decades, high costs kept radar out of range for most recreational boaters (forgive the pun!). Radar was also impractical. On sunny days, screen glare made for difficult viewing—an inevitable problem on any small, exposed boat. But over the years, the cost of radar has decreased, and technological innovations (such as LCD displays) allow for an affordable and practical installation on nearly any vessel.

Unfortunately, little information is available to recreational boaters on selecting and using radar. This chapter focuses on the practical applications of radar for navigation and safety. See Chapter 25 for details regarding the installation, operation, functions, and performance of radar.

Range Settings for Recreational Boaters

Radar manufacturers often tout their product's range as a selling point. But even the most powerful radar can "see" only as far as the horizon. Objects (or *targets*) that lie beyond the curve of the Earth remain out of view. This limit-

ing factor cannot be overcome, but range improves with height. Just as you can see farther distances while dangling above the deck in a bosun's chair, a radar can peer farther across the water if it, too, is hung high above the boat. Since smaller vessels cannot offer much additional height, however, a costlier long-range radar system is overkill. This is one reason why more than 90 percent of recreational boaters use radar at ranges less than three miles—but there are other reasons, too.

Large vessels need much longer ranges. It takes many miles to execute a turn with a large ship, so commercial mariners need as much advance warning as they can get. In this sense, the size of the ship is advantageous because the radar can be mounted higher, thus providing a much longer view to the horizon.

Recreational boats, on the other hand, have much better maneuverability. For the most part, you'll need to focus your attention on nearby boats, although you may have occasion to look farther for shorelines or for higher-altitude weather conditions. Figures 15-1 through 15-3

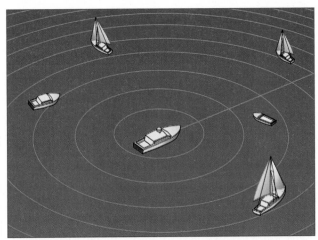

FIGURE 15-1. *At short ranges (less than 3 miles), you'll keep tabs on other boats. You might also use the radar to find a particular navigation aid, or a shoreline in poor visibility.*

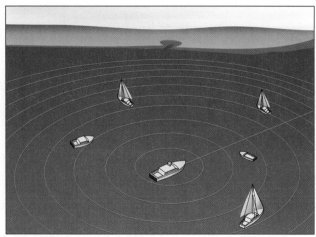

FIGURE 15-2. *At mid-ranges (3 to 5 miles), you'll look for shoreline features to help navigate and determine position. On a small recreational boat, the radar sits low above the water. Therefore, unless there are very large boats that peek above the horizon, the radar won't see much beyond a few miles. Nonetheless, these ranges can help you spot large, dangerous ships when you're crossing shipping lanes.*

FIGURE 15-3. *At the longer-range scales (beyond 5 miles), boats and land features likely lie below the visible radar horizon. However, the radar detects large rainsqualls in the atmosphere. When the weather suggests the possibility of storms, be sure to check the long-range scales from time to time.*

demonstrate how short-range, mid-range, and long-range settings can each uniquely aid the recreational boater.

Radar Display

Radar is not as intuitive as many boaters would like. The images seem to provide a fuzzy view of the world. The granularity of images on the screen is a direct result of the way radar works (see Chapter 25). Images on the screen change from sweep to sweep, sometimes disappearing and then reappearing. Shorelines are blocky and ill-defined. Boats

look much larger than they should. The smaller size of recreational-boat radars only add to this granularity, and occasionally miss small boats altogether. Until you grow accustomed to using the screen, you need to know what to look for. Using radar might be frustrating at first, but once you get the hang of it, you'll wonder how you ever got along without it.

Most displays also present a group of numerical data fields corresponding to settings of the radar. There also are data fields corresponding to inputs from other sources, such as a GPS. These are explained later in this chapter.

Visual Relationships

Images on a radar screen do not precisely correspond with the size and shape of the scanned objects. To get an idea of what the display looks like, imagine a wide-tipped black marker tracing the features on a paper chart. The wide swath of ink distorts the fine details of the shoreline and obscures the true size and shape of navigation aids and hazards. A radar display is no different. Small features such as bights and narrow inlets may blend in with more predominant shoreline trends. Navigation aids may appear as blockish circles. Boats might look like blobs, and two closely spaced boats may appear as one.

To accurately interpret the objects on the screen, you need to familiarize yourself with the radar images and the objects they represent. In short, you need to practice. Using your radar in fair weather is perhaps the best way to practice. On a clear, sunny day, you'll be able to compare the images on your radar screen against the distant boats and shoreline features you see from your cockpit.

Orientation

No matter where you go, there you are—a saying that's as true on your radar display as it is in life. The exact center of the radar display is equivalent to the "you are here" sign on a rest-area highway map. In other words, the display's center represents your boat (or, more precisely, the location of your antenna). Whether you're sailing at seven knots or motoring at forty knots, your position will always be in the center of the display. As far as the radar is concerned, you are the very center of the universe. (Some radars allow you to slightly offset this center to get a more extended view on one side than the other. Figure 15-5 shows the scan center below the center of the display. This allows a greater visible range ahead of the boat than behind it. But we're getting a little ahead of ourselves.)

From the center of the display, an invisible line radiates outward from the boat's position and sweeps across the display like the second hand of a clock. This line corresponds with the signal beam from the radar antenna. From

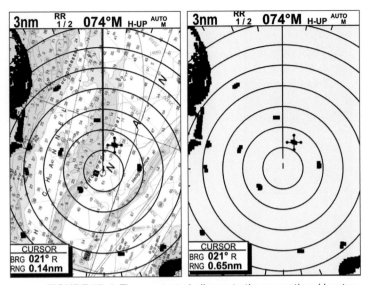

FIGURE 15-4. *The greatest challenge to the recreational boater is interpreting what appears on the radar screen. Isolated reflective objects such as buoys and boats appear as blobs. Their shape on the screen is more a result of the radar's resolution than the shape of the object. Echoes from land tend to take on an approximate shape of the shoreline. Radar echoes come from objects with some vertical shape, so the steeper the shoreline, the sharper the echo. Also, the radar cannot see "over" an intervening bluff or hilltop, so you tend to see just a portion of the land behind the shoreline. This figure is intended to provide a sense of what may appear on a radar screen from the charted area shown on the left.*

its mount above the deck, the radar antenna rotates, sending out its pulsing signal. When a pulse encounters an object, the pulse is reflected back toward the antenna. This returning pulse is called an *echo*. Echoes are received by the antenna and converted to images, called targets, on the screen. The farther a target lies from the boat, the farther its image will appear from the center of the display. As the antenna continues to rotate, the images are refreshed with each sweep of the beam.

HEADING-UP VERSUS NORTH-UP   Although it describes a circular rotation, a radar antenna has a forward reference point. The radar antenna is mounted such that the reference point aligns with the boat's bow. With the orientation of the antenna matching the orientation of the boat, the radar display becomes a little more intuitive. The top of the display represents the boat's heading. This is called a *heading-up* display. The heading-up display mode is most useful because it represents the world as viewed from the boat. A target that lies in front of the boat will appear toward the top center of the screen; a target behind the boat will appear toward the bottom center. The bearings on the display are thereby relative to the boat. They are measured from 0° at the top, clockwise to 180° at the bottom, and back toward 360° at the top.

Although the heading-up mode is usually more intuitive, the *north-up* mode is a useful feature when it's avail-

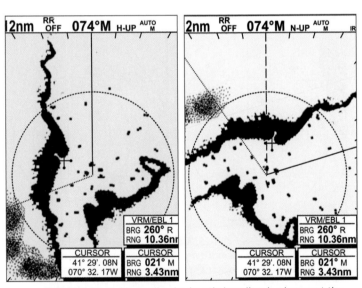

FIGURE 15-5. *Normally, the boat's heading is shown at the top of the display. The angle from the top corresponds with the relative bearing to a target. The distance of the target from the display center indicates its range from the boat. Heading-up is the natural choice for boating, because it relates with your visual horizon. However, if your radar receives input from a fluxgate compass or other external reference, you can reorient the screen to north-up. This is used occasionally when you want to compare radar images with those on a chartplotter.*

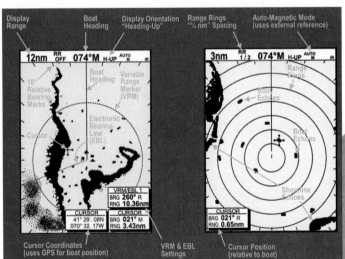

FIGURE 15-6. *Left: The range scale is 12 nm, the boat heading is 74° magnetic, the display is heading-up. There are no range rings displayed. In the boxes near the bottom of the display, you can see the coordinates of the cursor (the crossmark). These coordinates are derived using position information provided by an interfaced GPS. A variable range marker (VRM; dashed circle) has been set for 10.36 nm, and an electronic bearing line (EBL; dashed line) has been set at 260° relative. Right: Here the range setting is 3 nm. The range rings are turned on with ¹/₂ nm spacing. The VRM and EBL are off.*

able. To get access to north-up mode, you'll have to interface an electronic (fluxgate) compass with your radar, as discussed in Chapter 25. In this mode, the radar screen better matches charts when you want to compare shoreline features for locating your position; it also corresponds with the default setting on most GPS Map Screens. Further, in north-up mode, targets stay put on the screen when you alter course, rather than rotating clockwise in response to a left turn and vice versa. This offers advantages of continuity when you're tracking targets while engaged in collision avoidance maneuvers. But again, we're getting ahead of ourselves. (By the way, if it's important to you to have your radar and GPS orientations match, it is possible to set your GPS to heading-up as well, but that's not very common. Typically, boaters prefer to have charting and navigation instruments oriented with the chart, and radars and sonars oriented with the boat.)

Range Rings and Bearing Marks

Most radars will display a series of equally spaced concentric circles if you so choose. These *range rings* provide a quick visual reference for the range of an echo. The spacing is noted in a data field and depends on the range setting of the display. On most radar models, these rings can be turned off to provide a less cluttered display.

In addition, most radar models provide bearing marks at regular intervals. On most newer models, these are short lines arrayed around the perimeter of the display at some convenient increment, such as 10°. These marks provide a convenient reference for the bearing of a target.

EBL and VRM

Typical radars have two movable markers, an *electronic bearing line* (EBL) and a *variable range marker* (VRM). The EBL is a radial line that you can set to any relative direction on the display. Its bearing is presented as a data field for reference. The EBL is a convenient tool for measuring the relative bearing to a particular target. As you will learn shortly, it also can be useful in collision avoidance.

The VRM is a circle of constant range. It can be set to measure the range to a particular target. The VRM can also be set at a particular range, such as ¼ nm, to give you a frame of reference for targets that warrant particular attention.

Many new radars feature two or more sets of these EBL and VRM lines. Some also allow you to offset them to a reference other than the center of the scan. Their positions (bearing and range) are reported numerically on the display.

The EBL typically appears as a dashed radial line from the center of the display, and the VRM as a dashed circle. If there are two sets of EBLs and VRMs available, one typically has long dashes and the other shorter dashes to distinguish between them.

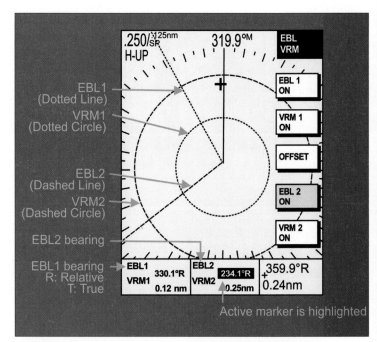

FIGURE 15-7. *This radar permits setting two EBLs and two VRMs. The EBL is useful for determining a bearing to another boat or for aligning with a charted object to help get a fix. The VRM helps determine target ranges. Each EBL and VRM can be individually selected and adjusted.*

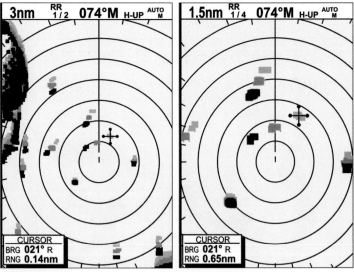

FIGURE 15-8. *Radar paints a new picture each time the antenna sweeps by. When you are moving, everything in the display appears to move. These two graphics show a 3 nm range scale with land features, and a 1.5 nm scale just showing nearby targets. The radar can be set to display only the most recent scan, or to show a series of successive scans at diminished intensities. The latter setting creates a trail that can be used to determine the relative motions of targets.*

In addition, most radar screens provide a movable cursor. You can scroll the cursor over a target and observe the corresponding range and bearing in a data field.

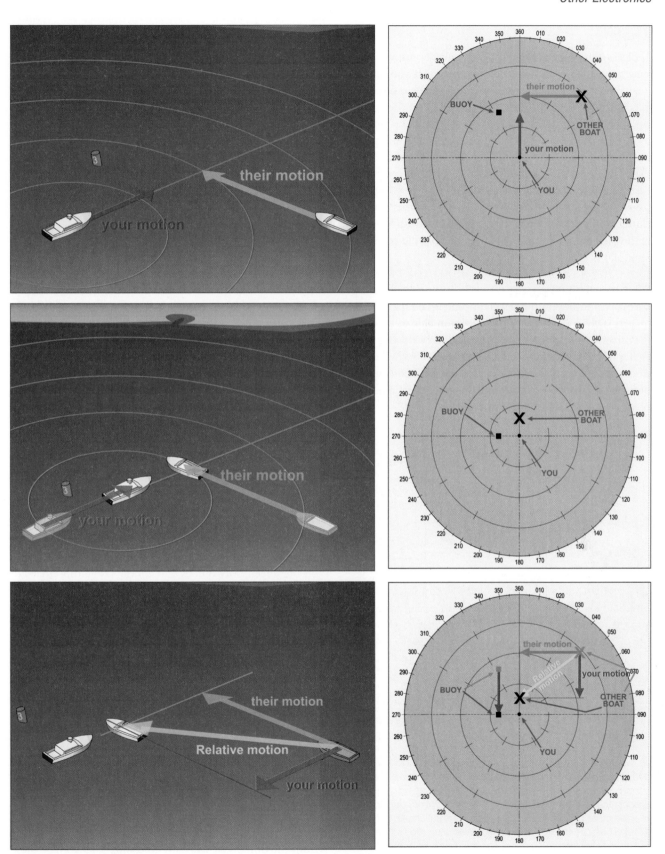

FIGURE 15-9. *Perhaps the most complicated concept to grasp in a radar display is relative motion. Because you are moving, everything on the screen appears to be moving—even stationary targets such as buoys and shorelines. The relative motion of the can buoy in this radar plot is straight downscreen at a speed that matches your boat speed—the sure sign of a stationary target. But what about that crossing boat? He's moving somewhat faster than you on a course perpendicular to yours, but his relative motion is toward your position at the center of the screen, passing just ahead of you. Remember, since he's approaching from your starboard side, he's the stand-on vessel. Maybe you should have turned to starboard to give him a wider berth.*

Trails

Typical radars scan at roughly 24 sweeps per minute, each time painting a new picture on the screen. If you make a mental note of the positions of returning echoes on the display and observe each successive scan, you can determine which way targets are moving relative to you. To help in this process, most radars will display a "target trail" from previous scans if you so select. Usually, the older echoes are presented at decreasing levels of intensity to avoid confusion. Also, on most radars you can set the number of sweeps (or time) for the trails. (If they are set too long, they tend to clutter up the display.) The trails can be very useful for interpreting the paths of other boats and to help avoid collisions.

DIRECTIONAL RELATIONSHIPS AND RELATIVE MOTION

When you are moving, the screen is constantly changing. Virtually nothing on the screen appears to be fixed. Fixed objects such as shorelines and navigation aids move down the screen at a rate of speed corresponding with your boat. Other boats move across the screen as well, but their directions and rates of apparent movement are independent. The only objects that appear to lie still are other boats that happen to match your speed and direction.

The directions of motion for other boats appear relative to yours, and their apparent speeds are also relative. Consequently, a relatively slow boat that approaches head-on will appear to move quite rapidly (his boat speed plus yours). And let's say you're gaining on another vessel on the same track; both of you might be moving quickly in the same direction, but the other boat will appear as though it's approaching you slowly.

It can all be rather confusing. But, as a recreational boater, you don't necessarily need to know the true courses and speeds of other boats. You need to focus only on movement patterns that represent a risk of collision. Be aware of any boat that closes directly on the center of the display. That's a collision course.

Connecting Radar with GPS

Radar and GPS are complementary navigation tools. In some cases, they can be linked to each other. When the two units are connected, the radar screen can display information from GPS (i.e., position, speed, track, crosstrack error, and bearing and distance to the active waypoint). This frees you to view different displays on the GPS (such as the Highway Screen), while simultaneously keeping tabs on other important information via the radar.

Collision Avoidance

Collision avoidance is the most important use of radar. To do this effectively, set the radar range between a half mile and a mile. It's also a good idea to set the variable range marker to about a quarter mile. A dashed circle will appear on the screen. Any echoes that appear inside this circle are within a quarter mile of your boat. These targets require your attention. In this case, you are most interested in the relative motions of the boats within your field of view.

Predicting Collisions

Targets that approach your location (at the center of the screen) represent a threat of collision. The direction of the trail provides a sense of the oncoming boat's *relative* motion—its motion with respect to you. (Determining the other boat's *actual* course is a problem of vector resolution and usually involves the use of a plotting board. But that is of less consequence to recreational boaters.) To evaluate the risk of collision, you need to mentally extend the other boat's relative motion. (Note that the natural yaw of your boat will result in some minor changes in your heading. The echoes from the other boat will shift accordingly, so average these out when you envision the extended path of the other boat.)

USING EBL You can use your EBL to help evaluate collision risk. Simply rotate the electronic bearing line onto the

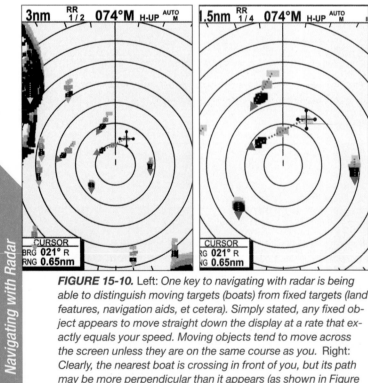

FIGURE 15-10. Left: *One key to navigating with radar is being able to distinguish moving targets (boats) from fixed targets (land features, navigation aids, et cetera). Simply stated, any fixed object appears to move straight down the display at a rate that exactly equals your speed. Moving objects tend to move across the screen unless they are on the same course as you.* Right: *Clearly, the nearest boat is crossing in front of you, but its path may be more perpendicular than it appears (as shown in Figure 15-9). The boat at 11:00 is moving slower than the first one and probably in the same direction. The two boats at 3:00 and 8:00 appear to be moving down the screen, but they are actually moving in the same direction you are—they're just not going as fast as you. When there's a stationary target on screen, use its relative motion to help you decipher what other boats are really doing.*

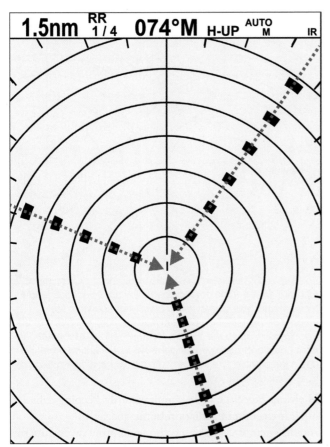

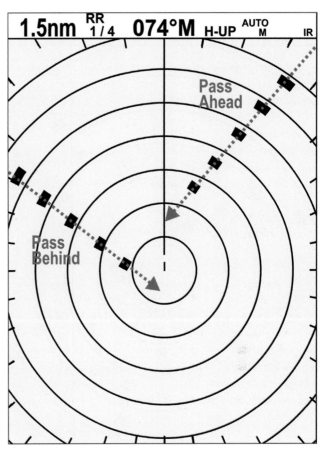

FIGURE 15-11. *Any target that retains the same relative bearing as it approaches is on a likely collision course. Three examples are shown in the figure. In each case, the path of the other boat continues directly toward the center of the display. Each is on a collision course. You are the give-way vessel to the boat approaching from 0130, but stand-on vessel to the overtaking boat and the one approaching from port.*

FIGURE 15-12. *Any boat whose relative bearing is changing will skirt the center of the display (and miss your boat) unless one of you alters course.*

other boat and observe. If it follows the EBL line toward you, a risk of collision exists. (This situation is analogous to using visual relative bearings to predict collisions; see Chapter 11. The corresponding radar display is shown in Figure 15-11.)

RATE OF CLOSURE The radar screen can also help you determine the *rate of closure*, or how long it will take for the other boat to reach you under current conditions. First, count how many seconds it takes for the oncoming target to span the distance between two range rings. Then multiply the number of seconds by the number of rings that remain between you and the oncoming boat. This indicates how much time you have until a collision could potentially occur.

PREDICTING A MISS If the extended path looks as though it will pass in front of you, it's likely that the target boat will too. Likewise, if the extended path appears to go behind you, so too will the target boat. (You can estimate how close the other boat will come by comparing the closest point on that extrapolated path with the radar's range scale.) If the

other boat turns, it will take a new path on the screen. Just make sure that this new path is not converging with the display's center of scan.

Suppose the object is fixed or at rest. The only way it can pose a risk is if it appears to be straight ahead and closing (moving straight down the heading-up display).

Effect of a Boat Turn or Change of Speed on the Display

Collision avoidance using radar almost sounds too simple. In most cases it is. There is one complication, though. Suppose you turn. Now *all* of the objects on the display will rotate relative to you. The display orientation tracks the heading of your boat, so if you turn, everything on the screen will appear to move in the opposite direction (see Figure 15-13). This can cause some confusion, because the image trails become distorted until you have a sufficient number of sweeps at the new heading to clarify the display. In the figure, you can see that the tracks are all disrupted but regain their patterns. However, your turn had the effect of altering potential collisions into misses. The boat to your left was closing at a high rate of speed; now it will pass ahead. The other two boats will pass behind you.

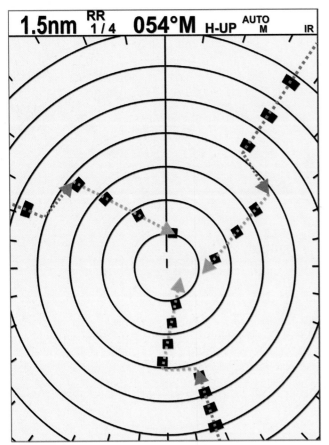

FIGURE 15-13. *Any turn that you execute will temporarily confuse the display. In this example (updated from Figure 15-11), you turned to port. You need to wait for a few sweeps to determine whether any of the other boats still presents a risk of collision. Because you are now moving in a different direction, it's unlikely that any of these three boats will now pose a collision risk. Note that a turn to starboard is preferred under the international rules of the road, but a turn to port, if done early and obviously, is also acceptable.*

If you change speed, other boats will acquire a new motion relative to yours (even if the other boat did not change its course or speed). Figure 15-14 shows two examples updated from the scenario shown in Figure 15-11. In the first, only two of the boats are shown. In this scenario, your speed is fixed. The boat at one o'clock has increased speed and will now pass in front of you. The second boat, at 10 o'clock, has slowed, and will fall away behind you. In the second scenario, all three boats from Figure 15-11 have retained their respective speeds, but you take action by speeding up. Note that all of the other boats begin to fall off as you move away from them.

If the other boat changes direction or speed (but you do not), the display is not disrupted. The relative motion of the other boat changes, and you simply need to monitor this new target trail to determine whether it poses a collision risk. If you both change speed or direction, you need to wait to observe the trail for a few sweeps after the changes have settled in.

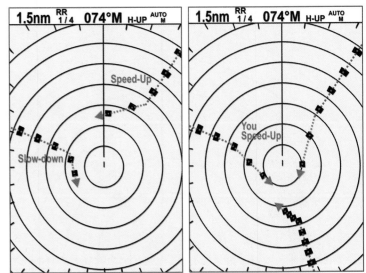

FIGURE 15-14. *If the other boat speeds up, its echoes tend to move across your display more quickly, as shown in the graphic on the left. If it slows down, its echoes will move more in a direction down the display. If you speed up, all the echoes from boats approaching you will move in a direction more down the display. The echoes from a boat traveling toward you from behind will fall off.*

If the other boat is within the quarter-mile zone, you should attempt visual observation and properly execute the rules of the road to avoid collision. The same principles apply under adverse visibility or at night. If there is any doubt, it pays to attempt radio contact to determine the other's intentions. You can also use sound signals.

Radar Navigation

To use the radar for navigation, you need to be able to recognize and identify what you see on the display. Navigation aids can provide excellent point targets from which you can derive your position. However, how do you know which buoy you are looking at? With other boats and potentially multiple buoys in the area, it can be difficult to distinguish the identity of a particular buoy. Sometimes you can use nearby shoreline features to help you identify the buoy. Generally, shorelines are less ambiguous than navigation aids. By zooming out to a display range that shows a reasonable section of shoreline, you can compare the radar profile with your chart and pinpoint which section is within view.

Appearance of Shorelines and Land-Based Objects on a Radar Screen

Radar echoes are dependent upon two features of the object being viewed—its reflectivity to radar signals and its aspect angle to the radar. Good reflectors such as metal return stronger signals than wooden objects. And objects that are vertical provide good surfaces visible to the radar.

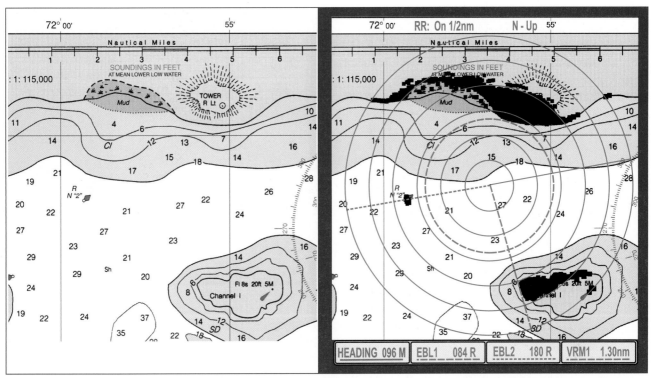

FIGURE 15-15A. *The graphic on the left shows a section of a training chart used by The U.S. Power Squadrons. The image on the right depicts which of those features would appear on a radar screen (black). Note that the buoy shows as a discrete echo. The shoreline's leading edge appears as a solid echo, except in the region of the mud and swamp where the returns are patchy. The tower on the hill to the north cannot be seen, and only the face of the hill is visible. The same is true for Channel Island. Only the near side of the island can be seen—the rest is masked by intervening topography.*

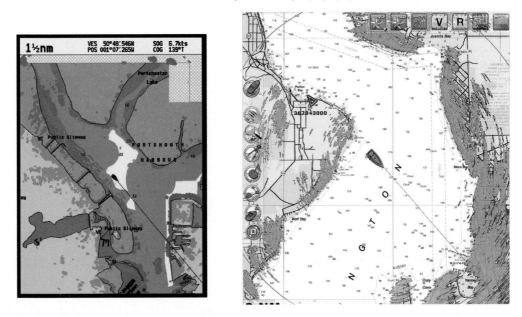

FIGURE 15-15B. Left: *This radar screen shows a radar image overlaid on a digital chart. Note the shape of the echoes and how hey compare with the charted shoreline. If you mentally remove the chart, you still could deduce your position, although it would not be as easy. (Courtesy: Raymarine)* Right: *Another view of a radar image shows how well the radar returns correspond with fixed shoreline features and the chart. Other returns are likely to come from boats. Note the green triangle in the radar blind spot behind your vessel. That is a plotted AIS target (see Chapter 19). (Courtesy: Furuno)*

What does all that mean to the recreational boater? Ground is a decent reflector, and it is generally high enough to show up on the radar screen. However, a marsh is low and flat and may not return a solid echo. Also, the radar will see most of a rise in the land that faces the radar, but it will not see the back side. Therefore, you will tend to see the leading edges of shorelines in somewhat blocky detail, and solid returns to some distance inland on the visible sides of slopes.

As previously outlined, radar paints with a broad brush, so it does not detect detailed features such as a narrow inlet until you are close enough that its larger relative size permits distinction.

Objects on land, such as towers, are generally not seen, because their echoes are masked by the landmass around them. An isolated high tower on the far side of a hill may return a discrete echo, but it might be difficult to determine with any confidence whether the echo on the screen comes from a particular tower.

If a shoreline in the foreground is followed by a stretch of open water, such as an interior bay, and if that shoreline is not so high as to obscure the radar signals, then you may be able to see the far shoreline across the bay (see Figure 15-16). The land appears as echoes, whereas the water does not.

Also, as mentioned at the beginning of this chapter, radar can see only as far as the horizon. The range depends upon the height of the antenna. In a typical installation, your antenna will be ten to twelve feet above the surface of the water. This means you can potentially see a water-level object at a distance of roughly four nautical miles. If the shoreline lies beyond that, you will see only that portion of the land that extends above the radar horizon. For instance, land at an elevation of twelve feet can be seen from another four nautical miles away (a total of eight nautical miles), but you need to recognize that the shoreline you see is not necessarily the shoreline on the chart. You are looking at the twelve-foot topo line on shore. So, unless there's a twelve-foot cliff jutting out of the water, it's likely that your radar is detecting a point farther inland.

Navigating with Radar and GPS

Radar can be connected to a GPS receiver to form a single powerful navigation tool. Most GPS receivers and radars can communicate using the NMEA 0183 protocol. This standard for connections is used on almost all electronic equipment. By connecting just two wires, the radar can display GPS information such as current position and speed, bearing and distance to the active waypoint, and other data fields. Even better, most radars plot the active GPS waypoint on the radar screen. The waypoint appears within a dashed circle, and a dashed line extends from the waypoint to the center of the display. This feature is aptly named a "lollipop" display (see Figure 15-16). Now you can use the radar to steer toward that waypoint. Just follow the lollipop's "stick" to the sweet spot—your waypoint.

If the active waypoint is a buoy or navigation aid with a radar reflector, it should appear within the lollipop. Now you have an unambiguous identification of that

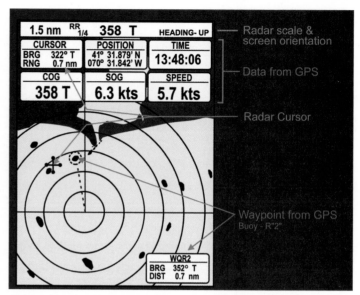

FIGURE 15-16. *When you connect your radar with your GPS, most of the pertinent GPS information is displayed on your radar screen. In addition, the radar creates a "lollipop" display to help distinguish the echoes from the waypoint. The radar places a dashed circle around the waypoint and a dashed line from the center of the display to the circle. If you are navigating to that waypoint, you simply align the lollipop with the heading line on the radar screen.*

buoy. If there is no radar image within the circle, and you expect one based on the type of buoy, you should look to other parts of the radar screen to verify your position.

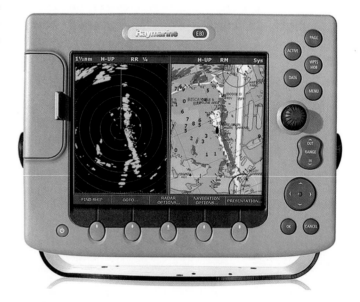

FIGURE 15-17. *This split-screen view shows a radar screen on the left and a digital chart with radar overlay on the right. Note that the general shoreline features are shown near the boat and on shorelines nominally at right angles to the boat, but the channel to the SSE of the boat is obscured on radar. (Courtesy: Raymarine)*

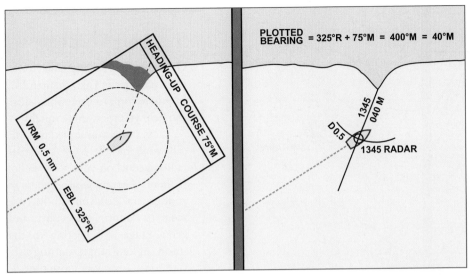

FIGURE 15-18. *In this example, the radar display is heading-up. Note a prominent shoreline feature, then use your cursor or EBL and VRM to measure the range and relative bearing to that feature. Next, you'll need to convert the relative bearing to a magnetic (or true) bearing. Then you can plot your location on your chart.*

you determine that the bearing is 40° M. Plot that bearing. The range to the point of land is 0.5 nm. Simply draw an arc of that radius from the point to where it intersects with the bearing. That is your position.

Last, label the plotted position with the time followed by "Radar" (for example, "1345 Radar").

PLOTTING BY RANGE AND BEARING: BUOYS By combining your recognition of the shoreline with the echo from a nearby buoy, you can significantly improve the quality of your fix. However, using nav aids for radar navigation can be tricky. Often, it's difficult to determine whether you're looking at a buoy or a boat. You can tell whether the object is moving or at rest by observing the target trail, but that doesn't eliminate the possibility that you're looking at a boat at anchor. If there are multiple returns from that locale, there may be boats fishing near the aid. If so, you should select a more isolated object. However, if there is a distinguishable pattern of buoys, and you feel confident that your display corresponds with the chart, you can get a decent fix on your position. Simply refine the range and bearing markers to coincide with your selected navigation aid, then plot those measurements.

PLOTTING BY RANGE ALONE There are instances when you will not find a sharply defined feature along the shoreline. Look for sections of shoreline where you can unambiguously measure range (as shown in Figure 15-19).

Then adjust the VRM to measure the distance to each shore. Next, using your drawing compass, draw an arc at that radius for each of the locations measured. Because you are using distance, your exact placement of the compass center is not critical. Your location is at the intersection of these arcs.

Radar Avoidance Techniques

Chapter 24 describes a number of avoidance techniques while underway. This section describes the details of some techniques using radar.

TRACKING A SHORELINE For obvious reasons, shorelines are hazardous to boaters. What better place to run aground than the ground itself? Your radar can help you safely navigate along shorelines, even under conditions of restricted visibility.

Navigating with Radar Alone

Suppose your GPS has failed, or at least is suspect. Or you are navigating near land and want to make sure you stay far enough away. Radar provides your real relative position and can be more reliable than using the GPS. You can navigate using your radar alone, but it will take an extra measure of attention.

PLOTTING BY RANGE AND BEARING: SHORELINES Shorelines provide somewhat unambiguous radar targets that you can use to plot your location on a chart. Look for a prominent point or feature along a shoreline presented on the screen. Usually, this is a sharp point of land with an identifiable profile that you can match to the chart (as shown in Figure 15-18). The accuracy of your position depends upon the sharpness of the shoreline feature you have used. If the shoreline is a vertical bluff, its position will be more precisely fixed than if it is a gradually sloping beach.

Using your radar's electronic bearing line (EBL), you can place a radial bearing line through the image at that point. Then set the variable range marker (VRM) so the circle intersects that same point. Read the bearing and range in the respective data fields. (Alternatively, some radars allow you to place the cursor over the point and read bearing and range directly.)

Next, you need to calculate the magnetic bearing, so you can plot it on your chart. In this example, the relative bearing is 325° and the magnetic heading of the boat is 075° M. Using the formula:

$$MB = RB + MH$$

(magnetic bearing = relative bearing + magnetic heading)

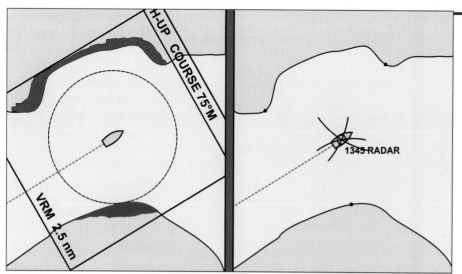

FIGURE 15-19. *In this example, while coasting a long shoreline, the navigator must pick points that can be located with confidence on a chart. He finds three points that are high enough to return an unambiguous reflection and are closer to the boat than the shore on either side. Bearings and ranges to these three points agree with each other perfectly, making a fix the navigator can be sure of.*

The easiest way to avoid the shoreline is to set the VRM at the minimum safe distance of approach. Navigate until the VRM just touches the shoreline, and proceed until you reach your destination. At this close range, you are likely to see the harbor or inlet on your radar and can use that to navigate to your destination.

RADAR DANGER CIRCLE   Chapter 7 describes danger circles as a planning tool to stay away from hazards. Radar can be used to avoid them. First, you need to associate the danger area with a prominent feature that can be identified on your radar. Then measure a minimum approach radius from the prominent feature. From there, you simply set your VRM at that same radius and ensure that the prominent land feature never enters within the VRM setting while you are navigating nearby. Radar has an advantage over GPS because it shows you the shoreline, whereas the GPS could potentially have an erroneous position stored for the waypoint.

Tracking Weather

Generally, you set the radar to reduce rain clutter (see Chapter 25), but there comes a time when radar can help you spot severe squalls.

As a rule, you should periodically tune into the NOAA weather radio channel on your VHF radio. If there's a severe weather alert in your general area, you can then use radar to confirm the report, and get a range and bearing to the storm. At long range, spotting a severe storm gives you more time to seek shelter.

Set the radar on or near its longest range. Because the severe weather is at high altitude, you have a direct line of sight to the storm cell. You will be looking for a large mass that appears to be moving. The shape and motion should correspond with what you would expect of a storm squall. Typically, a squall will appear as a band of dense echoes that moves forward at a steady rate. By judging its rate of advance, you will be able to determine your strategies and whether you can make port before it hits.

Radar returns from rain generally have a speckled pattern of random dots. They also tend to undulate. These dots do not reappear at the same locations. The overall limits of the dot patterns provide a sense of the size of the storm cell. In many areas, cold fronts are associated with strong squall-line thunderstorms, which are dangerous. If there are any indications that such storms are approaching, you should periodically set the radar to the long-range mode, turn down the rain clutter setting, and look for any unusual returns. Once a storm is spotted, you can tell the direction and rate of advance, and prepare your actions accordingly.

CHAPTER

16

Using Depth in Navigation

Sonar is the underwater equivalent of radar. In its full implementation, sonar provides a view of the seabed and objects all around the underside of the boat. Simpler versions of sonar—depth sounders and fishfinders—look only downward. Unfortunately, these devices do not give an indication of what is coming—only what is directly below or (in the case of a fishfinder) what you have already passed. Nonetheless, up-to-the-minute depth information can help you navigate.

FIGURE 16-1. *Depth sounders can be useful supplements for navigation.*

Depth Sounders versus Sonars and Fishfinders

A depth sounder consists of a processing and display unit and a transducer. The control unit prompts the transducer to send an acoustic pulse downward into the water; then it "listens" to the returns before sending another pulse. (These acoustical frequencies are above the range of human hearing.) When the pulse signal hits the bottom, an echo returns to the transducer. The depth of the water is determined by measuring the round-trip time of the echoes. Because there are numerous objects that could return an echo (including fish!), the depth sounder control unit is designed to look for the relatively solid return that is expected from the sea bottom. That depth is displayed on the control unit, usually in feet. The depth is continuously measured and displayed. The most basic type of depth sounder provides a numeric display representing the instantaneous depth beneath you.

It's important to recognize that the depth reported by the depth sounder is measured from the transducer. So, if the

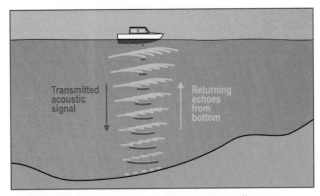

FIGURE 16-2. *Depth sounders function by sending a sequence of acoustic sound pulses downward from a transducer mounted in the boat. The transducer listens between pulses for the returning echoes. The time to make a round trip is directly related to the depth.*

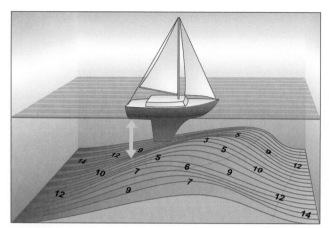

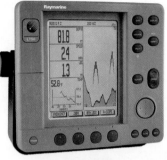

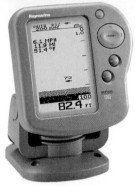

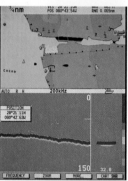

FIGURE 16-3. The depth sounder is not measuring the depth of the water. It is measuring the depth from where the transducer is mounted on the boat. Many depth sounders can be adjusted with an offset to account for this difference. Then you must subtract the draft of the boat from the depth reading to determine your clearance.

transducer is mounted at the waterline of the boat, for instance, you need to measure the boat's draft and subtract it from the reading to know the exact clearance between the deepest portion of your keel or running gear and the sea bottom. Some depth sounders enable you to offset the depth indicated on the display to account for the draft of the boat.

A fishfinder is a variation on the depth sounder. It uses a similar transponder and works the same way. The greatest difference is that the fishfinder displays *all* returning echoes on screen in graphic form. The intensity of each image corresponds to the strength of the return.

Fishfinders also display a historical record of depths below the boat. The newest data represent what currently lies beneath your boat; the display extending off to the left shows the depths and objects that you have already passed over. As you move, your fishfinder "paints" a picture. The undulations of the bottom show as a band at the bottom of the display. Smaller objects, such as fish, show up as discrete echoes above the bottom, and can be distinguished by their finite size. The longer the fish, the longer the echo. Return intensity also provides some information regarding the character of the bottom. A sharply delineated band usually means a hard bottom; a blurry return is likely to be mud.

Fishfinders and depth sounders are special-case applications of sonar. In both cases, the beam from these devices is fixed in direction—downward. Sonars have the capability to steer the beam, much like a radar, though sonars offered to recreational boaters have limited scanning ability.

Some sonars scan back and forth immediately in front of the boat and directly under it. These sonars are designed particularly for avoiding obstacles ahead. However, the range looking ahead is limited to hundreds of feet rather than miles. A fast boat can quickly overrun the image and get into trouble. Other sonars scan sideways. These provide an image of what lies to port and starboard as well as

FIGURE 16-4. Fishfinders are a special type of depth sounder. They record the echoes on a screen as the boat moves. The picture on the screen depicts the sea bottom lying directly under the boat alongside a brief record of the sea bottom from moments before. The bottom appears as a continuous wavy line reflecting changes in depth. Fish appear as isolated objects at shallower depths. Some fishfinders recognize the pattern for a fish and replace it with a fish symbol on the screen. Others show the actual echoes that appear as upside-down "V"s.

below. These are more useful for staying within a narrow channel.

The performance of a sounder, whether for finding depth or fish, is dependent upon the transducer. Typically, there are two frequency ranges available. Each has its advantages and disadvantages. A 200 kHz transducer has a narrower beam that provides a higher-resolution picture, but its depth is limited. A 50 kHz transducer has a broader beam and thus far less resolution, but it penetrates deeper into the water.

Some sounders use transducers that transmit on both frequencies and then compare the results. It's the best of both worlds, but it adds cost. Transducers are available with various transmitted power levels and comparable differences in range capability.

Transducers for through-hull mounting require custom installation and a hole drilled through the boat's hull. Unless you're familiar with installing and sealing through-hull fittings, you should let a professional do this. The transducer must be mounted so its face is parallel with the sea bottom, so some fairing may be required. The most popular fishfinder transducer is easily installed on the face of the transom, with the head extending just below the hull.

FIGURE 16-5A. *Sonar is a more sophisticated application of the depth sounder. Instead of a transducer that looks only downward, these sonars actually scan in front of the boat or side to side. The former presents an image of depths to come rather than what lies directly beneath. Obviously, this is a more useful tool for hazard avoidance. The screen on the left shows a top view of the boat as the sonar scans from side to side. On the right-hand screen, the vertical profile shows a shallow area dead ahead. (Courtesy: Interphase)*

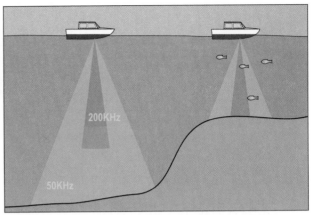

FIGURE 16-6. *Transducers come in two basic frequency ranges (50 kHz and 200 kHz). The higher-frequency transducer has a narrower beam and thus provides greater resolution. It also has a shallower depth of penetration in the water.*

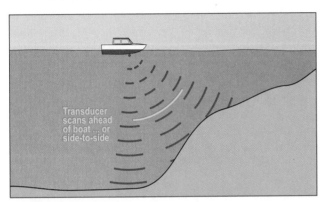

FIGURE 16-5B. *The right-hand screen from the previous panel is illustrated here. The transducer is scanning ahead of the boat.*

FIGURE 16-7. *Some depth sounders come with dual frequency transducers to provide both deeper coverage as well as higher resolution at shallower depths. This system from Raymarine shows the 200 kHz image on the top and the 50 kHz image just below it. Note that the lower image is smoother and the bottom is better defined, while the upper image shows various images above the bottom, which may be fish. The corresponding chart is shown on this unit in the lower half of the display. (Courtesy: Raymarine)*

This location is subject to turbulence while underway, so these units work better at slow speeds (as when fishing). Turbulence causes air bubbles and eddies, which disrupt the signal transmission.

Another popular mount is inside the hull. This works reasonably well for solid fiberglass hulls, which transmit sound rather well. The transducer face must be in solid contact with the hull. Because the hull is seldom flat and horizontal, the transducer is often mounted in an interior box that is bonded to the hull and filled with water to facilitate sound transmission.

Navigating with a Depth Sounder

Although the depth sounder itself may not indicate upcoming hazards, using it with other instruments and charts can help you find your way and anticipate what's to come.

Using Depth with GPS and Charts

Depth provides a good and quick way to cross-check your other electronics, such as the GPS. By locating your GPS-reported position on a chart, you can compare the depth in-

dicated on the chart with your depth-sounder reading—taking into account the state of the tide. Even more useful is the change in depths as you pass over shoal areas, as indicated on the charts. If the changes in depth as reported by the sounder match the profile of the charted depths, you can be reasonably comfortable with the GPS position, particularly if the depth profile has sharp and defined changes.

Although depth is not a definitive check, it is a good indicator when you get a match, and it does not take a great deal of time to compare. Obviously, this comparison is easier when using a chartplotter or computer navigation that overlays the GPS position on a chart.

Using Depth without GPS

If the GPS is suspect, you can use depth as a coarse backup navigator. Using whatever limited information you may have about your charted position, you can compare the depth profile shown by the sounder with the chart as you

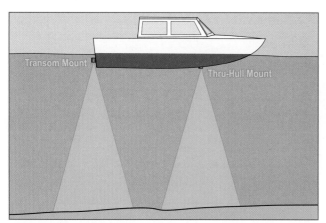

FIGURE 16-8. *Transducers can be mounted at a number of lo-cations. Most fishfinders use transom-mounted transducers. This is more convenient for installation. The transducer is mounted just at or below the waterline. Others are mounted by cutting a hole through the hull and sealing the transducer. Some are mounted inside and send signals through the hull into the water. The sensitivity of these units is lessened by the boat's construction materials.*

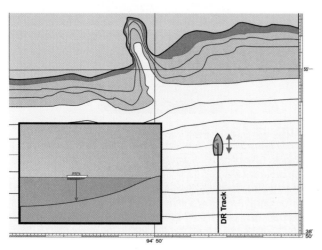

FIGURE 16-9. *Here a boat approaches shore across steadily decreasing depth contours. Operating without GPS and in poor visibility, the navigator is using depth readings to double-check his DR plot. The depth reading at the time of his DR po-sition is in rough agreement (within the range of the line seg-ment shown next to the boat on the DR plot), which gives him more confidence in his dead reckoning.*

move. For example, you should proceed using dead reckon-ing and plot your course steered. You can compare your DR position estimates with the depth provided by the sounder, and refine your DR accordingly. This technique works best when you are approaching a shoreline where the depth steadily decreases toward shore. As you near land, you may prefer to follow a depth profile along the shoreline. Select a depth contour that is likely to take you near a visible navi-gation aid or landmark that will indicate where to turn into the harbor.

You should also consider using a technique called the *intentional miss.* If you are not sure about your position

while well off from the harbor, aim some distance to the left or right of the direction you believe to be correct. In other words, plan to miss the harbor in a known direction. Now, when you reach the desired depth, turn in the direction of the harbor and follow that contour until you find it. If you had navigated directly toward your best estimate of the har-bor's location and missed, you would not know which way to go when you reached shallower water. By intentionally missing to one side, you increase your probability of follow-ing the profile in the proper direction.

Using Depth with Radar

Even if the GPS has failed, the sounder can help you refine your position estimate when used in conjunction with your radar. By adjusting the radar to achieve a view of the shore-line, you can develop a sense of your general location by us-ing your charts for comparison. If you are far enough out, only higher elevations along or inside the shoreline will re-turn echoes. Nevertheless, radar will give you a sense of your relative location along the shoreline; and the depth sounder will help you more precisely pinpoint your position by matching the local depth profile.

With the radar providing a view of the shoreline, you know the direction to land. As you near the shore, the radar will display greater detail, and the shore itself will become more distinct. You may now be able to identify your general location using radar alone but still not have distinct landmarks to achieve a worthwhile fix. The depth profile reported by the sounder can be used to refine your position estimate and enable you to plot a path to your destination.

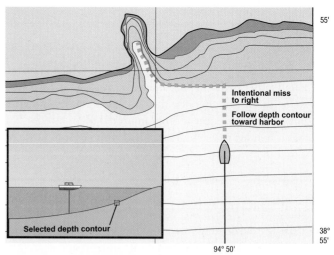

FIGURE 16-10. *The navigator in Figure 16-9 is using a tech-nique called the* intentional miss. *Using your best estimate of the course to your destination, plan to intentionally miss to one side—in this case, to the right. Now, using depth alone, navi-gate toward shore until you reach a predetermined depth con-tour. Turn and follow that contour along the shoreline until you see features of your harbor or you notice the turn in the con-tour. This is your approach channel.*

Using Radio in Navigation

Radio can be an essential tool, especially in an emergency. Marine VHF-FM is the radio of choice. Although recreational boaters are not required to own or operate a VHF radio, it's highly recommended that you do so. VHF radios are offered in both fixed and handheld configurations.

In an Emergency

The major justification for having a VHF radio is safety. In the event of an emergency, you are likely to reach the U.S. Coast Guard directly, if you are within range. Upon receiving an emergency call, the USCG can use your signal to isolate your position and effect a rescue.

Channel 16—International Distress, Safety, and Calling

On VHF radio, one channel is designated for initiating calls and distress. Channel 16 is monitored by all USCG stations and boats, and must also be monitored by all commercial marine traffic. Recreational boaters also use channel 16 for emergencies. If you have a radio, it is sound practice to monitor channel 16. Even if it's just one of a number of channels that you scan, tuning to channel 16 enhances the chances that an emergency call will be heard. If the calling party is out of the Coast Guard's direct range, another boat may be able to relay the distress call to the Coast Guard.

Channel 16 is also used to initiate calls for regular traffic. If you have not prearranged another calling channel, you initiate a call on channel 16, then switch to a working channel as explained later in the chapter under "Routine Calls."

The net effect is that there is a lot of traffic on channel 16. Even with distress getting top priority, some calls could be missed. In high-traffic areas, channel 9 is sometimes designated as the preferred calling frequency, with channel 16 reserved for distress.

FIGURE 17-1. *VHF radios are not navigation tools, but their use is essential to navigation. Fixed-mount units offer greater transmitting power and longer and higher antennas, and thus, a much longer range capability. Handheld VHF radios are popular and useful for short-range communication and as a backup. (Courtesy: Raymarine, ICOM, Standard Horizon)*

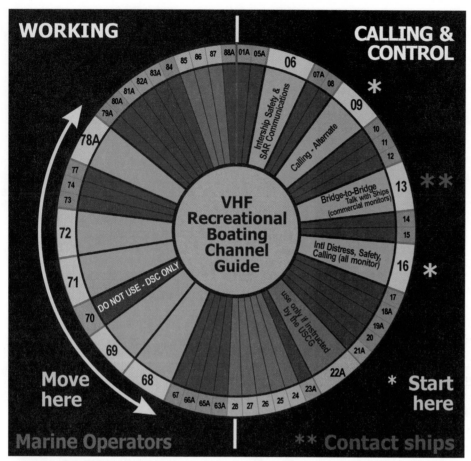

FIGURE 17-2. *There is a wide group of VHF channels, but only a limited number are open to recreational boaters. You generally make contact using channel 16 or 9, then switch to a working channel for communication. Recreational boaters have channels 68, 69, 71, 72, and 78A as working channels. Channel 13 is used to communicate with commercial ships and bridges. Channel 16 is used for international distress as well.*

DSC

A new worldwide system called the Global Marine Distress and Safety System (GMDSS) has been adopted, and the USCG is in the process of upgrading to accommodate these new features. Under GMDSS, any VHF radio designed after 1999 includes a special channel for digital selective calling (DSC). DSC uses channel 70 to send a digitally coded message. With digital calling, a significant amount of traffic can be accommodated over a single channel. In addition, under GMDSS, the DSC channel also transmits a unique address tied to your radio with your identity and your GPS coordinates. (To transmit your coordinates, the radio must be connected to a GPS receiver.) Unfortunately, only fixed VHF radios are mandated for DSC capability, but some handheld DSC models are available.

A distress call initiated on a DSC-equipped radio is received by all other DSC radios and sounds an alarm. It also acknowledges the receipt of the distress alert back to the sending radio and switches that radio to channel 16. All DSC radios receiving the alert are automatically switched to channel 16. The calling party then verbally reports emergency information (see "Mayday," below), which can be heard by all other radios within range. The USCG is in the process of implementing DSC within its high-ground stations. Meanwhile, all regular channel 16 emergency calls are received as well. The United States does not require recreational boaters to replace any older analog designs. The analog radios are fully functional but cannot

FIGURE 17-3. *Digital selective calling is a mandatory requirement in all new fixed radio designs (although earlier designs without DSC can still be sold). DSC uses channel 70 as a digital calling channel. You can issue a distress call using DSC, and all DSC radios within your range are automatically switched to hear your call. This saves time and the risk of being unheard on a too-busy channel 16. By connecting your DSC-VHF radio with your GPS, your position is automatically transmitted as well. Additionally, you can signal another individual DSC receiver and switch its channel to your selected working channel for a more private conversation, much like a cell phone call. Some handheld VHF radios are being offered with DSC as well.*

send or receive DSC alerts. Analog radios can tune to channel 70, but under no circumstances should you transmit voice over that frequency, and you will not be able to understand the digital tones.

In order to be fully functional, you need to register your DSC-equipped radio and get a Marine Mobile Service Identifier (MMSI) number assigned. The registration process records basic information about the boat and its owner, so the information is immediately available to rescuers in the event of a distress call. (Currently, BoatU.S. is one of the registering organizations in the United States for recreational boats.)

DSC radios are equipped with a red button—often with a safety cover over it—that you press in the event of a distress call. It automatically transmits your call, MMSI, and coordinates (assuming your radio is interfaced with GPS). Any DSC receiver within range will sound an alarm to alert the crew and immediately switch to channel 16 for a response. If your radio sounds a DSC alarm, you should wait briefly and listen to see whether the Coast Guard answers the call. If they do not, you should answer the distress call. There is a possibility that the Coast Guard will hear your response even if they did not hear the original

call. In essence, you could become a relay between the Coast Guard and the calling party.

DSC also can be used to selectively call other parties, either individually or in groups. You must have their individual or group MMSI numbers to make these calls. Upon receiving the call, the selected radio or radios will sound an alert and switch to a preselected working channel for talking.

DSC calls include your MMSI number and (if GPS is interfaced) your coordinates. Newer GPS chartplotters connected to your DSC radio can display the location of the calling party upon receiving a DSC call. This is particularly useful for distress calls but may be convenient for coordinating a rendezvous with other boats as well.

Routine Calls

Routine calls on an analog VHF radio (i.e., without DSC) are initiated on channel 16. You must first listen to be sure the channel is clear and you will not step on another communication. After pressing the button on the microphone, you identify the name of the called boat (up to three times), followed by the name of your boat and call sign (if you have one). All of this must take less than thirty seconds. Next, listen. If there

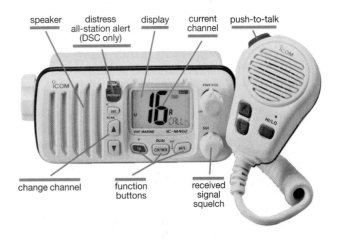

speaker   distress   display   current   push-to-talk
all-station alert   channel
(DSC only)

change channel   function buttons   received signal squelch

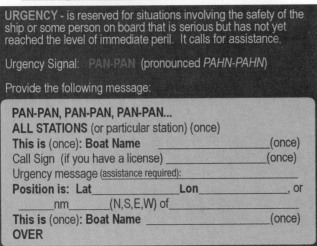

URGENCY - is reserved for situations involving the safety of the ship or some person on board that is serious but has not yet reached the level of immediate peril. It calls for assistance.

Urgency Signal: **PAN-PAN** (pronounced *PAHN-PAHN*)

Provide the following message:

PAN-PAN, PAN-PAN, PAN-PAN...
ALL STATIONS (or particular station) (once)
This is (once): Boat Name _____ (once)
Call Sign (if you have a license) _____ (once)
Urgency message (assistance required): _____
Position is: Lat_____**Lon**_____, or
_____nm_____(N,S,E,W) of_____
This is (once): **Boat Name** _____ (once)
OVER

SAFETY - is reserved for information regarding navigation safety.

Safety Signal: **SÉCURITÉ** (pronounced *SAY-CUR-I-TAY*)

Provide the following message:

SÉCURITÉ, SÉCURITÉ, SÉCURITÉ....
ALL STATIONS (once)
This is (once): **Boat Name** _____ (once)
Channel # for message: _____
OUT (go to channel, repeat above & provide message)

FIGURE 17-4. *Distress calls come in three levels. You use channel 16 (unless using DSC) to initiate these calls. First, listen to make sure that the channel is clear. Press the microphone button, then clearly provide the information shown in the graphic. Pan-Pan calls are for lesser emergencies, such as fuel outage or non-life-threatening injuries. Sécurité calls are made to inform boaters of potential hazards such as a floating log.*

is no answer, you can repeat the call in two minutes. You can repeat the call once more after two minutes, but if it still isn't answered you must wait another 15 minutes and start over.

The receiving party will answer on channel 16 with your boat name and theirs, and indicate what channel you should switch to for further communication. Channels 68, 69, 71, 72, and 78A are designated for such communications between recreational boaters.

Safety and Distress Calls

Safety and distress calls are categorized into three levels under the heading "Emergency Calls." This is an internationally recognized protocol. You should be well versed in these calls and be prepared to use them. It's a good idea to write down the key information about your boat and itemize other information. That will facilitate a brief, crisp call in the event of an emergency.

MAYDAY Mayday repeated three times indicates immediate peril and risk to human life. This call is the highest level of priority. Anyone hearing this call on channel 16 should cease any activity on that channel and await an answer from the Coast Guard. If, after waiting for a reasonable time, no response is heard, answer the call yourself by repeating the information. Then relay the information to the Coast Guard.

When placing a Mayday call, you need to provide several key pieces of information, as illustrated in Figure 17-5.

The entire emergency process is designed to maximize the potential for your call to be heard. If the Coast Guard cannot hear your call because you are out of range, there is a good chance that someone on another boat at an intermediate position will hear your message and relay it.

PAN-PAN Conditions of emergency or potential emergency falling below the threshold of immediate risk to life are treated under a separate category called Pan-Pan (pronounced *pahn-pahn*). The radio procedures are similar.

SÉCURITÉ The third, and lowest, level of emergency call is called Sécurité (pronounced *say-cur-i-tay*). These calls are used to announce the presence of a navigational risk such as floating logs.

Weather Radio

From a navigation perspective, the weather reports and forecasts transmitted on VHF frequencies are extremely valuable. NOAA broadcasts continuously on seven frequencies across almost all areas of the United States, using a network of 800 transmitters across all 50 states. The Canadian government also broadcasts on a number of these frequencies.

Your VHF radio is designed to receive these transmissions, when you select one of the receive-only weather frequencies on your transceiver. You will not be able to monitor VHF marine traffic or transmit while you are monitoring the weather channels. Because VHF is nominally a line-of-sight transmission system, you will be able to receive the transmissions for some forty nautical miles or so from the station. Adjacent stations operate at different frequencies (for example, wx1, wx2, et cetera) to avoid interference.

The reports continuously provide weather information for users on land as well as marine reports. The reports are updated hourly to reflect the latest data. For the most part, these reports use a computer-generated voice, repeating every few minutes.

Fixed versus Handheld VHF

You should consider a fixed-mount VHF for your boat. This may be the only means of communicating to get help in the event of an emergency. Fixed units operate at up to 25 watts of power, whereas handheld units are limited to about 5 watts. All VHF radios must have a 1-watt setting for short-range communications to minimize stepping on other users over a wide area.

Along with your fixed VHF, you should choose the highest gain antenna that is practical on your boat, and mount it as high as possible. VHF is a line-of-sight communication, so the higher you place your antenna, the greater your range. Longer antennas have more directional gain than short ones. Directional gain increases the effectiveness of the radio in horizontal directions. This is equivalent to increasing the radio's power as well as the sensitivity of its receiver.

A handheld VHF has only a short, inefficient antenna that is not very high above the water. You can expect to get a few miles out of a handheld radio, whereas a fixed unit may be able to reach a USCG tower from 20 nautical miles away or greater.

DISTRESS - is reserved for situations involving risk of life and/or grave and immediate danger. It calls for immediate assistance. It has priority over all other forms of traffic.

Distress Signal: MAYDAY
Provide the following message:

MAYDAY, MAYDAY, MAYDAY...
This is (once): Boat Name _____ (3 times)
Call Sign (if you have a license):_____ (once)
MAYDAY, Boat Name _____
Position is: Lat_____ Lon_____, or
_____nm_____(N,S,E,W) of_____
Nature of Distress _____
Assistance Required _____
Boat description _____
No. of persons on board _____, other_____
OVER

FIGURE 17-5. Mayday is the highest level of emergency call. It is made only when there is real risk to life. Mayday calls have priority over all other forms of traffic.

Using an Electronic Compass

Many boat owners are opting for electronic compasses, which provide more accurate heading information than their magnetic couterparts and can be interfaced with other electronics to export data. These data can help guide autopilots and orient radar displays to match your charts. Nonetheless, it's still a good idea to keep an old-fashioned magnetic compass on board. If you should lose your GPS due to power failure, it would be a shame to lose your only compass at the same time!

Types of Electronic Compasses

Fluxgate Compass

The most popular type of electronic compass is the fluxgate compass. It is a magnetic compass, and as such is subject to the Earth's magnetic field as well as onboard influences from metal and other electronics. The fundamental difference between electronic and mechanical compasses is in the way the magnetic field is sensed. On a traditional compass, a card with an embedded magnet is suspended on a pin and sealed in a liquid-filled globe. The card spins until the magnet aligns with magnetic north. The configuration is designed to let the card seek a level position even as the boat heels or pitches at sea. The biggest problems with these compasses are mechanical limitations that may inhibit how accurately the card points to magnetic north, and the need for compensation on the boat. (Compensating a compass to reduce deviation is described in Chapter 4.)

A fluxgate compass uses coils of wire to sense the Earth's magnetic field. Two sense coils are wound in opposite directions, and a drive coil is used to create a local magnetic field. The Earth's magnetic field adds to the drive coil field on one side and subtracts from it on the other. The other two coils sense the relative proportions on each side and these determine the direction of the Earth's magnetic field. The fluxgate compass display is usually presented both as a digital heading readout and a graphic simulation of an analog compass card. Since the fluxgate compass is not required to turn like a traditional compass, accuracy is improved. However, the sensor electronics need to be nominally horizontal to achieve the best accuracy, so for marine use, the sensor is mounted on a gimballed platform.

In addition to providing an electrical data output to electronic devices, perhaps the greatest advantage of a fluxgate compass over traditional compasses is its ability to self-compensate. The microprocessor that converts the electronic sensor output to a direction also enables self-compensation. When the boat is turned through a series of slow circles, the microprocessor computes and corrects for the error at each and every angle. Typically, a good fluxgate compass is accurate to within 1° or better. Their moderate cost also makes them popular.

A fluxgate compass can also display your heading in degrees true. Thanks to the embedded microprocessor, you enter your local magnetic variation and it performs the calculations and adjusts the display.

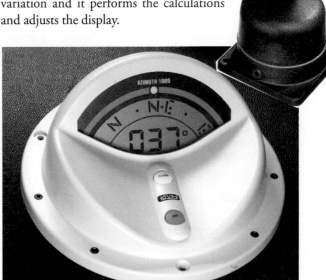

FIGURE 18-1. *Fluxgate compasses come in self-contained display and compass units such as the KVH Azimuth 1000, or as a sealed fluxgate sensor that can be placed at an optimum location on the boat and connected with other electronics. (Courtesy: Raymarine, KVH)*

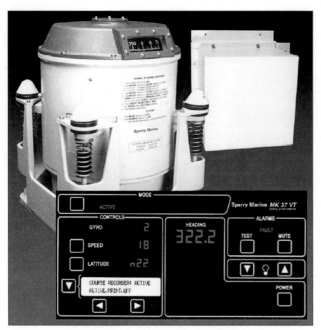

FIGURE 18-2. *The gyrocompass does not use a magnetic sensor. Instead, it uses a precision gyro that is set to a known bearing. Once set, the gyrocompass maintains precise heading information. These compasses are used on commercial and naval vessels. Very few recreational boats use one due to the high cost. (Courtesy: Sperry Marine)*

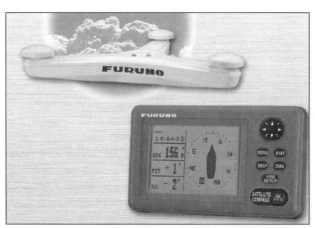

FIGURE 18-3. *A GPS compass typically uses three GPS receivers and antennas. The antennas are separated by several feet. The incoming GPS signals are compared and the direction between the antennas is sensed and processed to provide heading even when the boat is not moving. (Courtesy: Furuno)*

The processor also can average readings to provide the equivalent of different dampening levels of the heading indicator. Dampening is an inherent feature of a traditional compass: the viscosity of the liquid slows the movement of the compass card and provides a steadier reading. Powerboats and sailboats respond differently to the sea, and their compasses require different degrees of dampening to smooth out the reading. The fluxgate compass gives you the choice of how much you want the output dampened.

Gyrocompass

A gyrocompass is typically ten to forty times more expensive than a fluxgate compass. The gyrocompass does not use the Earth's magnetic field to maintain its alignment, so it is completely independent of local influences. The gyro needs to be preset to true north. Once set, it uses the gyroscopic effect of a turning wheel to maintain that direction. However, due to friction and other factors, the gyro drifts and must be updated periodically. Typically, these compasses are highly accurate and are used in offshore navigation, where a small angular error can result in a significant position error over time. These devices are common on larger commercial ships and on some yachts that use autopilots.

Many professional compass compensators use a gyrocompass to adjust a ship's magnetic compass. Given the high cost of gyrocompasses, few recreational boaters use them.

GPS Compass

The latest in highly accurate compass designs employs GPS in a special configuration. As explained earlier, GPS is not a compass. You must be moving in order to get a direction. However, GPS compass designers have overcome this limitation by building two or three GPS receivers into the same assembly (separated by about thirty inches). To obtain a directional reading, all the unit needs to do is compare the positions of each GPS antenna. This information alone would not be accurate enough, but using a special technique called phase tracking, the electronics can measure minute signal differences in each antenna. Those precise differences can be converted into a highly accurate direction, even when the GPS is not moving.

These devices achieve accuracies comparable with many gyrocompasses, without the need for external alignment. Because they use GPS, they are not subject to local magnetic influences and thus provide direction with respect to true north. But the GPS compasses on the market as of this writing are oriented toward commercial rather than recreational users. Prices are about half those of comparable gyrocompasses, and they're expected to drop further over time.

Using the Electronic Compass for Navigation

Once a fluxgate compass is installed on the boat, you need to calibrate it. Typically, you need to activate the calibration mode, then turn the boat in fairly slow, moderate-size circles until the unit reports that it is finished.

Next, you need to select both the appropriate dampening level for your boat and the north reference. If you choose to have the fluxgate compass display true north, you will be able to more quickly correlate direction with your charts. If you do this, make sure that you set your GPS to true north reference as well.

Remember that the compass is still a heading reference that reflects the pointing angle of the bow, not the movement of the boat over ground as reported by your GPS.

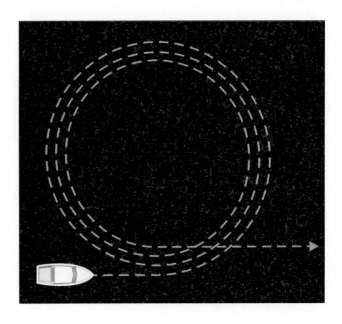

FIGURE 18-4. *The fluxgate compass initially requires that you run several slow circles to perform its internal compensation. It looks at the magnetic reading from every heading and computes the corrections, which are then stored in the unit's memory. Once calibrated, most fluxgate compasses constantly update their compensation to maintain their accuracy even if metal objects or electrical wiring is added or moved on the boat.*

Automatic Identification System

AIS brings a whole new dimension to your awareness and identification of other vessels. But before we talk about AIS, let's review how you might identify another vessel to avoid a collision using just your radio and radar. Here is a typical example:

The weather is hazy. You are in a 30-foot powerboat traveling northeast along the channel. You see at least a dozen boats on your radar and are concerned that a sailboat may be attempting to cross your bow on a port tack. You pick up your VHF microphone and place a call on channel 16. Here's what is likely to happen.

"Sailing vessel on my starboard bow, this is Longbow, *a 30-foot powerboat in the channel. It appears that you are making a turn to starboard. Do you intend to cross my bow, over?"*

*"*Longbow, *this is* Sailfree. *Are you the powerboat northbound near buoy 10, over?"*

*"*Sailfree, *this is* Longbow. *Negative, I am two miles southwest of that position, over."*

PAUSE

*"*Longbow, *this is* Seabreeze. *Are you in the vessel with a blue hull, over?"*

*"*Seabreeze, *this is* Longbow. *No, we have a white hull, over."*

AND SO ON...

This process of trial and error has been used for decades as vessels attempt to identify each other and communicate to share their intentions. Radar, covered in Chapter 15, is a superb tool, providing you with real-time imagery of objects around your boat. However, when you see an object on the screen, you have to ask yourself, "What or who is that?"

Now picture your chartplotter screen with other boats displayed at their respective positions along with their names and directions of travel. That comes from the Automatic Identification System. AIS is not on every boat or ship, so it does not replace radar, but it adds an important dimension—identification. With AIS, your exchange would be

much easier, since you now know the name and MMSI for the vessel in question. As a refresher, MMSI (Maritime Mobile Service Identifier) is a unique number assigned to a ship and its radio by which it can be individually signaled by another radio.

What Is AIS?

AIS incorporates a transponder mounted aboard a ship to transmit detailed information about that ship and its progress, and a receiver component to gather the same data from other vessels. There are two levels, or classes, of AIS—Class A and Class B. There is also the option to use just an AIS receiver, without a transponder. In each case the receiver intercepts AIS transmissions and can provide a wealth of information from a transmitting ship, including its name, MMSI, course, speed, and, if it is turning, the direction and rate of turn. When your AIS receiver is connected to your chartplotter or navigation computer, the positions of all ships

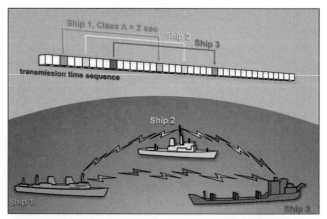

FIGURE 19-1. *Using the Automatic Identification System (AIS), ships transmit and receive information about their identities, positions, movements, and voyages. Two dedicated VHF channels are used, and transmissions are prioritized and staggered according to the class of AIS carried.*

within range that are transmitting AIS signals will be displayed.

This chapter provides an overview of AIS from a user's perspective, and explains the advantages of owning and knowing how to use AIS, in the form of either a simple receiver or a full transponder/receiver system. Properly used, AIS can provide a dramatic boost to your vessel's safety.

AIS operates on two VHF channels, sharing these channels between all boats and ships within antenna range. It is a system originally intended for commercial shipping for traffic control and inter-ship safety. However, AIS has quickly found its way onto a wide range of ships, other commercial vessels, and recreational craft. The AIS transponder incorporates its own GPS receiver to provide positional and navigation information to others. Using its GPS and often other data sources aboard ship, the AIS formulates messages that it transmits at specific intervals depending upon the class of AIS involved. Those messages are in different categories, which include vessel-specific information, voyage-specific information, and current position and motion information. More on that shortly.

AIS offers many advantages. Clearly, being able to identify a specific vessel and its actions is at the top of the list. AIS also can see in places that radar cannot. For example, vessels around a blind curve or masked to radar by intervening landmasses can be identified on AIS. The leading disadvantage, and why you still need radar, is that not every vessel has AIS on board.

Class A AIS

Class A is what you will find on most commercial ships. It is the higher-power version, offering 12.5 watts nominal transmitted power on VHF channels 87B and 88B. It also has a lower-power two-watt mode. The Class A AIS transponder must incorporate a display, an integral GPS receiver, and interface with the ship's GPS, heading sensor, and rate of turn indicator.

Messages are broadcast generally at two-second intervals, providing updated present position, heading, course over ground, speed over ground, and rate of turn information. Slow-moving or anchored ships broadcast at a longer interval. The ship's name, MMSI, and other relevant information are also transmitted at longer intervals.

Class A transponders are required on ocean-going vessels and most of those carrying passengers by international treaty and Coast Guard regulations. The detailed current requirements in international and U.S. waters are shown in the table on page 202; however, the list of required-carry vessels is evolving. AIS will probably be required on most commercial vessels eventually. The Class A carrying vessels generally are large, with limited maneuverability. They may

require considerable distance to turn or stop, and tend to travel at deceptively high speeds compared with recreational boats. The 12.5-watt transmitted power gives considerable range, so boats at quite a distance will be able to "see" these vessels and take action to avoid collisions.

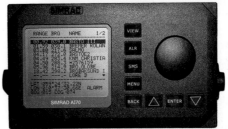

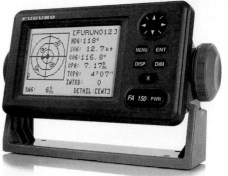

FIGURE 19-2. *AIS Class A receivers carry integral displays showing a wealth of information, including the identities, positions, and courses of AIS-transmitting vessels within antenna range. Full-capability AIS units are offered by many leading marine electronics manufacturers. Shown are examples of currently available transponders. Each has a transmitter and two receivers, one for each channel; displays show text information received from other vessels. (Courtesy: ACR, Simrad, L3 Communications, and Furuno)*

Information Transmitted by AIS Class A

One of the primary challenges in designing AIS was packing all the needed information into two VHF channels without one vessel stepping on the transmission of another. The resulting design uses a system of time slots in which all Class A transponders in range self-manage and decide when to transmit. For those who keep up with these technologies, it is called self-organizing time-division multiple access

INFORMATION TRANSMITTED BY COMMERCIAL VESSELS

Static Data. This is data entered into the AIS upon commissioning of the unit on the ship. Transmitted every 6 minutes.
- Vessel IMO Number
- MMSI (Maritime Mobile Service Identifier)
- Vessel name, port of call
- Call sign and name
- Length and beam
- Location of the GPS antenna on the ship (reported position on AIS) *[Aft distance from bow, distance to port or starboard from centerline]*

Voyage-Related Data. This data is manually entered via password-protected entry prior to voyage. Transmitted every 6 minutes.
- Ship's draft
- Hazardous cargo (type)
- Route plan
- Destination and ETA (at master's discretion)

Dynamic Data. This is data derived from on-board sensors. Transmitted according to the following interval:

At anchor	3 minutes
0–14 knots	10 seconds
0–14 knots and changing course	3½ seconds
14–23 knots	6 seconds
14–23 knots and changing course	2 seconds
Over 23 knots	2 seconds

- Ship's position, indicating accuracy and integrity of data (from GPS)
- Time in UTC (from GPS)
- Course over ground (from GPS)
- Speed over ground (from GPS)
- Heading (from electronic compass)
- Navigational status—"at anchor," "not under command," "underway," etc. (manually entered)
- Rate of turn (where available) (from rate gyro—part of autopilot)

Safety-Related Messages. Important information from authorities or vessels:
- Brief messages from ships or shore stations, may include notices to mariners, navigational warnings, weather, search and rescue communications, or ship-specific messages from Vessel Traffic Management

(STDMA). It uses the precise time accuracy from GPS to synchronize the sequential transmissions from a host of ships. There are 2,250 time slots allocated under this protocol. Each ship announces its projected time slots so others will avoid them. A new ship entering into range will take an unoccupied time slot and synchronize with others within listening range, and so on.

To gain efficiency, the information to be transmitted is arranged into three categories. The positional data, or *dynamic data*, is more time-sensitive and is therefore transmitted more frequently—nominally 2-second intervals in this case. Information about the vessel is not time-sensitive, so the name, MMSI, and other related data is transmitted at a less frequent interval. This information falls into two categories, *static data* about the ship itself, and *voyage-related data* that describes current mission information. There is also another category for *safety-related messages* that are equivalent to *Sécurité calls* made on voice VHF. If the vessel is stopped or at anchor, the position data does not change, so it is transmitted less frequently. It is still necessary to transmit this identifying information on a regular basis, as new ships will likely enter into its range and need to be advised. The table at left shows what is transmitted from Class A transponders.

Information to be transmitted about the vessel is entered into the AIS either permanently upon commissioning the ship or AIS, or prior to a voyage. Information about its position and navigation status is provided by an internal GPS, an electronic compass, and, optionally, a rate gyro often included in an autopilot system. The Class A AIS also interfaces with the ship's GPS. The AIS requires access to its own independent VHF antenna to transmit and receive messages, and to an independent GPS antenna.

The Class A AIS consists of two receivers, one for each of the two channels, and a single transmitter. The transmitter alternates transmissions between the two channels. The alternate channel receiver listens during transmissions.

The display unit presents summary information about each ship, usually cataloged by vessel MMSI or Name. The presented information includes the dynamic data plus two critical computations: CPA and TCPA.

Closest Point of Approach (CPA) is calculated based on the provided data from each vessel as compared with your own vessel's dynamic data. It tells you, given no change of course or speed for either vessel, the closest distance that will occur (or has occurred) between the two vessels. It computes this separately for each vessel.

Time to Closest Point of Approach (TCPA) is similarly calculated and indicates the amount of time from the present until each CPA will occur. These calculations are comparable to those performed with radar using ARPA (Automatic Radar Plotting Aid). You will base your decisions to communicate with any particular vessel and/or take evasive action largely based on CPA and TCPA.

The Class A AIS receivers interface with other ships' systems, including the radar, GPS, and chartplotting. Many radar units accept AIS input and will plot AIS targets along with internally computed ARPA targets to present a full picture of the local environment. Navigation software also plots AIS targets. With most systems, by scrolling over one of these targets, you will be presented with the static data for the vessel, usually in a data field or box. Having the vessel's name and MMSI makes it easy to communicate directly with the correct ship, particularly with a DSC-equipped radio that permits signaling a specific MMSI.

Carriage Requirements

The International Maritime Organization established mandatory carriage requirements for approved AIS equipment under the Safety of Life at Sea (SOLAS) convention. Local authorities can add to the list of vessels required to carry and operate AIS. In the United States, the Coast Guard manages AIS carriage based on U.S. law and regulations. The regulations are still evolving, so it would be wise to check periodically with the Coast Guard website under AIS for updates.

Class B AIS

The second type of AIS is Class B, which was approved in the U.S. in late 2009. This system is intended for smaller vessels and recreational boats. Class B has a lower transmitted power of two watts, and thus a shorter range. This is intentional, as the vessels carrying these transponders tend to be more localized and maneuverable than those carrying Class A. This is analogous to the low-power setting on certain VHF marine radio channels, leading to shorter range transmissions and allowing more vessels to share the limited available channels.

Class B AIS transponders also include one transmitter and two receivers. A display is not required, but certain LED indicators are. Usually, these transponders are integrated with an onboard chartplotter or computer to display received targets. The transmitted data format supports heading information, though most users do not connect their Class B AIS units to an electronic compass.

Class B uses the same VHF channels, but a different control protocol than Class A: Carrier Sense Time Division Multiple Access. CSTDMA requires that the Class B AIS listen to the AIS network to determine if the network is free of activity. Only if the network is free can it transmit its information. When possible, Class B is intended to provide updates on dynamic data at 30-second intervals. The Class B AIS must also listen for and comply with information from fixed AIS transmitters, called base stations (more on these later) and must minimize any interference with higher-ranked AIS or aids-to-navigation transmissions. All this means that in higher traffic areas, your Class B AIS may not be able to transmit at nominal 30-second intervals.

Because the density of Class B transponders in any given area may be very much greater than for Class A, the Class B transmissions are shorter and less frequent. As a result there are a number of items of information *not* transmitted by Class B as follows:

VESSELS REQUIRED TO CARRY AND OPERATE AIS

IMO Specified Carriage Requirement (vessels engaged in international voyages):

All ships of 300 gross tons or more

Cargo ships of 500 gross tons or more not engaged in international voyages

All passenger ships irrespective of size

U.S. Coast Guard Additional Carriage Requirement for Vessels Operating in U.S. Waters:

Self-propelled vessels of 65 feet or more in length, other than passenger and fishing vessels, in commercial service and on an international voyage

Same for U.S. voyages excepting passenger vessels certified to carry less than 151 passengers for hire in commercial service

Passenger vessels certificated to carry more than 150 passengers for hire

Towing vessels of 26 feet or more in length and more than 600 horsepower, in commercial service

---

CLASS B MESSAGE TRANSMISSION REQUIREMENTS

Static Data. Transmitted every 6 minutes, divided into two messages due to length; messages sent within one minute of each other.
- MMSI
- Boat name
- Ship type
- Call sign
- Dimensions
- Equipment vendor ID

Dynamic Data. Transmitted every 30 seconds over 2 knots, or 3 minutes under 2 knots.
- MMSI (programmed in unit)
- Time (from GPS)
- Position (from GPS)
- Speed over ground (from GPS)
- Course over ground (from GPS)
- True heading (from electronic compass, if installed)

FIGURE 19-3. *AIS Class B transponders are significantly less expensive than Class A units, but are subordinate to Class A in transmission priority. They use a different transmission control system and send out less information at less frequent intervals. They generally do not carry information displays, but can be connected to chartplotters or navigation software so that AIS targets can be plotted. (Courtesy: ACR, Raymarine, and Comar)*

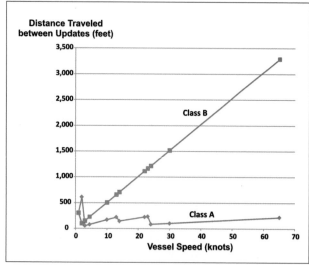

FIGURE 19-4. *There is a dramatic difference in the update intervals for Class A and Class B transponders. At slow speeds, they are nearly identical, but as vessel speed increases, the Class B vessel can be a considerable distance from its last reported position before its updated message may be received. The less frequent transmissions of Class B mean that a fast-moving vessel can be far from its reported position by the time its message is received by another AIS receiver.*

- Vessel IMO number
- Vessel ETA or destination
- Navigation status
- Safety messages (receive only)
- Rate of turn information
- Draft of vessel

The Class B message transmission requirements are shown in the table on page 203.

The Coast Guard does not recommend Class B transponders for vessels that operate at high speed or in close quarters, because of the lag time that may be involved in transmission of position. Class B has a longer interval between transmissions of dynamic messages, typically 30 seconds above two knots. However, the transmission updates can be further delayed in areas of high traffic density as your Class B receiver has lower priority. As you can see in Figure 19-4, a vessel using a Class B AIS while traveling at planing speed can move a considerable distance before transmitting an updated position. A recreational vessel, for example, going 30 knots is likely to be 1,500 feet or more from its reported position before an update is issued. This means that you must take considerable care in relying upon the present position reports of these boats. For the most part, the vessels issuing Class A AIS transmissions are within a few hundred feet of their reported positions.

The Class B AIS contains an internal GPS and connects to two dedicated antennas, one GPS and one VHF. Each unit is required to contain a GPS for position and course/speed over ground information. Class B does not require connection to an electronic compass. Connecting to a chartplotter or navigation software system enables plotting of AIS targets. Class B is a more moderately priced option for recreational boaters if they choose to be seen as well as to see.

AIS Receivers

You may not need a transponder or may not choose to spend what it takes to acquire and install one. Most recreational and pleasure craft operators are not required to carry and operate AIS, so it's up to you. However, you have the option to install just the receiver portion of AIS, so you can observe other AIS-carrying vessels at lower cost. What you lose is the opportunity for others with AIS receivers to see you.

From a system viewpoint, the authorities may prefer that everyone not operate an AIS transponder in high-traffic areas frequented by both commercial and recreational boats. Requiring AIS to be installed on all boats could lead to saturation of the available channels and significantly delayed position reporting. That is one of the reasons why installation of a transponder on a recreational vessel is still voluntary.

However, if you regularly operate your boat near commercial traffic, you would be wise to install an AIS receiver. There have been two types of receivers offered, single- and dual-channel. The dual-channel receiver is preferred because it mimics those on the transponder units and provides the same data. Single-channel units scan between the two AIS channels, and you run the risk of missing a transmission while you are tuned to the alternate channel. A missed Class B update means at least a minute between position reports for that vessel. Single-channel receivers are generally older products, and most companies have stopped making them.

AIS receivers generally do not contain an integral GPS. GPS input is provided from your onboard GPS. As with the transponders, AIS receivers also require a connection to a VHF antenna. Since you are not transmitting from your AIS, you can share your existing VHF antenna between the radio and the AIS, but you need an antenna splitter. Some receivers come with the splitter built in. The VHF antenna is connected to the AIS receiver, and a second cable connects the AIS receiver to your radio. If you choose a receiver without the splitter, plan on spending about $200 for a separate unit. If you get an AIS receiver with the built-in splitter, you will need to reroute your existing antenna cable to it. Remember, this is a line-of-sight system, so antenna height is an important factor for AIS as well as your radio.

A relative newcomer to the market is an AIS receiver integrated with a VHF marine radio. With this solution, you only need to connect to a single VHF antenna. It requires a GPS input, which it uses for both the AIS and the DSC radio functions. The radio/AIS has its own AIS display, unlike many of the other receivers, but it is really designed to work with a chartplotter or navigation computer, with which it can share position information as well as allow plotting of both DSC call position and AIS ship positions.

What AIS Does for You

Automatic Identification System is an ideal solution for quickly and positively identifying ships, particularly in areas of traffic. AIS also provides the locations of certain navigation aids, and can also receive special messages. With a chartplotting system interconnected, each transmitting ship's position is shown on the chart along with a vector indicating its direction of travel, and also indicating if it is underway or turning. AIS-transmitting navigation aid positions are also shown. Anyone familiar with racons will recognize the potential of AIS to replace that function over time. There is also a capability to transmit from a single location the locations of a host of navigation aids at different locations.

AIS Displayed Information

On a typical chartplotter, AIS targets are shown at elongated triangles with the sharp point indicating the course over ground.

By scrolling your cursor over any AIS ship icon, you will be presented with a host of information. Armed with this information, you can contact a particular ship by name or MMSI on your radio to identify yourself, indicate your intentions, or arrange clear passage around the ship. With AIS on most systems, by incorporating your own boat's information, you will be provided with two important pieces of information: closest point of approach (CPA), and time to closest point of approach (TCPA) of every transmitting ship in range. If the CPA with another vessel appears too

FIGURE 19-5. *The simplest and least expensive option for recreational vessels is an AIS receiver without a transponder. These allow reception of information from AIS-transmitting vessels within antenna range, but cannot send out data from the owner vessel. They require only a connection to a VHF antenna. Many have feed-through splitters so you can share your VHF radio's antenna. Most receivers today scan both dedicated AIS VHF channels so that incoming data is not missed. (Courtesy: Raymarine, ICOM, Furuno, and Garmin)*

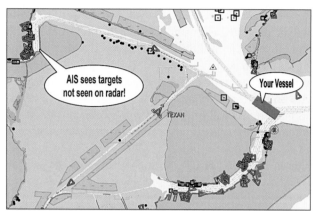

FIGURE 19-7. *Unlike radar, AIS can "see" around headlands and bends in the channel as long as targets are within VHF antenna range. It cannot, however, see obstructions and floating objects like buoys the way radar can. AIS also uniquely identifies each plotted target and its degree of danger of collision with your vessel. You can highlight a specific vessel and be presented with a great deal of information as shown to the left of the chart screen regarding the tug,* Texan. *(USCG)*

close for comfort, you should take evasive action and make it very clear to the other vessel. Obviously, the best way to accomplish that is to call the other vessel. It is a lot easier when you have its name and MMSI.

Remember, AIS is a supplement to radar, not a replacement, because not all vessels carry AIS. The plotted AIS symbols will take care of a lot of other vessels around you in traffic, but not necessarily all of them. Also, even though AIS can reveal other ships that may be masked on radar by land or other obstructions, it does not show landmasses and shows only selected navigation aids or landmasses, which radar does.

Other Uses for AIS

AIS was designed to include a number of related functions that can be of great help to mariners of all types. Here is a list of those services, followed by a brief summary of each.

- AIS base station
- AIS Aids to Navigation (ATONs)
- AIS search and rescue
- Search and Rescue Aircraft
- Search and Rescue Transmitter
- Vessel Traffic Service

AIS Base Station

An AIS base station is a fixed transponder that can send out a variety of information to aid in navigation or alert vessels to hazardous conditions, weather, or water conditions. The base station can also manage the allocation of time slots by excluding certain operators from using selected time slots.

AIS AIDS TO NAVIGATION. Aids to Navigation (ATONs) are often integrated with AIS. For example, a lighthouse or even a buoy can be equipped with an AIS transponder. Then that aid can transmit its location and status, normally every three minutes. These stations can be programmed to provide other safety information, such as weather or tidal data.

An AIS base station can be programmed to transmit the position and emulate a navigation aid elsewhere that does not have AIS installed. When this is done, the virtual aid is known as a *synthetic ATON.* It can even be programmed to show the location of a navigation aid that has been temporarily taken out of service or lost.

The base station AIS can emulate a *virtual* navigation aid or set of aids marking an area to avoid, such as the scene of a plane wreck. These electronic AIS aids will appear on

FIGURE 19-6. *Marine electronics manufacturers are now integrating AIS receivers into VHF radios. The combination units still require a GPS connection, both for AIS plot displays and for the radio's digital selective calling (DSC) feature. The display can be set to present nearby AIS targets or radio information. It requires only a VHF antenna; a connection to your GPS/chartplotter is recommended to provide position information for DSC and to plot DSC calls and AIS targets. (Courtesy: Standard Horizon)*

FIGURE 19-8. *An AIS target is shown on a chartplotter screen as a long triangle with the apex pointing in the direction of the target's travel. In this presentation, your vessel (black symbol) is dealing with three other vessels that could pose a collision risk as it navigates to the selected waypoint (red "X"). By scrolling over the vessel to the right, the display indicates the target's magnetic heading, speed over ground, distance away, and time to intersection at a plotted point.*

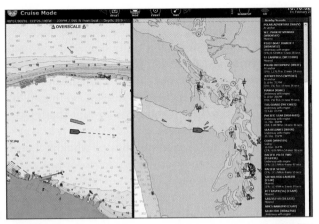

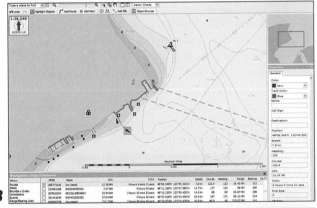

A

B

C

FIGURE 19-9. *Working with AIS targets and data can be easier on a computer screen through a navigation software program. Figure 19-9A shows small- and large-scale zoom levels of the same situation. It appears that you and the vessel to your port are converging. In the right-hand view, you can see other vessels reported by AIS along with a listing of the vessels by name. Figure 19-9B shows full data on 12 separate AIS targets with their respective CPAs and TCPAs, which can be toggled on or off for viewing. Figure 19-9C shows projected tracks from AIS targets with directional vectors. The dots at the ends of the dashed lines indicate where the vessels will be at a predetermined time from now given their current courses and speeds. Harbor Emperor has been highlighted for further information provided in the box. (Courtesy: Rose Point Naviga-*

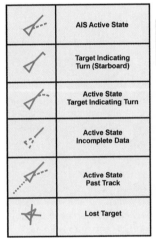

	AIS Active State
	Target Indicating Turn (Starboard)
	Active State Target Indicating Turn
	Active State Incomplete Data
	Active State Past Track
	Lost Target

FIGURE 19-10. *AIS target symbols are designed for quick recognition. Note that magnetic heading reported by a target's electronic compass may differ from the vessel's actual course over ground (COG) due to the influence of current.*

AIS SEARCH AND RESCUE TRANSMITTER (SART). This includes mobile equipment to assist in homing to its location, such as a lifeboat. You normally think of an EPIRB as a device for a lifeboat, but an AIS SART can be employed and intercepted within radio range to provide position messages when activated.

Vessel Traffic Service

AIS serves as a key component in VTS (Vessel Traffic Service) systems, providing identification, position, and relevant information to enable the VTS operators to manage ships in proximity to each other and to their assigned ports.

your chartplotter, navigation computer, or radar as if they were really there.

In order to operate an AIS aid to navigation, the operator must have prior approval of the Coast Guard and the FCC in the U.S.

AIS Search and Rescue

Search and rescue is a time-and-position sensitive service generally led by the Coast Guard. There are associated applications.

AIS SEARCH AND RESCUE AIRCRAFT. An aircraft-mobile AIS will normally provide reports at 10-second intervals. This information is used by SAR managers to coordinate activities by knowing the present location of the aircraft.

The Future of AIS

AIS offers a critically needed identification role that previously relied upon visual or radio verification, or in the case of radar, racon verification. This radio-based transponder system is limited to VHF radio range. However, there are multiple initiatives underway to use satellites to receive the AIS information and relay it over greater distances. This would be used for traffic management, security, and SAR operations. That may not have much direct effect on you as

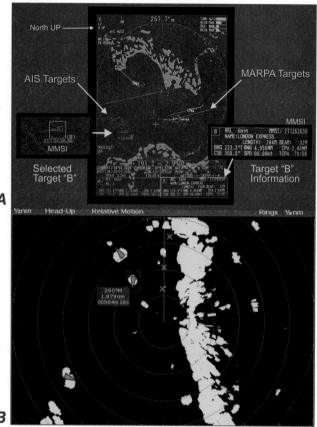

FIGURE 19-11A AND B. *AIS targets can be displayed directly on radar screens. This enables fusion of data from both systems. **A.** You can see AIS targets in red along with details about selected vessels (indicated by four corners shown around the symbol). This screen also shows MARPA targets being tracked on the radar. **B.** A typical recreational boat radar—you can see a nearby boat's echo on radar and its AIS symbol superimposed. (Courtesy: Furuno)*

a recreational boater unless someday you need to be rescued offshore.

What Should I Install?

You could choose a Class A transponder, but you are likely to spend several thousand dollars between transponder, antennas, and installation. If you are not operating a SOLAS-mandated vessel, your best choices are either a Class B transponder or an AIS receiver. The advantage to the transponder is other boats may see you and respond, thus providing more eyes on the situation, but this comes at a cost between $500 and $1,500, plus antenna. You can reasonably expect costs to go down over time as production quantities rise. The transponder requires access to a separate VHF antenna and a GPS antenna. You will want to connect it to your chartplotter or computer to display target information.

On the other hand, an AIS receiver alone is less complex to install and less expensive. Receivers range in price from $150 for a single-channel unit to almost $600 for a

high-end unit. Most receivers today carry an internal splitter to share your existing VHF antenna with your radio. Alternatively, you may find it less costly simply to add a second VHF antenna dedicated to your AIS. The AIS receiver requires data input from your ship's GPS in order to function. Most of the receivers have no displays, so to gain full benefit you need to have it connected to your chartplotter or navigation software system.

Ultimately, most recreational boaters who travel in areas where there is commercial or passenger-for-hire traffic will find it important to use AIS. As more active features become routine on AIS such as warnings, virtual navigation aids, AIS-identified navigation aids, and others, you will find it essential to have at least an AIS receiver. Otherwise, you will be somewhat blind to critical information that you could have displayed right on your chartplotter.

In the meantime, you can see how integral AIS is with radar in Figure 19-11A. This high-end radar screen displays both MARPA targets (ones you selected to be tracked) and AIS targets. The AIS targets are shown in red. Each of the targets is displayed in the local environment along with radar returns. By placing your cursor over any of the targets, you will be presented with a host of information. A similar display is shown for a typical recreational boat radar in Figure 19-11B. Here you can see a nearby boat's echo on radar and its AIS symbol superimposed. By highlighting this symbol, you are presented with the vessel's magnetic heading, its closest point of approach, and time to closest point of approach.

In some cases, you just want a simple display of the AIS data, so you can focus on what targets may represent danger. The display unit in Figure 19-12 provides just such a display, which connects to your AIS receiver. In this example, the darkened triangle represents just such a threat based on alarm criteria that you have selected.

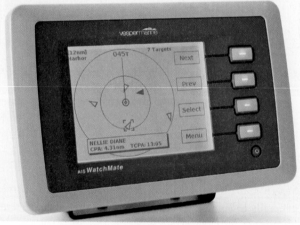

FIGURE 19-12. *Sometimes a simple display is best. This AIS Watchmate connects to an AIS transponder or receiver to provide a display of targets around you. The darkened triangle indicates a dangerous target, and the boxed triangle is the one highlighted to show CPA and TCPA information. (Courtesy: Vesper Marine)*

Using an Autopilot in Navigation

As skipper, you are required to maintain a constant lookout, so why would you want an autopilot? Actually, maintaining a course across undulating seas can be very tiring for the helmsman. The constant attention to steering also diverts focus from other important tasks. In reality, you can maintain a better lookout when an autopilot is operating, and you can pay more attention to your navigation.

Once considered a luxury, autopilots are finding their way onto boats of all sizes. As the name suggests, an auto-pilot steers the boat on a course set by the helmsman. Basically, autopilots are mechanical devices that mate with the steering gear, and take their commands from a control unit. They are driven electrically or hydraulically, with the electrical drive becoming increasingly popular on smaller boats.

Navigating with an Autopilot

The autopilot requires an external heading reference in order to function. Usually, this reference comes from an electronic compass (see Chapter 18).

To operate the autopilot, you simply set the desired course and activate the control. The mechanical gear then adjusts the rudder to correct for any differences between the heading you set and the reading from the electronic compass. How quickly the autopilot responds depends upon the dampening in the compass, any additional dampening in the autopilot, and the responsiveness of your boat to its helm.

FIGURE 20-1. *Autopilots were once considered expensive luxuries rather than serious navigation gear. Today, their costs are moderate and their features make them popular. A typical autopilot includes a display, a processor, and a means of controlling the rudder or ship's wheel.*

FIGURE 20-2A. *When you're boating in moderate-to-heavy seas, the waves tend to push the bow of the boat, causing a yaw, in this case to starboard.*

FIGURE 20-2B. *After you cross the wave crest, the boat will be drawn back in the opposite direction. As a result, you are constantly changing course. Maintaining a heading under these conditions can be tedious, tiring, and prone to errors. The autopilot is designed to handle these constant changes and average out the yawing effects.*

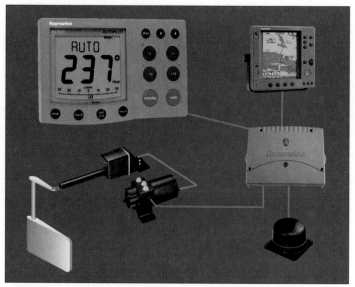

FIGURE 20-3. *A typical autopilot consists of a display unit, a control box, and an electromechanical device to control the rudder. Heading information is provided by a fluxgate compass. A GPS or chartplotter can be used to provide course information for the autopilot to follow. (Component images courtesy of Raymarine)*

Many autopilots offer a range of settings for responsiveness. Greater responsiveness maintains a tighter course by correcting more frequently. This is most useful in narrow channels or regions of restricted maneuverability. Lower responsiveness allows more deviation from the course line but conserves power required to drive the mechanical steering gear. Some units adjust to the sea state and recognize the repetitive motion of the waves. Then the autopilot responds only to actual changes in course rather than the natural reaction of the boat to the wave action.

All autopilots have a quick override feature that puts the unit in standby mode and allows the helmsman to steer. While active, a typical autopilot also allows the helmsman to make small and large changes to the set course to adjust the heading or to avoid an oncoming boat. Once clear, you can restore the original heading. Some units have a "dodge" control that allows a heading deviation (for a lobster pot or buoy), then automatically returns to the original course.

Many sailboats use autopilots to relieve the tyranny of the helm on long voyages. Some units are designed to move the tiller; others connect to the steering gear directly. Special features make some autopilots very useful for sailors. At the press of a button, auto-tack changes the course by approximately 100° to head on the complementary tack.

Most autopilots consist of several components:

- Control unit provides the user interface, display, and buttons, as well as the brains of the system.

- Heading sensor accepts directional input, usually from a fluxgate compass.

- Rudder sensor indicates the position of the rudder to the autopilot.

- Drive system is either hydraulic or electrical. Hy-

draulic systems contain a reversible pump and a hydraulic actuator. The pump is electrically powered and provides hydraulic drive to the actuator, which moves the steering gear. Electrical systems contain relays that control the power to a reversible electric motor that drives the actuator.

- Rate gyro is used on some advanced systems to detect tracking at sea. A rate gyro is a device that senses a change in direction and the rate of change, and provides that information to the control unit, where it is processed.

Using an Autopilot with GPS and Other Devices

By using a GPS to drive the autopilot, you can control the boat's actual track along a preset course toward your waypoint. Without the GPS, the autopilot steers to a boat heading (based on the helmsman's setting and a compass reference). In a crosswind or crosscurrent, without GPS, the boat simply goes where it is pointed. With GPS, the autopilot steers toward the active waypoint and maintains the boat on the original course line. If your course involves a sequence of waypoints, the GPS can drive the autopilot to follow the route to your destination.

Most autopilots are designed to accept steering inputs from a GPS or other devices via standard NMEA 0183 input commands. When the autopilot is set into a track mode, it takes its commands from the GPS. You still have the ability to manually adjust your course around obstacles or other boats, then return to the track mode. Usually, the

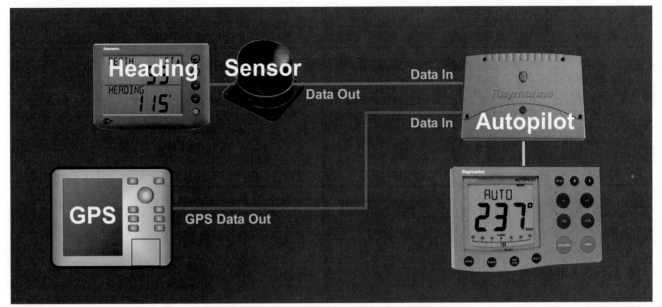

FIGURE 20-4. *A GPS receiver can be connected to the autopilot using the same NMEA 0183 interface that is used to connect GPS to radar and other equipment. The GPS data output and ground are connected to the autopilot data input and ground. (Component images courtesy of Raymarine)*

autopilot sounds an alarm as you approach one waypoint and again before switching to the new heading for a subsequent waypoint along a route. This provides you with the opportunity to ensure that the turn is safe, and to manually accept the turn before it is implemented. Most autopilots also accept crosstrack error information from GPS and display this information to alert you that you may be off the course centerline.

Another steering sensor that can be connected to the autopilot is a wind vane. Given an input from a wind vane and using the boat speed from the GPS, the autopilot can set a course with respect to either the true or apparent wind direction. This mode is designed for sailors, who shape their courses and sail trim to the wind.

SPECIAL TECHNIQUES

Navigating While Tacking into the Wind

Sailing toward the wind—going "to wind'ard," as the old schoonermen called it—brings a new set of challenges. Most cruising sailboats can sail about 45° from the wind direction, whereas racing sailboats can get a good bit closer—sometimes to within 40° or less. We say the typical cruising sailboat "tacks through 90°." If your planned destination falls in that 90-degree sector, you'll need to tack to get there. Your planned course is a straight line (called a rhumb line) from the waypoint just departed to the one ahead. In tacking, you'll zigzag across this rhumb line while making gradual progress along the base course.

Powerboats operating in heavy seas may decide—for reasons of comfort, safety, or both—to take oncoming waves at an angle rather than head-on; this too results in a tacking action.

Tacking adds to the navigation work, but a few straightforward techniques ease the work while helping you stay safe and optimizing the path to your objective.

Figure 21-1 shows a sailboat tacking and some of the data to be monitored. Here a boat tacking through 90° (between headings of about 195° on a starboard tack and 285° on a port tack) is zigzagging up a baseline course of 255° into a wind blowing from 240°. The object is to attain that upwind destination as efficiently as possible while avoiding hazards along the way. To do so, we need to answer two questions. While sailing each tack, how can we make the best progress on it? And how do we know when it's time to tack? GPS can help us with both questions.

Getting the Most out of Each Tack

In considering progress toward an upwind objective, we need to shift our thinking a bit. Up to now we've planned a course and used GPS and other tools to stay on it, but that's not how we sail to windward. Instead, the helmsman constantly monitors conditions, especially wind strength and direction, and makes course adjustments accordingly. He or she responds to favorable shifts (lifts) by heading up toward the wind and destination, and is forced by unfavorable shifts (headers, or what racing sailors call "knocks") to head off, away from the goal. Let's look more closely at what's going on here.

A sailboat's speed through the water depends greatly on its heading relative to the wind, as well as on wind speed. This relationship is sometimes shown on polar diagrams, such as those in Figure 21-2. This boat can sail no higher than 45° off the wind. Increasing that angle slightly increases our speed considerably but heads us farther from our destination on each tack, ultimately forcing us to sail a longer distance. Thus, we're interested in the optimum compromise between heading and speed. If you're lucky enough to have a polar diagram for your boat, you'll have an ideal to shoot for, but you may not duplicate the designer's or builder's data in your particular situation. Helmsmen traditionally find the optimum tacking angle by feel; GPS can help refine the process.

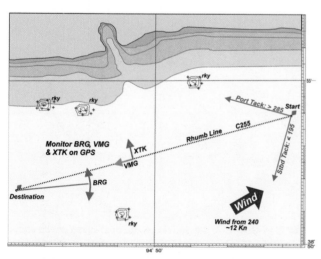

FIGURE 21-1. Sailing into the wind, or powering in heavy seas, means that you cannot go directly to your destination. Your GPS has several data fields that will help you: crosstrack error (XTK), velocity made good (VMG), and bearing (BRG).

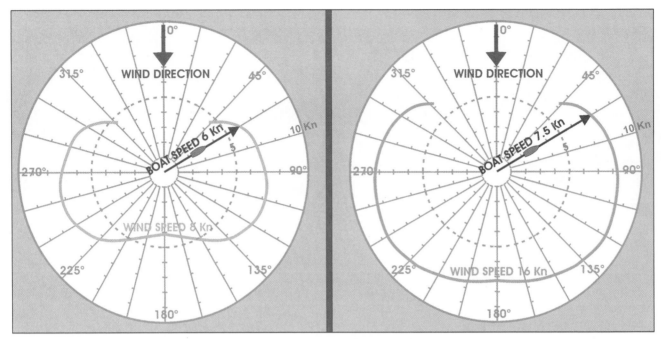

FIGURE 21-2. *Sailboat speed depends upon the angle of the boat's heading relative to the wind. Since this is a topic of great importance to racing sailors, many boat designers will provide polar diagrams for their boats. A polar diagram shows boat speed for various pointing directions relative to the wind. A separate curve is prepared for each wind speed. Two examples are shown: for 8 knots, and for 16 knots. Note that the maximum speed for this boat is achieved on a broad reach (a little over ninety degrees to the wind). The least speed is directly downwind. Within 45 degrees of the wind, the boat cannot make forward progress. In fact, the curve drops off significantly within 60 degress for most boats. You also can see that even with twice as much wind speed, at 60 degrees the boat speed only increases from 6 to 7.5 knots.*

To understand how, let's review the terms of engagement and the corresponding GPS functions. As a boat tacks upwind, its actual track will almost certainly not match its compass heading. All sailboats (and powerboats too) make some leeway or sideslip from the force of the wind. When you sail to windward, the wind and waves are driving you lower (away from the wind) than your intended course. Current may also be a factor (the only one that sometimes helps). The "Track" readout on your GPS receiver accounts for all these factors because it shows your actual course over ground (COG); your GPS speed is speed over ground (SOG).

The VMG (velocity made good) data readout on your GPS shows the vector component of your SOG that is toward your upwind destination (the active waypoint). It stands to reason, then, that the way to get the most out of each tack is to maximize VMG. That is true as long as we confine the discussion to *instantaneous* VMG.

Why the restriction to "instantaneous" VMG? Because, as a boat sails a windward tack, the angle between the boat's track and the destination (the active waypoint) continually increases. This causes the VMG to gradually decrease as you sail along (because you are heading less and less toward the mark). When the mark is abeam (at right angles to your heading), the VMG drops to zero even though the boat is still sailing well. Refer to the boat in Figure 21-6; it's sailing directly at the mark on its last tack,

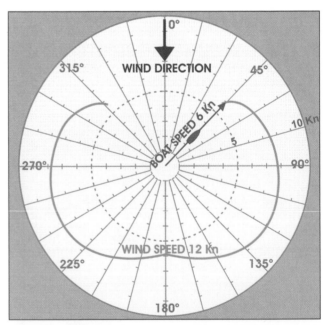

FIGURE 21-3. *At 12 knots, your expected boat speed will be about six knots at a 45-degree angle from the wind. At 50 degrees the effective speed increases about half a knot—a considerable improvement. However, this must be factored against the fact that your course at this direction will take you farther away from your intended objective. VMG is the ultimate measure. That is, your GPS can provide you with VMG so that you'll know just how quickly you're converging on your objective.*

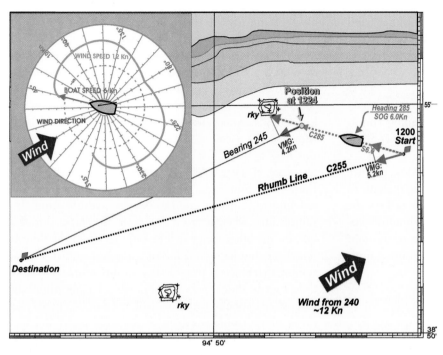

FIGURE 21-4A. *In this scenario, you are sailing at 45° off the wind, or on a heading of 285° on port tack. Looking at the polar diagram for a wind of 12 knots, you can see that your boat speed should be 6.0 knots on this heading. When you started at 1200 hours, the VMG (velocity made good) toward your destination indicated 5.2 knots. You have determined that you will tack when you reach a bearing to your destination of 245° in order to clear the rocks that lie ahead of your port-tack course. You arrive at this bearing 24 minutes later. Now, your VMG has dropped to 4.2 knots. Note your position.*

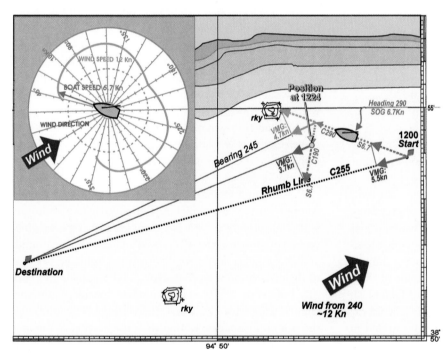

FIGURE 21-4B. *Now, let's repeat the same scenario, but this time, let's steer an additional 5° off the wind (50° instead of 45°) on a heading of 290°. Why would we do this? As you can see from the polar diagram, your boat speed at this heading should be 0.7 knot faster, or 6.7 knots. You are steering slightly farther away from your destination, but you will go faster. When you begin, your VMG is 5.5 knots (0.3 knot higher than before). You still plan to tack at a bearing of 245° to your destination, and you arrive there in less than 20 minutes. You tack to a new course of 190°, which also yields a speed of 6.7 knots. Now, let's see where 4 more minutes will get you. As you can see, at 1224 you are slightly closer to your destination than in the previous scenario, even though you steered a course farther from the rhumb line. Note that your VMG on the starboard tack is lower than on the port tack. This is due to the angle of the wind relative to the rhumb line, which favors port tack. This is a complex computation using charts and polar diagrams, which is why using VMG on your GPS can help you solve these complex problems.*

so its VMG equals its SOG, but just before it tacked, the mark was abeam and the VMG was zero, even though it was sailing a correct course. Thus, although an instantaneous drop in VMG signals a drop in effective speed, a more gradual drop in VMG may not. In this section, then, we focus on maximizing instantaneous VMG with heading and sail trim.

Finding the Best Angle and Trim

The desired heading and sail trim combination as you sail a tack is the one that gives the highest instantaneous VMG toward your upwind destination. When you find that combination, you'll be sailing "in the groove," as racing sailors call it.

In Figure 21-3, a heading of 50° off a 12-knot wind results in a boat speed increase of about half a knot over a heading of 45°. But steering 50° off the wind forces you ultimately to sail a greater distance to reach your destination.

What course is best? The one that gives you the maximum instantaneous VMG under the prevailing conditions. Changing the heading a small amount in either direction from there results in a lower VMG.

Adjustments to sail trim also affect VMG, so once you find your optimum heading, try adjusting the sails to increase the VMG still further. Then go back and try the heading again. It's an iterative process; by continuously optimizing sail trim and heading, a sailor adjusts to constant changes in wind speed and direction while ensuring optimum progress toward an upwind destination.

Knowing When to Tack

While you are sailing a particular tack—be it a zig or a zag—one of the key questions is, How far can I carry this tack? The answer depends upon three factors: (1) your safety, (2) efficient progress toward your objective, and (3) intangibles (the chance to get closer to an interesting boat or shore by carrying the current tack a few minutes longer; complaints from crew who are tired of having to trim the genoa to a new tack every few minutes; the delightful feel of wind and sun on your face on this tack; the necessity of readjusting your seat cushions and drink holder when the boat begins to heel to the new tack; and so on).

FOR SAFETY Of these factors, safety is paramount. The danger avoidance techniques in Chapters 5, 6, and 7 can help you maintain a safe passage while enjoying your indirect but steady march to windward. If the local prevailing winds blow from your regular destinations, it's wise to plot on the charts the lateral limits free of obstacles along often-used courses. You can then plot routes comprising rhumb-line courses between waypoints down the middle of these "fairways," and program these routes into your GPS. This enables you to use the GPS crosstrack alarm to avoid exceeding the lateral limits while you tack, as illustrated in Figure 21-5.

Of course, isolated and clustered hazards must be marked, as discussed in Chapter 6. And don't forget your mariner's eye. You still need a sharp lookout!

FOR OPTIMUM PROGRESS As you tack back and forth toward a windward objective, it's tempting to carry each tack as far as possible, until you're forced to tack by obstacles ahead. Indeed, there is much to be said for this strategy: tacking requires human energy, so reducing the number of tacks advances one of the primary goals of sailing, which is to relax. Then, too, tacking requires a turn through the wind and waves, and this slows a boat down; a minute or more might pass after each tack before the boat gets back up

to speed and the helmsman once more "finds the groove" on the new tack. But when your goal is optimum progress to windward, carrying each tack to its safe limit is not *always* the best thing to do, because the wind is almost never steady over time or from place to place.

Consider, for example, a sea breeze that springs up early on a summer afternoon as heated air over the land rises and cool sea air wafts in to replace it. A breeze such as this may well oscillate back and forth over 30° or more. Suppose, in such a breeze, you're sailing 45° from the rhumb-line course to a windward objective, but then you sail into a 21-degree header. Now you're 65° from the rhumb line, whereas, assuming your boat tacks through 90°, on the other tack you'll be only 25° from the rhumb line. Every header on one tack is a lift on the other. So, assuming that efficient progress is your foremost objective at the moment, should you tack? Probably. Racing sailors say that, when in doubt, you should sail the tack that heads you closer to your objective. And if the wind is shifting frequently and unpredictably, they say you should tack on every header. But what works for racing sailors with their nimble boats and big, eager crews doesn't work for everyone. The rest of us try to evaluate whether the header we've just sailed into is a persistent one; if it is, we may drive some way into it before tacking, so we can maintain the lift on the other tack. Or we may look ahead to see whether there's more wind on the water up there. Or we may look to windward to see how much wind sailboats up there are experiencing, and from what direction. Most likely we'll do all these things, as well as consult our crew's mood and our own, before deciding whether to tack. But can GPS help with this decision?

Only in a limited way, and only if your GPS model computes true VMG, which is your effective rate of closure with your objective. This is a complex and ever-changing vector computation factoring speed and course over ground and the angular departure of the latter from the bearing to the destination waypoint. Not all GPS models give you this bona fide VMG. Some models consider only the angular difference between your course over ground and the rhumb-line course (rather than the bearing to the upwind waypoint), which does not change as long as your track direction and speed do not change—not quite the same thing, and not as useful. This discussion assumes that you have access to true VMG.

As mentioned earlier in the chapter, all other things being equal, your true VMG decreases gradually but constantly along your tack as the relative bearing to your upwind destination grows increasingly wider. The VMG is highest when you commence each new tack and declines continuously as you progress. When the upwind waypoint is directly abeam—that is, when its relative bearing is 90° on a starboard tack or 270° on a port tack—the VMG is zero. If you continue on the same tack, the VMG will turn negative, reflecting that you are actually moving farther

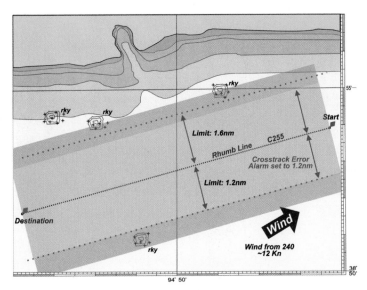

FIGURE 21-5. *Sailing to windward means that you will almost never be on your intended course line, or rhumb line. To stay safe, you can use GPS, but first you will need to look at the limits of the clear area on each side of the rhumb line. Using the crosstrack error function (also called "off course"), you can monitor the limits of travel away from the rhumb line. In this example, the clear path on the right side of the rhumb line is 1.6 nm to clear the rocks; on the left side it's 1.2 nm. Make sure your crosstrack error does not exceed those limits while tacking into seas.*

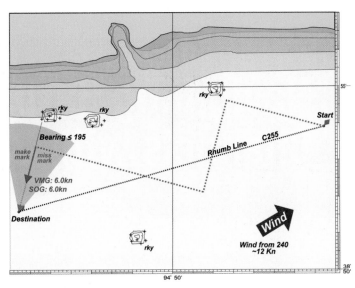

FIGURE 21-6. *The last leg to the destination uses bearing to determine when to tack. The initial analysis using the wind direction indicated that the starboard tack heading should be equal to or less than 200°. To ensure that, you need a bearing to the destination of, say, 195° before you make your final tack.*

away from your objective. A racing sailor would say that you have "overstood the mark."

The key is determining what level of decline from the highest value of VMG constitutes the best time to tack. You might decide to tack after a VMG drop of 20, 30, or 50 percent, based on what you've experienced on the tacks immediately preceding, on what you can see around you, and on all the other considerations alluded to above. Making the call is an art, not a science. Your VMG readout is just one more observation to consider, but it can be an especially useful one when current as well as wind varies across your course. Unlike wind, changes in a tidal current don't cause observable effects on heading, sails, heel angle, or the feel of the helm, but they *do* affect VMG, which your GPS is faithfully recording. Thus, tacking in response to a VMG that begins to decrease faster than it should may well prevent you from being set down from your objective by a foul tide.

WHEN TO MAKE THE FINAL TACK Sooner or later, as you zigzag your way inexorably "uphill" toward a windward objective, you get close enough to start wondering, Gee, if I tack now, can I fetch it? This is another decision that racing sailors and cruising sailors approach a little differently. The racer worries most about "overstanding"—that is, sailing beyond the *layline* (in racing parlance, the imaginary line along which a boat sailing close-hauled can just fetch the windward mark with no margin for error) before tacking, thereby sailing farther than necessary and ceding an advantage to more farsighted competitors. The cruising sailor, on the other hand, is more likely to worry about tacking too

soon; if he tacks, then can't fetch that windward destination, he'll have to tack once or twice more, and that means more work. What the racer calls overstanding the layline and tries to avoid, the cruiser calls money in the bank and tries to ensure.

Either way, the Bearing to Waypoint function of your GPS receiver can help you decide when to (hopefully) make that final tack. In Figure 21-6, you're exactly on the layline when the bearing to the waypoint equals your precalculated starboard tack angle. To put some money in the bank, hold your present tack just a little longer.

POWERBOATS Most of these concepts work for powerboats as well. In this case, you'll be tacking across waves at an angle that matches the capabilities of your boat and the prevailing conditions. If the VMG falls off while you're pointing as much into the waves as you feel comfortable doing, you might consider a tack. Wave action is likely to be variable along your cruise due to interaction with shorelines as well as the wind. By monitoring VMG, you can take advantage of these shifts by selecting the most favorable tack.

Chartplotters and Navigation Software

The techniques described above work with any GPS. If you have a chartplotter or a navigation computer that shows a chart on the screen, your safety is further ensured by watching for hazards and obstacles along each tack.

Navigating Harbors and Channels with Electronics

Navigating in tight channels or within harbors is tricky. Not only is there a higher risk of running aground, there's also an array of obstacles—docks, pylons, moving boats, moored boats, and so on. GPS, radar, and a depth sounder can enhance your safety in these cramped spaces. At night, in fog, or even under conditions of good visibility, your electronics can make a huge difference—if you know how to use them.

Good Visibility

During conditions of good visibility, your task is somewhat easier. Usually, a channel is marked by buoys. All you need to do is stay within the lateral marks and avoid other boats. This is when you should practice using your electronics.

GPS

Your GPS can get you to the channel or harbor, but it may not be accurate enough to safely guide you within. Nonetheless, monitor your GPS whenever you're boating in these areas. If your GPS comes equipped with a marine database, you may find that the stored navigation aids are not exactly where they are shown on the screen. If you have a chartplotter, you may find that the shoreline and channels are not exactly as they are shown on the screen. This could be a result of GPS error, but it is even more likely that shorelines and channels have shifted since the charts were last updated. Although it's handy to have an up-to-date built-in database in your GPS, you can create your own by using the mark feature.

MARKING A CHANNEL OR HARBOR Your marking strategy depends on the character of the harbor or channel. If it is wide, you would be wise to mark the buoys and beacons on the starboard side as you enter the harbor (red), and those on the starboard side as you depart (green). In this way, you have both sides of the channel or harbor stored in your GPS. Simply use the GPS Mark function as each buoy passes abeam. Going slowly improves the accuracy of the process.

If the channel is relatively narrow, you should mark its center. Using this technique, you should be

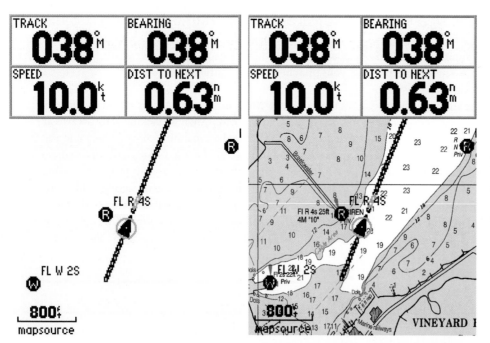

FIGURE 22-1. *Many GPS receiver models provide an error circle on the Map Screen that reflects the current estimated accuracy of the GPS. The screen on the left is from a Garmin GPS 76. On the right, the same screen has been superimposed on a chart segment to convey just how large this uncertainty is with respect to the harbor. Sometimes, this degree of accuracy is inadequate for navigating in a harbor or a narrow channel. If the GPS had been WAAS enabled, the accuracy would be significantly better (ten feet or less).*

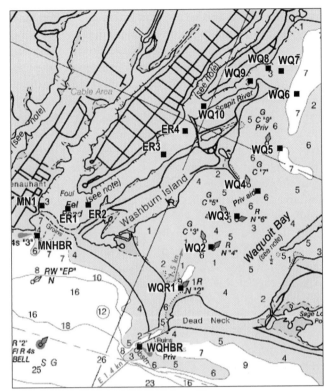

FIGURE 22-2. *As a matter of course, you should mark all the buoys along the channel into your harbor. In this example, most of the GPS waypoints represent the channel center between red and green buoys rather than the buoys themselves. Key navigation aids such as the harbor entry beacon are marked at the location of the actual aid, using latitude and longitude scaled from the chart. Often, the buoys within a harbor are not shown on a chart. The only way to get them in your GPS is to mark them as you pass. Recognize that they may be moved from time to time, so be prepared to update your corresponding waypoints. This digital chart segment demonstrates the downloaded waypoint positions.*

able to see the navigation aids on one or both sides when you reach that spot, even under adverse visibility.

But don't limit your marks to buoys and beacons. There may be some other helpful cues to guide you through turns or alert you to hazards.

The accuracy of your fix is important, as explained below. You will get a sense of the accuracy by comparing the location of marks on the screen with your visual observations of the buoys. You might find that the buoys are in a different location on the screen from when you marked them. It may be worthwhile to mark the same buoys over several transits on different days and at different times. Then edit the marks using the buoys' average coordinates.

ACCURACY GPS is accurate to about forty-five feet (or better) about ninety-five percent of the time. This is superb when you're at sea, but it's not always adequate when you're within a narrow channel. Actually, most GPS sets provide fixes within thirty-three feet most of the time—but this still may not be good enough.

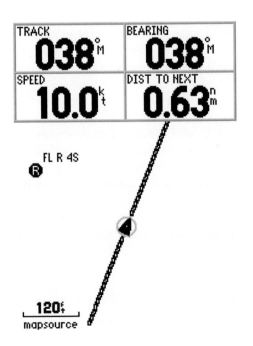

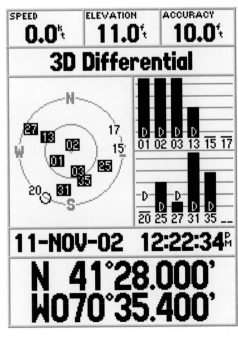

FIGURE 22-3. *This Satellite Screen reflects differential corrections being applied when Wide Area Augmentation System (WAAS) is enabled. WAAS is an FAA system designed to provide a higher degree of accuracy for aircraft, but it also works well for boaters. The "D" symbol on the signal bars indicates that WAAS corrections are applied to that satellite. The resultant accuracy is estimated at 10.0 feet. In the accompanying Map Screen, you can see that the circle remains nearly the same size as in Figure 22-1, but the screen is zoomed in by a factor of 6. In other words, your accuracy has improved.*

The Coast Guard has determined that helmsmen need an accuracy of fifteen feet or better to safely navigate within a channel. (This does not factor in the task of dealing with other boats!) This was used as a criterion for the Differential GPS (DGPS) program, which the Coast Guard developed and manages. Unfortunately, DGPS requires that you have a separate receiver and antenna to get the DGPS corrections that improve your position fix. However, with the advent of WAAS (Wide Area Augmentation System), most recreational boaters no longer use DGPS.

WAAS can provide accuracies to ten feet or better. The Federal Aviation Administration (FAA) developed the Wide Area Augmentation System for commercial aircraft navigation. Pilots needed a system with coverage over land as well as along the coasts. In addition, they were looking for an improvement in accuracy. Recreational boaters are the beneficiaries of this fine program. Fortunately, the corrections are transmitted from geostationary satellites (fixed in position relative to the Earth) on the GPS frequency. All you need is a WAAS-enabled GPS receiver and a clear view to a WAAS satellite. (Boaters—being on the water—usually have an unimpeded view.) There are two WAAS satellites for the United States, one over the Atlantic Ocean and one over the Pacific Ocean. Downloading the WAAS correction information initially takes a while, but subsequent updates come more quickly.

You need to make sure that you have the WAAS function enabled. To do this, use the Setup function in the GPS. You can tell when WAAS corrections are being received by viewing the Satellite Screen. Usually, a "D" appears on the satellite signal bars, or the Status Screen indicates something like "Differential 3-D Navigation." It's very important to know when you have a differential lock, because you won't want to count on this degree of accuracy if for some reason you do not have a WAAS fix. Always check.

TRACK MODE   Another GPS feature you may wish to use is its built-in *track* mode. Using this, the GPS plots where you have been in order to store track points (up to the limits of its memory). When you traverse the same channels and harbors often, you'll find that multiple tracks appear on your Map Screen, representing prior transits.

Radar

Why would you need radar when the visibility is good? Two reasons. First, this is your opportunity to develop familiarity with how these channels and harbors appear on your radar screen. Second, radar provides an extra set of eyes to help you identify nearby boats. Even in clear weather, the radar screen can help make you aware of nearby objects that your eyes miss.

On a clear day, concentrate on buoys and other fixed objects, noting how they appear on the screen relative to your position. It even makes sense to jot some notes on your chart. For example, the entrance to the harbor may not show on your radar until you're nearly lined up. Make a note of that and look for that view before entering the harbor next time.

You also should monitor the shoreline and features such as docks and piers, and compare these with your chart. When the weather turns ugly, you'll feel confident about features you see on the radar screen.

USING RADAR WITH GPS   As described at the end of Chapter 15, radar works with GPS if the two are interconnected. When you activate a waypoint in the GPS, its posi-

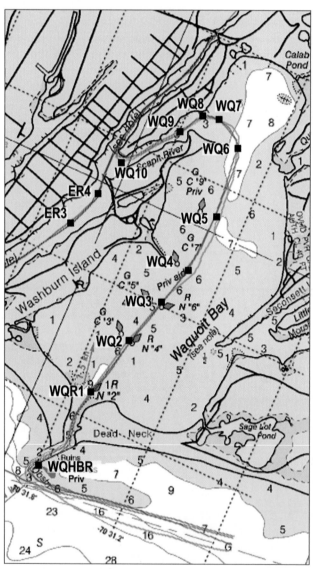

FIGURE 22-4. *The Track feature is available on most GPS models. Using the same digital chart section as Figure 22-2, tracks were downloaded from the GPS and overlaid on the chart. Note that the tracks pass directly over the waypoints. Even if you haven't recorded any waypoints, these tracks can help you navigate a channel simply by repeating a previous safe passage that had been stored in the GPS memory.*

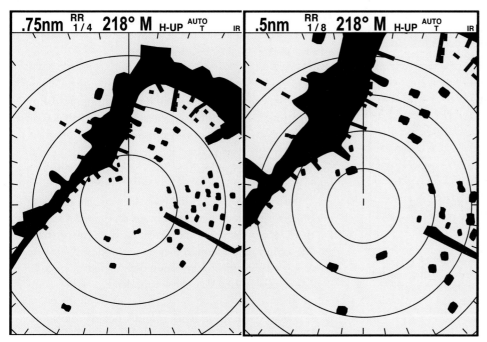

FIGURE 22-5. Left: *Radar can be invaluable for navigating a channel or harbor. In this example, you are entering Vineyard Haven Harbor. You see shoreline features, docks, and the barrier jetty clearly. You also can see a maze of moored boats. At this range, you can get a perspective of your position, but navigation may be difficult. Right: By using a closer range setting, you are able to distinguish other boats and nearby fixed features. Radar indicates the real positions of fixed objects more accurately than charts and GPS in close quarters.*

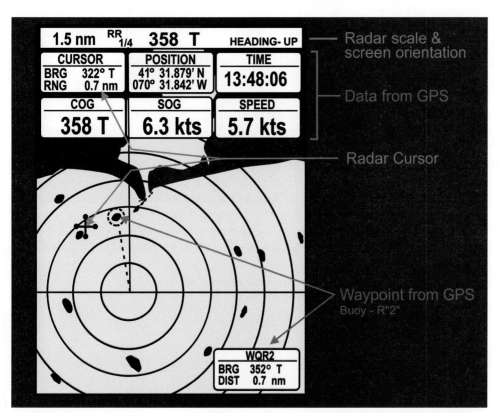

FIGURE 22-6. *When you are navigating toward your harbor, radar in conjunction with an active waypoint (in this case the safe-water buoy at the entrance to the harbor) can show you the way. The radar provides the shoreline features to help you recognize the harbor. The GPS helps to create the lollipop display that guides you to the proper navigation aid.*

tion is relayed to your radar screen, where it shows as a dotted circle. A dotted line extends from the center of the radar screen (your boat) directly to the circle to provide a direction. This presentation is what is known as the "lollipop" display. Generally, you'll use a heading-up display on your radar for these conditions; you can use this picture to steer the boat. Assuming there's a clear path to your next waypoint, just turn the boat such that the lollipop stands straight up. Now you're heading directly for it.

Depth Sounder

Your depth sounder becomes particularly important when you're traversing a channel. By definition, a channel is a deeper path in the water surrounded by shallower water. It may have been dredged or scoured by currents, but it is definitely where you want to be. Often, the edges beyond the channels contain hazards such as rocks.

Much like radar, your depth sounder measures the real conditions around you. In this case, you get a snapshot of the bottom. You need to factor in the current state of the tide. This can be done by quick observations (as well as by using the techniques described in Chapter 14). You should know the local tidal range to get a sense of how much higher the high-water level is compared with the sounding on the charts.

Monitor your depth sounder. It should read levels consistent with what you expect in the channel. If it doesn't, you may need to make some fine course adjustments and watch whether the depth decreases or increases. Obviously, increasing depth tends to indicate that you are moving toward the center of the channel and away from the edges. Note the depth readings on a good day, when you can see where you're going. Develop a sense of the bottom.

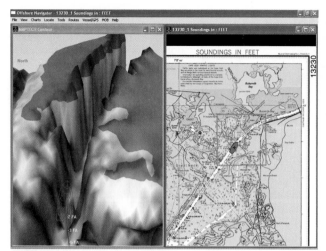

FIGURE 22-7. *Using bathymetric (underwater profile) charts available for computer-based navigation, you can track your progress relative to a channel. You can compare this with your depth sounder as a cross-check of your location.*

Limited Visibility

There's nothing as unsettling as being near hazards in the cramped quarters of a harbor or channel and not being able to see. It's easy to become disoriented at night, in fog, or in heavy precipitation. Just as airplane pilots are told to depend on their instruments, not their sense of direction, under these circumstances, you want to practice repeatedly with your instruments during good days. Stress runs high under adverse conditions. Mistakes come easily.

Navigating by Instruments

The key to navigating under these conditions is using your instruments. I say *instruments* because you cannot rely on any one instrument alone. If you have a GPS, radar, and depth sounder as well as a compass, the sum of what they tell you will keep you more safe.

GPS Your GPS, although being the primary instrument after your compass at sea, should take more of a backseat in close quarters. You'll want to navigate to the center of the channel using your best position information. You'll want to monitor progress relative to marked points along the path. You should use GPS to cue up these marks to observe on your radar.

RADAR Radar becomes a nearly essential instrument if you frequently encounter adverse visibility. Radar not only helps you fine-tune your position with respect to fixed objects, it is the only electronic means of monitoring other boats. This does not rule out or replace the need for a lookout and sound signals, but it offers you "eyes" where otherwise you might have none.

You'll want to use GPS and your charts to help you identify objects. Then look for those objects on the radar screen. Do they appear where you expect them to? If so, you can have confidence in your position. If they do not, your GPS may be indicating a slightly incorrect position. Rely on radar, not GPS, in these circumstances. Also, check your depth.

DEPTH SOUNDER Your depth sounder doesn't care about visibility above the water. It gives you the same information every time you transit the channel or harbor. After allowing for the present height of the tide, compare your depth reading with the charts and what your GPS and radar say your position should be. If all three match, you'll be even more confident. If they don't, make course corrections using the depth sounder, and look again at the radar.

PUTTING IT ALL TOGETHER It is possible to misidentify buoys you see on the radar screen if there are a number of them in the channel. You used GPS to help define your position. You used your chart to determine what ought to be there. You compared that data to targets on the radar screen to gauge your position. If there are any discrepancies, you may have misestimated your position. Go back to the radar and attempt to use other features, such as shoreline profile, to retune your position estimate. Is that new estimate within the accuracy limits of your GPS? Go back and forth among GPS, chart, and radar until you find a correlation of what they tell you. Meanwhile, use depth to adjust your position in the channel. If in doubt, stop and regroup. Use your radio to communicate with others. Let them know you are there and what you are doing. They can't see you either, and many of them do not have radar.

Navigating under Adverse Conditions

Every boater's skills are eventually tested by adverse conditions. Chapter 22 highlights the most challenging task of all—navigating in a narrow channel or harbor under conditions of limited visibility. This chapter highlights techniques that apply to navigating in open water.

Limited Visibility

In open water, boats are likely to be moving somewhat faster than in a harbor, even with limited visibility. This means that you need to be doubly alert. In harbors and channels, everyone posts extra lookouts. Usually, there are landmarks to help guide you. In open water, none of these may exist. You truly could be operating blind. GPS can help you maintain your course and reach your destination. The larger issue is the potential for collision with other boats along the way. This is where radar becomes invaluable.

Lookout and Sound Signals

You are required to post a lookout whenever your boat is underway. In many cases, that lookout is you. The lookout is searching within the limits of visibility for any sign of another boat, hazards, or navigation aids. If you are not alone, select someone else to be the lookout. Place him or her on the bow, if safe to do so, with lights, binoculars, sound signal, and certainly a life jacket.

You should reduce your speed to a rate that allows you to stop in half the distance of visibility. That way, if you see a boat at the limit of visibility, and the other boat sees you at the same time, you can both stop without colliding. (That is, as long as the other boater is as dutiful a lookout as you!)

The rules say you should sound a signal every two minutes. A substantial sound-producing device such as a horn should be used. Powerboats sound one long (four- to six-second) blast every two minutes. Sailboats (under sail alone) sound one long and two short (one-second) blasts

FIGURE 23-1. *Fog is perhaps the most intimidating condition a recreational boater faces. You cannot see other boats, and they cannot see you. Radar is the most valuable tool for navigating in fog, although radar may not pick up small boats. It is recommended that you set your radar on a short-range setting, because it enhances the returns from small targets. If you are near shipping lanes, periodically increase the range setting to check for large ships.*

every two minutes. If you're not underway, sound two long blasts every two minutes.

Navigating with Electronics

Having GPS and other navigation electronics aboard provides great comfort during conditions of adverse visibility.

You are far less likely to miss a buoy or a harbor. Unfortunately, other boaters are likely to be heading for those same marks. GPS can get you there, and depth sounders can help, but they don't warn you of other boats. Radar can help with navigation *and* look out for other boats. Thus, when visibility declines, radar should become your primary navigation instrument, with GPS support.

Radar

Radar can see what you cannot. It may make sense to shut off the automatic gain and filter controls. You'll want to advance the gain, and the rain filters, to a point where you have speckles on the display. Increase them to a point where there is too much noise or clutter on the display, then back them off until you have an acceptable level. You do this because you want to make sure you do not miss other boats.

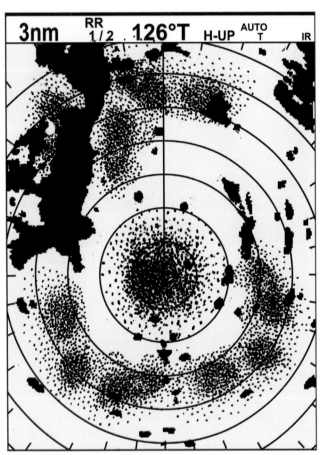

FIGURE 23-2. *Under adverse conditions, the radar screen can be populated with a great deal of clutter. Heavy nearby seas can cause echoes called sea clutter. Usually, sea clutter can be filtered by blanking out some of the closer returns. Fog and rain also cause clutter as diffuse echoes are returned from the atmospheric moisture. This clutter can make it difficult to see a real target. Both forms of clutter move and tend not to repeat from sweep to sweep. Controlling the radar is further explained in Chapter 25.*

In fog, you may get small speckles of reflection caused by the fog itself. That's okay, because they don't look like the returns from a boat.

Set the range scale to a close range, say one-quarter of a mile, unless you're in a major shipping lane, in which case half a mile is safer. At this setting, the radar's pulses will be optimized for short ranges. Set the VRM (variable range marker) to about one-tenth of a mile. If possible, have a different person monitoring the radar from the one tending the lookout.

Set the trail to help you distinguish moving objects from those that are fixed. The potential for collision makes your lookout for other boats the primary concern, and navigation becomes secondary.

Radio

Keep your VHF radio close at hand and ready for use. You'll use the radio more under adverse visibility than at any other time. Monitor channel 16 (and channel 13 as well if you're near shipping lanes or areas where you may encounter commercial boats). If your lookout or your radarperson notices anything, don't hesitate to place a call to "unknown vessel." Describe the vessel and its location relative to landmarks, your position, and the relative direction of the other boat from you. Indicate your position and your intent. This helps anyone in your proximity to understand what you'll

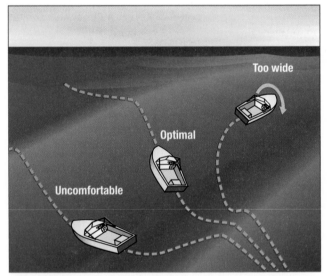

FIGURE 23-3A. *When the seas build, your best strategy is to take the oncoming waves at an angle rather than straight-on. (The angle can be somewhat critical and depends upon the boat. Typically a powerboat can take the waves at angles out to about 45 degrees.) This effectively stretches out the distance between wave crests and smoothes out the profile from crest to crest. If you take the waves at a sharper angle, you risk having the waves push the bow broadside—a precursor to a possible capsize.*

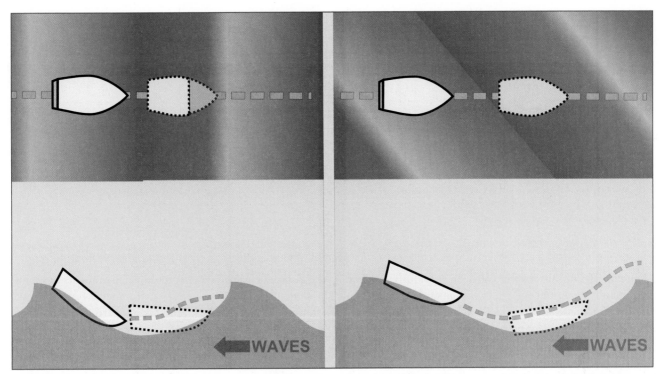

FIGURE 23-3B. *This diagram shows a cross section of the waves and the boat. Clearly, taking waves head-on leads to steeper slopes and shorter distances between crests. At 45 degrees, the same wave heights appear less severe and the crests are effectively spread out.*

be doing. If you have radar, indicate that you have the subject vessel on screen.

Wind and Sea

Adverse conditions come in many forms, of which limited visibility is just one. The sea and wind conditions add another element. In strong seas or winds, you may not be able to follow your chosen path to your destination. You need to pick directions that minimize the adverse effects, but still you want to get to an intermediate destination at least. For example, there may be a sheltered path close to shore where the seas are not as strong. In other cases, the shoaling near shore may cause waves to pile up and break. Under those conditions, you'd be better off in deeper water. You'll need to read the seas and conditions and seek opportunities to find more favorable conditions.

If you are heading into the seas, try taking them at an angle as shown in Figure 23-3. If you take them head-on, the slope to the crests is greater than when taking them at an angle. However, if you go too far, the waves will push the bow to turn the boat broadside to the waves. Then you run the risk of *broaching*—turning over. Set an angle into the waves that lets you maintain steering control.

Prepare the Crew and Boat for Heavy Seas

Make sure everyone is wearing a life jacket and all hatches are closed. Post a lookout for other boats or hazards.

Slow down to minimize pounding, but make sure you do not lose steerage. If sailing to windward, determine the best port and starboard tack headings that allow for efficient operation of the boat. (Use the techniques outlined in Chapter 21.)

A Last Word on Avoiding Danger

The material in this chapter has been previously touched on, but it is important enough to warrant a consolidated refresher and focused discussion. Avoiding danger is your primary task as a skipper and navigator. Electronics can help greatly, especially if you use multiple instruments to get different perspectives on your environment, but your own senses are also essential. Study your charts and maintain a constant lookout for clues to reinforce your position.

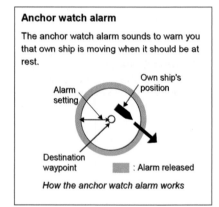

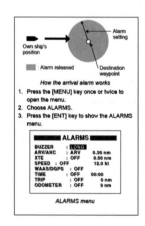

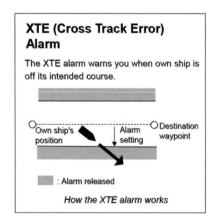

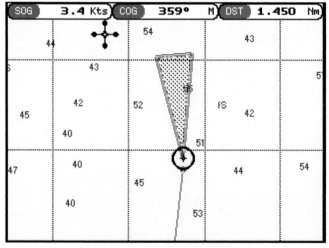

FIGURE 24-1. *Most GPS models provide alarms that work in conjunction with avoidance waypoints. But there are a number of other alarms you can utilize. Top left: The Alarm Screen from a Garmin GPS chartplotter. Anchor drag is an alarm that you can set to go off if your position changes by more than a preset amount. Top middle: The arrival alarm sounds when you've reached your destination. Top right: This Furuno diagram shows how the GPS anchor watch alarm works. Bottom left: The crosstrack error alarm sounds if your course has strayed beyond preset parameters. Bottom right: Using charted depth data, this C-Map alarm system will go off if you're heading toward shallow water. You can program the depth at which the alarm will sound.*

Chapter 7 describes how to preplan to avoid danger. Using these techniques, it is possible to prequalify an area rather that just a path, so you can roam freely outside risky areas. This approach does require careful attention to instruments, because any lapse can result in straying into danger. But you at least have three powerful tools at your command: (1) an intimate knowledge of surrounding waters based on experience and charts; (2) electronic alarms; and (3) visual bearings. And GPS and radar can help in other ways.

Electronic Alarms

When you're faced with watching for a number of potential hazards, alarms help. Without alarms, you're likely to find yourself within danger areas before you realize it. The key to alarms is making sure you'll hear (or see) and recognize them. Most GPS models permit you to set alarms for the following conditions (as described in Chapter 7).

1. **Avoidance or Proximity Waypoints**—you set a radius. When you enter within this radius, the alarm sounds.
2. **Anchor Watch**—you set a radius. If you leave the area bounded by the radius, an alarm sounds.
3. **Crosstrack Error**—you create an artificial course line through the center of a clear area. By establishing this as a route (even if there are only two waypoints) and activating it, you create an area bounded by the crosstrack error limits you establish on either side. If you stray outside the area, an alarm sounds.

Nevertheless, handheld GPS receivers and even chartplotters limit the number and types of alarms you can program. When you use a computer for navigation, you have far more flexibility. Many navigation programs allow you to define an area either to be avoided or to stay within. Depending on the program, the area can be defined by a circle (as in an avoidance waypoint), an ellipse, a square, or a user-defined polygon.

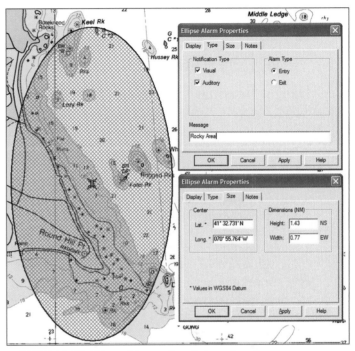

FIGURE 24-2B. *This avoidance alarm is based on an ellipse that can be drawn using the mouse. Its north-south and east-west dimensions can be independently adjusted to tailor the shape to its underlying region.*

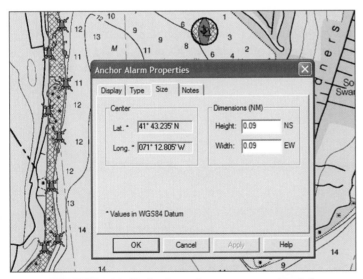

FIGURE 24-2A. *Navigation software on computers is far more flexible as to how areas can be identified and alarmed. The computer can be connected to an external audio to amplify the alarm sounds, which can be very useful. This anchor alarm setup screen allows you to enter the latitude, longitude, and lateral dimensions of the alarmed area (N-S and E-W). You can see the charted alarm above the setup panel. (Courtesy: Maptech)*

FIGURE 24-2C. *This setup screen provides information about the alarmed area to the left of the screen. You can create an alarmed area of any shape by making virtual fence posts with successive mouse clicks. Then you can set it to sound upon either entry or exit. In this case we have marked rocks so this is an entry alarm.*

Of these, the user-defined polygon is the most practical way of defining a large area. You simply plot a sequence of lines that clear the obstacles until you have completely enclosed the area in question. You draw the lines on the computer screen using mouse clicks. Then you set the alarm.

When you use the computer with GPS input, it will monitor your position and sound an alarm if you enter or leave the bounded area. You can add alarmed avoidance areas to mark isolated hazards within otherwise safe waters.

Visual Observations

Danger Bearings

Suppose, using the techniques in Chapter 7, you have defined a bearing from a landmark across the near side of a hazardous area. You measured and labeled this danger bearing by its direction and with the annotation NMT or NLT, meaning that you do not want to find yourself where the actual bearing from your position is more than or less than the prescribed bearing.

On the water, you monitor the bearing to that waypoint on your GPS. Because there is no alarm for this condition, you need to be alert. This is riskier than using an audible alarm, but it can be highly effective when experience and chart study put you so in tune with your surroundings that you know intuitively when a danger bearing is nearby.

Waypoints

It is also possible to mark hazards with ordinary waypoints carrying special symbols and names, as described in Chapter 7. You won't be able to define a radius, but you can place four waypoints at cardinal points relative to the hazardous

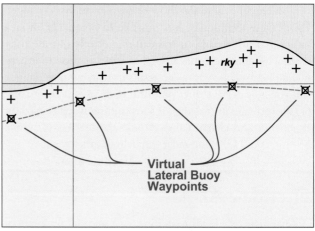

FIGURE 24-4. *In Chapter 7, you created your own lateral limits near the shoreline. On the water, your Map Screen displays these waypoints. Maintain your position to the proper side.*

area. This is similar to the placement of the cardinal navigation aids commonly deployed to mark such an area in Europe and Canada, though not in the United States.

While you are on the water, you monitor your position on the Map Screen to make sure you don't enter within the boundaries of the area delimited by cardinal waypoints.

Another technique using waypoints is to create an artificial string of "buoys" to mark a line or an area to be avoided. This is similar to a string of real-world navigation buoys marking the lateral edge of a channel.

Using Radar

Because radar offers a view of surrounding shorelines, navigation aids, and other features (including boats!), you can use it as a frame of reference to monitor hazardous areas.

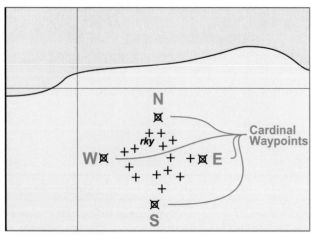

FIGURE 24-3. *In Chapter 7, you learned to enter cardinal waypoints to mark danger. On the water, you'll monitor your GPS to make sure you stay north of the north waypoint, south of the south waypoint, and so on.*

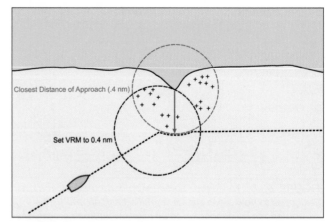

FIGURE 24-5. *Radar can be used to form a danger circle around a prominent point of land. You need to be able to recognize the features of the shoreline to use this technique. Set a VRM at the radius of the danger circle and ensure that the prominent land feature stays outside the VRM.*

Say you have plotted a radius to avoid a prominent feature such as a point of shoreline. On the water, set the radar's VRM to the radius you want to avoid. As long as the prominent shoreline feature doesn't enter within the VRM on the screen, you'll avoid the hazards, as described in Chapter 15. This technique can be used with buoys, but you must be able to clearly and quickly isolate the desired buoy in the image on the screen. Any uncertainty introduces risk. You can find your way home using radar to avoid coastal hazards along the way. For example, in Figure 24-6, you see rocky areas along the shore. By setting your VRM to a distance that will adequately clear the rocks, you can use the radar to steer toward shore. When the shoreline touches the VRM, you turn and run parallel to the shoreline until you locate your harbor. This technique works in all sorts of weather conditions and in darkness, and it is totally independent of GPS.

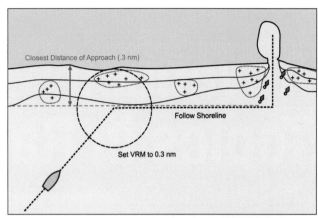

FIGURE 24-6. *Radar can help you stay clear of underwater hazards, too. In this example, you set the VRM to a radius that clears the rocks. Approach the coast until the VRM touches the shoreline, then parallel the shore until you reach the harbor.*

Advanced Topics in Radar

As described in Chapter 15, marine radar is now relatively inexpensive and available for use on virtually any boat. Radar gives you "vision" when outside visibility is restricted, and alerts you to danger even on clear days. Radar also complements other navigation devices, as previously described, and is the only navigation tool that shows you the locations and relative motions of nearby vessels. Chapter 15 introduces the use of radar in navigation. Here we take a closer look at radar tuning, controls, installation, and interpretation.

How Marine Radar Does Its Job

Radar is simple in concept. The radar transmitter emits pulses of *radio frequency* (RF) energy. Immediately after transmitting a pulse, the radar goes into a "listening" mode. Each pulse travels outward, dissipating energy as it goes. If the pulse encounters an object, some of the energy is reflected back toward the radar. The amount of returning energy depends upon the reflectivity of the material and its

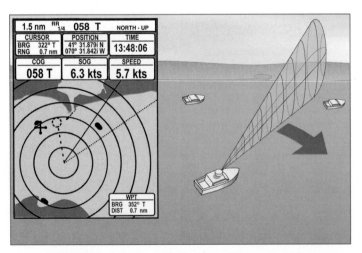

FIGURE 25-1. *Radar works by transmitting pulses from an antenna. As the antenna rotates, the pulses sweep the horizon. The distance to the target is determined by the round-trip time for the pulse to reach the target and return to the antenna.*

orientation (so as to mirror some of the energy back in the direction from which it came). The return pulse dissipates more energy until it reaches the radar antenna, where this weakened signal is received and processed.

The radar processor then determines the time taken by the pulse to make the round trip from antenna to target and back again, calculates target distance by dividing that time by two, then displays the target at that distance on the screen in the form of an image. To display the entire region around the boat, marine radar antennas rotate while transmitting a continuous stream of pulses. The returning pulses "paint" the objects seen by the radar onto a circular display, thus forming a complete view of your surroundings.

The Shape of Radar Returns

Because radar frequencies are not short enough in wavelength to produce high-definition images, the echo images from boats don't look like boats at all, but blobs on the screen. Shoreline features are blocky and ill defined, and navigation buoys can be indistinguishable from stationary boats unless you know what you're looking for and where to find it. Looking at a radar screen can be disappointing for the new user. Images appear as if they were generated using a wide marking pen rather than a sharpened pencil, and understanding these images takes practice.

The radar antenna contains an array of small, radiating elements designed to give a precise directional focus to the transmitted beam. The resultant beam is narrow but tall. Its narrowness focuses the signal's energy and helps the radar distinguish the direction of returned pulses and somewhat resolve their shapes. A narrow beam is essential to distinguish between objects that lie side by side. Beam width determines the minimum width of an image on the screen. This is called *bearing resolution*.

Contrary to intuition, a wider antenna array produces a narrower beam, but there are practical limitations. Recreational boaters are rarely blessed with enough space to accommodate a large antenna, and instead must use arrays of about

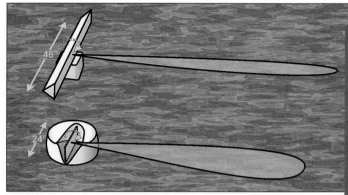

FIGURE 25-2B. *Two different types of antenna are offered. The round dome houses a rotating planar array antenna that is narrower than the one shown in the open array on the top. The wider the horizontal width of the antenna, the narrower the resulting horizontal beamwidth. Narrow beams mean greater gain and resolving capability.*

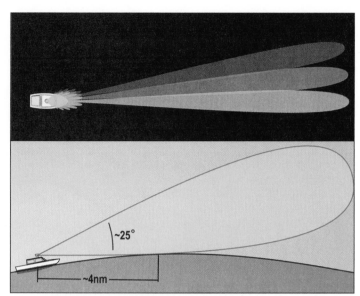

FIGURE 25-2A. *The antenna beam is narrow in azimuth (horizontal) and relatively broad in elevation (vertical). The narrow width is required to distinguish between closely spaced targets and to provide a reasonable representation of shoreline features. The beam's vertical width permits viewing targets as the boat pitches and rolls.*

To determine radar range, use the formula:

$$Range = 1.22 \times \sqrt{Height\ of\ Antenna}$$

To find how far beyond the horizon a tall object can be seen, use the following formula:

$$Range = 1.22 \times \left(\sqrt{Height\ of\ Antenna} + \sqrt{Height\ of\ Target} \right)$$

eighteen to twenty-four inches in diameter (usually housed within a circular radome that is transparent to RF). This produces an effective horizontal beam width of about 5° to 6°.

Although a narrow beam provides better image clarity, a tall beam is preferred. Because a boat pitches and rolls (and, if a sailboat, heels) at sea, you want to make certain that the beam will not just be pointing into the water, and the pulses reach their intended targets. And because radar displays your surroundings from a bird's-eye view, the height of the beam does not affect the clarity of the image. Typically, a sailboat radar has a vertical beam height of 25° to 30°. Even so, on a heeled sailboat, you may find that you are blind on the windward side when the beam points into the sky. That's why many new installations use a gimballed mount to keep the antenna level.

Just as a radar's beam width determines its bearing resolution (and thus the minimum "width" of a target, or even whether a tug and a barge two miles away appear as two separate targets or as one "wide" target), the duration of each transmitted pulse determines its *range resolution*—that is, the apparent radial "thickness" of a target on the screen. Range resolution is usually sharper than bearing resolution—that is, an echo on the screen from a target such as a boat is rarely as "thick" as it is "wide."

For better range resolution, shorter pulses are used. At shorter ranges, where less power is needed, the radar transmits short pulses and increases the rate at which they are sent. At longer radar ranges, to allow sufficient time for an echo to return from one pulse before the next pulse is transmitted, the pulse rate is slowed, but pulse length must be

increased at the same time to keep the average power transmitted from decreasing. That, in turn, reduces range resolution. All of this is accomplished automatically within the radar. As the operator you need only recognize that images from afar are not as well defined as those from nearby objects. Practically speaking, this is not a real problem for the boater, because long ranges are used for different purposes, as was explained in Chapter 15. Your radar manual includes a table of range settings with corresponding pulse lengths and repetition frequencies (prf).

Radar Range

Radars are marketed by their "range" capabilities. This is a bit of a misnomer, because range is usually limited by the horizon, and radar rarely provides any useful information at the stated maximum ranges. These stated ranges are based on how far the radar could detect an ideal target if it could "see" it—something that doesn't happen in real life.

Rather, the radar horizon is limited by the height of the radar antenna above the water. Typical recreational radars are mounted about ten feet above the water (sometimes higher on sailboats). At this height, the radar horizon is less than four nautical miles. Any object at sea level beyond

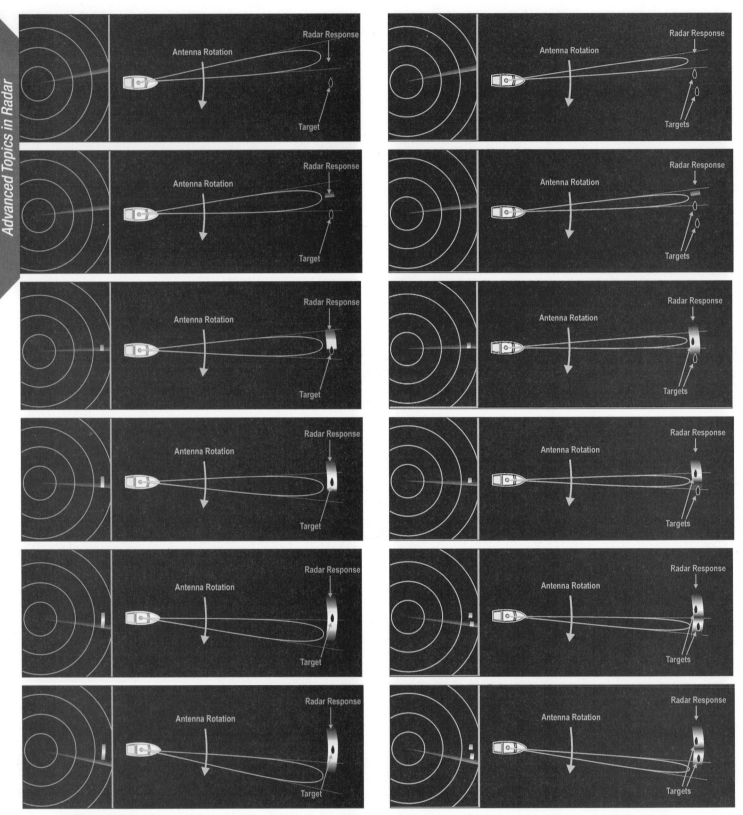

FIGURE 25-3. *Radar returns are a result of the signal hitting the target (images on left), and the shape of the target itself. But the shape of the beam affects the returning echoes, too. As the antenna beam's leading edge begins to hit the target, you will initially get a relatively weak return. As the antenna beam passes by, the echo becomes stronger. The echo begins to diminish when the trailing edge of the beam leaves the target. The resulting target presented on the screen is a composite of the target itself as extended by the width of the antenna beam. That is why you do not get sharp, pencil-point returns. If you had two targets instead of one (images on right), the width of the beam used in the previous example could mask the distinction between the two. In this example a wider antenna is used, with a narrower beamwidth. You can see how the narrow beam helps distinguish the two targets.*

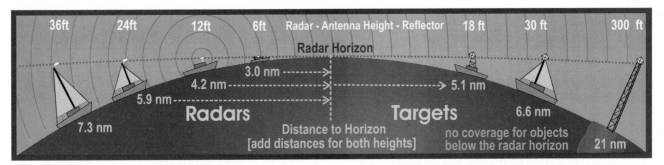

FIGURE 25-4. *Radar is a line-of-sight radio signal. (Actually, radio signals curve a bit so they reach about 4 percent farther than your visual horizon.) Consequently, you cannot see targets that lie below the radar horizon. Your radar's range is dependent upon how high you mount the antenna. Typically, recreational boats have their radars about 12 feet above the sea. This means you can see a target on the horizon at about 4.2 nm. If the target has a height of 18 feet, you may be able to see it up to about 9 nm.*

that range receives none of your radar's energy and cannot return an echo. At greater ranges, that portion of a taller object or boat above your radar horizon returns an echo, but its strength represents only that percentage of the target that was "illuminated." Larger boats may appear smaller than they are. Shorelines are masked; you see echoes from some point inland where the land is high enough to be illuminated by your radar. So if geometry is usually the limiting factor, what is the advantage of higher power or a bigger antenna? For most recreational boaters, not a lot.

In the absence of a horizon, a radar's effective range depends on its transmitted power and the narrowness of its horizontal beam width (often referred to as antenna "gain"). Most recreational marine radars offer either 2 or 4 kW of peak pulse power. Because the pulses are very short, the average power transmitted by the radar is quite low—typically a few watts or less. Practically speaking, a 4 kW radar can see farther than a 2 kW unit and provide stronger returns at shorter ranges. Similarly, a radar with a wider antenna array (narrower beam) can see farther than one with a smaller antenna. Because most recreational boaters operate their radars at ranges less than a few miles, these issues are of lesser concern. The larger antenna also provides sharper bearing resolution, however, as we have seen.

Radar is used differently on large commercial vessels. Antenna mounts on ships are typically high, providing ranges to the horizon of more than ten miles. Big vessels *need* to see farther, because they need miles to execute a turn. They maintain radar plots on other ships and boats to anticipate maneuvers. On a recreational boat, you can't see far, but for the most part your threats are nearby. You also have the ability to maneuver quickly. All of this means that your collision avoidance responses may be compressed into a few minutes or less.

The Radar Screen

A radar screen presents a circular view of the world around you centered on the boat, as described in Chapter 15. Most radar screens present a "heading-up" picture in which the

"view" over your boat's bow is straight up on the screen. As the antenna rotates (typically clockwise at about twenty-four rotations per minute), returns are painted on the screen. The image just in front of the sweep is about two and a half seconds older than the newly "refreshed" or "updated" image behind the sweep. It is important to observe the changes in an image from sweep to sweep, because that represents the target's motion relative to your boat.

Though heading-up is the natural orientation for radar—easier for the helmsman and watchkeepers because it corresponds to the real world around the boat—a north-up orientation also has advantages. Chief among these is that targets retain their places on the screen when you execute a turn, though their relative motions will subsequently change. In a heading-up display, in contrast, all images on the screen rotate counterclockwise when you turn to star-

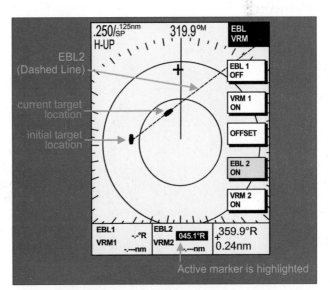

FIGURE 25-5. *Chapter 15 described the utility of EBLs and VRMs. Many modern radars extend their utility by allowing you to offset the EBL from the center of the display. Using the offset EBL, you can place the line over a moving boat and adjust its angle to correspond with its apparent motion. This can help you determine risk of collision and estimate the point of closest approach.*

board or clockwise when you turn to port. (Take a look back at Figure 15-13 to see this effect.) A north-up display is also somewhat easier to match to a nautical chart of surrounding waters. Still, most boaters prefer the intuitive advantage of a heading-up display. At any rate, a north-up display is unavailable unless your radar is interfaced with a fluxgate digital compass through the radar's NMEA input, as described in Chapter 27.

The radar screen can display a set of concentric circular rings, each ring denoting a range from your boat that depends on the active range setting of the radar. These rings can be turned off if they distract you. Also, a bearing scale is generally presented around the perimeter of the display. As

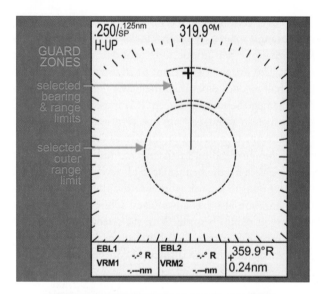

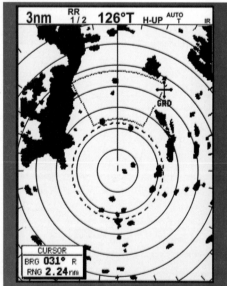

FIGURE 25-6. *Many radar models allow you to set a "guard zone." This is a radial box bounded by an inner and outer range and two bearings. Once set, any strong echo returning from within the box will sound an alarm. This can be useful as a supplemental technique to alert you to objects in front of your boat.*

described in Chapter 15, two user-selectable markers usually are provided to refine the position of a displayed target, or just for general reference: the EBL (electronic bearing line) and the VRM (variable range marker). Their positions are adjustable, and their values are provided in a digital readout somewhere on the display. They usually are represented by a dashed radiating line and a dashed circle, respectively. In addition, the radar display provides a cursor that can be moved anywhere on the screen; its range and bearing are continuously updated in a digital readout.

Using the EBL and the VRM together, you can determine the range and bearing to any object on the screen. If that object is fixed and charted, its range and bearing can be used to generate a position fix for the boat. The EBL and VRM are adjusted using buttons on the radar display unit.

New radars usually provide two or more sets of EBLs and VRMs. In addition, these often can be offset from the center of the scan, as shown in Figure 25-5. The offset EBL can be useful for tracking the relative motion of another boat. Collision bearings are described in Chapter 15. It is important to follow the path of a converging boat as it advances. The offset EBL can be placed over the return from a boat and rotated to follow the successive returns. In Figure 25-5, you can see that the other boat will pass in front of you at a distance indicated by the intersection of the offset EBL with your heading line (solid line).

Most radars also enable you to set up a *guard zone.* This is a section on the display associated with an alarm. You can set the inner radius of the guard zone, its outer radius, and two bearing limits, as shown in Figure 25-6. This curved box usually is set ahead of your boat; you are alerted any time a substantial echo is returned from this region. The guard zone helps with your watch just in case you missed a potential target.

The radar screen also includes a number of data fields reflecting the current setup for the radar, such as the display range (to the edge of the screen or outer ring), and the spacing of the range rings in nautical miles (or other units that you have selected). Usually, the radar indicates the display orientation as heading-up or north-up. Other settings of the radar also may be displayed. Setting up the radar is described in a later section.

The radar screen usually also provides for display of information supplied by a GPS. Once a GPS receiver is connected to the radar via the NMEA data-in port, the radar looks for specific information. Generally, the radar displays your GPS-reported position (latitude and longitude), boat speed over ground, course over ground, and bearing and distance to the active waypoint. These data are presented in digital data fields. In addition, most radars present a "lollipop" image superimposed on the radar image. The lollipop includes a dashed line extending from the boat toward the active waypoint. The active waypoint is enclosed within a displayed circle. This format enables the helmsman to steer so as to keep the dashed line and circle on the heading line. If the waypoint is beyond the range setting on the radar display, only the dashed line appears.

Installation and Alignment

A typical recreational marine radar consists of two units: the scanner and the display/processor. The scanner is the exterior antenna installed on the boat's superstructure or mast. Two types of scanners are offered. One uses a rotating antenna array on top of an electronics enclosure. These are seen on larger boats and feature larger antennas (24 to 48 inches) that may not fit practically into an enclosed radome. These antennas require enough clear space to rotate unimpeded, and generally do not work well on sailboats. The more popular recreational model uses a round radome within which the antenna and electronics are housed. Typically these are used for antennas from 16 to 24 inches in length. The scanner unit also houses the transmitter and receiver electronics and the controls and motor for rotating the antenna. The transmitter uses a magnetron tube to produce the high-power pulses. Magnetrons also are used in microwave ovens.

The scanner is connected to the display unit via a multiconductor cable. The cable provides power to the scanner and control signals to the transmitter and receiver, and carries the radar returns to the display unit. The display

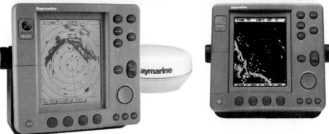

FIGURE 25-7. *Marine radar comes with two major components: the scanner/antenna and the display unit. (Courtesy: Raymarine)*

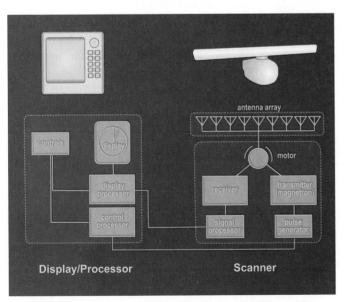

FIGURE 25-8. *The scanner unit contains the antenna array, a motor, a transmitter, and a receiver. The transmitter contains a magnetron tube controlled by a pulse generator; together they create and send signals through the array. A receiver senses the returning echoes. These echoes are processed to enhance their characteristics. The display/processor unit contains the controller for the radar, the control buttons, the display processor that controls the image, and the display itself.*

unit contains the controls for the radar, the display, and a processor to convert the radar returns into the appropriate display format. Most display units today use LCD screens, which are more durable, draw less power, and provide better visibility than the CRT displays they replace.

The scanner should be positioned as high as possible (because usable radar range is directly related to antenna height), and it should be angled so its base is nominally horizontal when the boat is at cruising speed. Even though the radar beam is rather "tall" (typically 25° to 30°), it still is better to focus that beam on the horizon. The radar should be placed at least several feet from other antennas used for communications and GPS. Also, to the extent possible, other antennas should be mounted at a height that does not fall directly within the radar beam. On a sailboat, it makes sense to use a gimballed, self-leveling antenna mount. When your boat is heeling under sail, as expressed above, even a tall beam may point into the water to leeward. Meanwhile, on the windward side, you may be looking for airplanes instead of boats. Many sailors opt for a gimballed mount on a pole at the transom instead of a higher mounting on the mast for this reason, though for the most part, even on a sailboat, a fixed mount will work.

It is a wise practice to mount the radar so the beam is not striking the helmsman or crew. This is microwave radiation, after all, and though it's nowhere near as intense as a microwave oven, why take a chance? Many boats have a radar arch on which to mount the radar above the crew and with a clear view of the horizon. Hardtops on boats also offer a good mounting surface. Often it is wise to mount the radar on a vertical post to further elevate its position.

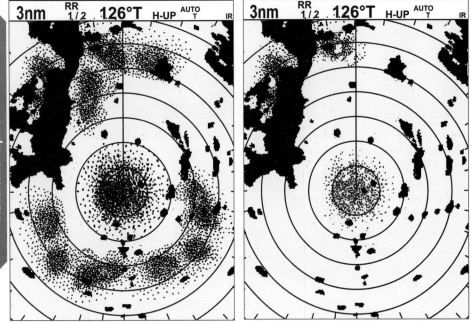

FIGURE 25-9. *Radar gain can be controlled via a button on the display/control unit. If you set the gain too high, clutter and noise will be amplified and show up as diffuse targets. Targets also will be enhanced, but they may be obscured by the noise. The best setting is obtained by turning up the gain until noise is seen on the display, then backing it off slightly until the noise mostly disappears. Most new radars have an automatic setting mode, which works well during normal, clear situations, but you should experiment with the manual settings to gain experience with them. Under adverse conditions, you may be better served by adjusting the controls manually.*

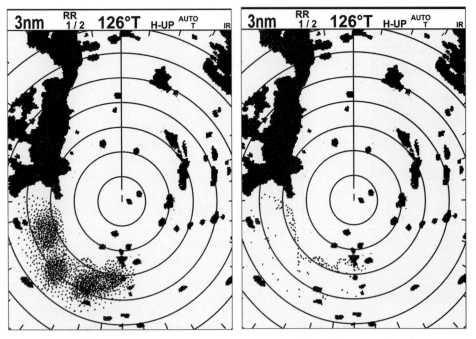

FIGURE 25-10. *Rain clutter or fog can obscure the display. Since the rain or fog is nearly transparent, it will return echoes at all ranges where it exists. This causes a snowy diffuse pattern on the display that can mask real targets. A special filter is available on the radar to control this. This filter senses the leading edge of a return and suppresses echoes behind the front edge to some degree. Properly setting this control will result in a much clearer display that will not mask true targets. Set the control until you see the rain clutter, then back it off slightly until the image is clearer.*

Radar Controls

The quality of the image on a radar screen is largely a function of local environmental conditions. However, your radar provides a group of controls to optimize that image. These controls can be intimidating until you understand what they do and why.

Gain

The gain control tunes the sensitivity of the receiver to incoming signals. If the gain is set too high, the screen becomes cluttered. If it is set too low, you miss seeing small boats and other objects. You should increase the gain until you see just a bit of noise in the background, then back off until the noise disappears. Noise shows as dots or speckles in the display that come and go randomly. Most radars offer an automatic gain control, which can be effective under many conditions. If you encounter squalls, however, you may be better advised to set your controls manually.

Rain Clutter

Radar can be useful for detecting rainsqualls at some distance, but rain, snow, or fog can mask returns from nearby boats and other targets. To combat this, radar manufacturers place a special filter in the system. With this filter turned up, you see the leading edge of a rainstorm; but much of the clutter beyond the leading edge is suppressed, so you may be able to see other targets in this region. These other returns are diminished somewhat by this filter, so it should be set carefully, to a point where the clutter is diminished just enough to see the targets. Many radars offer an automated rain clutter mode. If you are looking for distant storms or regions of fog and rain, you should temporarily reduce this filter setting so you can see the clutter.

Normally, rain or snow clutter is reflected from storm squalls and appears as a large number of small echoes continually changing in location and intensity. Sometimes these storms appear as hazy areas on the display. These cells usually can be seen at great distances due to their high altitudes. This can be useful for identifying an incoming squall, but you will want to minimize the setting at these ranges so the storm can be seen more easily.

Fog is a major concern, especially at closer ranges. Its appearance on the display may be similar to that of rain but more diffuse, with fewer small echoes. If this clutter makes it difficult to observe targets, reduce it with the rain clutter control. Often, you can use radar with the rain clutter control turned down low to observe distant fogbanks.

Sea Clutter

Sea clutter results from radar returns from waves near the boat—especially breaking waves. The result on the display often looks like strong echoes from all directions; on the screen it appears to be constantly changing. The sea clutter filter reduces the gain of the receiver slightly for short ranges while leaving the gain unaffected at other ranges. Simply adjust this control until the display speckles caused by sea clutter are reduced to an acceptable level. It is important not to reduce this level too much, or nearby targets such as small boats may be missed. With careful setting of this control, you may be able to see boats, even at very short ranges when sea clutter is present.

You can distinguish sea clutter from true targets by the fact that the clutter moves and changes on each sweep, whereas targets tend to be better defined and repeatable from sweep to sweep. In heavy seas, the display can become obliterated with strong sea returns out to the edge of the radar horizon (typically 3 nautical miles). Under these conditions, you will want to use the sea clutter control to minimize this.

The sea clutter control should be readjusted whenever the radar range scale is changed or when sea conditions change. Also recognize that the ideal sea clutter setting depends on the gain setting. If the gain is readjusted, make sure you readjust the sea clutter as well.

Tuning

The radar receiver must operate on the same frequency as the transmitter. Most radars provide an automatic tuning feature that operates with excellent success under most conditions. If you choose to tune the radar yourself, make sure the radar has been on for about twenty minutes so the mag-

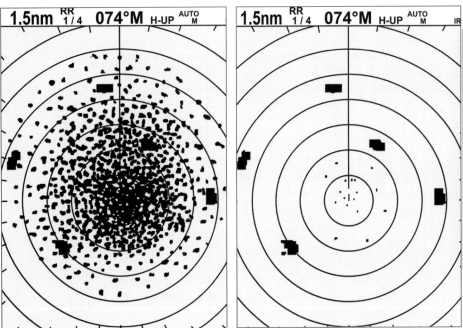

FIGURE 25-11. *Sea clutter generally comes from choppy seas near the boat. It can be confusing and can mask other targets. It will change from sweep to sweep much like rain, but its returns tend to be sharper. A special filter can adjust sea clutter by reducing nearby signal returns. Adjust this control so that the clutter diminishes just enough that you are comfortable that you are viewing real targets.*

netron (which creates the high power) has stabilized. You then tune to get the strongest return signal. Usually, this setting is adjusted prior to setting gain, rain clutter, and sea clutter.

The next group of controls has to do with how the processor and display handle information.

Electronic Bearing Line (EBL)

The EBL is usually set by a rocker switch, which advances or retards the angle of the line. Usually, this line is dashed to distinguish it from grid lines. The relative bearing of the line's current setting is displayed digitally on the radar screen. If the radar is connected to an external directional reference such as a fluxgate compass, the EBL can be set to provide magnetic or true bearing directions rather than relative bearings.

Variable Range Marker (VRM)

The VRM is usually set by another rocker switch, which increases or decreases the range setting.

Using the VRM, you can supply a movable reference ring to bound the region within which targets are of special concern to you. Because the VRM stays on the screen, it grows or shrinks as the range setting is changed on the radar, but its absolute value in yards or nautical miles remains constant until you change it.

Cursor

Many radars offer a cursor function, which in some cases replaces the two rocker switches described above to control the EBL and VRM. The cursor can also be used to quickly mark an object. The cursor's range and bearing from the boat are displayed on the screen.

Offset

Usually, your boat's position is shown at the center of your radar display, but you can reposition the center of the display downward on the screen to provide a longer view ahead, or to one side or another to provide a longer view either to port or starboard.

Range Rings

The range rings on the display can be turned off to provide a less cluttered display. Then the VRM, if selected, is the only range ring on the screen.

Ship's Heading

Your radar usually displays a line on the screen corresponding to the heading of your boat. On a heading-up display, this line points to the top of the display. If the radar screen

is reoriented to north-up, your heading line will point to its actual true or magnetic direction, according to the north reference used by the interfaced digital compass.

Trail

Older radars used a cathode ray tube (CRT) with highly persistent phosphors, which retained an image on the screen until the replacement image was painted. For moving objects, the result was a slowly fading trail showing where the image was on previous sweeps. On newer LCD screens, the image is mapped by the onboard processor and can be controlled in several ways. One of the options available is to create a trail of definable length corresponding to two or more sweeps of the radar; another is to show no trail at all. A target trail can be invaluable for assessing the risk of collision, as explained in Chapter 15.

Hold

The Hold function can be used to freeze the display temporarily for closer examination. Usually, this function resets to normal operation after a fixed time period, such as thirty seconds.

Guard Zone

Many radars permit you to set a guard zone. You select a near range, a far range, and two bearings, creating a box, as shown in Figure 25-6. When the radar detects a return within this trapezoidal-shaped guard zone, it sounds an alarm. Generally, you select a sector that represents a high potential for a collision.

Zoom

Some radars enable an operator to zoom the scale of the display around the location of the cursor for greater viewability. This does not change the basal settings of the radar, nor does it increase the resolution of the radar information.

Racons

Racons are special navigation aids designed to identify themselves in response to a radar signal striking them. These are active devices that send back a series of echoes after being struck by each radar pulse. These multiple echoes appear to extend outward from the navigation aid toward the perimeter of your radar display; they are coded to identify the nav aid. Thus, you can distinguish these aids from other echoes on your screen.

Racons are usually used for commercial traffic and therefore are located along major shipping channels, usually as an outer mark to help orient incoming ships from some distance away. Many recreational boaters never encounter a racon unless they operate at some distance offshore.

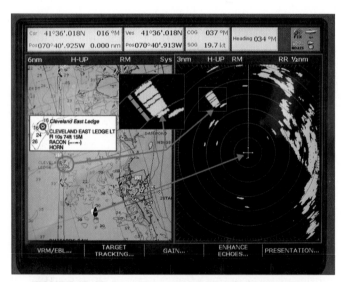

FIGURE 25-12. *In order to uniquely identify key navigation aids, a system called racon (which stands for radar beacon) is used. When your radar pulse hits the racon device attached to the navigation aid, it returns not only a normal echo, but adds a sequence of dots and dashes afterward extending in the range dimension. These appear farther than the racon and display as individual strong virtual echoes. The dots and dashes that appear represent the specific Morse code for the aid as shown on a chart (see inset). In this screenshot you can see a sequence of long-short-long-short, which is the code for Cleveland Ledge to port ahead. On the radar screen, you see a target in the same relative position. In addition, AIS systems, described in Chapter 19, are evolving to show labels on your screen for selected, identified navigation aids.*

Advanced Radar Systems

Radar systems have come a long way in recent decades. Not only are they considerably less expensive than their predecessors, but they perform far better and carry more advanced features. Most manufacturers offer a range of radar products with different peak power output and various-size antenna arrays—usually larger is better. With the advent of digital processing and digital displays, a whole new avenue has opened for even better systems. This section explains in layman's terms what these new radar systems can do, so you can decide whether such a system is worth your investment.

MARPA

Mini automatic radar plotting aid (MARPA) is a digital tool that can help the operator keep track of targets of concern. For example, Chapter 15 described how an EBL could be used to keep an eye on a target: if the target continues to move along the EBL toward the center of the display, that's a collision course. Even with multiple EBLs it would be a bit complex to track more than a couple of targets that way.

Enter MARPA. With most radar units so equipped, you can select multiple targets of interest using your cursor. The MARPA function then keeps tabs on these targets for you, comparing their sweep-to-sweep relative motions. While doing this, MARPA also computes the closest point of approach (CPA) and time to closest point of approach

(TCPA) for each target. CPA is the closest the other boat will come to you if both it and you remain on your current courses and speeds. TCPA is the time from present that the CPA will occur—in other words, how long you have to do something if required.

MARPA is an excellent tool to have and use, particularly if you are in a moderate- to high-density traffic area and need to keep track of several other vessels. In addition to providing information about the potential of a collision with CPA and TCPA, MARPA will provide you with real-time range and bearing information to each target. Some

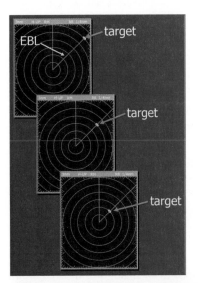

FIGURE 25-13. *This sequence of graphics shows that by placing an electronic bearing line (EBL) on a selected target, you can track its progress. Since this EBL originates at your boat, any target that follows the line toward you is on a collision course. This is a quick way to track a suspected target.*

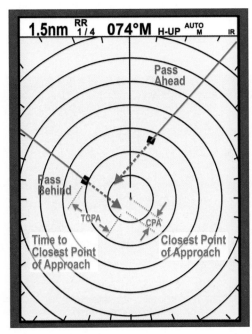

FIGURE 25-14. *The concept of closest point of approach (CPA) and time to closest point of approach (TCPA) is covered under MARPA later in this chapter and AIS in Chapter 19. These are two key parameters in determining the degree of risk to your vessel.*

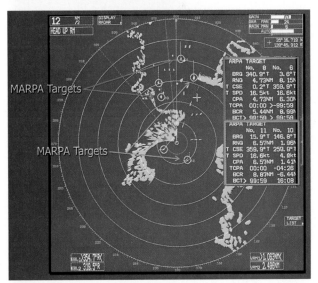

FIGURE 25-15. *Mini automatic radar plotting aid (MARPA) is a feature available on many radar units. More automated than the use of the EBL to track a target's approach, MARPA keeps tabs on targets for you. By simply placing your cursor over a suspected return and pressing the appropriate key, you enable the MARPA system to plot the path of the target and predict its path. MARPA provides CPA and TCPA for each target. Depending upon the radar model, you may be able to track ten to twenty targets simultaneously. (Courtesy: Furuno)*

FIGURE 25-16. *Several manufacturers offer what they call HD (high definition) radar. These radar units implement extensive digital signal processing to suppress clutter returns and sharpen the effective antenna resolving capability. Here is a sample of an HD scanner. Outside, it looks much like its non-HD counterparts. (Courtesy: Raymarine)*

systems will also provide the true headings and speeds of the activated MARPA targets. This requires some computation, since your radar shows relative motion involving your own speed and direction. All these movements must be factored out to get the true motion of other targets.

HD Radar

HD (high definition) radar has become very popular and is offered as a high-end system by major marine electronics manufacturers. HD radar uses digital signal processing to sharpen the resolution of targets shown while cleaning up clutter from the screen.

Radar was developed in an analog world. Even today, much of the terminology relates to analog filters that have been used for decades. Terms such as FTC and STC, which stand for fast time constant and sensitivity time control,

were originally the filters used to suppress rain clutter and sea clutter, respectively. These analog filters had relatively limited characteristics. Not only that, but the earlier radars had no memory, so the previous sweeps' results persisted on the CRT screen with carefully selected phosphors that retained the image for a while.

Today, in the digital world, the radar processor can store and analyze radar returns bit by bit, pulse by pulse, and sweep by sweep, and display the images pixel by pixel. To visualize what's happening, consider the following. The radar is transmitting short pulses of radio frequency energy at a relatively rapid rate. That means multiple pulses go out and strike objects, which return some of that energy back to the radar receiver. In earlier and less sophisticated systems, you simply decided which returns were great enough to warrant being displayed, and rejected the rest. You could set the gain, and deploy filters for rain and sea clutter to aid the decision process. Today, most systems store the results from previous sweeps and offer the opportunity to display a trail of returns from moving objects, or even track selected targets using MARPA.

The HD systems add yet more processing to the mix. They use more complex digital filtering to enhance and refine target returns, to remove clutter, and to enhance the displayed targets. In short, they analyze the returns looking for subtle characteristics that would indicate a desired target from clutter and noise. Perhaps the simplest way to look at it is to consider that clutter, such as rain, comes from many tiny moving raindrops. None stays fixed, so their returns are fleeting and constantly changing. The return from a boat is more constant. If you look at and compare each return with that from the next pulse headed to and back from the same

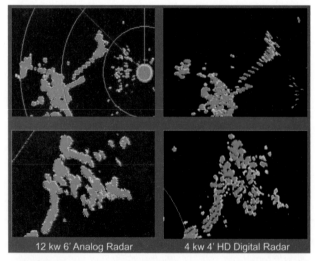

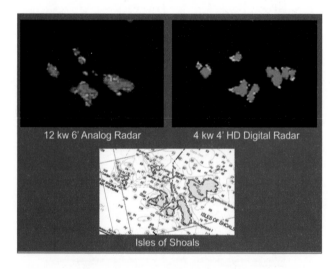

FIGURE 25-17. Left: *To see the effectiveness of HD, compare the return from a high-power 12 kw analog radar with a full 6-foot open-array antenna (left) with a return from an HD radar of only 4 kw with a 4-foot open array (right). The HD radar presents much more highly resolved returns with less clutter. The upper graphic, at 3/4 nm scale, shows individual targets; the lower, at 3 nm, shows distinct shorelines.* Right: *Two images shown are of the Isles of Shoals (chart inset shown) for the same two radar units on the 6 nm scale. Clearly the HD better reflects the shoreline features of the isles. (Courtesy: Raymarine)*

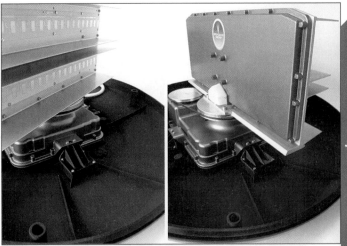

FIGURE 25-18. *Navico has embarked on a different approach to marine radar. Instead of transmitting very short pulses of high energy, they transmit essentially a continuous, low-power frequency-modulated signal. This means no magnetron is required, with its warm-up time and blanking of short ranges while the receiver is turned off as the transmitter is sending. Shown are the somewhat conventional looking radome (above) and the interior of this scanner (right). (Courtesy: Lowrance/Navico)*

direction at the same range, you can better determine which targets are constant (a possible boat) from those that are not (rain). In reality, many pulses strike the same area before the antenna moves on, so the processor can compare them all.

Now add a little more processing to compare what you found on a prior sweep with the current one. All targets are moving (relative to you, if you are moving), and moving targets are moving in various directions. However, boats don't move very far relative to each other in a single sweep. By carefully comparing these sweep-to-sweep returns with digital processing, the real target images can be further enhanced while clutter is further reduced. Some HD radar units can actually discriminate between two different closely spaced targets that otherwise might have appeared as one larger target.

Broadband Radar

Broadband Radar, developed by Navico for the recreational marine radar market, uses an entirely different alternative to traditional radar technology. Conventional radar transmits short pulses of very high power energy, typically 2 or 4 kilowatt pulses, while simultaneously protecting the path to the radar receiver. After a brief blanking period, it lets the receiver "listen" until it's time to transmit the next pulse. The radar then measures the round-trip transit time for the returning echo. Broadband Radar, on the other hand, transmits an essentially continuous low-power frequency-modulated signal that ramps up in frequency from a lower limit to an upper limit. Then it repeats. Since the transmissions are at low power, the receiver can stay on all the time and listen. The radar knows when it transmitted each frequency in the FM ramp. Distance is measured by comparing the time delay in the returning echo when the same frequencies are received.

One of the disadvantages of conventional radar is the

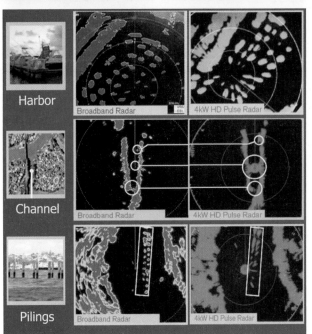

FIGURE 25-19. *The Broadband Radar, as it is known, produces even more refined returns close in, as you can see in these images comparing Broadband with HD radar. Boats and pilings take on a new definition of clarity. (Courtesy: Lowrance/Navico)*

blanking time before the receiver is turned on. This may be equivalent to losing the nearest tenth of a mile or more. Broadband Radar, being continuous, can detect nearby targets even in fog or darkness. Conventional radar employs a magnetron to create those high-power pulses, and it needs time to warm up. The Broadband Radar is low power and instantly available. Broadband Radar also has the capability to better resolve targets, making them more defined on the display.

The big disadvantage to Broadband Radar is that it does not use that high power to "punch through" to long ranges. While the claim is that the radar is nearly equivalent to a conventional 2 kilowatt radar in range coverage, its av-

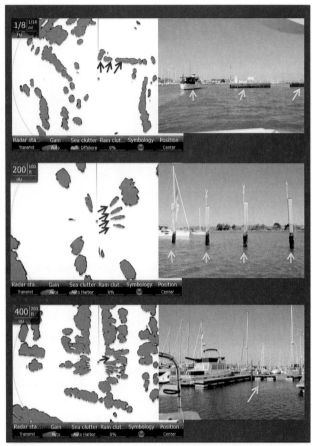

FIGURE 25-20. *Close-in, high-definition Broadband Radar is extremely useful. At the top, you can clearly distinguish the boat from the breakwater. In the center, the pilings are quite distinct. In the bottom, you can see the open slip along the marina fairway. (Courtesy: Lowrance/Navico)*

erage transmitted power is perhaps half the conventional radar's. Clearly, the Broadband Radar is an excellent complementary tool, providing close-in, all-weather coverage with excellent resolution. A prudent mariner may consider having both conventional and Broadband Radar aboard, using each for its respective strengths.

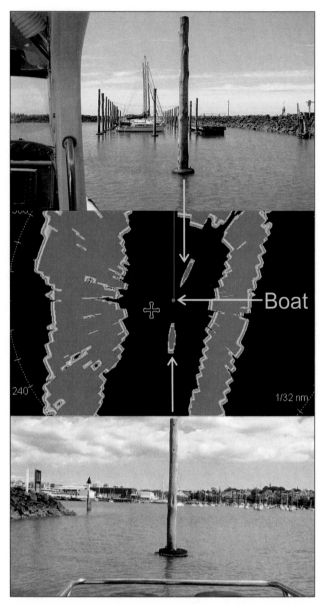

FIGURE 25-21. *With Broadband Radar, you can distinguish pilings close in. Imagine navigating this marina in deep fog or in total darkness. (Courtesy: Lowrance/Navico)*

Other Instrumentation

Beyond navigation instruments, there are a number of other tools available to recreational boaters. Wind, weather, and speed gauges can be added to a boat's data arsenal and help the boater make informed decisions.

Many of these instruments offer a repeater capability. The *repeater* is a secondary display that can be placed in the cockpit or on the flybridge to display information from instruments that may be located elsewhere on the boat. Many GPS models can accommodate inputs from these other instruments so the information can be combined into a single display, or incorporated with other navigation information to be passed on to other devices, such as an autopilot.

In addition to onboard instruments, today a great deal of information is available via satellite, especially for weather and water conditions. This information is collected and provided by companies using data from a variety of government agencies and independent services.

Instruments

Wind Sensors

Measuring wind on a moving boat is a challenge. The very fact that you are moving changes the apparent wind direction and speed. Apparent wind is well known to sailors and is used to their advantage in many instances. With electronics, you can see both apparent and true wind because the instrumentation factors in the speed and direction of the boat.

Traditionally, wind direction has been sensed by a vane, much like one you would mount on your house. Wind speed has been measured by an anemometer. These sensors are designed for the marine environment and typically are mounted near or at the top of a mast or masthead. Cables lead below to the electronics.

The electronic instruments take in the signals from the wind sensors, but they also have inputs from the boat's heading and speed instruments. By comparing the vectors

for wind and boat, the instrumentation presents wind speed and wind direction in either apparent or true dimensions.

True wind is more useful for determining sea conditions that result from the wind. Generally, the sea surface responds directly to the wind intensity, as amplified by the amount of time the wind has had an opportunity to affect the seas, and by the *fetch*—the amount of open water over which the wind has been blowing. Waves generally build up perpendicular to the wind direction (as modified by reflections from the shorelines). So, knowing the wind characteristics enables the mariner to estimate emerging sea conditions.

Wind direction and speed also are key forecasters of the weather. If you point your nose into the wind, the area of lower atmospheric pressure is typically 90° to 120° off to your right (in the northern hemisphere; off to your left in the southern hemisphere). Also, the wind direction tells you about emerging frontal conditions. For example, in the northern hemisphere, winds from the southeast generally precede a warm front. After the warm front passes,

FIGURE 25-1. *Wind instruments are gaining popularity even on powerboats. Sailors, especially, want to know the true and apparent direction of the wind. The instrumentation consists of an anemometer to measure wind speed and a vane to measure wind direction; both are mounted on the mast. The signals from these instruments are processed by a separate unit, and the results are displayed in the cockpit. Boat information such as course and speed are provided so the processor can calculate and display the speed and direction of true as well as apparent wind.*

FIGURE 25-2. *Devices that measure boat speed through the water employ paddle wheels, or optical sensors, to provide the source information for displays like these.*

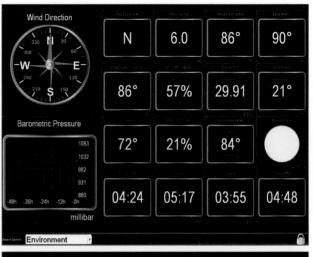

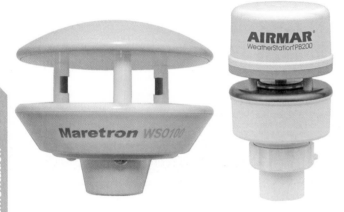

FIGURE 26-3. *Ultrasonic sensors have replaced the conventional mechanical vane and anemometer for measuring wind characteristics. These two examples from Maretron and Airmar measure wind direction and speed using the three vertical sensors with a high degree of accuracy. These units also can sense temperature, barometric pressure, and humidity to provide a complete profile of conditions to the helm. (Courtesy: Maretron and Airmar)*

FIGURE 26-5. *Weather services for inland and near coastal regions using information relayed by satellite are available to supplement onboard data collection. A number of chartplotter and navigation software producers have adopted one of these services to be integrated into their systems. The needed satellite receiver, shown here, when used with a companion antenna and a subscription to the service, provides a host of weather and sea-related information to the mariner. (Courtesy: Furuno)*

FIGURE 26-4. *The remote ultrasonic sensors provide data via a NMEA 2000 connection to the processor or computer. The system can provide a complete profile and a history of environmental conditions: wind direction, temperature, humidity, dew point, and barometric pressure (top); true wind and a host of data from other sensors, including GPS, water transducers, and sounder can also be displayed (above). (Courtesy: Maretron)*

winds veer and come from the southwest. Warm fronts usually precede associated cold fronts. After the cold front passes, the winds veer again, coming from the northwest.

Weather Instruments

A new generation of weather instruments has been developed using ultrasonic and other sensor technologies. Maretron and Airmar are two companies that offer these nonmechanical sensors.

The sensor unit employs an open cavity surrounded by sensors to measure wind direction and velocity. These replace traditional vane and anemometer instruments, which are still available. In addition to the wind sensor, these sensor units also measure air temperature, relative humidity, and barometric pressure. Some units include a built-in GPS and an electronic compass, which allow them

Other Instrumentation

to use boat speed and direction to calculate true wind data. Otherwise, the unit's data is integrated with the ship's GPS and compass for those computations. The units also can calculate dew point. The sensor unit can be mounted in any unobstructed area above the superstructure of the boat.

These sensor units use NMEA 2000 interfaces to provide data to specialized or multifunction displays, or to a PC. Maretron offers many other sensors and displays, all interfacing via NMEA 2000. Their display can present a host of weather-related data, both real time and historical based on inputs from their weather sensor. Alternatively, the sensor can be interfaced with a multifunction display or a PC. Airmar provides PC software for computing weather and displaying weather data.

In addition to wind instruments, you should consider

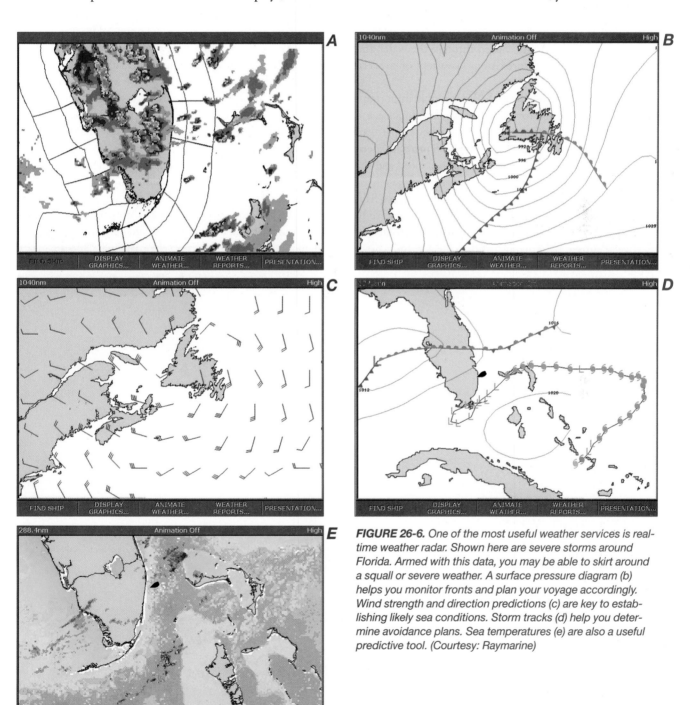

FIGURE 26-6. *One of the most useful weather services is real-time weather radar. Shown here are severe storms around Florida. Armed with this data, you may be able to skirt around a squall or severe weather. A surface pressure diagram (b) helps you monitor fronts and plan your voyage accordingly. Wind strength and direction predictions (c) are key to establishing likely sea conditions. Storm tracks (d) help you determine avoidance plans. Sea temperatures (e) are also a useful predictive tool. (Courtesy: Raymarine)*

a barometer and a sling psychrometer (or digital equivalent) for your instrumentation even if you have an ultrasonic weather station. The barometer can provide pressure trends that indicate approaching fronts and storms.

The psychrometer provides local temperature and dew point to help you anticipate fog.

Other Instruments

A variety of other instruments are available to the boater. Many of these also serve as remote repeaters at the helm, or even a second helm station. Speed through the water and temperature can be measured using a variety of modern sensors.

Monitoring speed through the water is important. Speed is directly related to the boat's hull performance and its engines or sails. In trimming the boat, the skipper usually wants to relate to water speed. The GPS provides speed over ground, which is the composite of boat speed and the effects of winds and currents.

Water temperature is of particular importance to fishermen since they are looking for conditions conducive to particular species of fish. Also, temperature is sometimes indicative of current patterns such as the Gulf Stream. Know-ing that you are traversing a current may be important to your navigation.

Satellite Weather Services

Satellite weather services have become mainstream features available to work with multifunction displays and marine networks. These services require that you add a specialized receiver and antenna to your boat. The receiver interfaces with the compatible display unit using the system network.

Two of the major services are provided by two parts of the same company, XM Weather and Sirius Weather. Each of these services derives its weather information from different sources, dating back to when they were separate companies.

Raymarine and Furuno use Sirius, while Garmin uses XM. You need to buy the receiver that is compatible with your multifunction display, and an antenna that is compatible with the receiver.

The weather services available are extensive, from real-time weather radar and satellite imagery to complete predictive weather maps with winds, fronts, and temperatures. Other services provide water temperatures and current information. These services generally are available up to about 200 miles or so from the coastline.

Connecting It All Together

27

Today, virtually any marine electronics device can be connected to another. Together, these devices produce an integrated approach to navigation with each part supporting the others. In Chapter 26, you found that wind instrumentation relies upon these interconnections to get boat speed and direction in order to calculate true wind speed and direction. Earlier, you learned that the GPS connected to your radar can help point you in the right direction by providing waypoint images on your radar screen in the form of a "lollipop" display. DSC radios derive their position information from GPS inputs. Autopilots can steer your boat using inputs from electronic compasses and GPS. The electronic compass can also supply information to the radar so that it can present your display as north-up instead of heading-up. All these devices can connect to a computer and software to display and process the information, and even relay it to other devices.

Sound complicated? Not really, but it often makes sense to have a professional installer hook it all up. This chapter provides a brief overview of how these interconnections work. A basic understanding may help you understand what the instruments are telling you, or make a repair onboard. It also provides some information to help you be an informed buyer.

Basic Interconnections

Most marine electronics devices are designed to interface with others using standard protocols created by the National Marine Electronics Association (NMEA). The most common standard used by most manufacturers is NMEA 0183. A new standard called NMEA 2000 is now gaining popularity. NMEA 0183 may not be fast enough for some types of information, but key data can be transferred with updates generally around once per second, and this works for most applications.

Using NMEA 0183, most marine electronics devices have a wire or a connector with a pin for data out to send

information. Another electronic device can accept information using a wire or pin for data in. The connections are point to point, much like connecting your TV set to your DVD player. The only difference is that these wires or connector pins must be connected or soldered. (You will need to use marine-grade cables and connections and be sure to seal them against the elements.) In any event, the connection to any device using NMEA 0183 consists of two wires—one for data and the other for ground. Each device outputs a host of information in serial "sentences." The receiving device listens for each sentence of interest and uses the data contained therein.

GPS is a typical source of data that other devices can use. Generally, you can connect up to three other devices to your GPS without additional equipment. For example, you may want the GPS data to go to your radar, your autopilot, and your computer. To do this, simply split the GPS data-out signal three ways and connect each to the data-in ports of other devices. You can do this using a terminal block.

While you can split the data-out connection, you cannot connect several data sources to a single data-in connector. This is much like a party line telephone: several can

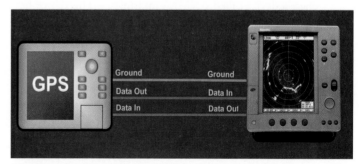

FIGURE 27-1. *Most radars and GPS units can interface using the NMEA 0183 protocol. This allows information from one unit to be received and processed by the other. The connections are much like how you connect a DVD player to a TV. The data-out from one unit goes to the data-in of the other. Generally, GPS outputs data to the radar, but there is less need for the radar to send information to the GPS.*

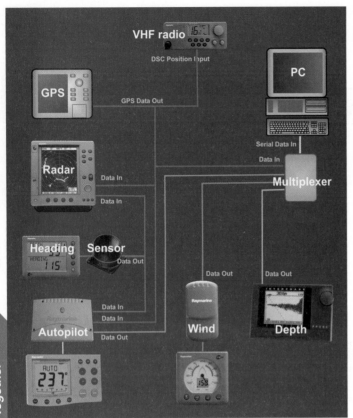

FIGURE 27-2. *With NMEA 0183, you can also interconnect a variety of other electronics. However, to avoid conflicts, only one device can be connected to a single input port of any device. In this example, a PC is being used aboard and you wish to connect a number of devices to it at the same time. To do this, you add a device called a multiplexer. The multiplexer receives all the inputs, stores the signals in a queue, then provides the signals to the PC sequentially. On the output side, you can generally split an outgoing signal to up to three different devices before you need to add a signal enhancer (not shown).*

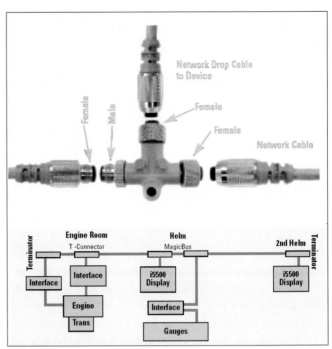

FIGURE 27-3. *NMEA 2000 provides for simpler interconnection by "daisy-chaining" all devices on the same central bus. You simply add a "T" connector in the line to add another device, then a cable from the "T" to the next device. The T's at each end are terminated with special connectors. Although NMEA 2000 offers greater flexibility and speed, it does not add much that NMEA 0183 cannot already provide for most boaters. Consequently, NMEA 2000 adoption has been slow. Most equipment manufacturers continue to offer the NMEA 0183 interfaces. However, with an adapter, you can connect NMEA 0183 devices into a NMEA 2000 system.*

talk at the same time, but no one is clearly understood. If you have only one input on your device, but multiple sources that need to be connected to it, you need to purchase a device called a NMEA multiplexer. This device has multiple inputs and listens to what each data source has to say, temporarily stores the information, and then relays the information sequentially to the device's single input port. However, with some careful planning, you can interconnect most of your equipment without resorting to multiplexers. Besides, many of today's electronic devices now provide multiple data-in ports (for example, data-in1, data-in2). You can define each of these inputs using the setup menus for that device. NMEA 0183 deals only with data; power to the units is separate.

NMEA 2000

NMEA members complained that the 0183 standard was too slow and limited. As a result, a new standard called NMEA 2000 was developed and finally finished in 2002.

Instead of point-to-point wiring, the new system allows any device to tap into a single *bus* (a cable) that provides both data and unit power. Each end of the bus is terminated, and each unit is connected to the bus via a T connector. The bus also connects to the boat's power source. This system is based on a design originally intended for automobiles, called CANbus. The marine standards are unique, however, and any device certified to meet those standards should be able to communicate with any other device on the bus.

Manufacturers had been slow to adopt the new standard because it was faster, but not fast enough for multiple radar, chartplotter, or sonar screens (see the next section).

However, with the advent of electronic engine controls, engine manufacturers saw NMEA 2000 as the ideal interconnect. Other sensor companies making weather instruments also saw advantages to using this new protocol. As a result, the manufacturers of electronic navigation equipment have slowly been adding connectors on their devices for both NMEA 0183 and 2000. Today, using this new protocol, multifunction displays and computers connected to the bus can present GPS position, engine status, weather instrumentation, radio status, AIS, DSC positions, and much more. Still, NMEA 2000 is not fast enough for

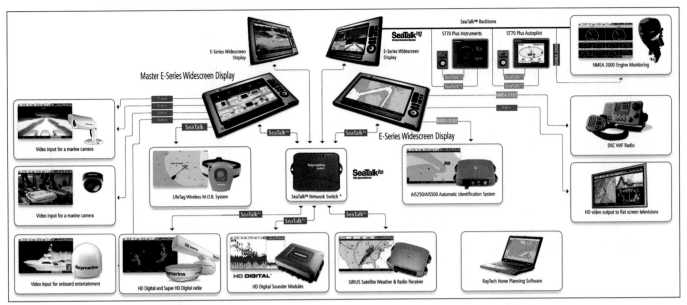

FIGURE 27-4. *Raymarine utilizes several levels of connectivity for various instruments. Its core interconnect is SeaTalk high-speed (purple) for sensor and display/processor connections. Other instruments connect via SeaTalk ng (gold), which is a NMEA 2000-compatible (dark blue) backbone. More traditional instruments may use SeaTalk (a legacy Raymarine interconnect) or NMEA 0183 (red), which is supported by most instruments. (Courtesy: Raymarine)*

sonar/fishfinder, chartplotter, and radar screens to be shared across multiple displays.

With an adapter, NMEA 0183 devices can connect to the NMEA 2000 bus, but we can expect most navigation devices to continue to offer NMEA 0183 connections as well for quite some time to come.

Higher-Speed Connections

Some skippers have multiple navigation and helm stations on their boats. In these instances, it makes sense to have radar, chartplotter, and sounder/fishfinder screens available at all locations. The complexity of the radar or chartplotter screen necessitates higher speed than either of the NMEA formats can accommodate, so several manufacturers have created their own proprietary connection systems. Unfortunately, these systems are unique to their equipment brands and are not likely to work with other brands for the high-speed data. Also, in order to make interconnecting their devices easier, several manufacturers have created their own versions of the CANbus, which may or may not interoperate with NMEA 2000 devices from other manufacturers. However, you can still use the NMEA interconnects for other data.

At the center of most marine "networks" is one or more multifunction displays that can present all of the information available on the boat, from charts, to radar, to sounder, to video. Since the format for much of this data is unique to each brand and model of equipment, you'll need to exercise a certain amount of brand loyalty for the multi-

function displays, the radar scanner, and the sounder unit in order to share them in multiple locations, along with their attendant unique cabling and interconnects.

Several major manufacturers offer their own systems for high-speed networks. With these high-speed connections, display units can share tasks, such as radar, chartplotter, and fishfinder. The most popular brands are Raymarine, Furuno, and Garmin. Most high-speed networks are variants of the popular Ethernet protocol used in most computer networks. As identified above, they may also offer their own proprietary version of CANbus for other data. Virtually all permit the use of NMEA 0183 standard interconnects, and many devices also support the NMEA 2000 standards as well. You'll need to read the manuals carefully or use a professional installer to make sure you are connecting compatible devices and ports.

Raymarine's network system is called SeaTalk. There are several levels of SeaTalk, including an older, legacy SeaTalk with relatively low-speed connectivity—on the order of NMEA 0183. The second is called SeaTalk2, which is a proprietary extension to NMEA 2000 using similar technology but applicable only to Raymarine products. The third is SeaTalk hs, which is a high-speed, plug-and-play Ethernet-based 100-megabit-per-second marine network used for sharing radar, chartplotter, sonar, and weather data. It can be connected with up to seven displays and a digital sounder module. The fourth and newest is SeaTalk ng, which is an updated version of SeaTalk2. It can connect with NMEA 2000 as long as other legacy systems are not connected through other devices to the bus. Since Raymarine's product line consists of devices from various genera-

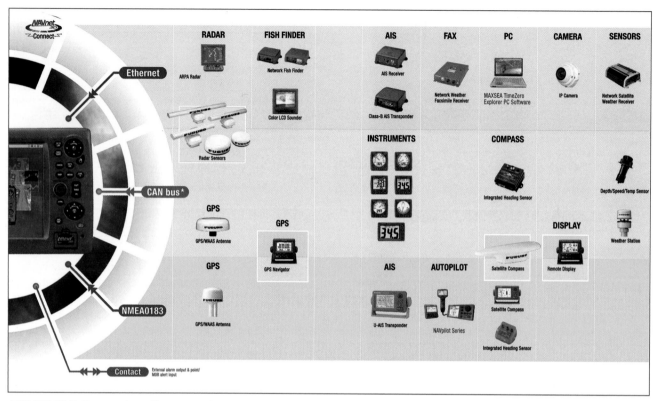

FIGURE 27-5. *Furuno also utilizes a set of connectivity tools. Its high-speed connections are accomplished via NavNet, which is Ethernet compatible. Instruments are connected via CANbus (which is nominally NMEA 2000 compliant) or NMEA 0183, as indicated in the graphic. (Courtesy: Furuno)*

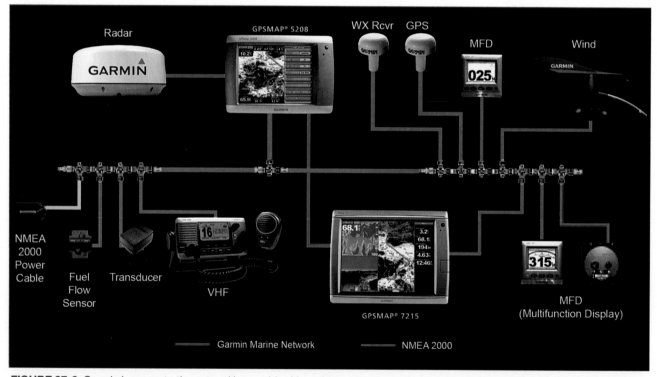

FIGURE 27-6. *Garmin is newer to the networking world, with a wide range of marine sensors and instruments. Its core connectivity is via NMEA 2000 and Garmin Marine Network, which is also an Ethernet derivative. Most of its devices also accept NMEA 0183 for slower-speed connections. (Courtesy: Garmin)*

Connecting It All Together

tions, you will need to look carefully at each device and which of the above protocols are supported.

Furuno uses a different approach called NavNet, which employs the commercial TCP/IP Ethernet protocol for high-speed data. There are two generations of NavNet, with the original called NavNet1/VX2. NavNet 3D is a new technology and is compatible only with NavNet3D devices. Up to ten multifunction displays can be connected on a single NavNet 3D network. Radar, sounder, IP camera, points, routes, tracks, navigation data, and system settings are all shared via Ethernet on the NavNet 3D network; however, charts and satellite photos cannot be shared across the network. These need to be loaded into the internal memory of each multifunction display in the network. In principle, both network generations use Ethernet and distribute connectivity through a hub.

It is important to use marinized equipment and cabling when installing a NavNet network. The NavNet 3D approach uses Ethernet for primary devices such as radar, multifunction display, AIS, PC, camera, and other sensors. It uses

a CANbus for connectivity to GPS sensors, instruments, and electronic compass, as well as depth, speed, water temperature, and weather sensors. It uses NMEA 0183 for some GPS sensors, AIS, autopilot, and electronic compasses.

Garmin has moved significantly into networked systems. It uses an Ethernet-based proprietary network system to connect its multifunction displays with radar, sounder, and satellite weather equipment. It also uses NMEA 0183 and NMEA 2000 interfaces for other interconnections that include a variety of instruments. Most of Garmin's higher-end chartplotters and displays have this Ethernet networking capability.

As a final note on marine networks, virtually every installation is a hybrid of multiple protocols (NMEA 0183, NMEA 2000, video, Ethernet, and proprietary). It is certainly possible for the recreational boater to install his/her own equipment but care should be taken to plan and select the particular type of interconnect with each unit. Make sure you carefully document the installation and consider interconnections when adding new equipment.

Electronic Navigation Tools and Rules—A Summary

28

This book describes a wide range of electronic devices that make your navigation easier and safer. Like most boaters, you probably have a limited budget and limited space to install all these electronic devices. So, which ones should you choose? This chapter will help you evaluate and prioritize your needs when equipping or upgrading your boat.

This chapter also provides a checklist of items, procedures, and tips that should be followed to ensure your safety.

Equipment Priority List

Obviously, your equipment priorities are somewhat influenced by your boating region. For example, on the West Coast around Santa Barbara, the depth drops precipitously just offshore, but fog is frequent. A boater there might consider radar a higher priority than a depth sounder. On the East Coast near Cape Cod, there are considerable shoals and hazardous rocks. A depth sounder and radio may take higher priority in that region.

Locality notwithstanding, here is a list of equipment to consider, along with a brief explanation of why.

1. **Magnetic Compass**—Many boats come with a magnetic compass already installed. Nonetheless, this should be the first item on your upgrade list. The compass is your primary navigation tool. It works in congruence with the electronics, yet it also works independently if your electronics should fail. Get the best compass you can afford and the biggest one you can fit on the boat. With compasses, size does matter. A four- to five-inch compass with a top-reading card is preferred. Make sure you select the right type for your boat—sailboat compasses are dampened differently from powerboat compasses.

2. **Hand Bearing Compass**—Because the compass is so important, it's a good idea to have a spare (even though the ship's compass is unlikely to fail). The hand bearing compass can help you double-check your navigation by providing you with bearings to landmarks. These devices are moderately priced and easy to store.

3. **GPS**—Most boaters use GPS as the primary tool to determine their position. It provides your coordinates to a level of accuracy that no other device can match. If you use a handheld GPS, get a bracket and plug-in power source. To work properly, the antenna must be pointed upward. These units are designed to be used with the face tilted slightly back from vertical. Check the signal bars on the Satellite Screen to make sure you are receiving signals from all directions. If any satellites are blocked, consider moving to a different location or using an external antenna. If you have an external antenna, mount it as low and as close to the center of the boat as you can without blocking it from the sky. Some sailors with nice tall masts will ask, "Why not put the GPS on top of the mast?" The answer is simple: the mast moves and it imparts a velocity to the GPS that is different from that of the boat. You want the GPS as close to the center of motion of the boat as you can to minimize erroneous readings.

4. **VHF Radio**—This is your means of summoning help in the event of an emergency. VHF radios are a source of NOAA weather broadcasts and other important information, and they allow you to communicate with other nearby boats. Some boaters place the radio higher than the GPS in priority. That depends upon the environment where you boat. Consider a fixed-mount unit, because it has considerably greater range. A handheld backup is not a bad idea, either.

5. **Depth Sounder**—This device is moderately priced and easy to install. Knowing the depth under your boat can provide you with an extra dimension of safety. Checking the chart soundings against your depth sounder can help you double-check your position. Sonars and fishfinders represent a step up in cost and sophistication. If you are cruising, a forward-scanning sonar is a great tool. If you are a fisherman, the choice is obvious.

6. **Spare GPS**—It may appear redundant, but if you are using GPS as your primary navigation tool, you should have a backup. Store the same waypoints in the backup as you have in the primary. Many people buy a handheld GPS, then later upgrade to a chartplotter. Keep the handheld as a spare. If you

use a handheld as your primary navigation tool, consider purchasing a stripped-down handheld as a spare.

7. **Chartplotter**—Most recreational boats do not have chart tables, so tracking your progress on a paper chart can be a chore. A chartplotter places a digital chart on the screen along with your GPS position. You need chart chips for your boating waters in addition to paper charts. Alternatively, if your boat has a suitable location or housing for it, a computer with navigation software and digital charts performs the same functions with even more features.

8. **Radar**—Other than GPS, radar is one of the only tools that can be used alone to navigate. The priority for selecting a radar depends upon your boating environment and whether you go out at night. In areas of fog, radar is an indispensable safety tool. It becomes your "eyes" during conditions of limited visibility. Today, radar is becoming a moderately priced accessory. Installation adds another cost, because the radar must be mounted above obstructions and people.

9. **Autopilot**—Although viewed as a convenience, an autopilot can be a real safety tool for long cruises where fatigue can become a factor at the helm.

10. **Electronic Compass**—The fluxgate compass is more precise and accurate than a mechanical magnetic compass. It is self-compensating as well. Generally, it is easy to install and use. These features make the fluxgate compass a nearly ideal ship's compass; however, they are electronic—and, well, you know the rest of the story. Make sure you have a magnetic ship's compass and also a hand bearing compass just in case you lose power. Other electronic instruments, like autopilots, for example, need heading references, so an electronic compass becomes essential with these devices. A radar also can use the electronic compass for a heading reference so you can display a north-up display.

11. **Wind Instruments**—These are handy for planning and useful for supporting your local weather predictions. They can also be helpful for sailors planning their navigation to windward, or for powerboaters in heavy seas.

Checklist

As a summary and a checklist, here is a hierarchy of rules and tips to consider. They are arranged with the highest priority near the top. Obviously, some items depend upon your selection of instrumentation and type of boating.

1. **Always carry paper charts for your boating waters**—Even if you have digital charts, it is imperative that you have paper charts for the regions where you intend to cruise. Keep them protected but near the helm for ready reference. Waterproof charts are preferable.

2. **Annotate those charts with waypoint names that you use in your GPS**—This prevents the accidental selection of a wrong waypoint.

3. **Plot and label legs onto your charts for ready reference on the water**—Use these legs as a matter of habit rather than taking shortcuts. Following prequalified paths may add a little length to a trip, but it adds to your safety and helps you keep track of where you are.

4. **Use waypoint names that have regional meaning**—Waypoints are just names or numbers in your GPS; you need to have clear labels so you select the proper waypoints for navigation (for example, FHR2 for Falmouth Harbor Red "2"). Also, because the GPS organizes your waypoints alphabetically, using a regional prefix in your naming convention is tantamount to organizing the waypoints by location.

5. **Check your electronics before you leave the harbor**—No matter how well electronics are constructed, the marine environment plays havoc with them, especially connections. Inspect the electronics visually for damage, and run them through their paces. It's a great deal easier to fix any problems while stationed on the dock than while rolling on the seas.

6. **Check the weather forecasts before you leave**—Weather can pose the greatest risk to boaters. Look for approaching fronts, especially cold fronts that may be driving severe squalls. Also, look at the dew point spread for where you're going. If the spread is narrow and the temperatures are likely to drop, plan for fog.

7. **Store your waypoints in your spare GPS**—Having a spare GPS is important, but it should have the same waypoints that you've stored in your primary GPS. Should you ever need to use the spare, you will be able to continue your navigation with minimal interruption.

8. **Carry extra batteries and/or an alternate 12-volt power source**—When you accept electronic navigation as your primary means of navigation, you need to recognize the importance of backup power sources. Carry extra batteries for your GPS, even if you normally power it from the boat's batteries. Also, carry a spare, portable 12-volt power source just in case the boat's batteries fail.

9. **Carry tide tables, cruising guides, and local facility information**—Tide and current tables are essential if you cruise in areas with any significant tidal action. Cruising guides can be useful in making contact with harbors and marinas along the way.

10. **Carry instruction manuals and supporting material**—This book, as well as Nigel Calder's *How to Read a Nautical Chart, GPS for Mariners,* and *Rules of the Road* (required for boats greater than twelve meters in length) should all find a home on your boat. Also, be sure to stow the instruction manuals for all your equipment.

11. **Bring aboard a support kit**—Don't leave port without pencils, erasers, a notebook and paper, plotting tools, and a calculator.

Measuring Compass 29 Deviation Using GPS

When you purchase a new compass, you should select the best you can afford and the biggest you can reasonably fit on your boat. Before installation, you should check the reliability of the compass, then zero it (away from the boat or other magnetic disturbances) to check its basic alignment. To check its reliability, take the compass to an area that's away from metallic objects, then align it with a distant object. Now temporarily turn it, then return to the original heading. If the card repeatedly returns to the same reading, your compass is likely to be reliable—even if it is not yet accurate. Try this at several different headings.

Accuracy refers to the compass's ability to reflect its actual orientation. To ensure accuracy, you'll need to zero it. Start by mounting the compass on a rectangular board and ensure that the lubber line of the compass is parallel with the edge of the board.

Carefully align the board in a north-south direction. It helps to have a topo map with a grid reference, or at the very least a good compass that has already been checked. As a reference, mark a line along one edge of the compass board, or place a second board (which you will fix in place as a reference) against the north-south edge of the compass board. You will be aligning all four edges of the compass board with this fixed board.

Check the compass reading to see whether it aligns with north. Then rotate the board 180° and check the south heading. If these two reading are off in the same direction (west or east), determine the average for north and south. Now with the compass board aligned with north, turn the north-south compensating screw until half of the difference is removed. Then turn the board to the south and repeat the process. Repeat until both the north and south headings are as close as you can get them.

Next, turn the board so the compass faces to the east, then west. Then repeat the above process by turning the east-west adjusting screw. When east and west are aligned as closely as you can, return to the north-south direction.

Check the alignment north and south, and again take out half the remaining error using the north-south adjustment on each pass. Return to the east-west alignment and do the same thing using the east-west adjustment.

As a result of each pass at alignment, the compass should come closer to exact alignment on all four cardinal points (north, south, east, and west). When you are finished, note any residual error and jot that on a deviation table if it is significant. Once you have zeroed the compass, you will have confidence in its accuracy.

Once the compass is on the boat, you're in a whole new ball game. Local influences affect the magnetic field around the compass. Making matters worse, the compass is mounted near the helm, where the majority of your instruments and electronics are located.

Accurate Compass Navigation

Deviation Changes with Heading

It's important to recognize that onboard influences on the compass vary as you turn your boat. That is because these objects have a different orientation with respect to the compass and affect the magnetic field onboard differently for each heading. For example, it is not uncommon to find that the compass is quite accurate while you're navigating north or south, but far off when navigating east or west. This may be due to the row of instruments that typically occupy side-by-side positions at the helm close to the compass. When you head north or south, these instruments may be perpendicular to the magnetic field, but when you turn, they align along the path of the magnetic field and the compass and have a larger effect on the magnetic field near the compass.

Although compasses may be affected by outside influences there are three ways to overcome this. Compensation is the first.

Compensation

Using a professional compass adjuster to fine-tune your compass on the boat is highly recommended. This process, called *compensation*, should remove almost all the effects of shipboard influences on the compass. Once the compass is properly compensated, its residual deviation should be less than about 2° or 3° across all heading directions. If your compass is compensated to this accuracy—which may be as close as you can hold a course anyway—you can ignore the extra step of correcting each course for deviation. (However, please note that even after a professional compass adjustment, deviation might be affected by the addition or redistribution of gear on the boat.)

A professional compass adjuster uses his or her own heading reference—usually a gyrocompass. (The gyrocompass must be initially aligned using a known reference, but afterward it maintains its orientation to north independent of the Earth's magnetic field, so it will not be affected by any of the objects on the boat that cause deviation in the ship's compass.) The adjuster uses your compass's two internal magnets to compensate for errors. One magnet adjusts for north-south headings, and the other adjusts for east-west. However, if the deviation is significant, the internal magnets may not be enough. Under these circumstances, the compass adjuster mounts external magnets on the compass.

Unfortunately, a qualified compass adjuster may be difficult to find. You may need to live with the deviation of your compass, or adjust it yourself. Adjusting compasses takes quite a bit of skill and experience. Although you can do it yourself, the process is complicated and beyond the scope of this book. For more information, you can refer to documents available from the U.S. Power Squadrons.

Noting Deviation or Compass Heading

The other two approaches to dealing with compass deviation are not mechanical. The first approach is to build a deviation table for your compass and use it to calculate accurate headings. (A sample deviation table is shown in Figure 28-4.) The second approach is to steer courses based on visible landmarks and label the corresponding compass headings on the chart for future reference. Let's say you're on a leg that's heading for a nun buoy marking a harbor entrance; the compass reads 030°. You would then label your course as "C030 C." (The second "C" notes

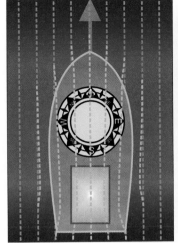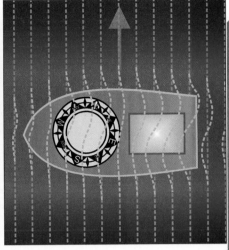

FIGURE 29-1. *Even if you have a high-quality magnetic compass, influences on the boat affect its readings. Metal objects (such as engines) and electronics have a significant effect on the local magnetic field, and their effects vary with the heading of the boat. The difference between magnetic north and the compass reading is called* deviation. *Electronic instruments are often quite close to the compass. They are generally set in a row facing the helmsman. When the boat is pointing north or south, the instruments are perpendicular to magnetic north and cause little deviation. However, when the boat is turned to point east or west, and the row of instruments is parallel to magnetic north, the magnetic field tends to bend toward the instruments, producing greater deviation.*

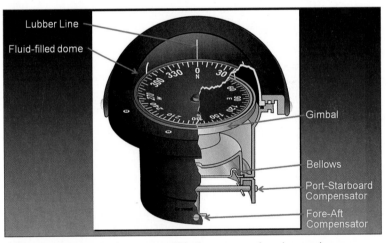

FIGURE 29-2. *A pair of magnets within the compass housing can be rotated to compensate for deviation. A compass adjuster aligns the boat with magnetic north and adjusts the north-south compensating magnet. He then aligns the boat with magnetic west and adjusts the other magnet. The adjuster repeats this process for different headings until the compass is as accurate as possible. Any residual inaccuracy is recorded in a table so the helmsman can calculate for deviation while underway.*

that this is a compass course.) Next time you're on that leg, regardless of visibility, you'll know the correct compass heading for that course.

Recognize that the deviation table or the compass labels on the charts are useful only on your boat—and only as long as you do not significantly reconfigure any equipment and thus change your compass's deviation.

FIGURE 29-3. *On larger ships, particularly with steel hulls, internal compensating magnets are inadequate. This compass provides external iron spheres known as* quadrantal correctors *that can be adjusted to compensate for deviation. These are rarely if ever needed on recreational boats. (Courtesy: Danforth)*

Determining Deviation

When you install the compass on your boat, or make significant changes to other equipment on the boat, you should check your compass deviation on various headings as an important part of planning your navigation. To do this, you should prepare yourself before going on the water. As you'll see shortly, you will need to preplan the legs you will travel to check your compass, and issues such as tidal currents and winds can be a source of error.

Also recognize that the power status of electronics and wiring can affect the compass. The compass deviation can change significantly depending on whether a particular device is turned on or off, or even depending on its mode of operation. It pays to check these effects by turning equipment on and off while monitoring the compass. In general, you should build your deviation table while running all the usual equipment on your boat. (One such piece of equipment that can have a considerable effect on the compass is a windshield wiper. Usually, it's turned on only under adverse conditions and limited visibility—precisely when you're most reliant on your compass. It's important to be aware of

this effect, but it may be too complicated or erratic to include in a deviation table. Instead, when adverse conditions arise, you can periodically stop the wiper and confirm your compass heading before turning it on again.) If the equipment that you use varies from time to time, check the influence of each. If a specific device is used intermittently and its power status is a factor, you might consider moving it away from the compass.

Underway, what you do around the compass can have a profound effect on its deviation, as well. For example, putting a cellular phone, keys, or tools nearby is perhaps the greatest cause of off-course navigation. Keep these objects away from the compass. It's easy to check their effect: simply move them away and note whether the compass heading changes. You may need to do this for different headings. Also, be aware of gear that you bring off and on the boat, especially if it is placed within a few feet of the compass.

You can reduce, if not eliminate, some of the adverse effects on your ship's compass. First, remove any unnecessary equipment from the vicinity of the compass. Make sure there are no loose tools or other metallic or electrical devices near the helm that do not belong there.

Next, check the wiring near the helm station, including any wiring behind panels. All the wire pairs should be twisted around each other. This tends to cause the magnetic fields from each wire to cancel each other. Attempt to route wiring away from the compass as much as practical.

Keep in mind, too, that adding new equipment and gear or moving it to different locations can alter the magnetic influences on the boat. Therefore, you should regularly check your compass. Fortunately, GPS can help.

Using GPS

Your GPS can be used to check your compass and to build a deviation table. First, you must recognize that the compass and the GPS receiver are measuring different things. As explained earlier, GPS is not a compass. It provides an accurate indication of your boat's direction of actual motion over the ground. However, you must be moving to get this

SAMPLE DEVIATION TABLE*					
Magnetic	**Deviation**	**Compass**	**Magnetic**	**Deviation**	**Compass**
000°	1°W	001°	180°	0°	180°
045°	2°W	047°	225°	2°E	223°
090°	2°W	092°	270°	1°E	269°
135°	1°W	136°	315°	1°E	314°

For headings between those listed, use the closest listed deviation.

FIGURE 29-4. *Using the techniques described in this chapter, you can build a deviation table for your compass, like the sample above, that will allow you to steer accurate headings despite any magnetic influences on your boat.*

reading. You cannot compare compass headings with GPS tracks while tied up to the dock.

Along those lines, recognize that your compass measures the direction in which the bow of the boat is pointed—not necessarily your course over ground. As was explained in Chapter 12, currents and winds can push you sideways. GPS displays your course over ground; the compass provides your boat heading. In a crosscurrent, you may be "crabbing" into the current.

Therefore, the key to using GPS for comparison with your compass is to make sure that you are not being influenced by a crosswind or crosscurrent. This can be determined by looking at the crosstrack error, as explained below.

LOCATION You will want to locate areas where you can make straight runs of a half mile or so while checking your compass. This requires open water and the absence of obstacles. It is preferred that you have landmarks to steer toward. A range is ideal. These landmarks should be located such that you can make a nominal northerly, southerly, easterly, or westerly run, but it's preferable to do more than one direction. To effectively measure the compass's deviation, you'll make at least eight runs going both ways in the four cardinal directions. You'll use these to compensate your compass. Ideally, you will also run the 45-degree intercardinals as well to check and record any residual deviation.

CONDITIONS If at all possible, select bays or sheltered areas that are less susceptible to currents, wind, and waves. If you stay away from main channels, current effects may be minimized. Otherwise, plan on making runs during periods of slack water. If your boat's track is susceptible to wind, consider waiting for a windless day, or reduce your boat's windage by removing canvas or sails. It's better to select calm conditions when the water is relatively flat. Your boat will yaw over waves and make it virtually impossible to get precise readings from your compass.

PREPARATION Store the coordinates of the selected landmarks in your GPS and mark the intended course lines on your chart. Set up your GPS to display the Highway Screen, course line, bearing to the landmark, and crosstrack error.

Prepare a notepad for recording your readings. Plan to note the compass heading and GPS track at least once per minute while underway. Also make a column for recording crosstrack error.

BEFORE YOU LEAVE THE DOCK You should have a hand bearing compass on your boat. It can be used as a supplementary tool in developing a deviation table. First, you should check the hand bearing compass away from the boat, as recommended for your main compass (described above). Sight in various directions, swing it away, then return to see how well the compass repeats the same readings.

While on the dock, use your hand bearing compass to take a bearing on a distant object. Then board your boat and take bearings of the same object from different locations on the deck. How does the reading change with each location? Note the locations with the least effect for future use on the water.

While you're still at the dock (but away from shore-based metallic objects), point along the bow and compare the hand bearing compass reading with the ship's compass. Do they match? Doing this accomplishes two things. First, if they match, you'll have some degree of confidence in your ship's compass *and* your hand bearing compass. Second, you'll get a sense of how various locations on the boat are influencing the readings from your hand bearing compass.

You also can get a sense of the influences around the ship's compass. (However, don't place the compasses side by side, as they will interact with each other.) Use your hand bearing compass as your gauge. As long as its reading corresponds with the reading you took while on the dock, you are in a region of minimal impact.

Execution

Using your GPS, move to a starting point that is nominally in a cardinal direction from the selected landmark. Now steer toward the landmark by eye, not by compass. Have your GPS ready with the selected landmark activated.

You begin by making north and south runs. Make your runs at a steady but low speed. Record the compass heading, GPS track, and crosstrack error once every minute. If the crosstrack error builds, you can continue, but you should plan on repeating the measurement at a later time. When you get to the end of the run, simply reverse direction and measure the reciprocal course. If current did not affect you on the first run, it will not have an effect on the reciprocal.

Then make east and west runs. If these are reasonably good, you should expect that the compass will be good for other headings. It pays to check the deviation for at least four increments; eight are preferred.

Now look at your results. Average the readings and see how closely the compass and GPS compare. If they are close (less than 3°), your compass probably does not require compensation. You can make the 45-degree runs, but it is unlikely that they will produce widely different results. Note the deviation and be prepared to use it on longer runs.

If there is significant deviation, either proceed to have it compensated or build a more detailed deviation table. In this case, you'll want to make runs at the 45-degree intercardinal headings (NE, SE, SW, NW). If the 45-degree deviations are nominally halfway between the corresponding north-south and east-west deviations, you can interpolate the deviations for other headings from these. But if the pattern appears irregular, you'll want to measure the deviation for other headings. At a minimum, you'll want to add 30-

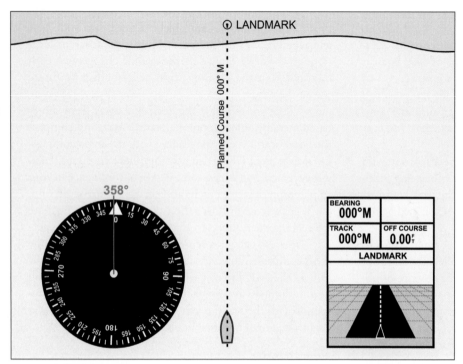

FIGURE 29-5. *To measure deviation, align your boat using a distant landmark. The bearing should correspond with one of the cardinal directions you want to check: N, S, E, or W. The visible landmark must be entered into the GPS; you'll compare the GPS bearing to that landmark with the compass reading as you proceed toward it.*

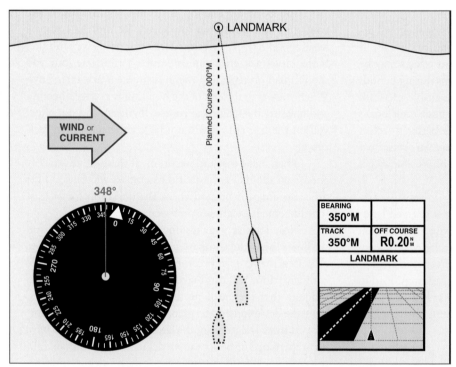

FIGURE 29-6. *Even in a crosscurrent you can get an indication of compass deviation. Point toward a landmark you have activated in your GPS. As you proceed, maintain the heading of the boat toward the landmark and repeatedly compare the compass reading with the GPS bearing to the landmark. Because you'll drift sideways in the current, the bearing and compass heading will change while you proceed. Take a series of readings, then average them to derive an approximate deviation. In this example, you have drifted to the right, so the actual bearing to the landmark, which was 000° M initially, has dropped to 350° M. Meanwhile the compass heading has dropped from 358° to 348°. Thus, the deviation on a northerly heading is 2° east.*

degree increments around the compass.

USING LANDMARKS IN A CROSSCURRENT It is possible to make deviation measurements even in the presence of crosscurrent or crosswind. It takes more concentration and some timely action.

You'll need to have the landmarks stored as waypoints in the GPS, as above. Again, you'll steer to the landmark. Activate the landmark's waypoint in the GPS while you're underway. Immediately look at the GPS bearing to the landmark and the compass reading. Record both; the difference is your deviation. Make a series of paired readings in this fashion. You'll note that both the GPS bearing and the compass reading change over time, because your aspect angle to the landmark is affected by the cross motion caused by the wind or current.

WITHOUT LANDMARKS One of the advantages of using a landmark stored in the GPS is that you can use the data fields to provide useful information. If you do not have a prominent charted landmark, you still can measure deviation, but the accuracy may not be as good. Pick out some feature of a distant shoreline or along the horizon, and make the run steering to that spot. Even a cloud formation along the horizon may suffice. Without a waypoint activated in the GPS, you won't get crosstrack error or bearing, but you will get track—reflecting your course over ground. In this case, monitor your compass heading as you progress along the leg. If your heading continues to change in one direction, you're being influenced by a crosswind or crosscurrent, and the track won't correspond with the heading of the boat.

Measuring Deviation While You Cruise

The methods described above represent a structured approach to building a deviation table. That process should be undertaken from time to time, but there is an easier alternative. As a normal task while cruising, you should monitor your GPS track and compass heading. Whenever you find that the crosstrack error is minimal, you can make an observation for the current heading of the boat.

Normally, you'll be cruising along prequalified legs that are plotted on your chart. The magnetic headings should be annotated on the chart. Monitor your compass and GPS while attempting to stay in the center of the course line. The GPS track should correspond with the plotted magnetic course direction. This provides confidence that you truly are on the defined leg. Any compass reading that differs represents deviation. Jot that deviation on a notepad or on your plotted course, or label the compass course on the line for future reference.

Over a period of time, you will build a fairly good deviation table for your compass. In addition, you will maintain a constant reference check on your compass. If you choose not to use a deviation table to correct your courses from magnetic to compass, then consider labeling frequently used course lines with your corresponding compass courses for future reference.

Using Digital Charts

Digital charts help make your GPS more practical by minimizing the chance for errors. They also ease the task of planning and managing your waypoints and routes. With this appendix plus simple planning software and digital charts (that you can download at no cost from the Internet), you will learn how to use digital charts. Live navigation software—which turns your laptop computer and interfaced GPS into a sophisticated chartplotter—is available from a number of sources.

You can go to www.weekendnavigator.net for links to all the tools you need. The software used in these examples is Rose Point's Coastal Express Viewer, which can be downloaded free through a link on www.weekendnavigator.net or directly from www.rosepointnav.com.

The charts used in the exercises can be downloaded free from www.weekendnavigator.com, or you can get the latest versions directly from NOAA at www.nos.noaa.gov. All U.S. raster navigational charts (RNCs) are available free from this site and can be used with Coastal Express Viewer.

What Is Needed?

Rose Point's Coastal Express Viewer software (free download):

- Reads digital charts

- Creates routes, waypoints, marks, and chart annotations

- Prints chart packages and route plans

- Provides chart symbols, a cruising guide, and light lists

- Provides access to Rose Point via the Internet

The digital charts available at www.weekendnavigator.net include:

- Detailed sample charts—Martha's Vineyard to Block Island

- Nautical charts

Digital Charts

Digital charts greatly simplify the process of planning for GPS navigation because you plan your paths directly on a chart. The resultant waypoints and legs are accurate. If you upgrade to the full Coastal Express software (upgrade via an unlock code at www.rosepointnav.com), you can upload these waypoints directly into your GPS, and follow along on your computer screen as you navigate. In addition, this software computes a wealth of information about your plotted courses, including course directions, leg distances, total trip distance, and more. At the heart of digital charting is the calibrated representation of a chart or map. There are two basic types of digital charts, raster and vector. The charts recommended for these exercises are raster charts, although the same exercises can be performed with vector charts as well using different software. The full version of Coastal Explorer from Rose Point Navigation will work with raster, vector, photo charts, topo maps, and more.

Working with digital charts is much the same whether the charts are viewed on a computer or a chartplotter. Thus, the exercises in this appendix will be useful to you no matter which direction you take in the future.

The RNCs (BSB format) are used by almost all the navigation software programs on the market. You can also update your software at nominal cost to live navigation software.

In addition, many new charting software programs today will work with some form of vector charts. Free vector charts, called ENCs (electronic navigation charts), are also available directly from NOAA and will work with some navigation programs.

If you have a handheld GPS without charting capability, you will find digital charts to be very useful. You can plan your routes and waypoints in a snap on the computer, then transcribe or upload them to your GPS (with the upgrade). While on the water, you simply follow the planned routes knowing that they were prequalified. Even if you use a charting-capable handheld GPS or a chartplotter, you will find that it is somewhat easier to plan using digital charts on a computer, then upload into your chartplotter or GPS.

The software used in the exercises in this appendix is available at no cost from Rose Point Navigation. Whether you download the charts from *www.weekendnavigator.net* or directly from NOAA, these are real navigation charts, which makes the exercises realistic. The software is designed to work on PCs with Windows operating systems.

You will be able to work with any downloaded charts as well as plot courses and waypoints. Coastal Express (full version) is designed to interface with most popular GPS receiver models, so data can be uploaded to the GPS or downloaded from GPS into the program. The software provides an effective GPS route and waypoint editor.

Installing the Coastal Express Software

You must install the Coastal Express Viewer program on your computer in order to use the charts you download. Installation of the software is easy, as explained below.

Downloading and Installing Chart Navigator Viewer

Go to *www.weekendnavigator.net* for the link or directly to *www.rosepointnav.com*. Look for the link to Coastal Express Viewer Edition. Then click on DOWNLOAD. In most instances you will be asked whether you want to run or save the software. It is recommended that you click SAVE. You may be presented with a choice for either a 32-bit or 64-bit version (depends upon whether you have the 64-bit version of Windows installed on your computer). Select the appropriate version and save it to a folder of your choice.

Once the download completes, double-click the downloaded file that appears in the folder you selected. This will install your Coastal Express application. Once that process is completed, you may run your software application and delete the download from your Desktop.

Downloading Charts

Go to *www.weekendnavigator.net* and select Exercise Charts to download the following. It is best to create a folder called Charts or a similar name you will recognize. You will be downloading the following chart numbers:

13218	Martha's Vineyard to Block Island	1:80,000	shown
13221	Narragansett Bay	1:40,000	shown
13223	Narragansett Bay and Approaches	1:20,000	shown
13228	Westport River and Approaches	1:20,000	extra
13229	South Coast Cape Cod & Buzzards Bay	1:20,000	extra
13232	New Bedford Harbor and Approaches	1:20,000	extra

Alternatively, you can go to *www.charts.noaa.gov* and select Click Here to Download NOAA raster navigational charts. This will take you to a downloader page where you have a choice to download up to twenty specific RNCs (best if all you want is the set above), or you can select sets of charts by Coast Guard district or state. The charts will be downloaded in a zip file. Coastal Express can be directed to the zip file to directly install the charts for use by the software.

You can go back to the NOAA site at any time and select additional charts or update the charts that you have with the latest available on the NOAA server. Remember, chart information is updated weekly through *Local Notices to Mariners*. These updates are regularly added to the stored charts at NOAA.

Using the Coastal Express Viewer

Using Coastal Express Viewer is easy and intuitive. This software was selected because it and the related Rose Point programs are considered to be the easiest to use of all navigation software programs. Most planning software available on the market performs similar functions.

This program reads any BSB format raster chart, as do most other navigation software applications. Developing skills using this program will help you plan on almost any chartplotter or software; the functions are virtually the same even if the menus and screens are slightly different. This appendix provides a quick-start guide to using this program.

Rose Point Navigation Systems Coastal Explorer Viewer and Express Editions Overview

The following sections were provided by Rose Point Navigation.

Coastal Explorer Viewer is a raster chartviewer with basic route planning tools and a simple navigation simulator. Viewer is intended to provide an introduction to Rose Point Navigation Systems and to electronic charting in general. Viewer may be upgraded to Coastal Explorer Express for a nominal charge. Express adds support for GPS navigation, tide and current predictions, access to weather forecasts (using an Internet connection), an advanced ship's log, integrated guidebooks, and much more.

Viewer works with industry standard BSB format raster charts, available free of charge for the entire U.S. coastline directly from NOAA, which is the official charting agency in the United States. Charts are available in this format from many other sources for areas outside of the United States (but most are not free).

Raster charts are electronic images of normal paper charts, so they are familiar to anyone who is used to using paper charts.

Viewer uses a technique commonly referred to as quilting to combine multiple charts of similar scales in order to fill its window with chart information even when you are nearing the edge of an individual chart. You are free to move around the chart and zoom in or out, and Viewer will automatically select the best chart or combination of charts for the display. This lets you concentrate on where in the world you want to look rather than trying to figure out which charts to open.

Viewer lets you create several types of marks on your chart: marks, routes, and range/bearing lines (RBLs). A mark identifies a point (latitude and longitude) and has an optional name or label, and an optional icon. You can use marks to place notes on the chart as waypoints, points of interest, or whatever you want. Routes are made up of a sequence of waypoints and legs and are the basis of a voyage plan (a waypoint marks a spot where the route takes a turn, and a leg indicates the path between two waypoints). A range/bearing line is a line that is used to measure the distance (range) and angle (bearing) between two points on the chart.

Like most chartplotters, Viewer is considered to be a "supplementary aid to

FIGURE A-1.

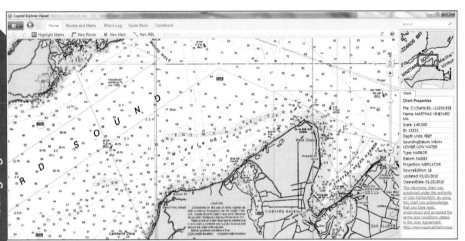

FIGURE A-2. *The Coastal Express Viewer screen shows a section of chart in the main field. On the right is a wider chart view showing the region covered in the main panel. Properties of the chart displayed are provided in the panel below the inset. On the right side of the chart view, you can see a zoom slider to move in for a larger-scale chart or a better view, or move out. The symbol on top of the slider offers choices for chart view relative to the boat. The I symbol below offers access to additional information.*

navigation" and not a "primary navigation tool." A warning message to that effect is displayed each time the program is started. You may disable the warning message by checking the Don't Show This Message Again option.

The major components of the window above (Figure A-2) include:

1. **Title Bar**—This is a standard Windows title bar with a standard system menu and MINIMIZE, MAXIMIZE, RESTORE, and CLOSE buttons.

2. **Tab/Status Bar**—Immediately below the title bar is a multipurpose bar that normally provides tabbed access to various "browsers," PREVIOUS and NEXT PLACE buttons, and a search tool. When the cursor is pointing at the chart, this bar changes to show information about the chart at the location of the mouse cursor. Some messages will also appear in this bar in order to let the user know of certain events, or ask questions that do not necessarily need an immediate answer.

3. **Toolbar**—The next bar down is a context-sensitive toolbar. The buttons that appear on this toolbar depend on which tab is active, and sometimes what object is selected on the chart, or what mode the user is in.

4. **Chart**—Most of the screen is occupied by the chart. On the right side of the chart display you'll see several controls: Follow Mode, Scale, and Info.

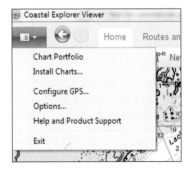

FIGURE A-3. *The box at the upper left of the screen offers a drop-down menu of choices to handle charts, configure GPS (not available with the Viewer), and options for displaying information.*

5. **Chart Overview**—The smaller chart panel to the right of the main chart shows an overview of the area seen in the main chart. A small box outlines the exact area displayed in the main chart; this box may be moved around to scroll through the main chart.

6. **Properties Panel**—Below the Chart Overview is a panel that shows details about the last thing in the main chart that the user clicked on. This might be read-only information about the chart, or changeable information about a mark, route, or range/bearing line.

The Main Menu

The first button on the tab/status bar is called the MENU button, which provides access to chart management features, program options, and the help system. Click the MENU button to access the menu that contains the following commands:

1. **Chart Portfolio**—Displays a list of the charts installed on your computer and provides access to chart management features.

2. **Install Charts**—Displays a window that helps you install charts to the Chart Portfolio.

3. **Configure GPS**—Displays a window used for configuring the GPS COM Port. (Requires upgrade to Express.)

4. **Options**—Displays a window containing all of the program options.

5. **Help and Product Support**—Displays a window that provides access to help, product support, license activation and information, and program version information.

6. **Exit**—Exits the program.

The Home Tab

Coastal Explorer Viewer starts with the home tab selected, and that is where you'll probably spend most of your time. The home tab's toolbar contains these controls:

1. **Undo and Redo**—The UNDO button will undo the last change you made to a route, mark, or range/bearing line. You can undo accidental deletes, moves, creates, and other changes, and you can undo more than once. The REDO button will undo an undo and can also be used more than once.

2. **Highlight Marks**—The HIGHLIGHT MARKS button will wash out the chart image a bit so that your routes and marks stand out more. This can be very handy when working on a route in areas where the chart contains a lot of information.

3. **New Route**—The NEW ROUTE button lets you start creating a new route. When you click this button, you will be in New Route mode and the toolbar will change to show some instructions and a DONE button. You may now click on the chart to place your waypoints; each click will add another waypoint. You may also move the mouse near the edge of the chart to scroll in that direction. When you are done

adding waypoints, click a second time on the last waypoint, press the Esc key, or click Done in the toolbar.

4. **New Mark**—The New Mark button lets you create a new mark on the chart. When you click this button, you will be in New Mark mode and the toolbar will change to show some instructions and a Cancel button. You may now click on the chart to place your new mark and then use the Properties panel to give it a name or a different icon. If you decide not to create a new mark and want to get out of New Mark mode, press the Esc key or click the Cancel button on the toolbar.

5. **New RBL**—The New RBL button lets you create a new range/bearing line on the chart. When you click this button, you will be in New Range/Bearing Line mode and the toolbar will change to show some instructions and a Cancel button. You may now click on the chart twice, once to place the start of your new range/bearing line, and then to place the end of the range/bearing line. The range and bearing of your line will be displayed along its length. If you decide not to create a new range/bearing line and want to get out of New Range/Bearing Line mode, press the Esc key or click the Cancel button on the toolbar.

6. **New Event**—The New Event button creates a new event mark at your boat's location. Event marks are useful for quickly marking the location of your boat on the chart and include the date and time the mark was created. The **F5** key may also be used to create a new event mark. (If you do not have a GPS connected and are not using the navigation simulator, this option will be disabled.)

7. **Sync**—The Sync button is used to check for software, data, and chart updates as well as to upload any logbook entries you may have made to the Coastal Explorer Network. (Most of the actions that this button can take depend on you having upgraded to Coastal Explorer Express and having an active Coastal Explorer Network subscription; however, it will at least check for Coastal Explorer Viewer software updates.)

8. **Help**—The Help button will display the built-in help viewer. Each toolbar has its own Help button, which will display help for that toolbar and/or browser.

The Toolbar When a Mark or Route Is Selected

When a mark is selected on the chart, the toolbar will change. All of the New buttons will be replaced with a single New button that displays a menu containing Route, Mark, and Range/Bearing Line, and Delete and Send To GPS buttons are added. A similar change is made when a route is selected, but an Activate Route button is also added.

1. **Delete**—The Delete button will simply delete the selected mark or route. You can also use the Delete key on the keyboard.

2. **Send To GPS**—The Send To GPS button requires the Coastal Explorer Express upgrade and will transfer the selected mark or route to a compatible GPS connected to the PC.

3. **Activate Route**—The Activate Route button is used to begin navigation along the selected route. Real navigation requires a Coastal Explorer Express upgrade to enable the use of a GPS, but Coastal Explorer Viewer contains a navigation simulator that may be used for practice.

You can get back to the standard home tab toolbar by clicking on the chart away from any marks or routes. That will deselect the selected mark and show the standard toolbar.

The Routes and Marks Tab

The routes and marks tab has a toolbar that is very similar to the home tab, but the Sync, Tools, and Help buttons are replaced with Import and Export buttons. Both of these buttons require the Coastal Explorer Express upgrade and are used to read marks and routes in files made with other programs or to write marks and routes to a file to be used by another program.

The routes and marks tab also displays a list of routes, marks, range/bearing lines, or waypoints below the toolbar. These lists provide an alternate way to see, select, and manipulate what routes and marks you've created, and are the only way to see routes and marks that have been hidden. (Each entry in the list has a check box that controls whether or not it is visible on the chart.)

Ship's Log Tab

The ship's log tab is used to create blog entries, review the blog, and access recorded tracks and events.

FIGURE A-4. Selections are made across the top of the screen by choosing an appropriate tab. Just below the tabs are features available to the user such as creating a route, mark, or range/bearing line.

FIGURE A-5. By selecting the routes and marks tab, you are presented with a list of those that you have entered and are stored with the charts.

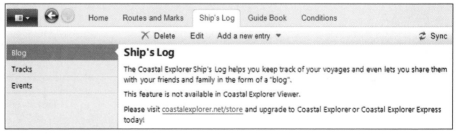

FIGURE A-6. Upgrading from the Viewer edition enables a host of real-time navigation and logging features, which can be shared with others.

The Blog

A blog (or web log) is a type of website that is normally created and maintained by someone to provide regularly updated news or information to interested readers. Blogs have become a very popular way to share cruising photos and stories with friends, family, or the world.

The ability to easily maintain your own blog about your cruising adventures is included as part of a Coastal Explorer Network subscription. You can decide whether to share your blog with the general public, only your friends and family, or keep it all to yourself. You can access your blog by logging into the Coastal Explorer Network with any web browser or through Coastal Explorer Express. Using Coastal Explorer Express, you can even create new blog entries when your computer is not connected to the Internet. All of your new entries will be sent to the blog the next time you use the SYNC button and are connected to the Internet. Syncing will also make sure that your computer has a complete and up-to-date copy of your entire blog so you can read it when your computer is no longer connected to the Internet.

Create a new blog entry with the Add a New Entry option on the ship's log toolbar. Each entry has a date and time, which is normally set to the time you created the entry, but you can change it if your entry will describe something that took place in the past. Entries also have a location, which is automatically set to your boat's location, but you can change that if the entry is for a different place. You will normally want to give your entry a title and type your notes in the content box. You can also attach photos if you want. When you are done, click the DONE button on the toolbar.

Entries may be changed by using the EDIT button on the toolbar. This will display the entry in the same form as when you created it in the first place. Make your changes and click the DONE button to finish.

When you are connected to the Internet, use the SYNC button to send any changes you've made to your blog to the Coastal Explorer Network and to update your copy of the blog with any changes that were made using other computers.

Tracks

Tracks are recordings of the courses that your boat has taken. When tracking is enabled, a new track is created when you start Coastal Explorer or use the Start New Track option.

You can enable and disable tracking by right-clicking on your boat and selecting the Enable Tracking option from the menu.

The Start New Track option is also on the boat's menu.

All of the tracks you record appear on the chart and in the Tracks list, which is part of the ship's log.

Large tracks can consume a lot of system resources, so if you notice that Coastal Explorer is starting slow or is acting sluggish, it may be due to excessive tracks, and you should consider deleting any you don't really need (possibly after exporting them to a file in case you need them later).

Events

An Event is a special type of mark that is created at your boat's location and given a name that is the date and time the event was created. They are useful to mark events such as dropping crab pots, catching a fish, spotting something you want to write about later in your blog, et cetera.

You can create an event by using the New Event option on the home toolbar, the New Event option on the routes and marks toolbar, or pressing the **F5** key.

Events show up on the chart just like a normal mark and appear in the Events list in the ship's log.

Guide Book Tab

The guide book tab is used to access the Coastal Explorer Network Community Guide Book, the Atlantic Cruising Club's Guides to Marinas, Panoramio photos, and other guide book information. Everything on the guide book tab requires an upgrade to Coastal Explorer Express.

The guide book toolbar provides commands for adding a new place to the Coastal Explorer Network Community Guide Book (see below), synchronizing (updating) the information on your computer with the Coastal Explorer Network, and showing (or hiding) various guide book layers on the charts.

The Coastal Explorer Network Community Guide Book

The Coastal Explorer Network includes a guide book made by the user community. This guide book contains information about marinas, anchorages, fuel docks, restaurants, and many other types of places.

To view the Coastal Explorer Network Community Guide Book, select the guide book tab and look on the chart for Coastal Explorer symbols. Each symbol represents a place in the guide book. Click on a symbol to see that place in the guide book browser. (If you don't see any Coastal Explorer symbols, make sure the Coastal Explorer Network Community Guide Book option is enabled in the SHOW menu on the guide book toolbar.)

Coastal Explorer Network Community Guide Book places also appear in the Search Results panel when their title (the name of the place) matches what you enter.

You can add to the community guide book by clicking on the Add a New Place button on the toolbar. Enter the name of the place and a description. You may also attach photos if you have any. Please keep in mind that anything you add to the guide book will be visible to many other Coastal Explorer Network members, so entries such as "this is where I keep my boat" are not really appropriate (though they are great for your own blog in the ship's log).

Installing the community guide book requires Internet access, but the guide is then stored on your computer for use when you are not connected.

Atlantic Cruising Club's Guides to Marinas

Rose Point Navigation Systems and the Atlantic Cruising Club have teamed up to provide you with Atlantic Cruising Club's (ACC) highly detailed, boater-biased Guides to Marinas built right in to Coastal Explorer Express.

Basic marina information from ACC's guides is available as part of your Coastal Explorer Network subscription. To have all of ACC's marina and What's Nearby information available in Coastal Explorer Express, including lots of photos, simply purchase one or more of the regional Atlantic Cruising Club's Guides to Marinas and install ACC's Digital Guide on your computer.

If you would like to explore the free marina information set, please use Main Menu > Options > Synchronization > Atlantic Cruising Club's Marina Guide to select the regions you are interested in.

Once you have subscribed to the marina data for a particular region, the ACC marina icons will appear on the chart and the ACC Guide entry will appear in the guide book browser.

Installing the ACC Guide requires Internet access, but the guide is then stored on your computer for use when you are not connected.

Panoramio Photos

Panoramio is a community-powered website for exploring places through photography. Rose Point and Panoramio have teamed up to provide access to Panoramio's millions of photographs right on the Coastal Explorer Express charts.

The Panoramio feature requires Internet access during its use.

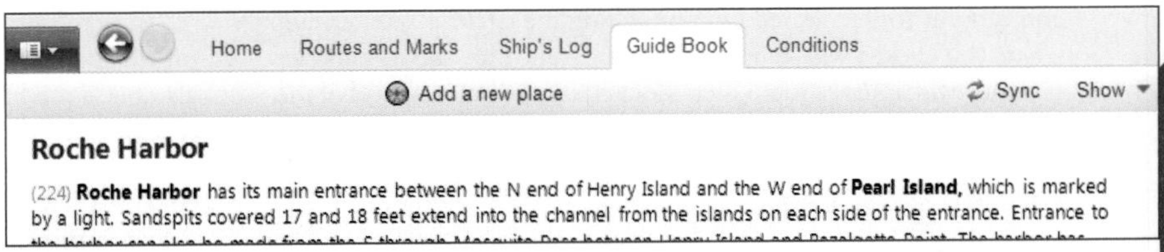

FIGURE A-7. *A guide book provides local information on specific harbors and ports.*

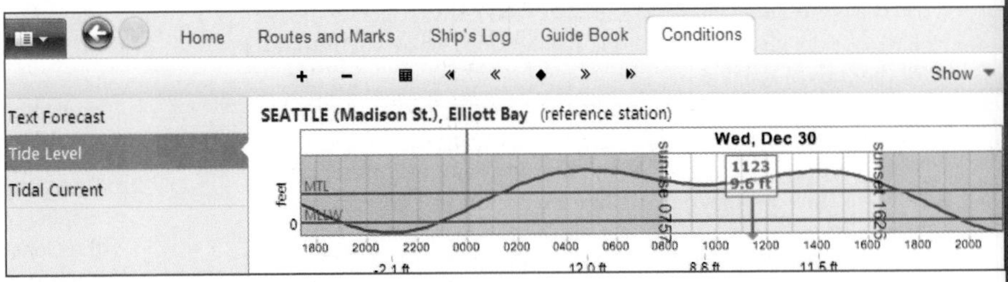

FIGURE A-8. *With the upgrade from the Viewer, tide information is available for all charts. Selected locations are available on the Viewer as a sample.*

Conditions Tab

The conditions tab is used to access tide level and tidal current predictions as well as weather forecasts. Most of this requires an upgrade to Coastal Explorer Express, but several tide and current stations are accessible in Coastal Explorer.

Once a tide or a current station has been selected, the buttons on the conditions tab's toolbar let you zoom in and out on the graph, select a day to view predictions, or scroll back and forth through time.

Virtual Time

Coastal Explorer lets you see tide level and tidal current predictions for times other than right now by using the concept of virtual time.

The virtual time affects the tide bars and current arrows that are displayed on the chart as well as the tide or current graph seen in the conditions browser.

Normally the virtual time is the same as the current real time, and as the real time changes, so does the virtual time. However, when you use any of the time changing functions in the conditions toolbar, the virtual time is set to the time you select and is paused so as not to advance with the real time. The time changing functions let you move forward and backward in time by one hour or one day and to resume real time.

Whenever a virtual time is in effect, the Virtual Time panel will appear in the lower right corner of the Chart panel to let you know what that virtual time is. You can always go back to real time by clicking on this panel.

FIGURE A-9. *Since the Viewer is a planning tool, you can select a virtual time.*

The Search Box

Coastal Explorer Viewer contains an extensive gazetteer for the United States that lets you find places on the chart simply by entering their name in the search box, which can be found on the far right side of the tab/status bar. As you type (or pause typing) in the box, a list of places that match will appear below the search box. If you see the place you are searching for, just click on it to

FIGURE A-10. *A search box is available to help answer your questions.*

scroll the chart to that location. If you want to see the list again, click on the magnifying glass inside the search box.

Creating and Manipulating Marks

You can create a new mark with the New Mark option on the home and routes and marks toolbars. After selecting the New Mark option, click on the chart at the location where you want the mark. The **F7** key will also let you create a new mark regardless of which toolbar is active.

You can move a mark to a new location on the chart by dragging it with the mouse.

Clicking on a mark will select it and display its properties in the Properties panel. You can use that panel to change the mark's name, hide or show the name on the chart, change the color of the name, change the icon, change the position to a specific latitude and longitude, lock the position so you don't accidentally drag it with the mouse, add an arrival circle (if you use the mark as a waypoint, this is how close you need to get in order to "have arrived" at it), or add notes about the mark.

Right-clicking on a mark will display a menu of commands that either are shortcuts to some of the properties or are toolbar buttons.

Creating and Manipulating Routes

You can create a new route with the New Route option on the home and routes and marks toolbars. After selecting the New Route option, click on the chart at the location where you want each waypoint. After placing your waypoints, press the DONE button on the toolbar (or the ESC key). The **F8** key will also let you create a new route regardless of which toolbar is active.

When you click on a route, it becomes selected and its properties appear in the Properties panel. You can change the route's name, see how long it is, and add some notes.

Right-clicking on a route displays a menu of commands for that route.

When you click on a route to select it, you will see three orange circles. One will appear at the location where you clicked, and the other two will be near the first and last waypoints of the route. These orange circles let you add new waypoints to the route and make it incredibly easy to fine-tune a route that was created as a rough draft. Click and drag on any of the orange circles to create a new waypoint and move it to the desired location. Using the circle at the location where you clicked will split that leg of the route into two legs and let you move the intersection. Using the circles at the start and end of the route will let you add new waypoints to the start and end of the route.

Creating and Manipulating Range/Bearing Lines

You can create a new range/bearing line with the New RBL option on the home and routes and marks toolbars. After selecting the New RBL option, click on the chart at the locations where you want each of the ends of the line.

A whole range/bearing line can be dragged to a new location by dragging the line itself, and either end can be moved to a new location by dragging just the appropriate end of the line.

When a range/bearing line is selected, its properties appear in the Properties panel. You can give the line a name, change its color, see its range and bearing, or add some notes.

Right-clicking on a range/bearing line displays a menu of commands that affect that line.

Using the Chart

The chart may be scrolled to a new location in several ways:

- By dragging the chart.
- By clicking near the edge of the chart (where the cursor changes to a large white arrow).
- By using the arrow keys.
- By dragging the outline box in the Chart Overview panel.
- By searching for a place using the search box.
- By using the Follow Boat option (use of a GPS requires an upgrade to Coastal Explorer Express).

The chart scale may be changed in several ways:

- By using the wheel on your mouse (if it has one).
- By using the + or – keys on your keyboard.
- By using the scale sliding control on the right edge of the chart.
- By holding down the wheel button of your mouse and dragging a box around the area where you want to zoom in to see.
- By holding down the right button of your mouse, dragging a box around the area where you want to zoom in to see, and then selecting the Zoom In command from the menu that appears when you let go of the button.

Above the chart scale slider on the right edge of the chart is a button with a boat in it. This button controls the Follow Boat option, which may be used to automatically scroll the chart as your boat moves. The symbol on the button indicates the state of the Follow Boat option, which can be any of these:

1. **Don't Follow**—automatic scrolling is disabled.
2. **Follow Boat**—automatic scrolling is enabled and will scroll the chart in order to keep the boat near the center of the window.
3. **Look Ahead**—automatic scrolling is enabled and will scroll the chart in order to keep the boat near the bottom of the window (so that you can see farther ahead).

Scrolling the chart manually will select Don't Follow. Click on this button to select Follow or Look Ahead modes. (You can also press the HOME key on your keyboard to select Follow Boat or Look Ahead mode.)

Below the chart scale slider is an INFO button that lets you control a few details of the chart display. Pressing the button will display a menu that contains these options:

1. **Tide Stations**—This option enables and disables the display of tide station symbols (which are magenta diamonds) on the chart. If you have the Coastal Explorer Express upgrade, these symbols will indicate the predicted tide level and whether it is falling or rising. With Coastal Explorer Viewer, only the location of the station is indicated.

2. **Current Stations**—This option enables and disables the display of current station symbols on the chart. If you have the Coastal Explorer Express upgrade, these symbols will appear as magenta arrows indicating the predicted direction and speed of the current. With Coastal Explorer Viewer, only the location of the station is indicated.

3. **Distance Scale**—This option enables and disables the display of a distance scale at the bottom of the chart.

4. **Chart Outlines**—This option enables and disables the display of magenta outlines indicating where all of your charts are even when the scale of the chart prevents it from being used in the current display.

Right-clicking on the chart will display a menu containing these options:

1. **Move Boat Here**—This option starts Simulated Navigation mode and moves your simulated boat to the location you indicated on the chart.

2. **Charts Here**—This option leads to a list of charts that cover the point where you clicked the right mouse button. Each chart has a check next to it indicating that the chart should be used in the quilt. If you need to temporarily remove a chart from the quilt, you can select that chart from this list to remove its check. You can enable the chart again in the same way. Changes made to chart quilting this way are temporary, and all of the charts will be enabled the next time you start the program. If you want to permanently disable a chart, use the Chart Portfolio.

3. **Insert Guide Book Place**—This option requires the Coastal Explorer Express upgrade and is used to add a new place to the Coastal Explorer Network Community Guide Book.

4. **Guide Book**, **Tide Level Prediction**, **Tidal Current Prediction**, and **Weather**—These options are shortcuts to the guide book and conditions browsers that find the appropriate type of station that is closest to the location on the chart of your click.

5. **Properties**—This displays properties of the chart in the Properties panel.

Simulated Navigation Mode

Coastal Explorer Viewer includes a feature that allows you to practice navigating a route. To activate the feature, press the CTRL+SHIFT+UP ARROW key, or right-click on the chart and select the Move Boat Here option from the menu. This will display a flashing boat symbol near the center of the chart.

The following table shows various keys that can be used to control your virtual boat:

KEY FUNCTION	
Ctrl+Shift+Up Arrow	speed up by 5 knots
Ctrl+Shift+Down Arrow	slow down by 5 knots
Ctrl+Shift+Left Arrow	change heading by 5 degrees to port
Ctrl+Shift+Right Arrow	change heading by 5 degrees to starboard

You can also drag the boat symbol around with the mouse or right-click anywhere in the chart window and select the Move Boat Here option to place the boat in a specific location.

The Navigation Information Panel

When you activate a route, a Navigation Information panel will appear between the Chart Overview and the Properties panel.

The Navigation Information panel displays the following information:

- The latitude and longitude of your boat's position as indicated by your GPS or the navigation simulator.

- Your speed over ground (SOG) as indicated by your GPS or the navigation simulator.

- Your course over ground (COG) as indicated by your GPS or the navigation simulator.

- The bearing to the active waypoint (BRG).

- The distance to the active waypoint (DST).

- As you arrive at, or pass, waypoints on your active route, Coastal Explorer Express will automatically select the next waypoint until you reach your final destination.

The Chart Portfolio

The Chart Portfolio is accessed via the TOOLS button on the home tab.

The Chart Portfolio displays a list of all the currently installed charts. Each chart is displayed with its ID (chart number), name (title), scale, type, last update, and folder.

This list can be sorted by clicking on the column heading for the column you would like to sort by.

Each chart has a check box next to it. This check box controls whether or not a chart is used in the quilt. If you have a chart that does not work well, and you do not want to delete it or move it to a place where Coastal Explorer Viewer won't find it, you can turn off this check box to prevent it from being used.

Selecting a chart shows additional information about that chart in the Properties panel and a thumbnail image of the chart above the Properties panel.

The toolbar has a box listing all the storage devices on the computer. A specific drive may be selected from this list in order to show only charts on the drive. Normally this list shows charts on all local hard drives.

The toolbar also has a button to display the Install Charts window, but this feature may also be accessed from the home tab's TOOLS menu.

To leave the Chart Portfolio and return to Coastal Explorer Viewer, click the home tab or the CLOSE button on the toolbar.

The Install Charts Window

The Install Charts window is used to install or update charts from a CD-ROM, DVDROM, portable storage device, or zip file. You can get to the Install Charts window by selecting Install Charts from the Main Menu.

The Install Charts window provides several ways of installing charts. The method to select depends on where you are getting the charts.

If you have a subscription to the Coastal Explorer Network, the easiest way to install and update charts is to use the first option—to select one or more regions of charts that you want to install. Once you have selected your chart regions, Coastal Explorer Express will download those charts or check for updates to those charts whenever you start the program (if you are connected to the Internet) or use the SYNC button on the toolbar.

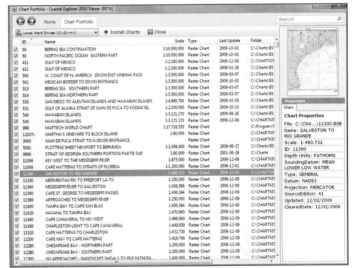

FIGURE A-14. *The Chart Portfolio provides an opportunity to deselect a chart from view. It provides each chart number and name, its scale, type of chart, date of the last update, and stored location. Details of a highlighted chart are shown in the information panel to the right.*

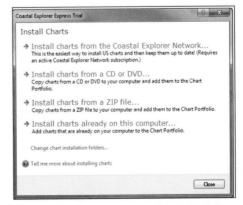

FIGURE A-15. *Installing charts is facilitated by options. If you subscribe to the Coastal Explorer Network, you can get them directly. Alternatively you can install charts from a CD or DVD, or from a zip file. If you go to NOAA directly, it provides your selected charts in a zip file.*

If you have a CD/DVD or some other removable storage device that contains charts, use the Install Charts from a CD or DVD option and follow the directions in the program.

If you have downloaded charts from the Internet in the form of a zip file, use the Install Charts from a Zip File option to have Coastal Explorer extract the chart files from that zip file and copy them to your hard drive.

If you have charts on your computer that are not in a folder that Coastal Explorer is using for charts, you can tell Coastal Explorer about those charts by using the Install Charts Already on This Computer option.

Finally, to tell Coastal Explorer where on your computer you want it to install charts, use the Change Chart Installation Folder option.

The Configure GPS Window

This window is used to select and configure the COM port used to connect a GPS to a PC. The left side of the window lists all COM ports currently available on the PC. Select the one being used for the GPS and then select the appropriate interface type and baud rate on the right.

Coastal Explorer Express can use either the NMEA 0183 interface, used by most GPS receivers, or the Garmin interface, used by many Garmin handheld GPS receivers. (Most Garmin GPS receivers can use either the NMEA 0183 or the Garmin interface; be sure to select the same interface in both Coastal Explorer Express and the Garmin device.)

The baud rate option controls the speed at which data flows through the COM port. It is important that both Coastal Explorer Express and your GPS are using the same baud rate. Most NMEA 0183 GPS receivers use a baud rate of 4800: however, your GPS may require a different baud rate, which would be

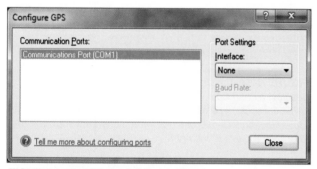

FIGURE A-16. *With the full Coastal Express program, you can select the GPS interface.*

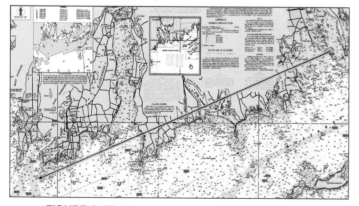

FIGURE A-17.

indicated in its reference manual. The Garmin interface usually requires a baud rate of 9600.

The Options Window

The Options window provides access to all program options. These options are in categories including:

1. **Measurements**—These options control the units and format used for various measurements.

2. **Synchronization**—These options are relevant only for the Coastal Explorer Express upgrade. This page of options is changed to an advertisement for Coastal Explorer Express when that upgrade has not been installed.

Sample Cruise with Digital Charts

Now that you know how to push the buttons on the Coastal Express, it's time to dive into the best features of the program. The principle charting techniques described above are:

1. **Route**—Routes for navigation

2. **Range/Bearing**—Point-to-point measurements

3. **Mark**—Waypoints/points for navigation or reference

This section demonstrates these functions and the chart manipulation features of the software using a sample cruise.

New Bedford to Newport

You are planning a route from New Bedford, MA, to Newport, RI. This route takes you along Buzzards Bay to Narragansett Bay in a generally WSW direction. You will discover a wide range of conditions along this route. In fact, the United States Power Squadrons, the U.S. Coast Guard Auxiliary, and many maritime academies use a special version of a chart of this region for training (called the 1210Tr chart). (You can follow along with the figures given below, but it's recommended that you open the Coastal Express Viewer software and follow along on your computer.)

You should start by scrolling to the region from Newport, RI, to New Bedford, MA (on chart number 13218, Martha's Vineyard to Block Island). Click anywhere on the chart and the chart being viewed will be listed in the Properties panel to the right. You zoom in or out sliding the vertical bar on the right of the main screen or by clicking the "+" or "−" icons above or below it. This chart is of a small enough scale to include both your starting point and destination. Generally, this is the best way to start a route plan.

Now, you will create a two-point route. To accomplish this, select the route icon. In this case, you start the route at the outer buoys at New Bedford harbor and end it at the outer buoy near the entrance to Newport harbor, as shown in Figure A-17. Move the "+" cursor to the location outside New Bedford harbor and left-click. Then move to the buoy outside Newport harbor and left-click again, but do it twice without moving the cursor. This ends your route generation for the time being. You have complete flexibility to move or edit these points in the future. Obviously, you cannot take this route, because it goes over land; however, it does represent the shortest distance between those two points. You need to tailor that route—first to get out it out over the water, then again for safe passage. For the most part, it's preferable to place waypoints near navigation aids, if possible. On the water, this provides a visible reference for confirmation as you achieve the waypoint.

To add these points, you need to move the hand cursor over any part of the route line. Left-click and this will highlight the route and place a magenta circle at the location of your cursor, which now adds a "+" sign and a pop-up box to Insert a New Waypoint. By left-clicking again, a new waypoint is created. Now, left-click, hold, and drag the new waypoint to its new location. Your first moved point should be placed on G "5," off Slocums Neck. Place the waypoint as best you can on the chart, and zoom in for a closer view. If this is open water, the position of the waypoint may not be critical. Using this view, you can add the next waypoint at G "3" using the same technique. This zoomed view also eases your task of looking along the route line for potential hazards. Seeing none, it's time to zoom back out a bit. Insert the next waypoint at the buoy RW "SR" off Sakonnet Point, as shown in Figure A-6. If you want a better view, zoom in until the chart on the screen changes to a larger scale version (chart number 13221_1 will appear, which is a 1:40,000-scale chart rather than the 1:80,000 scale on 13218). It's generally best to use your original chart as the baseline for planning, because you get to see your route in perspective, then scale or zoom in for a better look. You can now see the great advantage to digital charts. Instead of drawing lines sequentially from start to destination, you can make simple routes and tune them as you go along. You also can zoom in and out to select the view; zooming in will often produce a larger scale chart to get a more detailed presentation. The initial corrected route is shown in Figure A-20, but we're not finished yet.

Next, you extend and fine-tune the route at each end into the respective harbors. Starting with New Bedford, you move your

hand icon over to the first waypoint (Figure A-21). Adjust the zoom so you can see the state pier in the harbor (your starting point) and your first waypoint outside the harbor. Now, you will want to add waypoints at the beginning of the route. You do this by scrolling over and clicking on the route near but not on the first waypoint. This produces a magenta line and circle extending beyond the first waypoint. Now, left-click twice within the circle to create a new waypoint. Move the cursor to the next location and repeat until you have created three waypoints, starting with the one at the state pier to your original first waypoint just outside the harbor. After you have finished, zoom out and move over to the last waypoint—currently at the entrance to Newport. Repeat the process of clicking on the route, and adding waypoints using the magenta circle at the end of the former route. Zooming in, you will advance to chart number 13223_1. This is a 1:20,000-scale chart of Narragansett Bay including Newport harbor, as shown in Figure A-23. Add waypoints at the end of the route just as you did at the beginning. Add five waypoints as shown. You can edit any of these waypoints at will. You should scan along the route just to be sure that there are no hazards lurking near the planned route. Add waypoints to refine the route, or delete any extras. Once you are finished, you can place the cursor on the route and right-click to access the Properties panel. Here you will see the total route length. On the screen, the course direction and distance for each leg are plotted about mid-leg. If you want to see the waypoint coordinates, go to the routes and marks

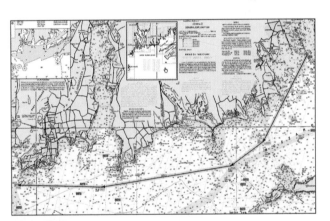

FIGURE A-20.

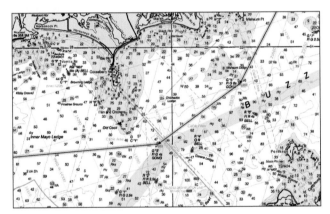

FIGURE A-18.

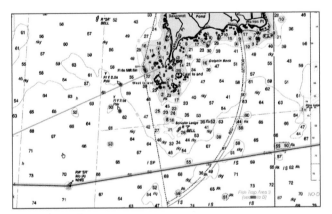

FIGURE A-19.

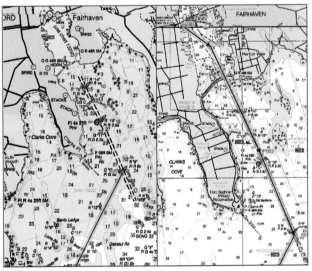

FIGURE A-21.   **FIGURE A-22.**

Using Digital Charts

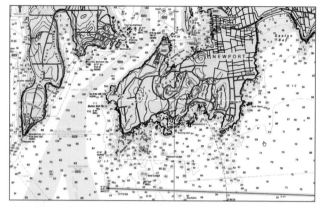

FIGURE A-23.

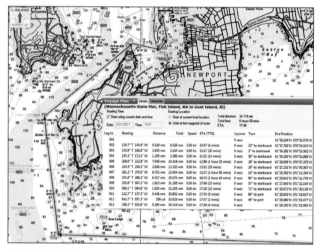

FIGURE A-24.

FIGURE A-25.

tab at the top of the screen and go down on the left side to select Waypoints. This provides a list of all waypoints along with their coordinates. If you want to see the return courses for each leg, scroll

onto the route and right-click. Select Reverse Route. The leg arrow directions will change, and the leg course directions will correctly indicate the reverse path.

If you have the full version of Coastal Explorer, you will have the option to present a tabulated voyage plan along with the opportunity to select leg speed to compute leg and route transit times. A sample of this voyage plan is shown in Figure A-24. With the full software package, the route information can also be printed in tabular form, as shown in Figure A-26. In addition, you can print the accompanying charts.

Once you are satisfied with the route, you can upload it into your GPS if you upgrade to Coastal Express. The software will upload all the waypoints and the route that goes with it. Simply right-click on the route and select Send to GPS. Select the appropriate GPS, make sure it is connected, and press START.

The waypoints are automatically named by number within the program unless you choose to change them. You can do that by accessing the waypoints in the routes and marks tab, selecting waypoints, and then highlighting a particular waypoint. In the Properties panel, you can change a waypoint's name, its color and icon (as shown on the viewer), its coordinates, and its arrival circle radius (used by the software). The arrival circle radius determines just how close you need to be to the waypoint coordinates for the software to recognize that you have arrived at the waypoint. Your GPS will have its own criteria independent of the software. It is recommended that you select to rename the waypoints using no more characters than your GPS can store. You also can add notes to each waypoint for future reference.

When the upload occurs, the waypoints and the route are transferred to the GPS. Depending upon your software, you can present a variety of charts. The Viewer and the low-cost upgrade to live navigation use only raster charts, but the full Coastal Explorer and many other programs can display other chart formats, including vector charts (ENCs), photo charts, topo maps, and bottom profiles. A number of companies produce various chart formats for navigation software.

Maptech produces various digital charts that expand upon the types of cartography that can be presented, all geo-referenced to the same coordinate system. As an example, you can bring up a topographic chart of the same area you have been observing on a nautical chart. This can be useful in helping you recognize landmarks and the topography of the shoreline. If you are using radar, this chart helps you determine the slope of the shoreline, which impacts radar returns.

A sample of your route termination in Newport harbor on a topo chart is shown in Figure A-27. It's easy to spot because it is listed as "topo" rather than "nautical." Note that your route is shown on this chart as well.

Another alternative form is the photo chart. This type of chart is created from aerial mapping photographs or satellite photographs. The photo chart also is geo-referenced to your coordinate system. It allows you to get a photographic view of the area. One of the interesting characteristics of these photo charts is how well they show shoals and shallow areas. For example, notice the shallow area off Castle Hill in Newport harbor (Figure A-28).

Digital charts also allow you to array and link charts side by side so you can get different views. To do this, under the Charts drop-down menu, select Link Two Charts to a Location. This brings up a menu of available charts. Select the other chart that you would like to see next to the one on the screen. In Figure A-29, we selected the topo chart corresponding to the Newport harbor nautical chart.

To get a perspective of a harbor, you can select Aerial Photographs. In the Options menu under the View drop-down menu, go to the overlays tab and click on the box for Picture Icons. Now your charts show camera symbols with arrows. The camera symbol indicates an available aerial photograph. The arrow shows the direction of the view from the camera. These photographs are available for challenging areas such as Sakonnet Point and the surrounding rocks. This is a region close to your route where you certainly want to stay clear (Figure A-28).

You might be concerned about how close your route will bring you to the rocks, and the bell buoy that marks them. You can use the Range/Bearing Line feature to determine this. To access the RBL, you can use the icon bar. Clicking the button converts the cursor to an arrow with a "+" sign. Place the cursor over your course line and left-click to anchor the first point. Your cursor is still the arrow with the "+" for the placement of the second point. As you move the cursor, an arrow will extend from the first point. The arrow will be labeled with the bearing and the distance to the cursor. When you click on the second point, the RBL is anchored in position and will stay until deleted (or hidden). You can find all of your RBLs under the routes and marks tab.

You can reverse the RBL to get the reciprocal bearing or delete it by right-clicking on the line and selecting the appropriate item in the drop-down menu.

Marks are particularly useful for annotating the chart with information provided by the Coast Guard's *Local Notices to Mariners*, or your personal observations.

To begin, click the mark icon and the cursor will change into the arrow with the "+" sign.

Move the arrow over the desired location and left-click. A symbol and the name NEW MARK will appear at that location. In the Properties panel to the right, the name NEW MARK will appear. You can change its name, its symbol and color, its coordinates, and its arrival circle radius, and add notes explaining what the mark represents. Your list of marks can be found under the routes and marks tab.

Now that you have followed along planning this cruise, you're ready to take off on your own. Navigate around this region. Download more charts and take a look at your home waters.

Now that you understand how to plan with digital charts, you will feel far more comfortable doing so on a chartplotter. If you're ready to do real planning for your waters, you may want to

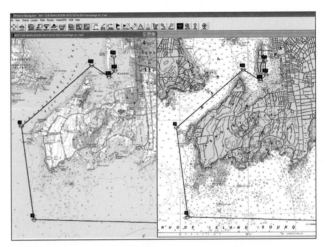

FIGURE A-26.

FIGURE A-27.

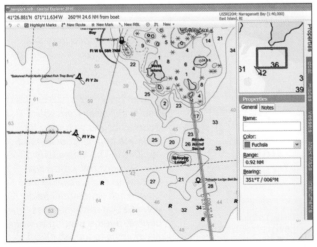

FIGURE A-28.

check out the Maptech selection of digital and paper charts on its website, www.maptech.com. If you are ready to navigate live using a computer and digital charts, simply go to Rose Point, www.rosepointnav.com, and upgrade your viewer software.

Also, look into the host of planning and navigation programs available across the market. Many of these companies are listed in Appendix 3. Since software is ever-evolving, please refer to www.weekendnavigator.net for updates and other useful information.

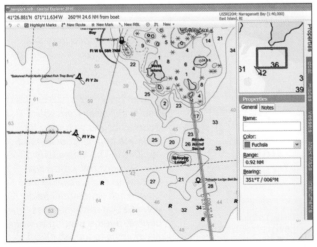

FIGURE A-29.

GPS Display Overview— A Side-by-Side Comparison

Throughout *The Weekend Navigator* we've looked at the various displays and data windows that your GPS provides. Still, it's a topic that's worth revisiting. The following pictorial takes us step-by-step through a real-world boating situation. This incremental approach gives us the benefit of seeing how all the GPS features interrelate.

When using the GPS, you can view only one "screen" at a time—you'd have to switch back and forth to compare the Map Screen with the Highway Screen. This section hopes to further your understanding of these screens by placing them side by side so that you can see how each uniquely conveys an identical situation.

The data fields on a GPS provide meaningful information, but their names and definitions can be somewhat confusing. Looking at these data fields and seeing how they relate to a changing situation will give you a much clearer understanding of what they indicate.

In this pictorial, you started out heading to your active waypoint "R2," but something went wrong.

OFF COURSE—HEADING AWAY FROM THE ORIGINAL COURSE LINE.

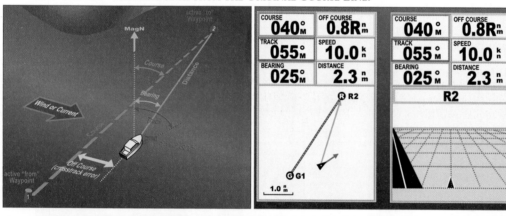

Left: *Let's say you've been pushed away from your original course line by a strong wind or current. Even though you've maintained your original heading, the boat continues to move away from the intended course line and the waypoint.* Center: *The Map Screen shows that your position is off the course line and pointed away from the waypoint.* Right: *The Highway Screen paints a similar, yet direr picture—your waypoint has completely slipped from the screen. Looking at the data fields we see that your track is to the right (055°). As you continue, your bearing to the waypoint will change. Off course is to the right (0.8 nm) and increasing steadily.*

OFF COURSE—ORIGINAL TRACK.

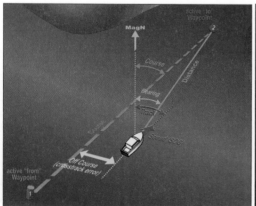
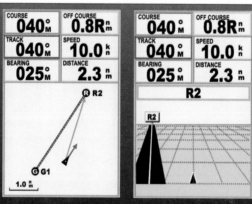

You're still away from your course but you've turned to steer the original course heading (040°). The Map and Highway Screens both show that you're moving parallel to the course line. In the data fields you see that track matches course, but the bearing to your waypoint is to the left (025°). Off course is to the right and will remain constant until you change your track.

OFF COURSE—POINTING TOWARD WAYPOINT.

Now you've turned toward the waypoint, but you're still to the right of the course line (as indicated by the yellow arrow in the left panel). It's interesting to note that the position arrow on the Highway Screen puts you to the right of highway, but the highway itself extends to the center of the screen—meaning that you're pointed toward the waypoint. Taking a look at the data fields, we see that track and bearing match one another (025°), but they're different from course (040°). Off course is to the right (0.8 nm), but this number will slowly diminish as you approach the waypoint.

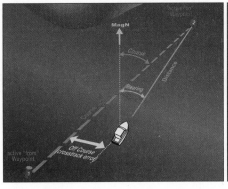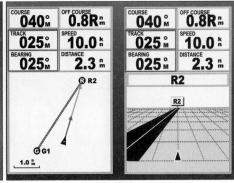

OFF COURSE—HEADING BACK TO ORIGINAL COURSE.

Since you're such a diligent student of navigation, you've decided to return to your pre-qualified course line and continue safely from there. To do so, you steer sharply to port. Note that the Highway Screen has changed drastically (right). It shows that you are heading back toward the highway; the waypoint is no longer visible on the screen. The data fields, too, are drastically different—none of the fields match. Your track is sharply to port (350°), and your bearing to the waypoint (025°) differs from course (040°). (It's important to note that throughout these examples, the course data field never changes—and it won't. That field will not change until you activate a different waypoint.) Off course is to the right (0.8 nm), but this number will diminish rapidly.

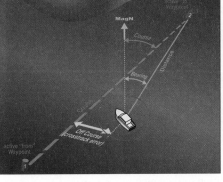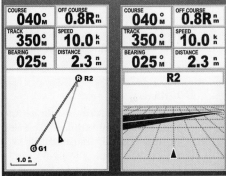

ON THE COURSE LINE—WRONG TRACK.

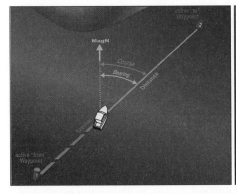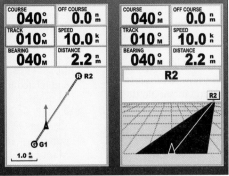

Finally, you're back on the course line—course and bearing match one another (040°). Off course is zero. However, your track is to the left of the course line (010°). If you continue in this direction, you'll soon be off course again.

ON COURSE.

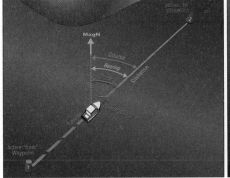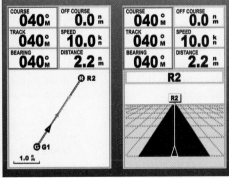

This is how everything should look. Note that the boat (left) is on the course line and heading in the direction of the active waypoint ("R2"). The position arrow on the Map Screen (center) is aligned with the course line. The position arrow on the Highway Screen (right) is exactly at the center of the highway and heading directly for the waypoint. The data windows for track, course, and bearing all have the same value. Off course is zero and will stay that way. Bon voyage!

GPS Display Overview

Resources and References

Throughout the book, a number of resources are identified for boaters seeking additional information. This appendix provides a summary list for ready access.

Books

Brogdon, Bill. *Boat Navigation for the Rest of Us*. 2nd ed. Camden, ME: International Marine, 2001. Filled with practical tips for the small-boat skipper, particularly in the use of the seaman's eye. The author has 30 years of Coast Guard experience.

Calder, Nigel. *How to Read a Nautical Chart*. Camden, ME: International Marine, 2003. (Second edition forthcoming May 2012.) Provides a complete reference to electronic and paper charts and chart symbology. It covers U.S. and international symbols and charts, explains how charts are created and their accuracy standards, and provides additional valuable information. It serves as a replacement for *Chart No. 1*.

Hubbard, Richard. *Boater's Bowditch*. Camden, ME: International Marine, 1998, 2000. An excellent reference for traditional, electronic, and celestial navigation. It also covers topics such as weather and oceanography.

Sweet, Robert J. *GPS for Mariners, Second Edition*. Camden, ME: International Marine, 2011. Explains how to use and operate a GPS. It covers buttons, screens, and menus on the GPS, and explains how to store and activate waypoints and routes. It also covers advanced navigation topics using GPS, chartplotters, and computers, including how to interconnect electronic equipment with GPS on your boat.

Government Agencies

Australian Hydrographic Service provides charts and predictions of tides and currents for Australia and environs. The website is www.hydro.gov.au.

British Admiralty (The United Kingdom Hydrographic Office) provides charts and predictions of tides and currents for major regions of the world. The website is www.ukho.gov.uk.

Canadian Hydrographic Service provides chart information across Canada and Canadian waters. It also provides tide and current predictions. The website is www.charts.gc.ca.

Canadian Office of Boating Safety provides information on safe boating and boating courses to Canadians. The website is www.tc.gc.ca/eng/marinesafety/marinesafety/debs-obs-menu-1362.htm.

Hydrographic and Oceanographic Department, Japan Coast Guard, provides charts and services in the region around Japan. The website is www.kaiho.mlit.go.jp.

International Hydrographic Organization (IHO) provides international standards for charts and cartography. The website is www.iho.shom.fr.

NGA (National Geospatial-Intelligence Agency), part of the U.S. Department of Defense, is a resource for charting and navigation information outside U.S. waters. It provides the pilot charts with offshore current and weather information. The main website is www1.nga.mil/ProductsServices/NauticalHydrographic/.

NOAA (National Oceanic and Atmospheric Administration) is responsible for chart development, tide and current information, weather information, and related research. The main website is www.noaa.gov.

NOS (National Ocean Service), a division of NOAA, is responsible for charts and tide and current predictions. The website is www.nos.noaa.gov

Office of Boating Safety is part of the United States Coast Guard. It analyzes and provides boating safety statistics and analyses, lists boat defects and recalls, and provides information for recreational boaters. The website is www.uscgboating.org.

Office of Coast Survey is the part of NOS that provides charts and related information. The website is www.nauticalcharts.noaa.gov.

USCG (United States Coast Guard) is part of the Homeland Security Department. It is tasked with controlling the U.S. waterways. It also provides chart updates via the Notices to Mariners and many resources on boating safety. Its navigation center (NavCen) is an excellent online resource. The main website is www.uscg.mil. The navigation center can be found at www.navcen.uscg.gov.

U.S. Navy has been a major factor in the development of navigation and navigation electronics for many decades. The website is www.navy.mil.

Organizations

American Canoe Association (ACA) focuses on paddlesports, including canoes and kayaks. Formal training programs are offered to paddlers and instructors to further the safety of the sport. The main website is www.americancanoe.org.

ABYC www.abyc.com American Boat and Yacht Council provides standards for marine equipment and installation to support safe voyaging. ABYC also trains and certifies marine technicians.

BoatUS www.boatus.com Boat Owners Association of the United States represents boaters to government authorities, provides services to boaters, and operates a foundation providing information and safety resources to boaters.

Canadian Power and Sail Squadrons (CPS) provides education and services to boaters throughout Canada. CPS has some 33,000 members and has been instrumental in public and member training across the country. The main website is www.cps-ecp.ca.

International Association of Marine Aids to Navigation and Lighthouse Authorities (IALA) provides standards for navigation aids throughout the world. The website is www.ialathree.org.

International Hydrographic Organization (IHO) provides international standards for cartography. The website is www.iho.shom.fr.

International Maritime Organization (IMO) provides international standards for safety at sea, and cleaner oceans. The website is www.imo.org.

National Association of State Boating Law Administrators www.nasbla.org provides support to state and federal authorities for safe boating through education standards, and training of boating authorities.

National Boating Federation www.n-b-f.org supports boating and yacht clubs for safe boating and legislative advocacy.

National Safe Boating Council www.safeboatingcouncil.org provides resources to boaters to support safe and enjoyable boating working with the boating community of organizations, marine companies, and the federal and state authorities.

National Water Safety Congress www.watersafetycongress.org works with the U.S. Army Corps of Engineers and Coast Guard to assist in boating safety.

United States Coast Guard Auxiliary (CGAux) provides volunteer support for the U.S. Coast Guard. Members support missions such as search and rescue, vessel safety checks and patrols (both sea and air) freeing up USCG resources for critical missions. Some 1,500 flotillas also support public education. The main website is www.cgaux.org.

United States Power Squadrons (USPS) serves all types of boaters and considers itself "America's Boating Club." USPS has a robust educational program for the public and for members. With more than 50,000 members in some 450 squadrons throughout the U.S. and Japan, it supports NOAA with its Cooperative Charting Program, providing updated information for charts, and the USCG with vessel safety checks. Visit www.usps.org.

United States Sailing Association (US Sailing) is the national governing body of sailing. US Sailing provides training and governance for sailing, and powerboat training through yacht clubs, associations, and affiliate schools. Their website is www.ussailing.org.

Companies

ACR www.acrelectronics.com is a leading producer of AIS, EPRIB, Personal Location Beacons, and rescue equipment.

Airmar www.airmartechnology.com produces ultrasonic transducers and sensing technology products.

Argonaut www.argonautcomputer.com produces a line of marine computers and displays.

Comar Systems www.comarsystems.com produces AIS transponders for marine applications.

Davis provides a wide range of navigation products, including handheld compasses, sextants, plotting instruments, and instructional material. The main website is www.davisnet.com.

Furuno Marine Electronics produces wide range of quality navigation electronics and interoperable components with a recog-

nized reputation. The main website is www.furuno.com.

Garmin, Ltd., is the world's leading producer of GPS products. Its line of handheld GPS models and chartplotters offers extensive features and leading edge technologies. The main website is www.garmin.com.

GPSNavX www.gpsnavx.com is a producer of navigation softare for the Mac operating system. They offer GPSNavX and MacENC.

Icom America, Inc., produces quality marine radios, both VHF and SSB. The company is recognized as a leading resource for communications equipment on both recreational and commercial boats. The main website is www.icomamerica.com.

Interphase is well known for depth sounders and sonar; it also produces GPS/chartplotters. It is one of the few sources for scanning sonar. The main website is www.interphase.com.

Jeppesen Marine (C-Map) is a leading producer of vector digital charts used in chartplotters. The vector charts are developed from master charts from NOAA and other hydrographic agencies and refined with additional information collected by the company. The main website is jeppesen.com/marine/lightmarine.

JRC (Japan Radio Co., Ltd.) provides a wide range of navigation electronics, including radar, GPS, chartplotters, and depth sounders. The website is www.jrcamerica.com.

L3 Communications www.l-3.com produces AIS transceivers.

Lowrance Electronics, Inc., is long known for handheld GPS units and marine electronics. The website is www.lowrance.com.

MacGPSPro www.macgpspro.com produces charting and mapping navigation solutions for the Mac operating system.

Magellan (part of Thales Navigation, Inc.) produces a complete line of handheld GPS models and is known for its automotive GPS systems. The main website is www.magellangps.com.

Maptech is a provider of digital charting products including packaged versions of NOAA charts and navigation software. Web site is www.maptechnavigation.com.

Maretron www.maretron.com is a producer of electronic sensors, interconnects and software for marine applications including ultrasonic weather instruments described in this book.

MarinePC www.marinepc.com produces marine computers and display components and systems.

MaxSea Marine Software, provider of quality navigation software, is known for offshore and commercial packages as well as recreational boater software. The website is www.maxsea.com.

Navionics produces vector digital chart chips used in some of the leading brands of chartplotters. Navionics is known for its ability to use both raster and vector cartography. The website is www.navionics.com.

Navico owns a number of navigation brands including B&G, Eagle, Lowrance, Northstar and Simrad. The website is www.navico.com.

Navsim Technology is a producer of navigation software for personal computers. The main web site is www.navsim.com

Nobeltec is one of the leading providers of navigation software. The website is www.nobeltec.com.

Nordhavn produces a line of ocean-capable yachts known worldwide for offshore voyaging and cruising. The main website is www.nordhavn.com

Northstar Technologies, Inc. has a reputation for quality GPS chartplotters. The website is www.northstarcmc.com.

OceanGrafix provides up to date NOAA charts on demand through selected dealers and direct shipment. The also provide NGA charts for much of the world. The website is www.oceangrafix.com

Plastimo is well known for its quality dual-use handheld and ship's marine compasses. The main website is www.plastimo.com.

Raymarine has a broad range of electronic navigation equipment, including GPS, radar, chartplotters, autopilots, radios, and marine instruments. Many of the photographs shown throughout the book were provided by Raymarine. The main website is www.raymarine.com.

Richardsons' Maptech is a leading private producer of nautical charts in printed format. Charts are provided in waterproof flip-fold, and chart book formats by area or region. The website is www.richardsonscharts.com.

Ritchie Navigation is well known as a producer of quality marine compasses. Its product line extends from handheld compasses to large boat compasses. The main website is www.ritchienavigation.com.

Rose Point Navigation produces user-friendly and powerful navigation software solutions including Coastal Explorer. Navigation solutions include radar, fish finders, and engine interfaces. The main website is www.rosepointnav.com.

Silva is a lesser known but quality supplier of compasses and a wide range of other products. The main website is www.silva.se

Simrad, Inc., produces high-quality navigation electronics, including radar, chartplotters, and navigation instruments. The website is www.simrad-yachting.com.

SI-TEX produces GPS, chartplotters, depth sounders, and radar. The main website is www.si-tex.com.

Standard Horizon (part of Vertex Standard) is known for its VHF marine radios. It also produces GPS/chartplotters. The quality of this equipment is well known in the industry. The main website is www.standardhorizon.com.

Steiner binoculars and optical instruments are among the very best. The company is recognized for quality high-performance marine equipment. The main website is www.steiner-binoculars.com.

The CAPN (Star Technologies) produces the well-known The CAPN navigation software. The website is www.thecapn.com.

Weems & Plath is well known for its plotting and navigation instruments. The website is www.weems-plath.com.

Westport Yachts produces powerboats whose quality and features are recognized by serious yachtsmen. The website is www.westportyachtsales.com.

Software, Tips, Reviews, Information

Active Captain www.activecaptain.com provides up to date information relevant to boaters and cruisers including an interactive cruising guidebook, newsletters, access to boating resources, and access to products.

EasyGPS www.easygps.com free software that allows you to create, edit, and transfer waypoints and routes between your computer and your Garmin, Magellan, or Lowrance GPS.

G7toWin www.gpsinformation.net free software to exchange information between a PC and Garmin, Magellan, or Lowrance/Eagle GPS.

GPS Information www.gpsinformation.net great resource for reviews, tutorials, and links to all types of GPS resources.

GPS Nuts www.gpsnuts.com tutorials, tips, hardware and software reviews for general use of GPS.

MadMariner www.madmariner.com is a web resource for boaters with regular articles, tips, and product reviews. This is one of the most current and refreshed resources available to boaters.

Maps-GPS-Info www.maps-gps-info.com resources for GPS and maps, links to software.

OziExplorer www.oziexplorer.com well-respected charting software, shareware. Works with Garmin, Magellan, Eagle, Lowrance, and Brunton/Silva receivers and a PC.

Panbo www.panbo.com is a marine electronics weblog providing a host of informative articles, reviews and tips to make your navigation safer and more enjoyable. This is one of the first sites you should visit to get up to date information on navigation equipment and its use.

SeaClear www.sping.com/seaclear/ free charting software for Windows. Works with any GPS outputting NMEA 0183 messages. Displays position, waypoints, and routes on most BSB/KAP version 1 and 3 commercial charts (eg., Maptech).

Waypoint+ www.tapr.org/~kh2z/Waypoint/ free software to exchange routes, tracks, and waypoints from a Garmin GPS to a PC.

WxTide www.wxtide32.com offers a free windows program providing tide and current charts using perpetual tables.

Index